DAVID MCCAMPBELL

David McCampbell

*Top Ace of U.S. Naval Aviation
in World War II*

David Lee Russell

McFarland & Company, Inc., Publishers
Jefferson, North Carolina

LIBRARY OF CONGRESS CATALOGUING-IN-PUBLICATION DATA

Names: Russell, David Lee, 1947– author.
Title: David McCampbell : top ace of U.S. naval aviation
in World War II / David Lee Russell.
Other titles: Top ace of U.S. naval aviation in World War II
Description: Jefferson, North Carolina : McFarland & Company, Inc.,
Publishers, 2019 | Includes bibliographical references and index.
Identifiers: LCCN 2019018010 | ISBN 9781476677798
(paperback : acid free paper) ∞
Subjects: LCSH: McCampbell, David, 1910–1996. | United States.
Navy—Air Group Fifteen—Biography. | Fighter pilots—United States—
Biography. | United States. Navy—Officers—Biography. | United States.
Navy—Aviation—Biography. | World War, 1939–1945—Aerial operations,
American. | World War, 1939–1945—Naval operations, American. |
World War, 1939–1945—Campaigns—Pacific Area.
Classification: LCC D790.35 15th .M337 2019 | DDC 940.54/5973092 [B] —dc23
LC record available at https://lccn.loc.gov/2019018010

BRITISH LIBRARY CATALOGUING DATA ARE AVAILABLE

ISBN (print) 978-1-4766-7779-8
ISBN (ebook) 978-1-4766-3607-8

Front cover image: David McCampbell, USN, Commander,
Air Group Fifteen, poses in the cockpit of his F6F "Hellcat"
on board USS *Essex* (CV-9), circa late October 1944
(official U.S. Navy photograph # 80-G-K-2178,
now in the collections of the National Archives)

Printed in the United States of America

*McFarland & Company, Inc., Publishers
Box 611, Jefferson, North Carolina 28640
www.mcfarlandpub.com*

To my life partner, Harriet, and
to my grandchildren, Emilie and Ryan

Table of Contents

Acknowledgments

Barbara E. Kemp
Head, Reference & Instruction
Nimitz Library
U.S. Naval Academy
589 McNair Rd.
Annapolis, MD 21402

Rebecca L. Collier
Assistant Chief, Textual Reference Archives II Branch (RDT2)
National Archives and Record Administration
8601 Adelphi Rd, College Park, MD 20740

Paul A. Cogan
Archives II Reference Section (RDT2)
Textual Archives Services Division
National Archives and Record Administration
8601 Adelphi Rd, College Park, MD 20740

Hill Goodspeed
Historian and Artifact Collections Manager
National Naval Aviation Museum
1750 Radford Blvd, Suite C
Pensacola, FL 32508–5402

Bill Addison
Library Research Volunteer
National Naval Aviation Museum
1750 Radford Blvd, Suite C
Pensacola, FL 32508–5402

Peggie Penn
Paralegal Specialist
Chief of Naval Air Training
250 Lexington Blvd., Ste. 102
Corpus Christ, TX 78419–5041

Richard A. Marconi
Curator of Education
Historical Society of Palm Beach County
300 North Dixie Highway
West Palm Beach, FL 33401

Nicholas Golubov
Research & Curatorial Assistant
Historical Society of Palm Beach County
300 North Dixie Highway Suite 471
West Palm Beach, FL 33401

Introduction

"Aggressiveness was a fundamental to success in air-to-air combat and if you ever caught a fighter pilot in a defensive mood you had him licked before you started shooting."[1]—Captain David McCampbell, USN

When David McCampbell completed his flight training at the Naval Air Station, at Pensacola, Florida, and was designated a Naval Aviator on April 23, 1938, there were approximately 1,700 pilots in the U.S. Navy and Marine Corps. By the summer of 1941 before World War II started, there were around 4,600 pilots and during the war from 1941 to 1945, the U.S. Navy trained nearly 65,000 American and Allied Naval Aviators. With all these thousands of Naval Aviator pilots who were trained, with many participating in World War II, only one man was to become the Navy's Ace-of-Aces. That man was David McCampbell.[2]

When McCampbell received his Navy Wings there was no way of knowing he would become such a legendary figure. Nevertheless, as the circumstances materialized in the Pacific War in 1944, he was the man who was in the right place at the right time, with the right skills, the experience, the confidence, the aggressiveness, and the courage to meet the Japanese aviators and shoot their aircraft out of the Pacific skies.

He had a great deal going for him. McCampbell was aboard the latest class of fleet carrier, which was part of the most powerful naval weapon system known to man—the Fast Carrier Task Force. He was flying the best carrier-based fighter plane in the world, leading the best-trained naval aviators to attack and destroy enemy aircraft, ships, airfields and facilities during the apex of offensive naval action in the Central and Far-Western Pacific in the campaigns in the Marianas, the battles of Leyte Gulf, and Formosa. As the Commander of the most successful Carrier Air Group in the Pacific War, he led from the front to engage the enemy forces.

While it is natural to glorify those specific exploits of an exceptional warrior like David McCampbell, that is not the full scope of all that he saw and endured while serving his country. This book reveals in detail the true story of all-out war from the eyes of a Naval Aviator and his companions. In combat zones there was the seemingly endless daily grind of early morning missions to find and destroy Japanese aircraft, ships and ground targets, with death all around.

There were many ways to die in their war. Enemy air attacks, surface combatants, or submarines could sink the carrier they lived on. From the time they were catapulted off the carrier deck, they were at risk from being wounded or killed from enemy anti-aircraft shells, from fighter gunfire, from parts of their airplane being shot away, from failures of engines or other critical internal systems, from crashes in the sea or on land, from being taken prisoner to be tortured, shot or even beheaded, from becoming lost at sea and from other horrific causes. After having survived these mission dangers, even landing aboard their moving carrier was a death-defying event.

While David McCampbell was honored for his legendary accomplishments as the leading U.S. Navy Ace of World War II, his 31-year career reveals an incredible diversity of leadership roles and assignments in the service of his country. He commanded ships, training centers, aircraft test facilities, and carrier aircraft squadrons and held a variety of Navy and Defence Department senior staff positions.

In the pages of this book, you will discover the full life story of this unique Navy fighter pilot and hero, David McCampbell.

1

Birth of a Hero

"60 rats, hawks and fish"[1]

The skies were cloudy with scattered clouds high and cumulus clouds low. The surface winds were from the east-northeast from ten to twenty knots. Flying conditions were average. The carrier USS *Essex* was steaming in moderate seas through slight swells some 75 miles east of Polillo Island off the eastern coast of Luzon, the largest island in the Philippines. The date was October 24, 1944.

Sunrise was still over an hour off at 0530 when Commander David McCampbell's alarm went off. He crawled out of his rack to begin another day of war in the Pacific. He pulled on his old green coveralls with his escape kit in one of his pockets, and the rest of his flying gear in the other ones. He put on his brown shoes, lacing them up, got his .38 revolver and knife, and headed out his door. Turning to his right, he went down the ladder to cross the hangar deck and enter Wardroom 1 for breakfast.

He downed his usual three cups of coffee and then drank his orange juice. At 0630 he was in his office four decks up on the OS level looking over the weather report and the latest information. His office was just outside the ready room of the *Essex* fighter squadron. He went about his duties as the Commanding Officer of Carrier Air Group Fifteen. He was responsible for three aircraft squadrons aboard the *Essex*: Fighting Squadron 15 (VF-15) flying Hellcats; Bombing Squadron 15 (VB-15) flying Helldivers and Torpedo Squadron 15 (VT-15) flying Avengers.

For the following hour, McCampbell went to the fighter squadron's ready room to get weather updates, moved to the bridge to observe the launches of the sector search missions, and then retired to spent time doing necessary paper work at his desk. Around 0639 McCampbell went out on the bridge to see the last of his fighters take off for attack sweeps on the airfields around Manila. As the last F6F catapulted off the *Essex*, he reflected on the status of his fighter squadron. Now aboard the carrier he had only seven available fighter aircraft out of thirty-six. McCampbell then went back to his office to continue his paperwork.

Later, at around 0750, search radar operators on the *Essex* and the other carriers of Rear Admiral Sherman's Task Group picked up a group of about 40 bogeys coming in from the west. Soon a second group was discovered behind the first group, and then an even larger third group of bogeys appeared on the radar screens coming in on bearing 240° at a distance of sixty miles. At 0757 Admiral Marc Mitscher, the Commander of Fast Carrier Task Force 38 aboard his flagship carrier, the USS *Lexington* in Sherman's Task Group 38.3, sent out the message, "Hey Rube!,"[2] to the Manila fighter sweep pilots. This was an old circus cry for help, which was adopted for the Navy to indicate that its ships were under attack.[3]

3

At 0800 aboard the *Essex* the ship's general announcing system called out the warning of incoming Japanese aircraft and blurted out, "All fighter pilots, man your planes."[4] With him in the ready room are his plane captain, E.E. Carroll, his Intelligence Officer, and his yeoman. Commander McCampbell quickly explained his intensions as he headed out yelling from the passageway to Carroll to get his plane ready. Lugging his backpack, helmet, and oxygen mask, he dashed to the ladder. Just as he is about to open the door to the hangar deck, he was stopped by an officer who handed him orders from the chief of staff in the control tower of the carrier not to take off on the alert. Reluctantly, he went back to the fighter squadron's ready room, sat down, and began to strip off his flight gear.

A few minutes passed and suddenly the squawk box again called for all pilots to man their planes using the word "immediately."[5] Though he had standing orders not to participate in defensive scrambles, McCampbell assumed the chief of staff had changed his mind and headed to the hangar deck where his plane was waiting on the elevator. After all, this was an emergency. He put on the Mae West and parachute he had removed a few minutes earlier, and rushed to the flight deck.

After ascending in the elevator, his Grumman F6F-5 Hellcat fighter, nicknamed the "Minsi III,"[6] sporting twenty-one Japanese victory flags painted on the fuselage under his canopy, was spotted first on the catapult being fueled. McCampbell got strapped in the cockpit and started checking his gauges when he heard the air officer in the flight control bridge call out on the flight deck announcing system, "If the air commander's plane is not ready to go, send it below!"[7]

McCampbell's centerline external tank was full, but his two main wing tanks were half-empty. The deck crew had become confused by the on-again, off-again fueling orders for the CAG's Hellcat, and assigned the most inexperienced man to the final fueling job. He had filled the center belly tank first, and then turned to gassing up the main wing tanks. What the new "Airedale"[8] did not know was that often the first action a pilot took in combat was to immediately jettison the belly tank to lighten his fighter. McCampbell was faced with this most dangerous problem with only 275 gallons of fuel aboard, but it would have to live with it. He waved off the deck crew with their fuel hoses and signaled that he was ready to launch.[9]

The hydraulic catapult sent McCampbell's dark blue Hellcat down the flight deck and into the sky with seemingly no effort. Once airborne McCampbell flipped on his gun switches and fired a few rounds from each of his six guns. Great-He had no jams. McCampbell banked his plane to the left climbing and ordered his remaining fighters to join him on the inside of the turn. He was followed off the carrier by his wingman, Ensign Roy Rushing, who made a deck launch not using the catapult. Soon McCampbell saw Rushing closing on his left and behind.

Climbing to 6,000 feet at 0821, McCampbell with Rushing was joined by his remaining five fighters. He had hoped to have two divisions aloft, but his second division leader did not get a plane. With Japanese planes coming in at approximately 18,000 feet, McCampbell's group headed north and started climbing. The group flight director, Lieutenant (junior grade) John Connally, who later would serve as the Secretary of the Navy, Governor of Texas, Secretary of the Treasury and candidate for the Presidency, vectored the group to the enemy aircraft intercept point out 40 miles.

With less than a full load of fuel, McCampbell raced ahead of his other fighters except Rushing who was able to stay with him even though he had a full fuel load. At 0833 and reaching 12,000 feet some thirty miles from the carrier, McCampbell and Rushing spotted the bogeys as McCampbell radioed in to the *Essex* Combat Information Center (CIC),

"Rebel, this is Niner-Niner. Are there any friendlies in the area?"[10] The *Essex* responded to the negative. McCampbell came back, "Well, in that case, I have the enemy in sight."[11] He reported a formation of enemy planes with "60 rats, hawks and fish."[12] In Navy lingo "rats" were fighters, "hawks" were dive-bombers and "fish" were torpedo bombers.

Since the enemy fighters were flying 4,000 feet higher than their bombers at 21,000 feet, and McCampbell and Rushing were already higher in altitude than the other five Hellcats, McCampbell directed his combat team of five fighters to attack the bombers at the lower altitude. McCampbell and Rushing climbed somehow undetected to an altitude equal to the incoming enemy fighters. Still climbing they observed the Japanese fighters making a slow turn to the right, continuing around in an arc of 270°. Now positioned in a near perfect location for an attack, 2,000 feet above them and behind the enemy aircraft formation, they were ready to pounce on their prey.

Suddenly, the Japanese fighter group split into three V formations, which was a delight to McCampbell's eyes. It made attacking the planes easier. Noticing an enemy fighter lagging behind in one of the V formations, McCampbell dove down and closed on the fighter until he could see the "meatball"[13] insignia on the olive-drab fuselage. He pulled back slightly and leveled out putting the bogey fighter in the center of his gunsight. McCampbell fired his .50 caliber armor-piercing incendiary bullets from his six guns and watched his tracer rounds follow the target until they hit the fighter in the fuel tanks at the wing-root, igniting them with a "bright yellow flame"[14] with black smoke trailing behind it. The fighter dropped its nose and descended. No parachute was seen, and, in just seconds, the plane crashed into the sea.

As McCampbell scanned the area, he saw that Rushing had also separated a fighter from the formation and sent it trailing smoke to a sea crash. To their surprise, the Japanese seemed not to have reacted to the loss of two of their fighters. McCampbell and Rushing climbed back up 2,000 feet to prepare to repeat their attacks, as the second combat team of F6Fs below were in a real melee engaging the dive-bombers and torpedo planes.

McCampbell again found a target fighter lagging behind and attacked, holding down the trigger to direct seventy-five shells per minute to hit the Zeke. The enemy fighter seemed to stagger a bit, fell out of formation streaming smoke. Then a flash of yellow flame broke out as the fighter went out of control to its destruction in the sea below. This time the Japanese reacted to their lost planes and formed what American naval aviators called a "Lufberry"[15] circle. Like the circle formation that the Conestogas used in the Old West to defend against attacking Indians, the airborne version was a defensive maneuver with a tight counterclockwise circular formation of planes. The idea was that if an attacking plane entered the circle to attack a plane from the rear, it would be subject to being shot down from behind by the next plane in the Lufberry circle. Not many pilots in McCampbell's position would attempt to break into an enemy Lufberry, but he was not an average fighter pilot.[16]

McCampbell and Rushing climbed above to attempt to probe the Lufberry. McCampbell nosed over and dove down at nearly 300 knots on the Japanese formation with all six guns blazing at the nearest fighter he saw. The enemy pilot fired back and they passed each other in a flash with neither downing the other. The attack was repeated, but the result this time was bullet holes in McCampbell's wings. Rushing tried the same attack approach with no success either. McCampbell radioed to Rushing, "I told him I thought they must be running out of gas pretty soon and I knew we had plenty of gas so they'd have to head somewhere and that's when we would work them over.... These were the fighters only. The bombers had all scattered and had been pretty well taken care of."[17]

They circled above the Japanese for ten to fifteen minutes and finally the Japanese broke out of the Lufberry and headed home on a course of 325°. McCampbell recalled, "So Rushing and I followed them back to Manila. We were engaged with them for about an hour and thirty-five minutes. We finally, after much screaming for help, got one other man [Lieutenant (junior grade) Black] who shot down five planes] to help us out there for a little while, and he ran out of ammunition and turned off and went to the ship."[18]

McCampbell described the next actions of himself and Rushing as "a pair of wolves attacking sheep."[19] The attack method was to climb high and dive down to attack a pair of enemy fighters, then split with Rushing to the right and McCampbell taking the left one. After they shot down their prey, they would climb immediately on top, look for stragglers, and execute the attack plan again. McCampbell recalled that the enemy was keeping their formation and their weaving action, but he and Rushing just waited for the right time to attack again. They engaged three types of aircraft: Zekes (Zeros), Oscars (Nakajima army fighters) and Hamps (carrier-based Zeros).[20]

McCampbell found another laggard and he waited until he is just 900 feet from the enemy fighter. At that distance, Minsi III's shells will have a 92 percent chance to land within a three-foot pattern at the wing roots. The shells hit the Japanese fighter and suddenly it exploded and fell to the sea. His third victim does not bail out. Although McCampbell could not see him, Rushing downed his second victim in that last attack.

McCampbell went down for another diving pass to attack an Oscar or Hamp-not sure of which it was. He got into position and fired a short burst when he saw shell tracers going past his wing from his rear. He immediately pulled the stick back and powered away. After he leveled off, he saw another Hellcat fly past him from below. That fighter had also been firing at the same enemy plane he was firing on.

This time, with only Rushing behind him, McCampbell approached an Oscar and opened up his six guns at the wing roots, causing the fighter to begin streaming smoke, then dropping off and diving out of control to the water. This was his fourth victim. Two dive attacks later McCampbell downed a Tony in flames from a wide V formation for victim number five. The sixth victim, a Zeke, met it fate when McCampbell hit its fuel tanks.

After his sixth plane shot down, McCampbell checked his fuel gauge on the left corner of his instrument panel. It showed that he was perilously low. Ensign Rushing, who at this time had shot down four Japanese fighters, had plenty of fuel, but was running low on ammunition. They both continued to attack anyway, and soon McCampbell had one more kill to his name after making two more passes at the Japanese, and Rushing scored his fifth downing. Even though they knew that ever minute they were getting further away from the *Essex*, and increasing the chances that other Japanese fighters might meet them, they pressed on.

McCampbell took on another plane and scored hits with smoke trailing when the enemy fighter banked and got away. As he pulled up, McCampbell found himself without his wingman and began to be concerned. He checked his rear for bandits. Then, off in the distance, McCampbell saw some type of silhouette behind him. For once, a Japanese plane has decided to attack him. He rammed his throttle forward and powered ahead as the enemy plane continued to close on him.

Finally, McCampbell engaged his water injection into the engine cylinders, built up speed and called Rushing, "This is Rebel Leader, Roy, waggle your wings."[21] Thankfully, the wings of the closing fighter begin to move its wings up and down. McCampbell relaxed. It was Rushing with him now.

Rushing, now with six kills to his name, called McCampbell, "Dave, I'm out of ammunition."[22] McCampbell responded, "Roy, this is Dave. I've got a little left. Do you want to stay up here and watch, or go down on each pass with me?"[23] Rushing replied, "I'll go down with you."[24] So they continued ahead as McCampbell spotted an island up ahead. They are close to Luzon now and the risk of other planes attacking them was getting higher. Still, he saw a Zeke trailing behind a V formation too far and attacked with two short bursts from 900 feet away into the wing roots. The plane flashed into flames and nosed over to crash below, with no parachute seen. Victim eight was destroyed.

As the Luzon coast kept getting large in his windshield, McCampbell with Rushing headed in. At this point, the Japanese fighters have descended to 12,000 feet. McCampbell saw his ninth victim and attacked from its rear. As he fired on the fighter, he felt his guns fail to fire, but he continued to pull the trigger until the enemy plane jerked, rolled over and began to dive downward anyway with black smoke trailing. He had hit the fighters' fuel tanks as the fighter crashed. No parachute was seen.

Now McCampbell had no choice but to retire. His guns were out of ammunition and so were Ensign Rushing's guns. With nothing to fire at the enemy and with low fuel, McCampbell and Ensign Rushing headed back toward the carrier on a course heading of 145° using maximum fuel-economy engine rpms and a slow descent. McCampbell's instruments showed he was low on fuel in his tanks. He called, "Roy, I've only got forty-five gallons left. I'm slowing to thirteen fifty revolutions."[25] Rushing acknowledged and revealed that he had plenty of fuel, but would stay with him. They are now flying home slow at 130 knots.

Every few minutes McCampbell called the *Essex*. They hear only silence. They continued forward and finally the *Essex* answered McCampbell's radio call, but the news was not good. The carrier's flight deck was loaded with aircraft for a strike and would not be available to take them aboard for at least fifteen minutes. They are still sixty miles out from the *Essex*.

Things got even dodgier as the two slow returning Hellcats approached the American task force. Gunners on the USS *Hornet* mistook the Hellcats as enemy fighters and fired anti-aircraft shells at them. McCampbell and Rushing descended to an altitude nearly touching the waves and began weaving back and forth to avoid the friendly fire. McCampbell called on the radio, "Call off the dogs. We're friendlies, trying to get back to the *Essex*"[26] The firing stopped just as several Hellcats dove in on them ready to fire. Thankfully, they recognized the two lone fighters and broke off their attack.

Several minutes later, they saw the *Essex* and, to their dismay, the flight deck was still covered with strike aircraft. McCampbell checked his fuel gauge and was desperate now as he looked around. He spotted the *Lexington* nearby, but then discovered she had a full flight deck too. As McCampbell prepared to ditch his Hellcat, word came in that the *Langley* was completing her torpedo bomber launches and would be able to let him land in a few minutes.

McCampbell's fuel gauge revealed that he could not last a few minutes, but miraculously he was able to keep it aloft long enough to land. He continued in anyway and approached the stern of the *Langley* expecting to be waved off by the LSO. His fuel gauge showed he had passed the ten-gallon mark and was moving down toward zero. McCampbell pulled his stick close to his belly, banked his Hellcat into a sharp left turn and headed in with the LSO's yellow and red diagonal flags waving. He was now 30 feet from the stern of the carrier. The LSO crossed his throat with his right hand directing McCampbell to cut his engine and land. The Minsi III bounced on hitting the flight deck, caught the second wire and jerked forward for 90 feet until it stopped.

As his Hellcat came to a stop, the engine coughed and stopped before he had an opportunity to turn it off. There were only six rounds of ammunition left in one gun, and all the other guns were empty. McCampbell later discussed the mission,

> My claim of nine planes destroyed includes only those that were seen by my wingman and myself to flame or explode. Numerous others were seen with engine smoking and diving away, two of which were spinning apparently out of control, toward the water, and are claimed as probable. Others were hit and undoubtedly damaged. No attempt was made at the time to record types and angle of attack, in fact it was not until we had destroyed five planes and business was beginning to get good that I decided to keep a box score by marking on my instrument panel with a pencil...[27]

The estimate he gave was that the two of them shot down nine Zeros, three Hamps and three Oscars.

Aboard the *Langley* McCampbell downed sandwiches and coffee. After his fighter had been rearmed and refueled, he was in the air again on Combat Air Patrol (CAP) on "low patrol"[28] at an altitude of 2,000 feet guarding against torpedo plane attacks. McCampbell asked why he had been given that specific CAP duty. The response was "Admiral's orders."[29] It was then that he knew that Admiral Sherman was upset with him.

After an uneventful patrol, McCampbell landed on the *Essex*. He was immediately summoned to the flag bridge. He knew what was coming. McCampbell entered the Admiral's cabin and confronted the steely gaze and frown of Sherman's face as he looked up from his desk. "Dammit, I told you I didn't want you flying in these scrambles."[30] McCampbell tried to explain, but before he finished his unconvincing excuse, the admiral interrupted him and said, "Dammit, don't ever let it happen again."[31] In McCampbell's defense, Captain Brown, Sherman's Chief of Staff, interjected his comment, "Well, Admiral, we were sent out here to kill Japs, and that's exactly what Commander McCampbell did."[32]

After receiving his medicine, McCampbell headed toward his quarters where fellow pilots and Captain Weber, the commanding officer of the *Essex*, received him with congratulations. He had shot down nine enemy fighters in a single mission, a feat that had never been done before and it is doubtful that it ever would ever be equaled. He and his wingman had turned back a group of sixty enemy fighter planes and protected Task Group 38.3 from potentially serious damage.

October 24, 1944, was the day David McCampbell became a real American hero. In the Oval Office of the White House on January 10, 1945, President Franklin D. Roosevelt presented him with the Medal of Honor.[33]

2

Bessemer to Annapolis

"a good sailor and one not easily lost in the academic sea"[1]

The core roots of a heroic man of the sea do not always come from the coastal environs. And so it was for David McCampbell.

In the midst of the Southern steel economic miracle, on October 10, 1886, a John Luther Perry from McCalle, Alabama, died leaving his wife, Martha Frances Velma Calhoun, widowed with three small children: Elizabeth LaValle Perry, John Calhoun Perry and Henry David Perry. Martha and her three children moved to Bessemer, Alabama, to stay with her mother, Frances Woodruff Calhoun, and assist in running her boarding house on Carolina Avenue near the train station.

William Jacob Long, a man of means from Redkey, Indiana, had the vision of what the commercial growth of the steel industry in the Bessemer area could be and decided to travel to the town and stay at Frances's boarding house. He became interested in Martha and on November 5, 1890, he married her. Now he had a new wife and Martha had a man to help raise her three children. A year later on October 8, 1891, Martha gave William a son, Charles Allen Long.

The Long family prospered and grew along with the city of Bessemer. In 1887 William Long established *The Bessemer Cornice and Iron Works* in a new building on the corner of 2nd Avenue and 23rd. Street. A few years later, a Mr. Lewis, owner of *Lewis Hardware*, needed some financial help, so William Long purchased a 51 percent interest in the company, and later bought out Mr. Lewis altogether. This became *Long-Lewis Hardware Company*. In 1890 *Sullivan, Long & Haggerty Contractors Incorporated* was founded when two Irishmen needed funding to continue building sewers. William Long provided the partnership investment and the business flourished.[2]

On September 18, 1901, Elizabeth LaValle Perry married 26-year-old Andrew Jackson McCampbell at Bessemer. Andrew lived in a rented house on 19th Street in Bessemer and worked as a salesman at a local grocer. His father, William Daniel McCampbell, was a farmer in Jackson County, Alabama. His mother, Martha Jane Jenkins, married William in 1861 and they had five sons and three daughters. Andrew became a salesman at his father-in-law's *Long-Lewis Hardware*. The next year on August 18, 1902, they had their first child, a daughter named Frances Velma McCampbell.[3]

This whole story began on January 16, 1910, when a son was born, David McCampbell. Not much is known about David McCampbell's early life in Alabama except that the family owned ten cows during World War I. The cows were milked by an African American man and the milk was bottled by his mother and sister, and ultimately delivered by young David.

David did well in grade school through the 7th grade. He ranked second in his 6th grade class. David noted that his grades dropped off when the classes became more difficult. He developed an interest in swimming in Alabama when his father used to take the family to the lake every weekend when he was six, seven and eight years old. He was to develop his skills in the sport as the years progressed.[4]

In 1922 Andrew McCampbell moved his family to West Palm Beach, Florida, and soon opened *McCampbell's Furniture Store* on 330 Clematis Avenue. The store did well and eventually he added two more stores in the area. An advertisement in June 1930 declared, "If it goes in the Home you will find it at McCampbell's. Furniture and Floor coverings for every room in the house, stoves, refrigerators, glassware, crockery, cooking utensils, electric goods, for the kitchen and dining room. Trunks, bags and suit cases for your vacation, regular $1.00 square yard congoleum 50c per square yard. Good window shades, 3 × 6 feet for 59c. Special prices on Oil stoves and Gasoline pressure stoves in all sizes."[5]

The McCampbell' stores did well until the Stock Market Crash of 1929, when business dropped off. Store sales eventually deteriorated to the point that Andrew was forced to declare bankruptcy in 1934.

In 1923, a year after Andrew had moved the family to West Palm Beach, David's parents decided their thirteen-year-old son would follow his first cousin and attend the Staunton Military Academy in Staunton, Virginia. The Academy, founded in 1884, was considered one of America's most prestigious military academies.[6] It was also expensive for the 1920s, and cost some $1,200 per year when David attended.

David adjusted well to Staunton and the military discipline that was modeled after West Point. His professor of military science was from West Point, and the two assistant instructors served as sergeants in the Army in World War I. David was no scholar, performing average in his courses, but he graduated. David had lost a year when he had to leave Staunton in midyear due to serious sinus problems, graduating after his fifth year.

David was an Army ROTC participant at Staunton, and spent the summer of 1927 at Camp Meade, Maryland. Barry Goldwater (later the U.S. Senator from Arizona, 1953–1964) attended the ROTC camp that summer with him where they both won their expert riflemen badges. At Staunton, McCampbell headed ROTC Company E and Goldwater commanded Company B. David attained the rank of Army 2nd Lieutenant from the ROTC experience.

McCampbell and Goldwater shared a number of experiences together, mostly notably at the 1927 camp. McCampbell recalled that the college guys were mixed up with them in the ROTC work. The college boys went on a sit-down strike, while Barry Goldwater had all the prep school boys together with him and voted not to participate in the sit-down. A few days later the college guys returned to work. McCampbell remembered that a tall, husky guy drilled us in full gear and had us run in the sand, on the track for 15 minutes.[7]

McCampbell took part in football and baseball at Staunton, but swimming and diving were his sports. Back during his one year at home in West Palm Beach, he took up diving and continued to increase his swimming ability. He excelled in swimming underwater, having once won a watermelon for holding his breath for 25 yards. At Staunton, McCampbell had a good swimming coach that helped him develop further. He swam backstroke, and was one of the two team divers.

After graduation from Staunton in 1928, McCampbell wanted to attend the University of Alabama, but his mother would not let him go because his uncle had been a football hero there and eventually became an alcoholic. So David headed to his second choice, Georgia Tech in Atlanta, to pursue a degree in civil engineering. He was influenced in his degree program decision by the family construction business back in Bessemer, *Sullivan,*

Long & Haggerty, which built roads, schools, storm sewers, water systems and more. Based on the scholastic reputation of Staunton Military Academy, Georgia Tech did not require David to take an entrance exam.

At Georgia Tech, McCampbell's academic performance was good. He did well in algebra, plane and solid geometry, but failed his Spanish course. He credited his superior math grades to the advanced courses he had taken at Staunton.

David participated in sports at Tech. Though he spent six weeks on the freshman football team, he quit the day the team faced a scrimmage game with the varsity team. The varsity players' linemen weighed at least 220 pounds or more, and he weighed 156 pounds as a halfback. That was all it took to end his college football experience. As a member of the Tech swimming team, McCampbell swam the backstroke, and also took part in diving. He was not without an active social life, having attracted several girlfriends with his speedy Chrysler roadster, which few other men on campus had families wealthy enough to provide them.

During the 1928–1929 year at Georgia Tech, David joined the Navy ROTC (NROTC) and was able to make the 1929 summer cruise aboard the battleship USS *New York* (BB-34). His positive experience on the cruise influenced him to consider attending the Naval Academy at Annapolis, Maryland. With the events of the stock market crash of October 1929 and the end of the boom years in Florida, which created financial problems for his parents, David sought to reduce the burden of funding his college education by seeking an appointment to Annapolis and a resulting free education.

To gain admission to the Naval Academy, one had to be nominated by a U.S. Congressman, Senator, Vice President or the President, pass an entrance examination, as well as a medical examination. David applied for an appointment to Annapolis, and with the support of Andrew's political influence, David was able to get on the list of potential nominees. He was interviewed by the long-haired U.S. Senator, Park Trammell of Florida, and took two academic performance tests; one in English and the other in mathematics. He excelled in math having missed only one question, but barely passed the English exam. Senator Trammell named McCampbell as the first alternate behind a young man from Miami. Fortunately, for David, the Miami selectee failed his physical exam, thereby sending David McCampbell on his way to Annapolis.

As a plebe in his first year, David had no trouble adjusting to life at the Naval Academy. He had the advantage of having already lived under military discipline and hazing at Staunton. David recalled that at dinner he and other plebes were often required to "simulate [a] steam engine"[8] where they each alternated moving up and down like they were the cylinders of an engine.[9]

All the plebes ended up with nicknames. Having the last name of McCampbell, his nickname was naturally "Soupy"[10] after the Campbell soup product. During his years at Annapolis, David rarely received demerits. Once he had received ten demerits for not being out of bed and squared away when the reveille bell stopped ringing, and twenty demerits for sunbathing on the roof of the dormitory. Overall, he had no issues with the military life, even including the drilling and parades. David was to recall that he actually had more drills at Staunton than he did at Annapolis.[11]

Academically, David had no problems with the majority of the classes, but was forced to re-take exams in two Spanish courses, one mechanical drawing course and another for AC electricity. He took no special interest in his professional courses like ordnance and gunnery.

In the summer cruise after his first year at the Academy (his third-class summer cruise), McCampbell sailed aboard the 26,100-ton battleship USS *Arkansas* (BB-33) to Europe, visiting Edinburgh in Scotland, Cherbourg, France, Kiel, Germany, and Oslo, Norway. The cruise saw David standing engineering and bridge watches and sleeping in a hammock. At the Port of Cherbourg, David took five days leave and visited Paris. He took another five days off at Kiel and visited Hamburg.

As McCampbell entered his third year at Annapolis, he began to lose his interest and motivation. He even considered resigning and going to work in the family business in Alabama. He became even more discouraged after he learned that the Navy would probably only receive enough funding to commission half the class. Since David did not rank in the upper half of his class, he knew he would not be commissioned into the service.[12]

The bright spot in his life at Annapolis was in sports. It went out for baseball in his first year, but after a little run-in with his coach, Artie Doyle, he dropped out. After Doyle left the Naval Academy, David considered trying out for the baseball team again, but since he was unsatisfactory in a class, he could not try out.

McCampbell found satisfaction and success when he joined the freshman swimming team. Soon after joining, he decided to put all his effort in diving. He made the varsity swimming teams the last three years and moved up to senior diver in the third and fourth years.

The Naval Academy swim teams had eight swimming meets each season with Ivy League schools like Yale, the City College of New York, Harvard, Princeton, Rutgers, the University of Pennsylvania and two others. At the meets, David had the usual compulsory dives on the one-meter board, which included the front dive, back dive, the half gainer, and the jackknife. David then performed the optional dives with the one-and-a-half, the back one-and-a-half, the forward one-and-a-half with a half twist, the gained one-and-a-half, and the double somersault. He rarely worked off the high diving board.

David was a talented diver and took part in numerous regional swimming and diving championships. He became the A.A.U. Diving Champion for the Mid-Atlantic States in 1931 from the three-meter board, and was the Eastern Intercollegiate Diving Champion in

A 1933 Naval Academy Swim Team photograph, showing David McCampbell in the first row, third swimmer from the left (U.S. Naval Academy Class of 1933 Yearbook, page 480).

1932. He would have been able to represent the Naval Academy and the U.S. in diving in the 1932 Olympics, but with his failing grade in Spanish at the time, he could not attend. He finished fifth in the Nationals at Ann Arbor, Michigan, his last year.[13]

The 1933 Academy yearbook provided the highlights of the Swimming Team successes and accomplishments:

> The 1933 season looked promising despite the graduation of stars of the '32 squad. Returning were Captain Ray Thompson, fresh from National and Olympic triumphs, and Ashford, Davis, McCampbell, Hyland, Torrey.... In the first aquatic meet of the winter sports season, the mermen succeeded in outclassing the University of Virginia swimmers, 62–9.... Thompson and McCampbell, Navy's two intercollegiate champions, were the conspicuous performers of the day.[14]

McCampbell's interest in aviation was sparked in his youth in 1919 when his grandfather took him up several times in his old war-surplus Curtiss Jenny. From then on, he caught the flying bug. His interest in naval aviation took off during the Academy's "aviation"[15] summer before his second-class year (third year at Annapolis) when he flew on familiarization flights in twin-engine seaplanes. That summer the class stayed home at Annapolis.

Social life at the Academy mostly consisted of various arranged dances, but he eventually developed a relationship with a girl, Sally-Jane Heliker, who worked on the stage in New York. She would later become his second wife. He originally met her in West Palm Beach.

After his third year at the Naval Academy, he took part in the summer cruise aboard the battleship USS *Florida* (BB-30). His duties aboard were those of any other junior naval officer, and not like the previous summer duties that were those given to enlisted personnel. On that summer cruise, David visited the ports in Houston, Texas; Ponce, Puerto Rico; Cuba and Bermuda. David seemed to enjoy his cruises at sea.[16]

David McCampbell graduated from the Naval Academy with a B.S. in Marine Engineering on June 1, 1933. The U.S. Naval Academy Yearbook for the Class of 1933, called the "Lucky Bag," referred to him as follows:

David McCampbell
West Palm Beach, Florida
"Dave" "Mac"

> To attempt to describe this personage in the short space allotted here is a difficult task and must necessarily be sketchy. To begin with, Mac hails from Florida and has never been able to acclimate himself to the rigors of Maryland winters-or summers. He and the roommate have fought a four year battle over the question: 'Shall the windows be open or closed?' In academics Mac hasn't always had the wind abaft the beam, so to speak, but in rough weather he proved himself to be a good sailor and one not easily lost in the academic sea. In athletic fields of endeavor, Mac had had little or no difficulty in maintaining his superiority over others. For four years he has been the Navy's foremost fancy diver, and those who appreciate this most difficult and graceful art he has provided many hours of delightful entertainment. In fact, he so delighted the judges upon one occasion that they crowned him inter-collegiate champion. In addition to his diving, he has proven himself to be an outfielder of no mean ability. Mac's heart is torn between two loves; one Aphrodite, the other is Morpheus. Sometimes one has the upper hand, sometimes the other. He enjoys both to the fullest extent and is content with either. Mac will always find life enjoyable because he has an amiable disposition, because he is a gentleman, and because he is an optimist.[17]

The same day of his graduation, McCampbell received an honorable discharge from the Regular Navy and was commissioned as an Ensign in the U.S. Naval Reserve. Taking his disappointment in stride, David went to work for his family's business, *Sullivan, Long & Haggerty Contractors*, back in Bessemer, Alabama, as the boss of a crew building a storm sewer for $15 a week. He then decided to work in another family business, the *Birmingham Long-Lewis Hardware* store, for $11.00 per week. Since he didn't make enough money to drive back and forth between Bessemer and Birmingham, he got the idea to head out west to California and find a job.

After arriving in Los Angeles, he applied for work at the *Los Angeles Tribune* and an oil company, but they did not hire him. He was able to land a job as a riveter for Douglas Aircraft in Santa Monica. He worked on building DC-2s and DC-3s, having helped roll out the second DC-3 at the plant.

While living in Southern California, he became good friends with Buster Crabbe (Clarence L. Crabbe II), the renowned Los Angeles 1932 Olympic gold medal winner of the 400-meter freestyle, and soon to become a movie actor in the 1930s-1940s. David met Buster and his wife Virginia through an introduction by a fellow Annapolis classmate, Raymond W. Thompson, Jr. Raymond had been on the 1932 Olympic Swimming Team with Buster. David hit it off well with Buster, and he was invited to the Hollywood Athletic Club where he did some practice diving.[18]

3

Going Navy:
From Ships to Aviation

"I was comfortable in the air"[1]

After working for Douglas Aircraft for six months, McCampbell received an offer letter to rejoin the Regular Navy on Active Duty. He was delighted to have the opportunity to begin his professional career. He agreed to join and received a date-of-rank of May 29, 1934, as an Ensign. This date-of-rank gave him seniority over the graduating Naval Academy Class of 1934. He was given orders to report to the USS *Portland* at Portland, Maine, within 30 days. His official transfer from the Naval Reserve to the Regular Navy occurred on June 14, 1934.

McCampbell first drove cross-country in his car to visit his parents in West Palm Beach, and then proceeded north to meet the ship. On June 28, 1934, Ensign David McCampbell reported aboard the *Portland*. He was attached to the Engineering Department as an assistant heading the "E"[2] Division (Electrical). His E Division staff of sailors handled all shipboard electrical and interior communications equipment gear. Their primary responsibility was keeping the electrical generation equipment online for distribution throughout the ship. Reporting directly to McCampbell was a Warrant Officer who was a skilled electrician. He made Campbell's job easy.[3]

McCampbell stood engineering watches in the engine room the entire time he was assigned to the *Portland*. He became quite knowledgeable of all the control panels, dials and gauges down there, as well as the ship electrical circuit switchboard.

The *Portland* (CA-33) was a mammoth ship, a heavy cruiser of 9,950 tons, with a length of 610 feet and a beam of 66 feet at the widest point. The ship drew 22 feet of water from the keel to the waterline up forward. It was driven by four propellers powered by four steam-turbine engines giving it a total of 21,000 HP. Each engine was fed by steam from two boilers, fired by Navy Standard Fuel Oil, stored in 66 tanks of various sizes throughout the hull. The boilers were supplied ocean saltwater that was heated to create stream. With her power plant, the *Portland* allowed the ship to reach a top speed of 32 knots with all engines online. She could cruise at 15 knots with only two boilers lit, driving two engines.

The electrical system was powered by two auxiliary engines. The ship primarily used direct current (DC) except for certain systems like the radar gear and dental chair that required alternating current (AC).

Fresh water, converted from seawater by evaporators, was available, though somewhat rationed. It was stored in four 10,000-gallon tanks. Fresh water use for showers and shaving was available during certain hours of each day. Toilets were flushed by seawater.

USS *Portland* (CA 33) at Pearl Harbor, Hawaii, June 14, 1942, with her crew paraded on deck in "Whites" (Official U.S. Navy Photograph NH 97833, from the collections of the Naval Historical Center).

Of course, the real purpose of the *Portland* was to take the battle to enemy shipping using its armament. She had nine 8-inch guns, three in each of her two forward turrets, with one turret on the aft deck. On each side she had four 5-inch dual-purpose guns in single mounts. There were also a number of anti-aircraft (AA) guns available on the decks.[4]

In addition to his Engineering Department duties, McCampbell was given collateral duties as catapult officer, electronics expert, assistant gunnery officer of the port 5-inch gun battery and deep-sea diving officer. As catapult officer, he was responsible for one of the two catapults located amidships aboard the *Portland*. Aboard the cruiser were four Curtiss SOCs that were stored in a hangar. To launch one of the ships' Curtiss SOC "Seagull"[5] scout-observation planes, compressed air was engaged as air pressure increased to a peak as the pilot brought the aircraft engine to full power. When the pilot gave the signal, pins were taken out and the catapult shot the aircraft along the rails to get airborne.[6]

The Curtiss SOC-1 scout-observation biplane was a short-range floatplane designed for gunfire observation and scouting for the enemy fleets. The aircraft, with a wingspan of 36 feet, was powered by a Pratt & Whitney R-1340 single-row radial engine, and could attain a maximum speed of 162 m.p.h. The plane had a crew of two with a pilot and observer/gunner. The armament included a forward, fixed mounted, .30 caliber machine gun and a flexible mounted .30 caliber gun in the aft cockpit. The aircraft could carry two small bombs under the lower wings.[7]

After a flight, the Curtiss SOC-1 landed in the sea in the smooth wake of the cruiser and loaded aboard by a crane. In July of 1936, McCampbell became an Aircraft Gunnery Observer with Scouting Squadron 11 aboard the *Portland* after his predecessor, Ensign George F. Pittard, was injured when he got his finger caught on the hook used to lift the SOC, losing most of his finger. With his pilot, Ensign James A. Smith, McCampbell was quite active making catapult takeoff cycles as an observer.

As an Aircraft Gunnery Observer McCampbell was responsible for spotting from the aircraft where the ships' main battery shells or any gunnery bullet landed and gave firing corrections to the weapons directors aboard using Morse code. In those days, there was no voice communications from these aircraft, so aviators were required to learn to communicate by Morse code.

In an example of his purely observer role, McCampbell and his pilot Jimmy Smith were launched with another Curtiss SOC-1 in heavy fog off San Clemente Island. The second aircraft soon went down and McCampbell's aircraft circled about the downed plane relaying messages back to the *Portland*. They remained on station so long that were unable to make it back to the *Portland*. The USS *Chicago* picked them up and they spent the night there. Finally, the *Portland* picked up the crew of the downed SOC-1.[8]

One of real important side benefits of being an aviation observer was that those selected received 50 percent additional pay over their base pay. This was more important now to McCampbell because he had gotten married on June 26, 1936, to Susan Rankin.

Curtiss SOC-1 scout-observation aircraft (Bureau # 9979) in flight on July 2, 1939 (Official U.S. Navy Photograph # 80-G-5885 now in the collections of the National Archives).

Susan was born in Andalusia, Alabama, on September 18, 1914, but had moved to West
Palm Beach. After he received permission from the Captain, he got married in Honolulu,
Hawaii, when the *Portland* was there for an overhaul. To join McCampbell in Hawaii, Susan,
age 22, sailed from Los Angeles Harbor on June 26 aboard the S.S *Malolo*, arriving in Honolulu on July 2.

McCampbell and his new bride lived temporarily in a beach house on Waikiki. The
house belonged to an old architect friend he had known from Wilmington, Delaware, who
had retired in Honolulu. McCampbell made the eight-mile trip to work at Pearl Harbor
each day in his friend's Packard. After the wedding and time with her new husband, she
sailed from Honolulu aboard the S.S. *Monterey* on September 30 and arrived back home
in Los Angeles on October 5.[9]

The USS *Portland* had first arrived on June 10, 1933, at its new homeport in the Pacific
at Long Beach. Long Beach, a major naval base and shipyard, was the home at that time of
the U.S. Pacific Fleet. The same month McCampbell had reported aboard the *Portland*
(June 1934), Captain Herbert Leavy had turned over his command to Captain David M. Le
Breton. McCampbell's impression of his skipper was that he was "pretty tough"[10] and "very
distant from the crew and from the officers."[11] A real irritant with the Captain was his German shepherd dog named Oofie. The dog seemed to have issues with sea duty and had no
use for sailors trying to pet him. Once he peed on a main deck stanchion when an official
inspection was underway, leaving the Captain embarrassed and the deck crew that had to
clean up his mess mad.[12]

After serving as Captain of the Yard at the Pearl Harbor Navy Yard, in June of 1935
Captain Willis W. Bradley, Jr., took command of the *Portland*. He had a distinguished career
up to this point, having received the Medal of Honor for his extraordinary heroism by
extinguishing multiple fires caused by powder explosions as a Lieutenant while aboard the
USS *Pittsburgh* in World War I. He had numerous command tours, including as the Naval
Governor and Commander of Naval Station Guam in 1929.[13]

McCampbell was much impressed by Captain Bradley during his time aboard the
Portland. In May 1937 the *Portland* was at San Francisco celebrating the opening of the
Golden Gate Bridge. When underway approaching the new wonder of the world, Captain
Bradley turned to McCampbell, who was standing watch on the bridge of the *Portland* as
the Officer of the Deck, and said that McCampbell had the conn, as he walked back to the
chart room. McCampbell never forgot that day of celebration when he, as an Ensign, took
the *Portland* under the Golden Gate Bridge.[14]

McCampbell made numerous cruises while serving aboard the *Portland*. In the spring
of 1934, the *Portland* sailed with Cruiser Division Four and the fleet engaged in Fleet Problem XV through the Panama Canal, into the Caribbean and then along the Atlantic Coast
to New York. The purpose of the trip was to see how fast the Navy could transfer warships
from the Pacific to the Atlantic, as well as carry out the three-phased exercises to defend
an attack on the Panama Canal, to capture forward bases and to take part in a major fleet
engagement.[15]

The *Portland* sailed at high speed with the bow wave spraying mist for a hundred
yards along her gray-painted hull as her engines powered her to speeds more like a fast
destroyer. Though the *Portland* was homeported in Long Beach, McCampbell had reported
aboard her on June 28 while on the deployment along the East Coast to Portland, Maine.
The ship returned home in early November.

The 1935 Fleet Problem XVI took the *Portland* to Midway Island in the mid–Pacific
some thousand miles west of Hawaii. McCampbell served as the boat officer while the

Marines aboard the *Portland* did a practice landing onto Midway. There was no real liberty at Midway, but a few sailors were able to explore the "desolate place"[16] which consisted of a cable station, one man and his wife, a Jersey cow and some chickens. The fleet returned to training along the familiar waters of San Diego, Long Beach, San Francisco and Bremerton, Washington.

The year 1935 would turn out to be a special one for the *Portland*. On October 2 President Roosevelt and his party joined the *Portland* and a sister heavy cruiser, USS *Houston* (CA-30) at Long Beach. The President with a few others sailed with the *Houston*, while the presidential staff of four sailed aboard the *Portland*. The *Houston* had been specially modified with an elevator to allow the President to go from the main deck up to his stateroom unaided a few floors above. In the afternoon, the two cruisers sailed out of the harbor to sea with Roosevelt and his entourage to the thunder of a 21-gun salute from the other ships of the fleet. The ships steamed for two days at 15 knots and put down anchors at Magdalena Bay off Baja, California, Mexico to allow the guest to take in a little fishing.

On October 5, the ships sailed a few more hours and then set anchors in the open ocean for more fishing. This process of sailing a few hours and fishing continued for a week. The two cruisers reached the Cocos Islands, located some 550 km off Costa Rico, then headed to the Panama Canal where they made the canal transit.

On the Atlantic side, the fishing trip continued on to the San Blas Islands off the north coast of the Isthmus of Panama. McCampbell recalled that the island natives lived in huts built on stilts out in the sea. The leisurely fishing trip cruise continued as before until the ships reached Charleston, South Carolina. There the President and his party disembarked as the *Portland* logbook entry was recorded, "as escort to Houston, (S.O.P.A.) President of the United States."[17]

The spring 1936 Fleet Problem XVII was a five-phased war game exercise that focused on training in anti-submarine operations, testing fleet communications and training fleet air patrol squadrons. The exercise had the Fleet Battle Force engaging the opposition Scouting Force that included submarines. The exercises took place off the west coast of the U.S., Central America and in the Panama Canal Zone.[18]

The summer 1936 deployment of *Portland* with the fleet was a short visit to Panama for a brief canal transit, followed by training in Hawaiian waters. The *Portland* had participated in major war games in the Pacific triangle between Hawaii, Midway and the Aleutians before returning home in October. There was also the overhaul of the *Portland* at Pearl Harbor.

While at Pearl Harbor McCampbell with three other officers decided to take an eye exam in preparation for applying for flight training at Pensacola. They headed off to see the flight surgeon on the Naval Air Station on Ford Island. All four of the officers failed the eye exam because of a condition called hyperphoria, which was the tendency for the line of sight of one eye to deviate upward relative to that of the other eye. It is caused by a problem with the extra ocular muscles.

Not satisfied with the flight surgeon's diagnosis, McCampbell, along with a fellow officer, Frank Marshall, went into town to see a civilian optometrist. This doctor deemed their eyesight perfect, so they asked for the exam results in writing. They took the written statements from the civilian doctor back to the same flight surgeon they had seen before on a Friday, but the doctor said he had an exam and could not re-examine them that day, or Saturday or Sunday. Since the *Portland* departed Pearl at 8:00 a.m. on Monday, McCampbell and Marshall were unable to take another eye exam. Since flight physicals could only be given at Pearl Harbor, Norfolk, Coco Solo in Panama or aboard the USS *Saratoga*, McCampbell was delayed an entire year from applying to NAS Pensacola.[19]

In May of 1937, the *Portland* took part in the Fleet Problem XVIII that began in the waters off Alaska with port visits including Anchorage, Sitka and Valdex. McCampbell was able to pan for gold in a creek at Valdez. He recalled meeting a man who would fly his airplane fitted with skis up to his gold mine in the mountains. There he would load the plane with another load of gold ore and fly it back to Valdez, landing at low tide in the mud flats. McCampbell also did some salmon fishing in a mountain creek, where he could catch the fish with his bare hands. While off Alaska, the *Portland* went to a bay and fired four 5-inch shells to create an avalanche. McCampbell and his pilot then flew over the avalanche for one fantastic view.

The Fleet Problem exercises continued into the waters of the Hawaiian Islands and off Midway Island. The purpose of the exercises was to practice various tactics associated with attacking and seizing advanced bases. This was to be invaluable training in later Pacific War operations.[20]

When the *Portland* was in Bremerton for an overhaul, McCampbell's father had a major accident and was not expected to live. Granted 30 days of emergency leave, he travelled back home to West Palm Beach. While he was away, the *Portland* almost sunk when someone neglected to close the seacocks as the cruiser hit the water as it moved down the skids. McCampbell was fortunate to be away on leave as the incident created quite a flap and forced an investigation.

McCampbell was glad to get orders to NAS Pensacola for flight training and finally leave the *Portland* and all the duties he had to juggle. With orders issued, McCampbell was heading to the south. In June 1937, McCampbell's flying career finally got off the ground at Naval Air Station Pensacola where he reported for flight training. Naval flight training was a one-year period involving 465 hours of ground school and some 300 flight hours. Ground school was full-time the first six weeks and then he went to half days thereafter. The cadets learned navigation, powerplants, structures, aerodynamics, and radio code (Morse code).[21]

The flight training consisted of progressing through various squadrons with each covering different aircraft and flight instruction. McCampbell started out flying the floatplane NY in Squadron One, and was the first to solo in it under instructor Marine Captain S. Holmberg. He then moved up to fly the N2N. In Squadron Two he flew the N3Ns. Squadron Three involved flying OS2U land planes, while Squadron Four, under the flight instruction of Lieutenant Frank Turner, was in seaplanes and multi-engine torpedo planes.

During his training in Squadron Five,

Ensign David McCampbell. Photograph taken during his flight training at Naval Air Station (NAS) Pensacola, Florida in 1937 (National Museum of Naval Aviation, Emil Buehler Library, Ensign David S. McCampbell Aviation Training Jacket, Accession Number NNAM.1999.170.077).

McCampbell was flying stunts in SNJs and F4B-4s when his flight instructor, Lieutenant Fitzhugh Lee, gave him the highest grade possible, a 4.0, which was the only one he had ever given to any flight student.[22]

Spending a year assigned to Scouting Squadron 11 as an observer with his pilot, Jimmy Smith, letting him take over the controls of the Curtiss SOC-1, McCampbell was already used to flying in a floatplane. At Pensacola McCampbell had little difficulty getting through flight training. McCampbell explained, "Well, the main thing was that I was comfortable in the air. Having been an observer for a year helped with that aspect, and other than that, it was just following instruction."[23]

He was comfortable in the air, but some of his fellow trainees never gained that feeling and either dropped out or washed out having received too many "downed"[24] flights (a down in flight training is a failed check flight). McCampbell had two downed flights; one for not locking the tail wheel before he took off, and the other for violating a low altitude restriction.[25]

While at Pensacola, McCampbell was promoted to Lieutenant (junior grade). Some of those going through flight training with McCampbell were Lieutenant (junior grade) Frank G. Marshall and Lieutenant (junior grade) George F. Pittard, Jr., from the *Portland*, a former Annapolis classmate Lieutenant (junior grade) Robert S. Camera, Lieutenant (junior grade) Albert P. "Scoofer"[26] Coffin, Lieutenant (junior grade) William I. Martin, Ensign Raymond E. Doll and Ensign Edward C. Outlaw.

The social life on and off the base in Pensacola was active. There were dances every weekend at the Officer's Club that McCampbell attended. The drinking was heavy at the club and there were known to be occasional skinny-dipping episodes in Escambia Bay. In town, there was the San Carlos Hotel and a roadhouse between town and the base that he visited on occasion. Since McCampbell was married, his social life was more limited than others in his class.

David McCampbell graduated from flight training and received his Naval Aviator wings on Saturday, April 23, 1938, placing in the top five of his class. After the event he and his fellow graduates headed to the Officer's Club to celebrate over drinks.[27]

4

VF-4 and the Ranger

"It was a happy ship…"[1]

Having finished his flight training at NAS Pensacola ranked in the top five of his class, McCampbell was able to select any open fleet position available. He requested assignment to a fighter squadron. Thus, the new Naval Aviator, Lieutenant (junior grade) David McCampbell, received orders in June 1938 to Fighting Squadron Four (VF-4) aboard the carrier USS *Ranger*. He joined the squadron at North Island Naval Air Station on the Coronado peninsula across the harbor from San Diego.[2]

When he arrived aboard his new squadron, he was assigned as the wingman for Lieutenant (junior grade) Joseph C. Clifton. Clifton, hailing from Paducah, Kentucky, was nicknamed "Jumping Joe"[3] during a football game against Tennessee when, as a defensive fullback at the University of Kentucky, he recovered a fumble and jumped through two guards and ran for a 73-yard touchdown. He went on to the Naval Academy in 1926 where he was named an All-Eastern Fullback and received honorable mention as All-American in 1930.[4]

Clifton was an interesting guy with a few quirks. He loved to play polo and his wealthy wife encouraged it by giving him two polo ponies. When Clifton returned to the carrier from missions, he would get a blanket from his mechanic and put the blanket over the engine of his aircraft. He also had a "nervous tic"[5] that revealed itself when flying with him. He would push on the cockpit dashboard often with both hands, which gave McCampbell a real challenge staying on Clifton's wing.

McCampbell had no difficulty qualifying for carrier ops including takeoffs and landings, except for night landings. Out with two other pilots in the fall of 1938 on their initial qualification flight for night landing, he headed in first to land leaving the standard 3-plane division. He landed with no problem except being a little long. McCampbell took off again, clearing the flight deck for the next plane.

The second pilot in the division had an unsuccessful landing and crashed into the net barrier designed to stop planes that did not catch an arresting wire with his tailhook. The plane was cleared from the flight deck and the third pilot landed, but also crashed into the barrier. While waiting for the flight deck to be cleared while circling in the pattern, McCampbell raised his wheels and tailhook. Finally, the green light signal to come aboard was visible. McCampbell lined up, lowered his wheels and landed on the flight deck, but his plane hit the barrier. He had forgotten to lower his tailhook. Surprised, McCampbell received credit for both night landings and was deemed fully qualified.

McCampbell soon learned that his second landing was credited to him because the "wheels-and-hook-down-man"[6] supporting the Landing Signal Officer (LSO) had not shined his light on his tailhook before the landing. The LSO had decided to pass McCampbell's landing due to the error of his enlisted man.

He got his landing credit, but McCampbell suffered when he hit the barrier. On the bridge of his nose, McCampbell hit the long tube-shaped gunsight positioned directly in front of him in the cockpit through the windshield. It was an enduring scar and visual reminder of the event.[7]

McCampbell served as wingman for Clifton for a year and gave him due credit by stating, "I always tell people that I learned how to fly, really, by flying on Joe Clifton."[8] It was not long before McCampbell had earned the "E"[9] in both gunnery and bombing for which no other pilot in VF-4 held. He was now recognized as one of the top pilots in the squadron.[10]

VF-4 flew Grumman F3F-1 fighters. They entered the fleet in 1936, and were the last biplane fighters utilized by the U.S. armed services. Highly maneuverable, with a great rate of climb, they could reach a top speed of 264 mph.

With Joe Clifton, McCampbell gained experience in flight tactics while participating in exercises escorting bombers and torpedo planes, and fending off attacking fighter aggres-

Grumman F3F-1 Fighters of Fighting Squadron Four (VF-4) from USS *Ranger* (CV-4) in flight over the Southern California coast. Photograph is dated January 1939. Plane in the foreground is Bureau # 0261 (original photograph # NH 91168 is in the collections of the Aviation History Branch, Naval Historical Center).

sors. He and others also acted as the aggressor fighters against seaplanes and other aircraft. Air-to-air tactics were learned through dogfights with aggressor fighter aircraft, each fitted with small gun cameras. After the exercises the film was processed and action between aircraft was analyzed and critiqued by the gunnery officer, Lieutenant Edward A. Hannegan.

Dive-bombing exercises were often conducted by dropping special practice bombs on the old battleship *Utah* (BB-31) which had been reconfigured back in 1931 as a mobile target ship (hull number AG-16). Training exercises were not only conducted within their own carrier squadrons, but were also held with other aircraft from other carriers and ships.

Because of his superior flying skills as well as his seniority, McCampbell became a division leader in his second year in the squadron. He also participated with his squadron in the Cleveland Air Races one year. McCampbell recalled the event: "We performed as a squadron. I remembered we used to land and take off with the nine planes at the same time. The first division and second division would be nine planes each. We did a dive-bombing demonstration for them and a formation flying demonstration."[11]

McCampbell's first carrier assignment was aboard one of the most unique ships in the Navy at that time. From a design standpoint, the *Ranger* was a transitional carrier. The previous two carriers, *Lexington* (CV-2), and *Saratoga* (CV-3), were built on cruiser hulls when their construction had been canceled. The design for the *Ranger* (CV-4) in 1922 specified a new carrier design with greater speed and aircraft storage than the existing carriers in the fleet. Though she was the first U.S. Navy aircraft carrier built from the keel up, she had only ⅓ the tonnage of her two predecessors. She had a hull length of 730 feet, a flight deck of 769 feet, a top speed of 29.4 knots, and could carry 86 planes and a standard complement of 2,461 officer and men.

On September 26, 1931, the keel of the *Ranger* was laid at the Norfolk Navy Yard by the Newport News Shipbuilding & Dry Dock Company. She was launched 17 months later

USS *Ranger* (CV-4) underway at sea during the late 1930s (Official U.S. Navy Photograph # 80-G-428440, now in the collections of the National Archives).

and commissioned on Monday, June 4, 1934, when Mrs. Lou Henry Hoover, wife of Herbert Hoover, broke a bottle of grape juice over her bow. The ship builder was paid $2,160,000 by the government.[12]

After construction had started on the *Ranger*, the Navy took another look at the design of the small carrier that was restricted by ship category tonnage by the international Washington Naval Treaty. Though forced to build another small sized carrier (*Wasp* CV-7) to use up the remaining tonnage allowed under the same treaty restrictions, the following World War II carriers like the *Yorktown* (CV-5) and *Enterprise* (CV-6), that began construction in 1940, were 36 percent bigger than *Ranger*.

The new carrier design was focused on overcoming deficiencies found with the *Ranger* and *Wasp,* including being relatively slow, having no side hull protection against enemy gunfire and torpedoes, and the inability to launch aircraft in rough seas.

The *Ranger* was cruising the Atlantic conducting training and flying patrols until March 28, 1935, when she sailed to the Pacific via the Panama Canal, arriving at her new homeport at NAS North Island in San Diego on April 15. Since that date the carrier had been patrolling the West Coast from Alaska to as far south as Callao, Peru, and as far west as Hawaii.

Beginning in 1937 the *Ranger* was commanded by Captain John Sidney "Slew"[13] McCain (grandfather of Senator John McCain III). McCain graduated from the Naval Academy in 1906 and sailed around the world with the Navy battle fleet known as the "Great White Fleet"[14] from December 16, 1907, to February 22, 1909. His following assignments included the Asiatic Fleet, the Naval Base at San Diego, as executive officer of the cruiser USS *Colorado*, and in 1915 aboard the flagship of the Pacific Fleet, the cruiser USS *San Diego*.

In World War I McCain dodged German submarines on convoy duty in the North Atlantic, before he was transferred to the Bureau of Navigation in May 1918. In the 1920s and 1930s, McCain served aboard the *Maryland* (BB-46), *New Mexico* (BB-40), and *Nitro* (AE–2), before gaining his first command of the cargo ship USS *Sirius* (AK-15).

In 1935 McCain started flight training, and became one of the oldest naval aviators the following year. While serving until 1939 aboard the *Ranger*, McCain played a significant role in developing the carrier tactics which were to be so vital during the coming war.[15]

Because the carrier was not optimum for Pacific operations, on January 4, 1939, the *Ranger* departed San Diego for fleet operations in the Caribbean from Guantanamo Bay, Cuba. After the exercises, she sailed to her new homeport of Norfolk, Virginia, at a small grass field known as West Field, arriving April 18. From there she took up patrols along the East Coast and Caribbean. McCampbell lamented the duty station change to the East Coast because in those days he had to pay for his wife's travel since the Navy would not pick it up.

World War II began on September 1, 1939, when Hitler's Nazi forces invaded Poland, which prompted President Franklin D. Roosevelt to declare neutrality for the United States on the 5th. On September 4, the United States Navy took action when the CNO sent a dispatch to the Commander, Atlantic Squadron, which directed the "establishment of air and ship patrols to observe and report by classified means movement of warships of the belligerents within designated areas."[16] Operating from Bermuda, the *Ranger* took up these patrols along the shipping routes in the middle Atlantic up to Argentia, Newfoundland.[17]

McCampbell liked the *Rangers'* skipper and commented, "It was a happy ship under John Sidney McCain."[18] McCampbell also felt favorable towards the two commanding officers of VF-4 while he served on the *Ranger*. His first CO, Lieutenant Commander Wendell

G. Switzer, was seen as a better pilot, while in McCampbell's opinion Lieutenant Commander Albert K. Morehouse was "a little distant from squadron operations when he first arrived."[19] Morehouse came up to par fast with ops, but seemed to have trouble avoiding blacking out during dive bombing. This was a common issue with pilots, and McCampbell admitted he blacked out once when going into a half loop too aggressively when attacking a seaplane during exercises.[20]

5

LSO on the Wasp

"Who said a Wasp couldn't sting twice?"[1]

On April 25, 1940, Lieutenant (junior grade) David McCampbell was in Norfolk with Air Group 4 when the USS *Wasp* was commissioned at the Army Quartermaster Base in South Boston, Massachusetts, with Captain John Walter Reeves, Jr., in command. The *Wasp* Air Group Commander, Lieutenant Commander Grove B.H. Hall, was now McCampbell's new boss.

McCampbell's transfer and assignment to the *Wasp* occurred when the LSO, Lieutenant Frederick M. Reeder, decided he would retire from the Navy. That served to move his assistant LSO, Lieutenant (junior grade) Edmond G. Konrad, up to LSO of the Wasp Air Group. Over his objections, McCampbell was selected from VF-4 to join the Air Group as Assistant LSO. The downside of being assigned as an LSO was that there was not much flying. McCampbell only flew to and from the shore airfield for carrier landing practice.[2]

Konrad trained McCampbell to be an LSO, which was a critical role in getting the airplanes safely aboard the carrier. James Michener, in his book *The Bridges at Toko-Ri* (1953), perhaps described the role of the landing signal officer the best:

> There always came that exquisite moment of human judgment when one man—a man standing alone on the remotest corner of the ship, lashed by foul wind and storm—had to decide that the … [aircraft] roaring down upon him could make it. This solitary man had to judge the speed and height and the pitching of the deck and the wallowing of the sea and the oddities of this particular pilot and those additional imponderables that no man can explain. Then, at the last screaming second he had to make his decision and flash it to the pilot. He had only two choices. He could land the plane and risk the life of the pilot and the plane and the ship if he had judged wrong. Or he could wave-off and delay his decision until next time around.[3]

However you look at it, the LSO was the only person who was responsible for success or failure. Failure would usually mean injury or death on the carrier deck.

The LSO began his work as he stood on his platform at the back port corner of the flightdeck watching the naval aircraft turn from their base leg onto the course ("groove"[4]) lining up behind the carrier a hundred yards or so away. With his arms spread out holding striped paddles, the LSO monitored the glideslope of the aircraft approach in height, airspeed, altitude and line-up as he signaled with the paddles the status of what he saw. He also ensured the planes tailhook and wheels were down for the landing.

Adjusting his paddle signals as necessary, once the plane crossed the threshold of the rear flight deck and was in proper position to land, the LSO gave "the cut"[5] signal (slashing of the throat motion). Immediately the pilot cut the power throttle and dropped to land on the flight deck as the tailhook snagged an arresting wire that rapidly slowed and stopped the plane. If the tailhook does not catch one of the wires, the plane plowed into a barrier of high steel cables to stop it.

If the incoming plane was not positioned well for landing, or the flight deck was fouled, the LSO gave "the waveoff"[6] signal by waving his paddles crisscross over his head. At this point, the pilot pushed the throttle full forward and flew off to port to go around and try to land again.[7]

McCampbell spent three and a half years serving as an LSO aboard the *Wasp*. The training from Konrad was mostly on-the-job as he watched him handle the landings with precision. There was no radio communications between the LSO and the pilots on the *Wasp,* but there was an intercom to the carrier's bridge and the air officer.

Until the pilots became proficient at landing, the LSO on duty debriefed the pilots on their individual landing performance after the landing operations had completed. This feedback was critical because landing on a carrier was the most hair-raising event in a Naval Aviators' life. McCampbell recalled that the challenge was to judge how fast the plane was traveling. The object of landing was to move around the carrier in full-stall attitude with your engine set to three-quarter speed. At night the pilot looks at lights to see if he was too fast or too slow. Better judgment came by gaining more experience.[8]

Serving with Konrad and McCampbell was a Naval Aviation Pilot (NAP), Walter

LT David McCampbell, Landing Signal Officer, far left, bringing in planes aboard USS *Wasp* (CV-7) circa late 1941 or early 1942. Behind him is the Assistant Landing Signal Officer, Ensign George E. "Doc" Savage. In the catwalk in the lower center (back to front) are Len Ford (sailor), LT Hawley Russell and an unidentified man in the foreground. Caption details were provided by CAPT David McCampbell, USN (Ret.), in 1982, and further identification of the individuals shown is not available (Official U.S. Navy Photograph #80-G-K-687, now in the collection of the National Archives).

Gregg, who was their hook-and-wheels-down-man. Gregg's primary role, as an enlisted man who had earned his Navy wings, was to fly the Grumman J2F Duck amphibian utility plane or the old Vought OS2U Kingfisher floatplane when required. Though there had been NAP personnel flying since January 1920, at the end of 1927 there had been a total of only 108 NAPs and even after World War II by December 1947 only 5000 total NAPs had served. Gregg asked to be trained as an LSO, and before long he proved to be good at it. So here was a Naval Aviation Pilot who was a qualified LSO, which defined Gregg as certainly the rarest of the rare.[9]

In May of 1941, David McCampbell was promoted to Lieutenant. As the year had passed, Eddie Konrad left the *Wasp* and McCampbell replaced him as senior LSO, with NAP Gregg as the Assistant LSO. Later McCampbell brought in Lieutenant (junior grade) George E. "Doc"[10] Savage for training as an Assistant LSO.[11]

After her commissioning, the *Wasp* remained in Boston to be fitted out. The carrier sailed out on June 5, 1940, for radio direction finding gear calibration tests, and returned to Boston Harbor to complete fitting out. The *Wasp* got underway for Hampton Roads, and set its anchor on June 24. After four days, the carrier sailed out of the Roads with the USS *Morris* (DD-417) and joined up with the Air Group for the first time. En route to the Caribbean the Air Group pilots conducted carrier qualifications. McCampbell was one of the first to qualify before the carrier arrived at Guantanamo Bay to take part in the Independence Day ceremonies.

On July 9 the carrier Air Group suffered its first loss when a Vought SB2U-2 Vindicator crashed two miles from the *Wasp*. The *Morris,* as plane guard, and the carrier rushed at flank speed to the site, but the aircraft and crew of two were not recovered.

The *Wasp* departed Guantanamo Bay on July 11 and sailed for Hampton Roads, arriving on the 15th. The Air Group was disembarked and planes from the 1st Marine Air Group went to sea aboard the *Wasp* for qualification trials. The carrier Air Group trained on the southern drill grounds until the Marine Air Group returned and disembarked at Norfolk. The *Wasp* and her Air Group sailed to Boston for post-shakedown repairs. At Boston the *Wasp* honored President Franklin D. Roosevelt on his yacht, *Potomac* (AG-25), with a 21-gun salute at the Boston Navy Yard on August 10.

The carrier sailed from the Army Quartermaster Base on August 21 to conduct steering drills and full-power trials. The following day the *Wasp* departed for Norfolk with the *Ellis* (DD-154) as plane guard. En route the *Wasp* conducted takeoff and landing operations with her planes from Fighter Squadron 7 (VF-7) and Scouting Squadron 72 (VS-72). The *Wasp* ported at the Norfolk Navy Yard on August 28 for repair work on her turbines. She was drydocked during the period September 12–18.

On October 11, the *Wasp* joined Carrier Division 3 and relocated to the Norfolk Naval Operations Base (NOB Norfolk). Twenty-four Army Air Corps P-40s from the 8th Pursuit Group and 9 O-47As from the 2nd Observation Squadron were loaded aboard the *Wasp*. The carrier headed out to sea as the Army planes took off in a test to determine their takeoff run distances. This experiment was the first time that Army planes had taken off from a Navy carrier, and demonstrated that a carrier could successfully perform in a ferrying role as was utilized extensively in the war that was to come.

The *Wasp* sailed to Cuba and Guantanamo Bay accompanied by the *Plunkett* (DD-431) and *Niblack* (DD-424). En route the Air Group flew training flights with dive-bombing and gun firing. On October 19, they arrived and saluted the Commander of the Atlantic Squadron, Rear Admiral Hayne Ellis, aboard the *Texas* (BB-35).

During the rest of October and November the *Wasp* conducted qualification and

USS _Wasp_ (CV-7) entering Hampton Roads, Virginia, on May 26, 1942. An escorting destroyer is in the background (Official U.S. Navy Photograph # 80-G-12240, now in the collections of the National Archives).

refresher training flights. On November 26, the carrier departed back to the Norfolk Navy Yard, spending Christmas 1940 at home. After degaussing tests with the _Hannibal_ (AG-1), the _Wasp_ headed to Guantanamo Bay, arriving January 27, 1941. After conducting training exercises, she sailed backed to Hampton Roads on March 4.

Off Cape Hatteras, North Carolina, a lookout saw a red flare at 2245 and another one 14 minutes later. At 2329 the _Wasp_ located the 152-foot lumber schooner _George E. Klinck_ heading to Southwest Harbor, Maine. The vessel was having trouble as the sea state worsened. On March 8, as the schooner floundered, the _Wasp_ rescued the 8-man crew of the _Klinck_. Later that day the rescued crew disembarked and the _Wasp_ continued on to the drydock at the Norfolk Navy Yard to repair their turbines. While there, the _Wasp_ was fitted with the new CXAM-1 radar used for long-range detection of aircraft and ships.

After a trip to the Caribbean, returning on March 30, the carrier conducted flight and patrol operations between Hampton Roads and Newport, Rhode Island. Then the _Wasp_ sailed to Bermuda, arriving at Grassy Bay on May 12 to begin Atlantic Fleet's neutrality patrols in zones that had been extended eastward. The carrier patrolled between Bermuda and Hampton Roads until July 12.

On July 23, 1941, in late afternoon, resting at Pier 7 at NOB Norfolk, the _Wasp_ received aboard 32 Army Air Force (AAF) pilots. The next morning at 0630 cranes began hoisting on the deck of the carrier 30 Curtiss P-40C fighters and 3 PT-17 trainers from the AAF 33rd Pursuit Squadron of 8th Air Group from Mitchell Field, New York. The _Wasp_ was prepared to deliver these aircraft to Iceland as part of a new policy for United States forces to occupy Iceland and take a greater role in the Battle of the Atlantic. These Army planes would provide cover for the initial American forces.

On July 28 the *Wasp* went to sea accompanied by the *O'Brien* (DD-415) and *Walke* (DD-416) as plane guards. Within a few days the carrier was joined by another escort, the *Vincennes* (CA-44) and Task Force 16 made up of the *Mississippi* (BB-41), *Quincy* (CA-39), *Wichita* (CA-45), five destroyers, *Semmes* (AG-24), *American Legion* (AP-35), *Mizar* (AF-12), and *Almaack* (AK-27).

On August 6, the *Wasp* and her escorts left the Task Force, launched the AAF P40s and O-47As trainers to Iceland, and sailed for Norfolk, with an arrival on August 14. The carrier conducted refresher landings off the Virginia Capes on the 22nd, returned and then sailed on August 25 with the *Savannah* (CL-42), *Monssen* (DD-436) and *Kearny* (DD 432) for carrier flight operations in the Western Atlantic. On September 2 the *Wasp* and escorts set anchors in the Gulf of Paria, Trinidad.

Going to sea on the September 6, the carrier group took up Atlantic neutrality patrols by escorting British merchant ships to the mid-ocean meeting point (MOMP). Orders shifted the *Wasp's* patrols northward between the Grassy Bay, Bermuda and Little Placentia Bay, Newfoundland. The Atlantic war had escalated to the point that German warships and submarines began sinking American warships including the *Kearny* on October 17, the *Salinas* on the 28th and *Reuben James* (DD-245) on October 30. Meanwhile, on October 26 the Chief of Naval Operations, Admiral Harold R. Stark, ordered American warships to sink any German or Italian warships they encountered.[12]

The *Wasp* with its escorts continued their North Atlantic patrols and was lying at anchor at Grassy Bay on December 7, 1941, when the Japanese bombed Pearl Harbor. On that day the Wasp Air Group consisted of:

Fighting Squadron 71 (VF-71)-18 F4F-3s
Fighting Squadron 72 (VF-72)-17 F4F-3s, 2 SB2U-2s, 1 SNJ-3
Scouting Squadron 71 (VS-71)-4 SB2U-1, 13 SB2U-2s, 2 TBD-1s
Scouting Squadron 72 (VS-72)-18 SB2U-3s.[13]

Based on flawed intelligence, the U.S. Navy sent the *Wasp*, accompanied by the *Brooklyn* (CL-40), *Sterett* (DD-407) and *Wilson* (DD-408), to Martinique to determine if the Vichy French armed merchant cruiser *Barfleur* was trying to sail back to France. Discovering the French ship in port as directed, the *Wasp* with escorts sailed home and arrived at Hampton Roads on the December 22.

The carrier moved to the Norfolk Navy Yard on the December 24 for an overhaul. It remained there until it sailed on January 14, 1942, to NS Argentia, Newfoundland, and then Casco Bay, Maine. The *Wasp* departed on March 16 for Norfolk. The following morning at 0550, the bow of the carrier collided with the *Stack* (DD-406), punching a hole in the starboard side and flooded the number one fireroom. While still asleep, McCampbell heard the fire alarm set off by the command duty officer and got up to see what was happening. Smoke from the *Stack* was coming back toward the carrier and clouding over the bridge. The destroyer was able to steam away to the Philadelphia Navy Yard to repair the damage.

The *Wasp* arrived at Norfolk on January 21, but was back at Casco Bay three days later. On March 26 the carrier sailed with Rear Admiral John W. Wilcox who commanded Task Force 39 heading to reinforce the Royal Navy's Home Fleet. Sadly, Admiral Wilcox was washed overboard from his flagship *Washington* (BB-56) and drowned. Task Force 39 was joined by a naval force led by the light cruiser HMS *Edinburgh* on April 3 and escorted to Scapa Flow in the Orkney Islands.[14]

While at Scapa Flow, Royal Navy Captain Henry Fancourt landed a Gloster Gladiator on the *Wasp*. This was the first time a British aircraft had landed aboard a U.S. carrier. Though most of the British Home Fleet, designated TF 99, was covering the convoys to North Russia, the *Wasp* headed to Greenock, Scotland, on April 9. The next day the carrier was sailing up the Clyde River past the John Brown Clydebank Shipyard where the workers gave them a grand reception.

As part of Operation Calendar, the new mission for the *Wasp* was to ferry British fighter aircraft to Malta to regain air superiority from the Axis. The carriers' dive-bombers and torpedo planes were launched for land to make room for 47 Supermarine Spitfire Mk. V fighter planes of No. 603 Squadron RAF at Glasgow on 13 April. The next day the *Wasp* sailed in company with Force "W"[15] of the British Home Fleet, which included the cruisers HMS *Renown*, HMS *Cairo*, HMS *Charybdis* and destroyers *Madison* (DD-425) and *Lang* (DD-399).

The *Wasp* group passed the Straits of Gibraltar under darkness on April 19, and at 0400 the next morning at a position about halfway between Gibraltar and Malta, the *Wasp* launched 11 Grumman F4F Wildcat fighters as Combat Air Patrol (CAP) over Force W. Next, the Spitfires warmed up their engines in the hangar deck below and were brought up using the aft elevator (the first carrier fitted with a deck edge elevator). One after another the Spitfires were launched toward Malta. With their mission completed, the *Wasp* turned and sailed back to Scapa Flow.

Unfortunately, the relief British Spitfires were picked up by radar and Axis intelligence tracked the arrival force. The Germans sent air raids to Malta and destroyed most of the relief Spitfires on the ground at Ta'Qali airfield just minutes after their arrival. Within 48 hours all were destroyed. Prime Minister Churchill knew how serious the situation was on Malta and asked Roosevelt to have the *Wasp* make another ferry run to the embattled island. Roosevelt agreed and the *Wasp* was underway on May 3 from Scapa Flow with another group of Spitfire Vs as part of Operation Bowery. This time the carrier was accompanied by the British carrier HMS *Eagle,* which was also loaded with Spitfires.

Early on May 9 while sailing 1,000 yards ahead of the *Eagle* at the launch point, the *Wasp* launched her CAP of 11 F4F-4 fighters from VF-71. Sergeant-Pilot Herrington took off first at 0643, but lost engine power and crashed into the sea. He and his plane were not recovered. The remaining Spitfires launched successfully and formed up for the flight to Malta.

Bad luck came to another pilot, as Sergeant-Pilot Jerrold Alpine "Jerry"[16] Smith of the Royal Canadian Air Force accidently released his auxiliary fuel tank as he climbed to 2,000 feet. Without his lost fuel tank, Smith had no chance to reach Malta, Gibraltar or any Allied held territory. Southern France was out of the question and North Africa was held by the Germans. Considering his options, he rejected ditching and decided to attempt to land back aboard the *Wasp*.[17]

McCampbell recalled that once all the planes had been launched, the crash barrier was lowered, and the carrier sped up to allow as much wind as possible over the deck for the Royal Canadian pilot at risk. Smith was given the option to either execute a water landing or attempt to land aboard. He decided on a carrier landing. His major problem was that his aircraft did not have a landing hook. One of their senior officers said he was confident that he could pull it off. McCampbell was asked his advice as the LSO and he responded in the positive to land him aboard.[18]

McCampbell had briefed the Spitfire pilots the first day they came aboard on operational procedures and commented, "If you see me jumping into the net alongside my landing

USS *Wasp* (CV-7) Launching officer Lieutenant David McCampbell, USN, gets the ready signal from the pilot of a British Royal Air Force "Spitfire," just before it took off for Malta, May 9, 1942. This was *Wasp*'s second Malta reinforcement mission. Note deck crewmen holding the plane back. A Grumman F4F-4 "Wildcat" is in the background (Official U.S. Navy Photograph # 80-G-7085, National Archives collection).

signal officer platform when a plane's coming in, you know there's something wrong."[19] At least they knew that if the landing was looking bad, they should fly around and try again.

On his first approach to land, he was too high and fast, but did not respond to McCampbell's signals until he jumped into the LSO net. Remembering the briefing, Smith finally pulled up and went around for another try. His second approach was better, but he was still too fast and high. To respond to the reality and get him down, McCampbell called for a cut at 500 feet from the aft end of the deck versus the standard cut at 50 to 100 feet. Smith did cut and landed, but waited until he was halfway down the flight deck to use his hand brake. The plane slowed but continued forward toward the bow. McCampbell watched and thought the Spitfire would not make it. Fortunately, the plane stopped just short of the end of the flight deck. McCampbell later measured the distance himself, and it turned out to be just six feet short of disaster.

After the landing McCampbell quickly ran up to congratulate Smith on his excellent landing, took off his own hat and gave it to him. He told him that he must have had some real experience in Spitfires to execute such a landing, and that to his knowledge it had never been done before. Smith's answer was striking because he had only 127 hours of flying experience and had never flown a Spitfire before. In fact, he had never seen a carrier landing.[20]

That night McCampbell and the other Naval Aviators gave Smith a pair of Navy wings and pinned them on him. The *Wasp* sailed through the Straits of Gibraltar and three British Fairey Swordfish torpedo bombers flew out to pick Smith up and fly him back to Gibraltar. Smith finally got to Malta later, but was killed on August 10 chasing after a German JU 88 toward Sicily.

For the exceptional service to the British in the cause of Malta operations, Churchill sent a message on May 11 to the captain and ship's company of the *Wasp* declaring, "Many thanks to you all for the timely help. Who said a Wasp couldn't sting twice?"[21]

McCampbell recalled that no medals were awarded to the ships' officers or men as far as he knew, except movie star and Naval Reserve officer Douglas Fairbanks, Jr., who received the Legion of Merit when he was aboard the *Wasp* during the second ferry operation. Fairbanks served as the aide to Rear Admiral John L. Hall Jr., who was a liaison officer from the Commander U.S. Naval Forces Europe. McCampbell said, "he did nothing to deserve it."[22]

With the loss of the USS *Lexington* at the Battle of Coral Sea on May 8, the Navy decided to transfer the *Wasp* to the Pacific. The *Wasp* sailed immediately to Norfolk for repairs and alterations. On May 31, 1942, Captain Reeves was promoted to flag rank and the change-of-command gave command of the *Wasp* to Captain Forest Percival Sherman.

The *Wasp* departed Norfolk on June 6, 1942, in company with Rear Admiral Leigh Noyes' Task Force 37 with the new battleship *North Carolina* (BB-55), *Quincy* (CA-39), the *San Juan* (CL-54) and 6 destroyers. On June 10, the *Wasp* and re-designated Task Force 18 transited the Panama Canal. In an attempt to keep any possible enemy agents from knowing which ship it was, the name of the carrier was painted over and "Stinger"[23] was painted there.

The *Wasp* arrived at North Island Naval Air Station at San Diego on June 19. The carrier Air Group embarked the remainder of her aircraft compliment with Douglas SBD-3 Dauntless dive-bombers (replacing the old Vindicators), and Grumman TBF-1 Avenger torpedo bombers. The Air Group was briefed by Lieutenant Commander James H. Flatley Jr., who was fresh from serving as executive officer with VF-42 during the Battle of the Coral Sea. Flatley and the North Island staff covered tactics being used in the Pacific, though McCampbell was not present. He was able get leave to visit his parents in Los Angeles.[24]

In August 1942 the Wasp Air Group consisted of the following aircraft:

VF-71 with 29 F4F-4 Wildcat
VS-71 with 15 SDB-3 Dauntless
VS-72 with 15 SBD-3 Dauntless
VT-7 with 10 TBF-1 Avenger.[25]

With the strategic success of the Battle of Midway in June, the American military moved to take an aggressive offensive stance at Guadalcanal in the Solomon Islands. In support of this Operation Plan 1–42, on July 1 the *Wasp* headed to the Tonga Islands with the carriers *Enterprise* (CV-6) and *Saratoga* (CV-3), the fast battleship *North Carolina* (BB-55), six heavy cruisers, 16 destroyers, as well as a convoy of five transports loaded with the 2nd Marine Regiment.

This carrier group was designated Task Force 61.1 under the command of Rear Admiral Noyes who was embarked aboard the *Wasp*. As part of Operation Watchtower, the naval carrier forces role was to provide air support for amphibious invasion forces that were commanded by Rear Admiral Richmond K. Turner (TF 61.2). In overall tactical command of

TF 61 was Vice Admiral Frank Jack Fletcher who reported to the Commander of the South Pacific Area, Vice Admiral Robert Lee Ghormley, who was in strategic command of the Allied forces.[26]

After the Japanese had taken the nearby island of Tulagi during the Coral Sea battle, they discovered that the area near the north shore on Guadalcanal was appropriate for an airfield. On June 8, the Japanese had landed engineers to build a wharf. On the 20th Allied coastwatchers saw smoke coming from grass burning in a pasture near Lunga Point, which was assumed to be the airfield site. This was reported and confirmed by a reconnaissance flight on July 5.

While the *Wasp* and TF 61.1 were en route, on July 6, from a convoy of 12 ships, the Japanese landed 2,571 men from two construction units to build a 3,778-foot runway. Now the Japanese threat to Allied bases in the New Hebrides and New Caledonia area, as well as clear passage to Australia, was becoming an unfortunate reality.[27]

On July 18, the *Wasp* stopped at Tongatapu Island in Tonga's southern island group. Over the next several days the Pacific Service Force repaired the carriers' high-pressure steam turbine. The carrier then sailed with the task force to the Guadalcanal area.[28]

While preparations were underway for the Guadalcanal landing, the Air Group squadrons on the *Wasp* practiced day and night takeoff and landing operations. The original landing target date of August 1 was moved back to wait until all of the Marine transports arrived.

On the evening of August 6, the *Wasp,* accompanied by the *San Francisco* (CA-38), *Salt Lake City* (CA-25), and destroyers *Sterett, Lane, Aaron Ward, Stack, Laffey* and *Farenholt,* sailed westward toward Guadalcanal until midnight, and then headed east to reach her designated launch point 84 miles from Tulagi an hour before dawn.

At 0530 on August 7 the first flights of F4F-4s and SBD-3s scrambled down the flight deck for their takeoffs heading to their mission targets of Tulagi, Gavutu, Tanambogo, Halavo, Port Purvis, Haleta, Bungana, as well as a Japanese radio station referred to as "Asses' Ears."[29] At 0557 the CAP F4F fighters took to the skies. Lieutenant Shands and wingman Ensign S.W. Forrer headed down to the north coast of Gavatu, while two other F4F fighter sections made for the seaplane facilities at Tanambogo.

The simultaneous sunrise attacks were a surprise to the Japanese as Shands' fighters destroyed 15 Kawanishi flying boats and 7 Nakajima floatplane fighters flying close to the ground. Lieutenant Wright and Ensign Kenton eliminated three patrol planes each and a Japanese motorboat. The third section of Ensigns Reeves and Conklin took out two patrol planes and shared a fifth plane. As the F4Fs strafed the Japanese, they destroyed an aviation fuel truck and truck containing spare parts.

The SBDs deposited their bombs "on the money"[30] according to post-attack analysis, destroying the antiaircraft and shore gun batteries in the first wave.

At 0704 Lieutenant H.A. Romberg led his 12 Grumman TBF-1s off the carrier and provided close-air support for the Marines facing heavy enemy resistance east of Hill 281 in the Makambo-Sasapi sector, as well as the prison on Tulagi Island. The Japanese resistance was silenced. None of the Wasp's planes were shot down. Ensign Reeves in his F4F ran low on fuel and landed on the *Enterprise,* but the other squadron attackers landed back aboard the *Wasp.*[31]

The American invasion force of some 11,000 men met almost no opposition on August 7 from the Japanese on Guadalcanal largely because intelligence estimates had overestimated the strength of the enemy force at the airfield at Lunga Point at 5,275 men. Based on that flawed intelligence, Major General Alexander A. "Sunny Jim"[32] Vandergrift, Commander

of the 1st Marine Division, made the decision to move the landing to the east to flank the
Japanese. The bombardment and approaching Marines caused the Japanese to flee the airport leaving behind food, supplies and construction equipment and vehicles. Thirteen Japanese were found dead. Though there were problems landing the supplies from the
transports, the airfield was captured the next day, and renamed Henderson Field in honor
of a Marine aviator killed at Midway.

Marines went ashore on the southwest coast at Tugali at 0800 where little Japanese resistance was encountered. However, as the afternoon came, enemy resistance hardened as the
Marines advanced toward the southeast end of the island. As nightfall came, the Americans
were forced to pull back to a defensive line when they encountered the main Japanese force.
Night counter attacks were attempted, but failed. At daybreak of August 8, the Marines
were reinforced and cleared from the caves. By late in the afternoon the island was secured.

Another Marine force landed at Florida Island west of Tulagi at 0740 and at 0845 to
the east of Gavutu-Tanambogo flanking the islets. No Japanese troops were found on Florida
Island. A major Japanese force was found defending Gavutu and Tanambogo. The Marines
hit the beach at the seaplane ramp on the northwest coast of Gavutu at noon on the 7th.
The defending enemy was "holed up in caves and coconut log bunkers,"[33] but the Marines
secured Gavutu after only two hours, sadly with 10 percent casualties. An attempted landing
on Tanambogo at sunset was repulsed with high losses. Late morning on the eighth, Marines
attacked the causeway and after a fierce battle, the islet was secured as night fell.

The Marines lost 144 killed and 194 wounded at Tulagi and the nearby islets. The
Marine paratroopers had the heaviest losses with a 50 percent casualty rate. The Japanese
lost nearly their entire garrison of 900 men, with only 23 taken prisoner and 70 escaping
to Florida Island.[34]

At nightfall of the seventh, the *Wasp, Saratoga, Enterprise,* and screening warships
had repositioned southward. The next morning the *Wasp* returned and launched F4Fs
commanded by Lieutenant C.S. Moffett to provide CAP protection over the transport ships
until noon. Meanwhile, Lieutenant Commander E.M. Snowden led 12 of his Dauntless
SBD-3s off the flight deck to search a sector out some 220 miles from the carrier to cover
Santa Isabel Island and the New Georgia groups.

In the first two hours of the scouting patrol, the SBD pilots saw no Japanese aircraft,
but at 0815 Snowden saw a "Rufe"[35] Nakajima A6M2-N Type 2 Float Plane Fighter 40 miles
from Rekata Bay on Santa Isabel Island. He gave chase as the enemy fighter climbed in an
attempt to hide in the clouds. Snowden fired his .50-caliber guns and downed the plane in
the Solomon Sea.

Meanwhile, Rear Admiral Richmond K. Turner ordered all the transports to get underway when a large number of Japanese attack planes from Bougainville were discovered
heading toward the Guadalcanal. The *Wasp* prepared for action and sent Lieutenant Commander Eldridge and his VS-71 SBD-3s off Tulagi to Mbangi Island. In the rear seat behind
Eldridge was Aviation Chief Radioman L.A. Powers who saw a group of planes coming in
from the northeast. At first they thought the planes were friendlies, but quickly learned
they were Japanese. Suddenly six Zeros attacked the first section, but even after some 12
attack passes, the Japanese pilots did not shot down a single SBD.

The last section leader of VS-71, Lieutenant (junior grade) Robert L. Howard, located
a group of twin-engine G4M1 "Betty"[36] bombers heading straight for the American transports. Howard went into a dive toward the Mitsubishi Bettys, but unfortunately forgot to
turn his arming switch to "on."[37] After completing two attack runs with no effect, he realized
his mistake, but it was too late. At that moment four escorting Zeros attacked him. Rear

gunner, Seaman 2d Class Lawrence P. Lupo, did his best to keep the Zeros away as he hit several of the enemy fighters.

After having made eight runs at Howard's SBD, the Zeros had not scored any fatal hits. One Zero made a head-on attack at the SBD as Howard fired his fixed guns. The fighter caught fire, passed alongside the SBDs' left wing and crashed among the American landing craft below. Meanwhile, Lupo was firing his rear guns at another Zero engaging from the stern. Lupo successfully fought off the attacker. Finally, the Japanese fighters had had enough and flew off as Howard and his section returned to the *Wasp*.[38]

In what would become the most controversial decision of his career, at 1807 on August 8 Vice Admiral Fletcher recommended to General Ghormley that his Task Force 61.1 carrier group be withdrawn from Guadalcanal. Fletcher noted that he had lost in enemy attacks 21 of the 99 fighters he had started with, and his carriers were running low on fuel. Fletcher also factored in his decision the information Admiral Turner had earlier given him that all but five of his transports would be offloaded by end of second day, leaving just five cargo ships to finish offloading. Actually, the transport offloading was significantly behind schedule, but because of poor communications services between the two admirals, Fletcher had not received an up-to-date sitrep for some time.[39]

Ghormley approved the request and the *Wasp* sailed away from the Guadalcanal area along with the *Saratoga* and the *Enterprise*. As midnight of August 8 came, the Marine landings and carrier Task Force 61.1 had successfully accomplished their mission objectives. All Japanese resistance, except for snipers on Gavutu and Tanombogo, had ended, and the enemy air forces had been beaten back.

Unfortunately, the battle for Guadalcanal was not at an end. On August 9, opposing American and Japanese surface forces met in the Battle of Savo Island. The Japanese suffered little as Allied forces lost four cruisers including *Vincennes* and *Quincy* that had previously accompanied *Wasp* in Atlantic operations. The Japanese were slow to respond to the American invasion of Guadalcanal and Tulagi, but eventually they sent troop reinforcements and supplies as they continued to attack the Allied forces. The ships of Japan's "Tokyo Express"[40] would soon take control of the waters north of Guadalcanal, while *Enterprise*, *Saratoga* and *Wasp* operated to the southeast, waiting for the inevitable Japanese push to regain the two lost islands.

After moving south and refueling, the *Wasp* spent the following month patrolling and supporting resupply operations for Guadalcanal. The carrier did not take part in the Battle of the Eastern Solomons on August 24 during which the *Enterprise* was severely damaged by Japanese bombers. The carrier limped back to Pearl Harbor on the 26th for repairs.

A week later, on August 31, the *Saratoga* was hit by a torpedo from the Japanese submarine I-26, and was towed by the cruiser *Minneapolis* while the crew made temporary repairs. The carrier headed to Tongatabu and then sailed for Pearl Harbor for repairs. Now there were only two carriers in the southwest Pacific: *Hornet* (CV-8) and *Wasp*.

Escorting the transports carrying the 7th Marine Regiment to Guadalcanal for reinforcement on September 15, 1942, were the *Wasp, Hornet, North Carolina, Helena* (CL-50), *Salt Lake City* (CA-25), and 8 other warships. The *Wasp* was the duty carrier that morning and was located some 150 miles southeast of San Cristobal Island. The aircraft aboard the carrier that day were 32 F4F-4s, 28 SBD-3s and 10 TBF-1s. The carrier had been at General Quarters since two hours before dawn to 1000 when the search planes returned to the carrier. The planes were being refueled and rearmed for antisubmarine patrols. No enemy contacts were located on patrol except for a 5-engined flying boat that was shot down at 1215 by an F4F from the *Wasp*.[41]

At noon, the sound operator aboard the Japanese I-19 submarine detected heavy propeller noises. Some 50 minutes later the captain of the I-19, Commander Takakazu Kinashi, raised his periscope and peered out at a carrier, a cruiser and escort destroyers bearing 045T at 9 miles. Kinashi continues to track the American task force while trying to edge closer.[42]

Eight F4Fs of VF-17 and 18 SBDs of VS-71 were launched from the *Wasp* at 1420 into the wind from 120 degrees at 18–20 knots and recovered 8 F4Fs and 3 SBDs from earlier patrols. After the recovery operation, the carrier turned right at 16 knots to a course of 200° as planes were being refueled and positioned on the flight deck. Captain Sherman wrote in his After Action Report that he ordered 16 fighters to takeoff and to send the scout planes below. At that time the torpedo planes were armed but their fuel tanks were full of CO_2: "Scouts were fully fueled and armed with bombs. Fighters were fueled. All aircraft were complete with machine gun ammunition including incendiary. An exception to the foregoing existed for four fighters in the overhead which were unarmed and had tanks filled with CO_2."[43]

At 1444 on September 15, 1942, the Japanese I-19 submarine fired six type 95 Long Lance variant oxygen-propelled torpedoes at the enemy carrier from 50 degrees starboard at 985 yards. A few seconds later a lookout on the *Wasp* called out, "three torpedoes, three points forward of the starboard beam!"[44] The helmsman immediately reacted and turned the carrier from "right standard to right full"[45] but it was too late. Two of the torpedoes hit below the water line "between frame 30 and the bridge"[46] as the third one "broached and then submerged but was close to the surface when it hit 50 to 75 feet forward of the bridge...."[47] The three torpedoes hit in the area of the fuel tanks and magazines.[48]

Two of Commander Kinashi's torpedoes passed in front of the *Wasp*, passing astern of the cruiser *Helena* before one of them hit the destroyer *O'Brien* at 1451 on the bow causing structural damage. The sixth torpedo passed astern of the carrier just missing the *Lansdowne*, but striking the battleship *North Carolina* at 1452 on the port side at the No. 1 gun turret. The ship's bulkhead failed, resulting in some flooding.[49]

On the *Wasp* the torpedo blasts ripped through the front of the ship as ammunition in the starboard guns exploded, sending fragments everywhere up forward. Aircraft on the flight deck and in the hangar were lifted in the air by the blasts and fell downward breaking their landing gears as fire spread quickly. Planes in the overhead area broke loose and landed on the hangar deck.

The water mains in the forward section of the carrier had been broken, thereby leaving the crew no water to fight the fires. The forward engine room switchboard was down, along with several diesel generators and the forward turbo generator, which left the forward part of the carrier with no power or lights. The ship was listing between 10–15 degrees to starboard as oil and gasoline began burning on the water.

More explosives came from forward from gasoline tanks and ruptured gasoline lines, and destroyed ammunition, bombs, and torpedoes. Captain Sherman noted, "After the third hit I (Captain Sherman) slowed to 10 knots and put the rudder full left until the wind was on the starboard bow.... My object was to have the wind blow the fire away from the undamaged portion of the ship, keep the low side to windward, and back clear of burning oil. As the ship gathered sternway I slowed to five knots."[50]

Lieutenant McCampbell was just exiting his cabin located on a deck between the hangar and flight deck. He climbed up the ladder and was crossing the deck with the chief arresting gear officer discussing a frayed wire when the first torpedo hit. McCampbell thought the explosions were bombs and hide on the catwalk just under the overhang peering out to see the next bomb hit. He saw no bomb, but the next explosion blew the number two elevator 10 feet in the air. He felt vibrations moving from the bow to the stern and back, with one knocking him to the flight deck.

McCampbell headed aft to the LSO platform area, which was his designated abandon-ship assignment. There were no loudspeakers, or other communications to the bridge or air officer. Meanwhile, the ammunition and fire continued to increase as it worked itself aft. At 1505 a major internal explosion near the hangar occurred that blew the quad 1.1 inch mount off its base and sent hot gases up past the bridge on both sides. Rear Admiral Noyes on the starboard ladder was thrown on to the signal bridge with his hair and ears flash burned. Three men had died on the port walkway.

After the severe explosion and the *Wasp* had cleared the burning oil, Captain Sherman stopped the engines. By this time a significant number of men were already in the water. At 1515 the fire had spread to half the ship. Word from below decks told the story that with no water, the fire was now totally out of control. Having receiving situation reports from the Air Group Commander and Air Officer, and conferring with the Rear Adm. Leigh Noyes and the Executive Officer, Commander Fred C. Dickey, Sherman determined that the carrier could not be saved, and issued his order to abandon ship at 1520.[51]

McCampbell received no abandon-ship communications, but when he saw men going over the fantail, he took action. Many of the flight deck crew had gathered around the fantail as McCampbell and aviator Lieutenant (junior grade) Spencer Downs Wright of VS-71 began to lower an 18-man life raft over the stern. The raft ran out of rope with six to eight feet left to the water, so they had to jerk the pulley and let it fall. McCampbell was knocked off his feet.

They went back to the LSO platform and put lines down the side of the carrier. McCampbell directed men to use the lines over the side or go down to the hangar deck level and go over the side. After all the men in his area were off the ship, McCampbell decided it was time to get off. He took off his shoes and shirt, and thought about doing a "lay-out one-and-a-half with a full twist"[52] dive off the carrier. With so many people and debris in the water, he took the more prudent exit and jumped from the top of the large loudspeaker.

Though the usual distance from the flight deck to the sea was 45 feet, McCampbell's fall was some 56 to 58 feet. On his way down to the water his brain flashed that his insurance was up-to-date and other such thoughts as one would expect. It was a perfect jump, but he was shocked at hitting the water and remembered that he must have sank to about 20 feet down. After reaching the surface, he quickly swam away from the carrier as the explosions continued to fire off on board. It seemed to him that the ship was drifting down toward him faster that he could swim.[53]

Though supposedly required to wear the standard issue kapok life jacket in combat areas, McCampbell had not worn it because it was uncomfortable and too hot in the South Pacific. In its place he had worn an "illegal"[54] CO_2 life belt, but gave it away when a man at the abandon-ship station didn't have a life preserver. So McCampbell had jumped from the ship with no life jacket of any type, but had been able to get a pilot's life raft and threw if off the ship before he jumped. When he was in the water he tried to inflate it, but there was no CO_2 bottle in it. Later he would learn that the pilots had removed the CO_2 bottles because they were too hard to sit on in the cockpits.

McCampbell noted the gasoline fire on the water had moved to the port side by then, and he decided to swim over to the starboard side at the stern. There he saw three men-Chief Machinist Elmo D. Runyan, Fitzpatrick and another unknown man-trying to get onto a makeshift raft from lumber that had been thrown overboard tied together with their belts. McCampbell had gone over the side with two boxes of k-rations. He had recovered a water beaker, and decided to give his water and emergency rations to the raft-mates as he swam toward a destroyer some 300–400 yards away. Before he could get there, the destroyer headed off.

McCampbell saw a large life raft and swam over to it. In the raft was Ensign Jacob E. Hipp who was waving his paddle trying to keep the crowd of men, now three-deep, surrounding the raft from getting in. McCampbell took off swimming for another destroyer that had entered the area. On the way toward the destroyer, he ran into Captain Sherman resting on a large floating mattress and stayed a short while with him. Another destroyer, the *Farenholt,* came by and he continued his swimming that way until the motor whaleboat from the *Duncan* picked him up as darkness neared. Lieutenant David McCampbell had been in the water for some three and one-half hours.

In the stern of the motor whaleboat was Admiral Noyes wearing his "overseas cap, a flight shirt, leather flight jacket, and long under drawers."[55] McCampbell told the Admiral about Captain Sherman's mattress location and they "scooted over and picked him up, and then returned to the destroyer *Farenholt.*"[56]

Confident that all the men and injured were off the *Wasp,* at 1600 Captain Sherman had lowered himself by lifeline over the fantail into the water. The rescue operations had been delayed due to the Japanese submarine threat to the destroyers, which forced them to reposition periodically. Sherman reported that torpedo wakes were seen crossing the rescue area during the recovery.

As Task Force 18 departed the scene, Admiral Noyes ordered the *Lansdowne* to sink the *Wasp. Lansdowne* fired a Mark 15 torpedo at 1000 yards set to run at 15 feet under the keel of the carrier to inflict maximum damage. There was no explosion. The second torpedo was fired at 800 yards at keel depth, but again no result. Apparently, the magnetic influence exploders were still not working just as the Mark 14s had plagued the U.S submarine force since the war had begun. The destroyer disabled the magnetic influence exploders and fired three more torpedoes at a depth of 10 feet. Finally all three of the modified torpedoes detonated.

The *Wasp* sank by the bow at 2100. Of the 2046 men and 201 officers aboard the *Wasp* that day, 196 were killed and 85 were hospitalized. Approximately 400 men had minor injuries and were treated, but not hospitalized.[57]

A short while after coming aboard the *Farenholt*, McCampbell took a shower and used kerosene to get the oil off his body. He noted that the oil was still in his ears a month or so later. Afterwards he walked out on the deck nude and noticed the warrant gunner was still on the small raft that had been tied up to the large raft next to the destroyer. McCampbell dived into the sea and called out for a stretcher. The destroyers' chief engineer took his clothes off and dove into the water too and assisted him to get the warrant gunner aboard.

The *Farenholt* had taken aboard some 400 survivors, but the *Duncan* had taken about 900 men, which was so many people it affected the stability of the ship. Men were sent below decks to "sit in the corner … and not move from their spot during the night."[58] Eleven men died that evening aboard the destroyer. The next morning the Captain passed down the word for McCampbell to conduct the burial service, but he was able to get out of it.

The executive officer of the *Farenholt,* Lieutenant Alcorn G. Beckman, was a friend of McCampbell and offered his in-port cabin to him. He also gave him a pair of shorts and a ten-dollar bill to buy a shirt and pants in the small stores. Soon McCampbell and others aboard the *Farenholt* were transferred to the cruiser *Helena* before the ship moved to deliver the wounded to the hospital at Espiritu Santa, New Hebrides. McCampbell remembered that Ensign Mitchell was severely hurt when he was blown at the 5-inch gun mount and came to rest draped over the bridge railing. Courtney Shands gathered him and took him below deck.[59]

Then the *Helena* sailed with the other cruiser *Salt Lake City* and two destroyers to Noumea, New Caledonia. In Noumea McCampbell was able to put in a claim for some $1450 and later received $1200 for the personal gear he had lost. He lost about all he owned with the *Wasp* including his uniforms, clothes, cash, golf clubs, and more. He was transferred to a troop transport and made his way back to San Diego to lodge with the other survivors at the Hotel Del Coronado near the North Island Naval Air Station on Coronado Island.

While at the Hotel Del Coronado McCampbell waited like others to settle his accounts and receive back pay. He remembered the first evening when

> about five of us wanted to go out for dinner. Of course, we didn't have any transportation, so we decided to go there in the hotel. So we got to the door, and the man on the door there said, "You're not dressed. You can't go in here." The dining room. I said, "Look, for chrissakes, this is all the clothes we've got. We're survivors." And they finally let us in. No, I didn't have any other uniforms, just the one shirt and pair of pants, socks, till we got back to Norfolk. My wife was still in Norfolk.[60]

In October 1942, David McCampbell was promoted to Lieutenant Commander. He had been assigned to the *Wasp* for her entire life as a light carrier, had done his duty as an LSO aboard and survived the sinking. At this point, he had given 8 years and 5 months of active naval service to his country. It was time to begin an even more challenging part of his Navy career.[61]

6

Training Carrier Air Group 15

"The carriers are coming out faster than we can train people
to man them."[1]

After leaving the Hotel Del Coronado at San Diego, Lieutenant Commander McCampbell traveled home to Norfolk, Virginia, on 30 days survivor leave. While spending time with his wife, he received orders to proceed to the Naval Air Operational Training Command at Naval Air Station Jacksonville. The command was newly established to coordinate all operational air training activities of the Navy, with Rear Admiral Arthur B. Cook as the first commander.

McCampbell reported to NAS Melbourne in November 1942 and was further assigned to proceed to outlying Cecil Field where Ed Konrad, the ex-LSO officer from the *Wasp*, had command of fighter training. He served there for three weeks and then headed to Fort Lauderdale for a few weeks until NAS Melbourne was established. NAS Melbourne was commissioned on October 20, 1942, as Operational Training Unit 2 and with the mission to conduct advanced flight training for newly designated Naval Aviators to prepare them for squadron assignment and combat duties upon completion.

The creation of NAS Melbourne was part of a critical Navy program to train new pilots for the buildup of carrier task forces. The Naval Air Training had been done at NAS Norfolk and NAS San Diego up to this point, but these two facilities could not handle the number of pilots that had to be trained quickly for the war. To meet the operational training needs, the Navy built eight new Naval Auxiliary Air Stations; one in Georgia and seven on the east coast of Florida. Each new air station was organized to handle a specific need. NAS Melbourne was designated as a day fighter station.[2]

McCampbell was tasked to provide LSO training to pilots. He trained them and supervised their activities. At Melbourne McCampbell often flew a small light monoplane from the Taylor Aircraft Company called the "Cub."[3] Though he did not take part in any of the flight training programs there, he was able to get qualified in the Grumman F4F Wildcat fighter. He took gunnery flights and landing practice with the F4F.

Later in his tour at NAS Melbourne, he and one of his assistant LSOs flew the Grumman F6F fighters to Glenview, Illinois, to get checked out with carrier landings in the new Hellcat. They trained in takeoffs and landing aboard the USS *Sable* (IX-81) and the USS *Wolverine* (IX-64). These two former Great Lakes passenger steamers had been converted with flight decks for pilot carrier qualifications.

Having served as an LSO for three and one-half years aboard the *Wasp* and now saddled with the less-than-challenging repetition of LSO training at Melbourne, McCampbell was more than ready to find a way to get into a combat flying assignment. He appealed to his detail officer in Washington, but his response was, "No, we need you. The carriers are coming out faster than we can train people to man them."[4]

McCampbell next went for help to Commander David L. McDonald who was on the staff as second assistant operations officer. McDonald said, "Dave, when I get out of this job, I'll help you get out of yours."[5]

As it turned out, McCampbell got the most support from Commander Ernest W. Litch who was the chief of staff for the Naval Air Operational Command at NAS Jacksonville. Though Litch had served as the ship's navigator aboard the *Ranger*, McCampbell had never met him. After pleading his case, Litch answered, "Well, Dave, I'll tell you what you do. You go back and train two guys to take your place, and I'll tell the detail officer that you should be transferred, or request your transfer."[6] McCampbell declared, "Captain, I've already got two volunteers trained to take my place."[7] Immediately Litch picked up the phone and called the Navy detailer. He was given transfer orders within a month.[8]

At 0135 on October 27, 1942, just 42 days after the USS *Wasp* (CV-7) had been sunk by the Japanese submarine I-19, the *Hornet* (CV-8) went to its watery grave after a fierce attack the previous day by Japanese bombers and torpedo planes from the carrier *Shokaku* during the Battle of Santa Cruz Islands.

Back on August 3, 1942, the keel of USS *Kearsarge* (CV-12) had been laid by the Newport News Shipbuilding and Dry Dock Company, Newport News, Virginia. With the loss of the *Hornet* (CV-8), the carrier *Kearsarge* (CV-12) under construction was renamed the USS *Hornet* (CV-12) on January 21, 1943. The wife of the Secretary of the Navy, Mrs. Frank Knox, launched the new *Hornet* on August 30.[9]

Now that the *Hornet* was under construction, in early 1943 plans were set in motion for a new air group-Carrier Air Group 15 (CAG-15)-for the new carrier. CAG-15 was to be made up of three new squadrons that had to be formed: Fighting Squadron 15 (VF-15), Bombing Squadron 15 (VB-15) and Torpedo Squadron 15 (VT-15). The three CAG-15 squadrons to be formed were to be sent to different naval air stations for operational combat training. VF-15 was assigned to the new Naval Air Station Atlantic City in New Jersey, VB-15 to Creeds Auxiliary Air Station near Virginia Beach, and VT-15 to be stationed at Westerly, Rhode Island (site of the Westerly State Airport).

In the later summer of 1943 orders were sent to the designated naval officers to head up the new CAG-15 squadrons. Bombing Squadron 15 (VB-15) was initially commanded by Lieutenant Commander Irwin L. Dew who was a regular naval officer. Dew was also the new CAG-15 commanding officer. Torpedo Squadron 15 (VT-15) was temporarily under Ensign Charles G. Hurd.[10]

Lieutenant Commander David McCampbell's new orders spelled out that he was to be assigned as the commanding officer of Fighting Squadron 15 (VF-15). He was to report to NAS Atlantic City by August 1, 1943, to assume his duties. The squadron was officially commissioned on September 1, 1943, and consisted of 12 pilots and 8 enlisted personnel. Also attached to VF-15 were several surface officers: Lieutenant Robert McReynolds as Air Combat Intelligence Officer, Lieutenant Joseph J. O'Brien as the Administrative Officer and the Materials Officer, Lieutenant John R. Hoffman. There were also men attached to the Carrier Aircraft Service Unit (CASU) to maintain all the planes. Eventually VF-15 would be filled out with 45 pilots and 36 aircraft.[11]

Naval Air Station Atlantic City was commissioned on April 24, 1943, with Lieutenant Commander W.J. Junkerman as the first commanding officer. The ceremony was heard on the series called "Spirit of '43"[12] on the Columbia Broadcasting Radio Network. The airfield was constructed on 2,444 acres of land leased for twenty years in Egg Harbor Township,

New Jersey. The mission was originally to train crews for combat in carrier air groups including fighters, bombers and torpedo squadrons, but was shifted to fighter training only. This training included "low and high altitude gunnery tactics, field carrier landing practice, carrier qualifications, bombing, formation tactics, fighter direction, night operations and an associated ground school curriculum."[13]

McCampbell liked what he saw at NAS Atlantic City. He liked the new concrete runways, the standard Navy hangars, and a qualified field operations staff. VF-15 shared the airfield with VF-14 also tasked with training for combat. McCampbell and his officers lived in the comfort of the base bachelor officer's quarters (BOQ). On liberty they often traveled by bus to attend dinner dances and cocktail parties at the nearby Seaview Country Club some 12 miles away. On occasion, they headed just 16 miles away to Atlantic City or ventured further to Philadelphia or New York City.

McCampbell spent months at NAS Atlantic City building the staffing level of the squadron with qualified personnel and directing the training of VF-15. The new squadron was formed from pilots and men with varied backgrounds and skillsets. The executive officer (XO) was Lieutenant Commander Charles W. Brewer. Born in Oklahoma, he was a Naval Academy graduate from the class of 1934. The Senior Division Commander was Lieutenant James F. Rigg from the Great Lakes Operational Training Command where he trained aboard the USS *Wolverine*. Lieutenant George C. Duncan, who had completed flight training just six months before, was an Annapolis graduate, class of 1939, and had served aboard the USS *West Virginia* when it was attacked at Pearl Harbor.

Lieutenant (junior grade) John Strane joined VF-15 from two years duty as an advanced fighter tactics instructor at Pensacola. He had come with 100 hours in the F4F-4 Wildcat fighter. Lieutenant (junior grade) Roy Rushing had come from the Training Command where he served as a gunnery instructor. Ensign Ralph Foltz came to the squadron after completing training in photographic reconnaissance. Ensign Clarence Borley also joined the new squadron just before the tour to the Pacific.[14]

Another training instructor with experience was his nephew-in-law, Lieutenant Bert DeWayne Morris. McCampbell's niece, Patricia Ann O'Rourke, was married to Morris who was a well-known actor. Morris from Los Angeles completed high school, and attended Los Angeles Junior College. In 1936 while performing at the Pasadena Playhouse, a scout from Warner Brothers saw him and signed him to a contract. He debuted with a bit part in *China Clipper* (1936). His first major film was *Kid Galahad* (1937) when he co-starred with Humphrey Bogart as a boxer. In 1940 he got his private pilot's license preparing for a part in *Flight Angels* (1940). With World War II approaching and his newfound interest in flying, he decided to join the U.S. Naval Reserve for flight training at Pensacola.[15]

Back when McCampbell was still at Melbourne, Morris was a Navy primary flight instructor at Naval Air Station Hutchinson, Kansas, when he visited McCampbell to ask him to get him into fighters. McCampbell told him to give him a letter of request. Morris did, and McCampbell got him transferred, but the Navy assigned him to a PBY squadron because of his large size. McCampbell helped him with another letter to get him into his fighter training program at Melbourne and he followed him to VF-15.

McCampbell took pride in getting his first command and he became totally immersed in his duties. McCampbell trained his squadron in the typical pre-combat carrier air operations syllabus. They learned to get used to long range flying alone over water, flying on oxygen, navigation, combat aerobatics, simulated carrier takeoff and landings using the airfield, night carrier landing, and how to use a fighter-mounted camera. They practiced the Navy's standard fighter formation flying in two-plane sections and four-plane divisions, as well as dogfighting techniques above and below 10,000 feet altitude.[16]

McCampbell also taught using the fighter for dive-bombing. On visiting the designated skipper of the new *Hornet*, Captain Miles Rutherford Browning, at the shipyard at Newport News, he was told not to teach dive-bombing to his fighter pilots. McCampbell decided to ignore Browning's direction against training because he knew they were doing dive-bombing out in the Pacific.[17]

The tactics that were taught to the squadron pilots was influenced significantly by the characteristics of the aircraft utilized. VF-15 had been allocated the new Grumman F6F-3 Hellcat fighter, which they had to become familiar with during the training. The Hellcat was vastly improved over its predecessor the F4F. While the F6F design was originally developed as an upgrade to the F4F, the ultimate design was quite different. The F6F had a larger wing area, more powerful engine, better pilot visibility, strengthened airframe, a bullet-proof windshield, 212 pounds of cockpit armor, armored oil tank and cooler, and a self-sealing fuel tank.

The F6F-3 was powered by a 2,000 hp Pratt & Whitney R-2800–10 Double Wasp 18-cylinder, two-row radial piston engine giving it a top speed of 370 mph, a service ceiling of 37,200 feet, and a combat range of 1,590 miles with an external center-mounted 150-gallon disposable fuel tank. The plane was armed with six .50 inch Browning M2 machine guns (400 rounds per gun). Optionally, the fighter could carry up to two 1000-lbs bombs or six 5-inch rockets under the wing.[18]

McCampbell felt the F6F was an easy plane to fly and land. The F4F had been hard to land for many pilots. He told those men to keep off their brakes as much as you could and use the rudder to maintain directional control.[19]

By the end of September, VF-15 had 47 pilots. During training McCampbell lost two of the original pilots in crashes. Ensign J.A. Wakefield went down on a training flight on September 18, and Ensign D.F. Hoffman crashed two days later. The causes of these two accidents were never determined.

McCampbell had settled into the NAS Atlantic City life pretty well when, on November 15, 1943, VF-15 got orders to relocate to Pungo Auxiliary Air Station, near Virginia Beach, which served NAS Norfolk. The squadron went from a comfortable situation to what McCampbell called a "crude form of living."[20] The BOQ and enlisted barracks were 150-foot-long, basic single-story buildings with a single coal fired stove that, at most, heated to maybe 15 feet out from the fire. Needless to say, it was cold most of the time.

The man who stoked the coal stove came in at 0400 and made too much noise according to McCampbell. Everyone in VF-15 ate at the general mess hall and there was a canteen where one could get "gedunk"[21] food, cold drinks, personal items, etc. There were no recreation facilities at Pungo and the nearest bar was a public one called "The Officers' Club"[22] at Virginia Beach that sold high priced liquor. There were parties of course. The most notable party for the fighter pilots was after the commissioning of the *Hornet* on November 29. The event started out at the Portsmouth Officers' Club and hours later ended up at the Pungo general store.

While McCampbell and the VF-15 pilots deemed Pungo living conditions as below par, those in Bombing Fifteen training at Creeds Auxiliary Air Station felt they experienced far worse. They lived in Quonset huts, ate at a general mess, had a really poor canteen and worked in a single "barnlike"[23] hangar.

Actually, the most serious issue for VB-15 was the switch of aircraft during their operational training period. After the squadron was commissioned on September 1, 1943, the

VB-15 pilots started out flying the rugged, tried and true Douglas Dauntless SBD-5s that had delivered destruction to the Japanese by sinking six carriers from Pearl Harbor to Midway. These planes, crewed by a pilot and backseat gunner/radioman, had been the mainstay of the Navy's bombing threat in the war for two and one-half years until the Curtiss Helldivers came on the scene.[24]

For VB-15 the SB2C-1C Helldivers started arriving at Creeds on November 17, 1943. The plane was an all-metal mid-wing monoplane powered by a 14-cylinder air-cooled radial Wright R-2600–8 Double Cyclone engine with 1,700 HP that drove a three-bladed propeller. Like the SBD, the Helldiver was crewed by a pilot and rear gunner/radioman.

On paper, the advantages of the new Helldivers over the SBD-5s seemed to be positive enough to promise their success, but it was not to be. The SB2C-1C was faster by 30 mph, had a greater range, an internal bomb bay that could carry a 1,000 pound bomb or a torpedo, had two 20mm cannons in the wings, had manually folding wings for greater storage aboard the carrier, and could hold an impressive 78 degree dive angle.

But even after some 880 design modifications from the first prototype version, the Helldiver ultimately turned out to be difficult to fly. It was underpowered, had structural weaknesses, poor handling, and inadequate stability. The weight had increased from the prototype design of 7,122 to 10,114 pounds with the SB2C-1C, an incredible 42 percent. Per-

Two U.S. Navy Curtiss SB2C Helldiver dive-bombers of Bombing Squadron VB-1 in the landing circle of the aircraft carrier USS *Yorktown* (CV-10) in July 1944 (Official U.S. Navy Photograph # 80-G-376123, National Archives).

haps the most serious flaw in the SB2C was the poor aileron effectiveness, which made the plane close to being out of control at its 85-knot carrier landing approach speed.

Its pilots called the Helldiver the "Beast" and said "SB2C" stood for "Son of a Bitch 2nd Class."[25] The president of Curtiss, the manufacturer, Guy Vaughn, indicated that the Helldiver was "one of the biggest wartime crosses we had to bear."[26] The carrier commanders complained openly over the new dive-bomber, but since the Navy had put such a huge investment of development time and money on the Helldiver, they really had no choice but to force it down the throats of the commanders and on the dive-bomber squadrons.[27]

The transition by VB-15 to the Helldiver cost the pilots valuable training time in the new plane. In fact, when the time finally came to deploy aboard the *Hornet*, not one Bombing Fifteen' pilot had received over 15 hours of flight time in the new plane. This short training period was clearly insufficient for any aviator moving to a new aircraft, but was even more deficient in light of the variety of handling and stability problems with the SB2C-1C.

Bombing Fifteen had its share of tragic accidents in training. While on an instrument training flight on November 1, Ensign Harry G. Storey and Ensign John P. Walter died when they lost the wing of their SNJ trainer. Just two days later in a cloud training exercise two SBDs collided over Kitty Hawk, North Carolina, killing both pilots and gunners.[28]

Torpedo Squadron 15 trained with the TBF/M-1C Avenger torpedo bomber at Westerly, Rhode Island. The plane was designed to replace the outdated Douglas Devastator torpedo bomber and first saw combat in the Battle of Midway on June 4, 1942. The power plant was the Wright R-2600 Cyclone 14-cylinder radial piston engine with 1,700 hp. The top speed was 275 mph with an operational range of 1,000 miles and maximum ceiling of 30,000 feet. The range could be increased using three 335-gallon external fuel drop tanks.

The Avengers' cockpit was high on the fuselage and sported a greenhouse looking frame over the three crewmen. The flight crew was positioned in-line with the pilot up front, the bombardier in the middle and the tail gunner in the rear. The pilot controlled the two 12.7mm Browning machine guns in the wings. The bombardier had a seat in the lower part of the fuselage where he could control the torpedo or level bombing functions, as well as operate the defensive 7.62mm Browning machine gun pointed toward the rear. The internal bomb bay could carry the MK XIII-2 torpedo or up to 2,000 pounds of conventional drop bombs against surface targets. The tail gunner, who was seated in the rear under a rounded dome, controlled the 12.7mm Browning machine gun used to fight off enemy fighters during the attack runs.

The Avenger made use of a number of advanced features like electronically powered arresting hook, twin under wing main landing gears, retractable tail wheel, and powered wing folding. As production requirements increased for the Avenger at Grumman, the Navy decided to shift the production work to General Motors to take advantage of available resources at five of their factories. The newly tasked factories formed the "Eastern Aircraft Division"[29] where the Avengers were built under the new designation "TBM."[30]

On November 24, 1943, Carrier Group 15 carried out their first coordinated joint strike against a target. Two days after Christmas of 1943 some of air group moved to NAS Norfolk. At Norfolk McCampbell's VF-15 spent time getting organized and replaced some 16 engines in the F6Fs. The total number of pilots had to be reduced to 40 from 45, so McCampbell had each pilot vote on which pilot they would most like to go into combat with. He simply kept the top 40 pilots based on the secret voting and eliminated the five remaining. McCampbell was comfortable that the vote did reveal the pilots with the lowest performance or those that did not get along well with the others.

TBM-1C Avengers of VT-2 with wheels and arrester hooks down above the carrier Hornet (*Essex*-class) after a strike on Guam, July 18, 1944. Note rocket rails and ASB radar antennas under the wings (U.S. Navy Photograph).

Next McCampbell took his squadron out to qualify aboard the USS *Long Island* (CVE-1) in Chesapeake Bay. By the time January 13, 1944, arrived, all the squadrons of the group were embarked aboard the new *Hornet* as it headed out to an area off Bermuda on the shakedown cruise. It turned out to be the shortest shakedown cruise ever. Most shakedown cruises lasted at least a month in places like Jamaica or the Gulf of Paria off Venezuela, but this one saw the *Hornet* returning to Norfolk on January 30—a 17-day shakedown.

For VF-15 and McCampbell on the shakedown cruise, it was a period of continued training activities. The primary work was on takeoffs and landing operations, as well as formation flying. The Hellcats did practice strafing on a sled, while the dive-bombing and torpedo squadron crews bombed it.

Another important training cycle was navigating to and from the target over water. The pilots plotted the course to the target, and after the attack, each of them plotted a course back to the carrier. To aid the pilot in finding the carrier, which had obviously moved as much as 60 miles from their takeoff location, there was the YE-ZB homing system. Each carrier was equipped with a UHF (line-of-sight) transmitter than emitted a two-digit Morse code letter denoting 15 degrees of a circle. On returning home, the pilot would climb in altitude to get the best signal, and pick up the code letter. Based on that code letter, he knew within 15 degrees which quadrant angle it was in to the carrier. If the code letter changed, the pilot knew he was not heading directly toward the carrier and he would make a course correction.

While on the shakedown cruise, McCampbell had his pilots fly at different altitudes to note the range from the carrier they could pick up the signal. They observed that at 6,000 feet they could pick up the carrier at 60 miles. At 8,000 feet, the range was 80 miles, and at 4,000 feet at 40 miles away. The carrier used the YE-ZB homing system even while under radio silence since the quadrants codes were changed each day.[31]

The squadron with the most difficulty on the shakedown cruise was VB-15. During takeoff, Ensign Emmett Fletcher in his SB2C-1C Helldiver had his engine fail and as he tried to come around and land with low altitude and insufficient speed, he crashed into the sea. He died, but his radioman/gunner survived. Ensign Andrew Peterson and Radioman Leslie W. Gretter were killed when an aileron came off their Helldiver on a simulated bombing run on the *Hornet*.

The non-fatal accidents for Bombing 15 were almost unbelievable. On landing aboard the carrier, Ensign Alfred de Cesaro came in too fast, bounced his arresting hook, and hit the after gun mount which wrecked his plane and the guns. After the crash was cleaned up by damage control, Ensign Henry Harold Kramer jumped a barrier and crashed, as did Lieutenant Wilfred Saxton. Ensign Frank Eisenhart jumped two barriers and crashed his plane into Ensign David Hall's plane. Some planes hit the water in takeoff too.

The captain of the *Hornet*, Captain Miles M. Browning, was so frustrated he suspended flight operations and called the senior air group officers to the bridge. Lieutenant Commander Dew tried to defend VB-15, but Browning was not impressed. McCampbell chimed in and told Browning that the Helldiver was a new plane and the takeoff distance was not long enough. Browning said he was going by the manufacturer's stats for the Helldiver. McCampbell countered that the stats reflected those of a Navy test pilot at Patuxent not what a new aviator just learning the aircraft would need. On McCampbell's recommendation, Browning relented and gave the Helldiver pilots an additional 100 feet of deck to operate in. The accident rate was soon down.[32]

Though Captain Browning was a rather strict and tough commander, McCampbell had no problems with him. That did not mean he always agreed with him. In a briefing with the senior pilots in the wardroom on the shakedown cruise, Browning said, "Now, we're in a hurry to get out there in combat. They need us very badly. On this shakedown cruise, we're going to find out the guys that do the job and do it properly and the guys that don't. If you have one of those people under you that's not doing the job, you recognize it, then kick him aside and get rid of him when you get back to Norfolk."[33] McCampbell disagreed and felt that a man making a single mistake was worthy of more instruction. After all, most of the flight crews were "really novices"[34] since only a few of them had seen combat. Even McCampbell himself had not been in combat in a fighter yet.[35]

The Air Group would soon become disenchanted with life aboard the *Hornet* as the days continued. Captain Browning did not let Air Group 15 operate as its own entity aboard his ship as often was the case on many carriers. The air group commander and the squadron commanders were not able to handle the discipline of their airmen as they desired, but had to yield to the Captain's decisions. With Air Group 15 as V-5 Division of the carrier, the officers were assigned to various duties including intelligence, standing daily watches, serving in the medical department and others such general ship duties. The Captain showed little interest in the functions of an airman.

On February 2, 1944, CAG-15 moved back to NAS Norfolk as the *Hornet* went into drydock to correct problems encountered on the shakedown cruise. That same day Captain Browning relieved Commander William M. Drane as the air group commander, and Lieutenant Commander Irwin L. Dew as commanding officer of Bombing Squadron 15.

On February 9 newly promoted Commander McCampbell became the new commanding officer of Carrier Air Group 15, as Lieutenant Commander Charles W. Brewer moved up from his executive officer role to take over as the commander officer of VF-15. Captain Browning asked McCampbell to recommend a replacement squadron commander for VB-15. He told the captain about Art Giessar, but when Browning had the detail officer present Giessar with the squadron position, he declined. His reason for rejecting the job was that he had bad ears and could not do dive bombing. Strangely, he was currently serving at NAS Cape May as an instructor in dive-bombing.

Browning asked for another candidate, and McCampbell thought of James Mini from the Naval Academy class of 1935. Lieutenant Commander James Haile Mini took over VB-15 on February 13, 1944, but not without some strife. He and his wife were not too happy to leave since he was comfortable leading his shore duty commanding a training squadron at the time. Mini had served with carriers and had become a floatplane pilot. He was the senior aviator of a battleship fleet while serving on the USS *Arizona* when it was sunk at Pearl Harbor.

Mini had never flown a Helldiver SB2C-1C and had to qualify after he joined the air group. Though his first two carrier landings resulted in crashes into the barrier, McCampbell had helped him correct his landing technique with the Helldiver.

Lieutenant Commander Valdemar G. Lambert became the new commanding officer of Torpedo Squadron 15. Lambert had graduated from Southwestern Louisiana Institute and entered naval aviation training at Pensacola in 1936. After receiving his Wings and commission as an Ensign, he reported aboard the cruiser USS *Boise* as the aviation officer. Next, he served as a flight instructor at NAS Pensacola before taking command of a flying boat squadron stationed at Floyd Bennet Field in New York.[36]

After the men took some leave, on February 14, 1944, the USS *Hornet* with McCampbell and the squadrons of Carrier Air Group 15 sailed from Norfolk and cruised southward along the Atlantic coast. In transit to the Pacific for combat operations via the Panama Canal, the aircrews of CAG-15 continued to train. Unfortunately, there were more accidents. Off Cape Hatteras, North Carolina, a storm ragged, sending an SB2C over the side of the carrier and leaving ten other planes damaged. While conducting a simulated attack on the Panama Canal, Ensign O.G. Lippincott lost control of his plane and crashed in the jungle.

On February 18 around 1700 the *Hornet* pulled into the pier at Colon, Panama on the Caribbean Sea. The air group aircraft had already frown off to Panama Air Station. The next day at 0430 the carrier departed the port and entered the canal heading west. VF-15 airmen Elmer Cordray described what he saw: "Very warm here. I couldn't do the scenery here justice by trying to describe it. It's beautiful. We had very little clearance going through the locks. Hit port in Balboa in the afternoon. Starboard section got liberty, leaving me to stay aboard. Left Balboa this morning [February 20] at approximately 0930. Pacific very calm compared to the Atlantic."[37]

After passing through the canal, CAG-15 continued having accidents primarily from mechanical problems with the Helldiver aircraft. On February 27, 1944, the *Hornet* arrived at North Island Naval Air Station at San Diego. Two days later the *Hornet* departed for Pearl Harbor, Hawaii, arriving there and mooring at location Fox 9 at Ford Island on March 4, 1944.[38]

In his Pacific War journal ARM3c A.T. Graham of Bombing 15 recorded his thoughts about the trip to Pearl Harbor: "The cruise out was horrible. We were all hungry, over-crowded, the air-conditioning didn't work. Sweat held us adhesively to our leather seats. Officers ate three meals a day—had a snack stand besides. We stood in line for 2 to 3 hours to eat twice a day—and there wasn't much. This—coupled with that things looked as tho we'd be going straight out—didn't make anybody overly happy."[39]

In arriving in Hawaii Graham noted that Pearl Harbor was not as large as he had thought it would be, and even Diamond Head and Waikiki was not so spectacular. He felt Honolulu was too crowded, and full of barber shops and shoe stores.

When Air Group 15 arrived at Pearl Harbor, they were to receive a real shock. The Navy brass, with input from Captain Browning about problems with VB-15, decided that the air group had not reached the level of efficiency necessary to face the Japanese yet. Another factor in their decision was that Nimitz and his admirals wanted the F6F fighter pilots to be more proficient in fighter-bombing techniques. Since Browning had demanded that the fighter training be focused on shooting down Japanese planes, they had not received enough bombing experience.

To the dismay of VB-15s engineering officer, Ensign John D. Bridgers, Carrier Air Group 2 took possession of the aircraft of Carrier Air Group 15. He and his men had worked hard to get the aircraft to the required level of operational reliability just to leave them for another air group. Ensign Bridgers remarked, "Our being thrown off the *Hornet* was the equivalent of B'rer Rabbit being thrown in the briar patch."[40]

As a result of the identified deficiencies, especially with VB-15, Air Group 15 was detached from the *Hornet* and put ashore on Oahu for further advanced training. Air Group 2 replaced McCampbell's air group and sailed with the *Hornet* to forward combat operations on March 15, 1944. Meanwhile, VF-15 and the Air Group 15 staff headquarters went to NAS Kaneohe on the north shore of the island. VB-15 and VT-15 headed to NAS Barber's Point at the entrance to Pearl Harbor.

Having been separated from the *Hornet* and the air group split up on Oahu, the morale of the officers and men of Air Group 15 was decidedly down. VB-15 departed Barber's Point on March 8, but it was not until March 14 that all three squadrons of CAG-15 were reunited at NAS Puunene on the island of Maui.[41]

VB-15 sailed on the USS *Swann*, an old seaplane tender to Maui loaded with the squadron gear set on the fantail. They ate frankfurters and beans, and when it began to rain, they flipped over the lifeboats to keep dry. When dawn came, the ship was laying off Kahilui harbor as a formation of five fighters flew overhead. As the planes were moving back and forth below each other, one fighter fell into a spin when it hit a piece of wing flap. A white parachute suddenly appeared. Another fighter had a flame and smoke coming from its cowling. That plane fell straight down, winged over and crashed into the sea. Graham noted it was an unpleasant welcome to Maui.[42]

NAS Puunene was on 2,202 acres with two paved runways (6,800 feet and 6,500 feet) with taxiways, ramps, hangars and other buildings. Unfortunately, the facilities were designed to accommodate only one squadron, not three, and Air Group Eight was still there too. It was in a confused state for a while.[43]

At Puunene Air Group 15 spent six weeks of advanced training. The squadrons trained as a group and under their own officers. The various mechanical problems with the planes were also corrected. The only issue that persisted was the handling of discipline problems, which was in the hands of the base commanding officer and not McCampbell and the squadron commanders. The air group officers endured, but came to resent the intrusion into their area of authority.

McCampbell took the advice of the training officer of the Commander Air Force Pacific Fleet who said, "The fighters are now doing a lot of bombing, and if you haven't had any or hadn't had much, concentrate on that while you're here."[44] The approach to island attacks in the Pacific was sending in a fighter sweep first to strafe and drop bombs on the enemy fighters on the ground to eliminate the air threat. The bombs were hung on the wing mounts that did reduce the maneuverability of the fighter somewhat. The fighter pilots were briefed to jettison the bombs if they ran into enemy fighters in air-to-air combat.

The Air Group also took the opportunity to practice night field carrier landing. In addition, they conducted coordinated exercises with all three squadrons doing dive-bombing or making attacks on the island of Kanoolawe. Unfortunately, during their stay on Maui, VF-15 lost two fighter pilots. Lieutenant A. Grothaus crashed at sea in a midair collision with Ensign G.F. Butler just after a predawn takeoff. The two pilots had been practicing the Thach Weave. As a result of the collision, McCampbell's squadrons "did away with the Thach Weave completely, except for rare occasions, when our pilots would maybe get caught and a couple of other pilots would try and protect him."[45]

While at Puunene, like the other two Air Group squadrons, Ensign Bridgers and his engineering section strived to get his 36 Helldivers ready for battle. Air Group 15 passed their Operational Readiness Inspection and was ready to get their combat assignment with a carrier.

The social life for the Air Group personnel was almost too active as the men hit the bars in Wailuku and traveled to the estate of the Countess Alexa von Tempsky Zabriskie. After the Pearl Harbor attack, the Countess decided to entertain servicemen, especially Navy fighter pilots, with picnics, horseback riding, hunting and cookouts up in the mountains of Haleakala.

AOM 1/C Elmer Cordray wrote of his days on Maui:

> We didn't get any liberty the first week we were here, but finally one day they broke down and gave us a two day pass. Several of us went to Wailaku, a small town and stayed all night at the Grand Maui Hotel. Back at the base, we played several games of softball. In our game with the officers, Lt. Commander Brewer played with them that day. The chow here is really swell. All the ice tea and lemonade at noon and supper. At breakfast, had all the ice cold tomato juice, pineapple juice or grapefruit juice and cold milk we could drink. Ate plenty of ice cream and every day drank my share of cold apple juice. Just ten cents a can and a large can at that ... went over to Trade Winds beach swimming on our day off ... went through a sugar plantation and saw how sugar was made.[46]

Finally, on April 28, McCampbell's air group was ordered back to Pearl Harbor from NAS Puunene to board their assigned carrier, the USS *Essex* (CV-9). They were relieving Commander Philip H. Torrey Jr.'s Air Group 9 that needed a rest after serving in combat since they had come aboard in March 1943. The combat success of Air Group 9 would be a hard to top for McCampbell's untested Air Group 15.

The Air Group packed up their gear into transport planes on April 29, 1944, and flew from Puunene to Ford Island. At midnight that day, the officers and men of Air Group 15 began to board the carrier along with their 25 tons of baggage. Commander David McCampbell and his Air Group 15 were now ready to enter the Pacific War.[47]

7

Marcus and Wake Islands Raids

"Generally I'd just pound on my dashboard."[1]

McCampbell and his fellow officers and men of Air Group 15 were joining a carrier that had already engaged the Japanese in the Pacific and found success. The USS *Essex* had been built by Newport News Shipbuilding and Dry Dock Co., Newport News, Virginia, and was launched July 31, 1942, by Mrs. Artemus L. Gates, wife of the Assistant Secretary of the Navy for Air. She was the first carrier of the new Essex class of 27,000-ton aircraft carriers and was commissioned the last day of 1942.

Designed to accommodate 2,600 officers and men, the *Essex* was 820 feet long, had a beam of 147.5 feet, a draft of 28.4 feet and could make flank speeds of 33 knots driven by her four Westinghouse geared steam turbines. She was heavy armed for antiaircraft protection with 4-twin 5-inch .38 caliber guns, 4-single 5 inch .38 caliber guns, 8-quadruple 40mm .56 caliber guns and 46-single 20mm .78 caliber guns.[2]

After conducting sea trails in January, the *Essex* began testing her equipment around the Chesapeake Bay area. On February 17, 1943, an SNJ trainer made the first takeoff and landing aboard the carrier. In March, Air Group 9 embarked with 450 officers and men aboard the *Essex* with 36 F6F Hellcat fighters from VF-9, 18 TBF Avengers torpedo bombers of VT-9 and 36 SBD Dauntless dive-bombers of VB-9. On March 15 the *Essex* sailed south to the Gulf of Paria, Trinidad for a 25-day shakedown cruise, returning to the Norfolk Navy Yard at Portsmouth on April 9.

Designated as Task Group 28.19, the *Essex* sailed May 10, 1943, from Portsmouth toward the Panama Canal Zone. After clearing the canal on the 20th, the *Essex* headed to Pearl Harbor, arriving there on May 31. Like McCampbell's Air Group 15 would later partake, Air Group 9 spent ten weeks in Hawaii conducting advanced training while the *Essex* crews took gunnery practice.

After completing their shakedown and training cruises, the *Essex* with Air Group 9 aboard took off from Pearl Harbor on a series of successful combat deployments against the Japanese. As with TF 16, they conducted devastating attacks on Marcus Island (August 31), and for TF 14 hit Wake Island (October 5–6). Then they "hammered Rabaul harbor and its shore facilities"[3] on November 11, and as TG 50.3 hit enemy airfields in Operation Galvanic on Tarawa and Makin Atolls (November 18–26) and at Kwajalein Atoll (December 4).

The *Essex* with TG 58.2 participated in the second amphibious assault against the Marshall Islands (January 29–February 2, 1944), followed by strikes against the Truk Islands (February 17–18). With Fast Carrier Task Force 58 heading to the Marianas to attack Japanese supply lines, the *Essex* with Air Group 9 repelled a prolonged Japanese air attack, and proceeded to hit Saipan, Tinian and Guam (February 21–23).[4]

After the Marianas strike on February 23, the *Essex* turned eastward, arriving at Majuro Atoll on the 26th. The carrier was replenished, refueled and departed on the 28th to Pearl Harbor, arriving on March 4. Two days later the *Essex* sailed to San Francisco for an over-haul. The *Essex* arrived at the drydock at the Navy Yard at Hunters Point on March 10. The tired *Essex* crew and Air Group 9 were given well-deserved leave in San Francisco. After necessary repairs and installation of new equipment were completed, and sea trials had concluded, the *Essex* sailed toward Pearl Harbor on April 16, 1944.[5]

The *Essex* docked at Pier F-10 at Ford Island, Pearl Harbor on April 20. On the 24th the carrier went to sea for maneuvers and gunnery practice and returned on the April 28 prepared to take aboard McCampbell's Air Group 15. As they settled in on the *Essex* on April 30 there was a notable improvement over life back on the *Hornet*. Though the air group was again in Division V-5 in the carrier organization, the captain gave McCampbell and his squadron commanders' full authority over the discipline of their men. They were now able to maintain their duties as a separate entity aside.

McCampbell's Air Group 15 had joined the *Essex* with 122 pilots and a considerable inventory of 99 planes including 37 F6F-3 Hellcat fighters of VF-15, 36 SB2C-1C Helldiver dive-bombers of VB-15, 20 TBF/M-1C Avenger torpedo bombers of VT-15, and 6 F6F-3N Hellcat Night Fighters of VFN-77. The Night Fighters were equipped with AN/APS-4 radar in the starboard outer wing fairing.[6]

McCampbell's new boss was Captain Ralph Andrew Ofstie. He had taken over com-mand of the *Essex* from Captain Donald B. Duncan on November 6, 1943. Ofstie had an impressive array of assignments in his career. Born in 1897 in Eau Claire, Wisconsin, Ofstie graduated from the Naval Academy in June 1918, and served in World War I aboard the USS *Whipple* (DD-15) and the cruiser USS *Chattanooga* (CL-18) in the Eastern Atlantic. After the war, he saw duty aboard the USS *O'Bannon* (DD-177) and in 1920 he took flight training at NAS Pensacola. Graduating the next year, Ofstie served with VF-1 until 1924 when he became the Commanding Officer of Scouting Squadron Six (VS-6). He also had taken part in annual flight competitions between Army and Navy pilots using the Curtiss Marine seaplanes. On October 25, 1924, during the Schneider Cup Race in Bayshore Park, Maryland, Lieutenant Ofstie broke world speed records in the 100, 200 and 500 kilometers flying a Curtiss CR-3 seaplane.

From 1927 to 1929, he had duty as the Aviation Officer aboard the USS *Detroit* (CL-8). After serving at NAS Anacostia in the Flight Test Division until 1933, he went to sea aboard the USS *Saratoga* (CV-3) as Commanding Officer of VF-6 for two years. He was promoted to Lieutenant Commander and became Assistant Naval Attaché in Tokyo, then served as Navigator on the USS *Enterprise* (CV-3), with a temporary assignment as staff officer on the USS *Saratoga* (CV-3) in 1939. In 1940 Ofstie had duty as a staff officer on the USS *Yorktown* (CV-5), and the next year in London as Assistant Naval Attaché. In 1942, before commanding the *Essex*, he served as a Commander on the Pacific Fleet staff of Admiral Nimitz. Ofstie had known McCampbell from his Navy gunnery champion days before the war started.[7]

McCampbell's first encounter with Captain Ofstie after he boarded the *Essex* occurred when they both met halfway up the accommodation ladder as Ofstie said, "One piece of advice I want to give you, be sure you instruct your people to be very careful in their com-munications, to be as quiet as possible. We have one guy out here in the Pacific that you can hear him all over the Pacific, even without radio. I don't want any of that."[8] McCampbell saw little of Captain Ofstie during the remainder of his duty aboard the *Essex*.[9]

Shortly after McCampbell's air group came aboard the *Essex*, the Executive Officer,

Commander David L. McDonald, briefed the carrier crew over the loudspeaker. Part of his speech helped to give McCampbell's team the quality level of support and cooperation they needed as they undertook the dangerous job of naval aviation combat. McDonald said he wanted the people to realize that McCampbell's air group were new and they might start out perfectly as the last air group was, but he wanted them to treat the new group as well as the they had the old group. He told them that the new guys belong to the *Essex* and they would improve with more experience.[10]

On May 3, 1944, at 0800 the *Essex* got underway from their Ford Island dock heading for Majuro Atoll in the Marshalls. In company with the carrier were the new *Wasp* (CV-18, namesake of the *Wasp CV-7* sunk from under McCampbell on September 15, 1942), the *San Jacinto* (CVL-30), the *Henley* (DD-553), the *Reno* (CL-96), the *Dyson* (DD-572), the *Patterson* (DD-392), and the *San Diego* (CL-53). On the seventh, four more ships joined the group-*Converse* (DD-509), *Ausburne* (DD-570), *Wadleigh* (DD-689), and the *Spence* (DD-512).

As the *Essex* headed north from Hawaii into the wind, at 1100 Air Group 15 came over the horizon and entered the carrier landing pattern. The scout bombers, torpedo planes

USS *Essex* (CV-9) underway at 1615 hours during May 1943, in position 37 05'N, 74 15'E, as photographed from a blimp from squadron ZP-14. Among the aircraft parked on her flight deck are 24 SBD scout bombers (parked aft), about 11 F6F fighters (parked in after part of the midships area) and about 18 TBF/TBM torpedo planes (parked amidships) (Official U.S. Navy Photograph # 80-G-68097, now in the collections of the National Archives).

and F6F fighter planes descended to land aboard every 25 seconds. McCampbell was the first Hellcat that landed and after taxiing forward, the wings were folded upward. On the side of his fighter was painted the "Monsoon Maiden."[11]

After conducting training exercises in transit, the *Essex* and task group arrived at the 90-square mile anchorage at Majuro lagoon at 1430 on May 8 and birthed at position X-11. Though glad to finally be aboard a carrier heading to combat, the environmental conditions were rough. The only air conditioning was in the pilots' ready rooms, but none for the aircrewmen of Bombing 15 and Torpedo 15. The "suffocating"[12] temperature below decks was around 85° with 85 percent humidity. The flight suits were too hot and many of the crewmen just wore their skivvies. The men moved their bed mattresses on to the open decks to get any sea breeze they could to sleep.

The *Essex* spent a week at Majuro as Admiral Spruance prepared for a full invasion of the Marianas Islands to establish airfields within what the Japanese considered their inner empire. From the Marianas, the U.S. Army Air Force could bomb the mainland of Japan with their B-29s.

Since the planned Marianas invasion was still a month away, Admiral Mitscher, Captain Ofstie's boss, decided that *Essex*, *Wasp* and *San Jacinto* needed some combat experience. All three carriers had new air groups. Under the Task Group 58.6 commander, Rear Admiral A.E. Montgomery, the three carriers, in company with *Reno* (CL-96), *Boston* (CA-69), *San Diego* (CL-53), *Baltimore* (CA-68), *Canberra* (CA-70) and twelve destroyers, set sail on May 15 for Marcus Island some 1,700 miles away to the northwest.

The primary purpose of the mission was to "increase the security of our Marshall Islands holdings, and to reduce the future effectiveness of Marcus Island as an enemy operating base."[13] The Japanese at Marcus Island had tried to rebuild their damaged radio station and weather facility between the periodic raids from the American carriers every few months. It had become almost a standard real-world training exercise for every new carrier force in the Pacific.

TG 58.6 sailed for three days on a course to the east and the north of Kwajalein and Eniwetok until May 18 when they reached a refueling position 410 miles at 150° from Marcus Island. In the early evening, the *San Jacinto* with the *San Diego* and four destroyers was sent 400 miles to the north of Marcus to patrol for any enemy picket ships that might bring in Japanese aircraft to counter the air strikes, while the *Essex* and *Wasp* maintained continuous CAPs over the TG and rescue submarine.[14]

Morale for the air group had continued to be good as it had been at the anchorage, and it would have been "excellent"[15] if the air conditioning were provided below decks to the airmen. The condition of the VB 15 ready room aboard the *Essex* was detailed on the evening of May 17 on the way to Marcus Island:

Cigarette butts overflow in ashtrays and stray butts crunched underfoot, litter the deck, on both abeam bulkheads flight gear—suits, helmuts, masks, jackets, life jackets hang in lazy, reposing disarray. Wrappers, scraps of paper litter the deck, empty cigarette cartons. Into one chair seat—two pipes stuck—ready for instant smoking in the morning. Books, magazines are strewn about. "Disputed Passage" lay open on the deck—the wastepaper baskets are spilling over. Records are piled high next to the record player. On two bulkheads beside a pic of Chili Williams & one of Betty Grable, also Maria Montez, are maps of Marcus—our target. Stuck in front of the room is a Varga girl looking outward a soft-and-fluffy version of "The Thinker"—her trim legs nudging each other tenderly. On the blackboard is notice of a radio check—and the new "Bullsheet" [the squadron newspaper] is posted—along with the cleanup detail and some air intelligence information. On the bookcase—the books—their inspiring titles on their nonlustrous sides—dejectedly sleeping on the shelf. Decks of cards are stuck in beams along the bulkhead—and dungaree shirts have been slung over chair backs—it is much too hot to wear them below. At the back of the room lay tool boxes, gun cleaning paraphenalia: long-handled rods, caterpiller-like ramrod tips. That's the ready room tonight.[16]

In preparation for a combat mission, McCampbell would skip breakfast, except for perhaps an orange juice from the wardroom, and head to the ready room. He would do paperwork as necessary and listen to the briefing from the intelligence officer of the fighter squadron since he flew a fighter. As the commander of the air group, he could fly any aircraft type he wanted, but since he had trained as a fighter pilot, he flew the F6F. McCampbell never briefed the torpedo or dive-bomber pilots, but he did take part in the briefing for the fighter pilots.

The squadron intelligence officers got their information from the fleet intelligence officer before the mission. The squadron briefings to the pilots included Japanese plane and ship recognition and capabilities, target intelligence, anti-aircraft sites, and any other information gained from previous sorties. After the missions, the intelligence officers debriefed the flight crews and wrote down the event details. Then the intelligence officers along with the administrative officer would create the aircraft combat action reports which were submitted to the squadron commanders for review and approval, and then to McCampbell for final approval.

The challenge for McCampbell in editing the squadron action reports was to be consistent in what had been attacked and the level of damage inflicted. The reports had to be plausible and not be overly optimistic, and McCampbell had turned down a number of claims due to lack of evidence. He generally required confirmation of planes being downed by another pilot having seen it.

Even though the planes were initially equipped with camera guns, eventually McCampbell had them taken out because the pilots naturally followed the enemy planes they had hit all the way to the ground or until they exploded to make sure there was clear evidence. This approach resulted in pilots losing too much altitude, which was a major disadvantage during an engagement. The second reason for getting rid of the camera guns was that the action was too difficult to correlate with other action of other planes. Sometimes two attacking planes would be firing at the same enemy plane, and along with the vibrating camera shots too, nothing was clear-cut.

When the mission briefings were complete, planes were armed, fueled and prepared to sortie. When word came to launch, the pilots and flight crews left the ready rooms on the galley deck, and went up one level to the flight deck to meet their planes. There was no walk-around the plane inspection except for checking the rudder and the elevators. McCampbell trusted his plane captain, so after completing his quick inspection, he got into his cockpit. He was the only person who flew that specific F6F except in an emergency when they were short an aircraft.

Over time, the officers and men became like a family, though engaged in a deadly profession. The men who worked on the planes took great care of the men who flew them. McCampbell's mechanic would come to the ready room and talk with him about the aircraft. Once he asked McCampbell if he wanted him to make him a cigarette holder in the plane. McCampbell replied, "Yeah, that would be real neat."[17] Though the Air Group commander rarely smoked, the mechanic fabricated and riveted a piece of aluminum in the cockpit as a holder, and before each flight he made sure there was a fresh pack of cigarettes in it.[18]

The carrier strike group launched on May 19, 1944, for Marcus from 110 miles at 165° sailing at 20 knots. A preplanned 0500 launch of a Night Intruder strike over the target by four F6F-3Ns was canceled because of low winds over the carrier deck. At 0804 in heavy wind and overcast, the *Essex* launched 7 fighters, 8 torpedo bombers and 15 dive-bombers to attack the aircraft, airfields, and shipping. Just 35 minutes later Air Group 15 reached the south shore of the island. McCampbell arrived first and circled with three other F6Fs as CAP protection over the island at 8,000 feet. There was no Japanese fighter opposition to McCampbell's fighters. The remaining seven fighters began strafing the gun installations as the torpedo bombers targeted the storage dumps with 500-pound bombs from an altitude of 1,500 feet. They hit a concrete building and a few frame buildings. Using 100- and 500-pound bombs, the Helldivers dropped their bombs from 1,500 feet, with limited effect.

Lieutenant (junior grade) James N. Barnitz, better known as "bean bag" (top), and ARM3c Herbert N. Stienkemeyer (front), examine the battered rudder of their SB2C-1C Helldiver (Bu# 18208) they flew in raiding Marcus Island. Photographed on board USS *Essex* (CV-9), on 20 May 1944. In the background of the picture are two of Stienkemeyer's fellow gunners. To the left of the propeller is Charles Lossie Rowland, and to the right, partially obscured, is Stanley Nelson Whitby. Whitby was killed five months after this photograph was taken, shot down by the Japanese over the Pescadores Islands in October of 1944 (National Archives Photograph 80-G-373614).

Having been surprised with the fighter sweep, the Japanese gunners threw up light anti-aircraft fire at first, but soon through up heavy fire at the attackers. The torpedo bombers had come through a cloudbank and had little time to locate their targets to drop their bomb loads, yielding the expected results of misses. After the strike, the planes formed up and headed back to the carrier. Four of the Air Group fighters had been hit, which resulted in two engine changes. An F6F pilot, Lieutenant (junior grade) Robert Lloyd Stearns, was hit in the neck by a fragment of a 40mm anti-aircraft shell, earning him a Purple Heart, but still keeping him on flying status. Three torpedo planes and two dive-bombers were also damaged during the mission.

The second strike group took off from the *Essex* at 1031 with 11 fighters, 8 torpedo bombers and 9 dive-bombers. This attack, led by the Air Group Commander from the *Wasp*, encountered poor weather and the strike planes overran the island by nine miles. Once recovered, the dive-bombers and torpedo planes held back in a circle to give the fighters a chance to strafe the anti-aircraft guns. Then the bombers pounced on the enemy.

The eight torpedo bombers from the *Essex* were designated to drop their ordnance on a dispersal area at the wooded northern tip of the island. They came in on their bomb run at 1,500 feet at 300 mph and then pulled up. They were followed by the dive-bombers who descended from 14,000 feet to 8,000 feet at which point they broke off to attack their individual targets. At 2,000 feet they released their bombs with noticeable results. The attackers found an enemy vessel armed with three 20mm guns and began to strafe and bomb it. Two bombs landed astern and finally one hit amidships, which sent the crew jumping overboard.

Eleven American planes were damaged and a dive-bomber with pilot Ensign T.A. Woods and his gunner A. McPherson crashed in the sea, but were rescued. One gunner, ARM3c Edward Kyle McNaught, was hit by a glass marble shot fragment from a 3-inch anti-aircraft shell.

The third strike led by McCampbell headed out at 1324 with 10 fighters, 7 torpedo bombers and 14 dive-bombers to confront the worse weather of the day and severe anti-aircraft fire. McCampbell descended to lead the first strafing run when his F6F was hit in the fuselage and belly tank, and caught fire. He immediately dropped his burning belly tank and, thankfully, his fuselage fire went out in a few minutes. With hydraulic problems and his electrical system out, McCampbell flew to the rendezvous point to await his air group to gather.

The fighters continued to strafe the enemy guns flying at just 100 feet off the ground. Anti-aircraft gunners hit seven of the F6Fs and downed another in flames at around 1445 off the western shore of Marcus. Two fighters were directed to check for the downed flyer, but all they discovered were a dye marker and two oars hanging from a life raft.

While weaving about, the dive-bombers made their attacks at 800 feet as Japanese anti-aircraft guns peppered the sky with black smoke from 3-inch guns and white puffs from 20mm and 40mm guns. The torpedo bombers pressed through the cloud front and exited over the island, leaving little time to setup for attack runs. Their bombs did negligible damage. On their second runs trying to stay low and level using rockets, they had limited success as they dodged the anti-aircraft fire.

After all of the mission planes had landed back aboard the *Essex*, McCampbell counted heads and discovered that the fighter that had been downed on anti-aircraft fire was his wingman, Ensign Wesley Thomson Burnham. Also hit during the attack at 1300 was a Hell-diver piloted by Ensign Jared H. Dixon with his gunner ARM2c Sam Hogue. Dixon was flying as wingman for division leader Lieutenant John Broadhead, Jr., just before the last dive on the target. McCampbell listed them as missing.[19]

Having lost his wingman, Lieutenant (junior grade) Roy Rushing volunteered to be McCampbell's wingman. They were to become close partners in combat as the months progressed. McCampbell later commented about the qualities he looked for in a good wingman. He wanted him to stay close to him in action and provide him moral support when he needed it. He liked Roy and he was his wingman the rest of his tour. Sometimes Roy even came as close as three to four feet of McCampbell's wing that he had to motion to him to move away. McCampbell often communicated with Roy by pounding his dashboard with dots and dashes in Morse code to him.[20]

At 1445 after the third strike had launched, the SM radar on the *Essex* picked up a bogey bearing 170° at 30 miles. Two *Essex* CAP fighters were vectored to the target at 095° flying at low altitude. With the snooper hanging over the horizon at 32 miles running north and parallel on the east side of the carrier, the CAP located the Betty bomber at 1448 as it was dropping its bombs and disengaging to the east. Before the *Essex* fighters could attack, the Betty was downed by fighters from the *Wasp*.

The last strike on Marcus that day was launched at 1532 from the *Essex* with 11 fighters, 6 torpedo bombers and 7 dive-bombers. Again directed by the *Wasp* CAG commander, the attack was met with overcast weather and rainsqualls. The strafing of the anti-aircraft guns by the F6Fs was initiated, while the focus of the mission was bombing the runways. Torpedo bombers used 2000-pound bombs to make craters. Photographic evidence from reconnaissance planes taken after the attack revealed there were 36 bomb craters in runway number two. The last *Essex* strike planes plus a fighter from the *Wasp* landed aboard at 1825.

The second day of the Marcus strikes, May 20, *Essex* launched the first strike at 0634 with 12 fighters, 7 torpedo bombers and 8 dive-bombers. More anti-aircraft flak was propelled into the skies, but lessened somewhat after the fighters strafed the area. The torpedo bombers again had difficulty using their standard glide approaches to drop their bombs and fire their rockets, after they came out of clouds past their targets. Dive-bombers continued their standard approaches from 14,000 feet, then getting into their nose-down attitude at 12,000 feet and pulling out at 1,500 feet under the cloud cover for the drops.

With 10 fighters, 5 torpedo bombers and 14 dive-bombers, the second strike of the day took off at 0755 from the *Essex*. After their attack, the strike planes, with the CAP, were all recovered by 1100. Immediately, Captain Ofstie turned the carrier toward the rendezvous point with the *San Jacinto* group toward Wake Island to the southeast.

During the Marcus strikes, Air Group 15 had flown 178 sorties over the target, flew 24 sorties protecting the task group, dropped 424 bombs (79 tons) and fired 54 rockets on target. It had destroyed one enemy plane on the ground, one 130-foot long ship in the harbor, destroyed a water purification plant with five buildings and three tanks, twelve general buildings (plus six others damaged), two covered aircraft revetments, and other miscellaneous assets.

Air Group 15 lost two fighters and two bombers in the action, with two pilots and one aircrewman. A lifeguard submarine picked up the aircrew of one bomber. Two pilots and two aircrewmen were wounded.

At dawn on May 21, the Task Group joined with the *San Jacinto* search unit and made a course to the second rendezvous point with the tankers, which was set for May 22 some 525 miles southeast of Marcus Island. After refueling the carrier strike group moved to their planned launching point located 80 miles from Wake Island bearing 225° from the target.[21]

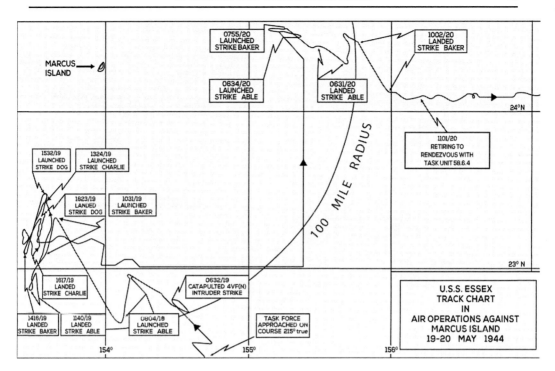

USS *Essex* Track Chart in Air Operations Against Marcus Island, May 19–20, 1944. Redrawn image based on *Essex* (CV-9) Action Report, March 30, 1944 (National Archives and Records Administration, College Park, Maryland).

The plan of attack for Wake Island was to conduct strikes all day starting at 0530. Bombardment by the heavy cruisers was supposed to be conducted, but it was canceled. The operational weather was "high thin scattered clouds at 2000 feet, with frequent rain squalls throughout the day."[22] The selection of the high priority targets was determined by the Joint Intelligence Center Pacific Ocean Area (JICPOA) based on recent photo interpretation.

Essex launched its first strike in winds at 15 knots at 0532 sending 12 fighters, 7 torpedo bombers and 9 dive-bombers. A CAP of eight fighters was also launched, as well as another 4 dive-bombers who flew the anti-snooper patrol at a sector arc at 20 miles from the carrier. The strike hit the air facilities at the airstrip with the bombers using 100-, 500- and 1,000-pound bombs.

At 0727 eleven fighters, eight torpedo bombers and eleven dive-bombers took off on the second strike from the *Essex*, led by the commanding officer of VF-15, Lieutenant Commander Brewer. Aircraft from the *San Jacinto* were also part of that strike. The target of the second strike was at Hell Point on Peale Island on the Wake Atoll.

Under continual threat of American carrier attacks, the Japanese had moved many of their installations on Wake underground. Anti-aircraft fire was lighter than at Marcus Island, but deadly enough to damage a fighter, and force a SB2C-1C dive-bomber to make a water landing from loss of engine power and sink. Pilot Ensign Conrad Crellin and his gunner, A.T. Graham, were rescued by a destroyer just as the third strike hit Wake Island.

Under the command of McCampbell, 12 fighters, 6 torpedo bombers and 13 dive-bombers launched at the 1006 for the third strike on Wake Island. Two F6F-Ns were also launched to provide the air cover for the rescue submarine. With heavy cloud cover, the

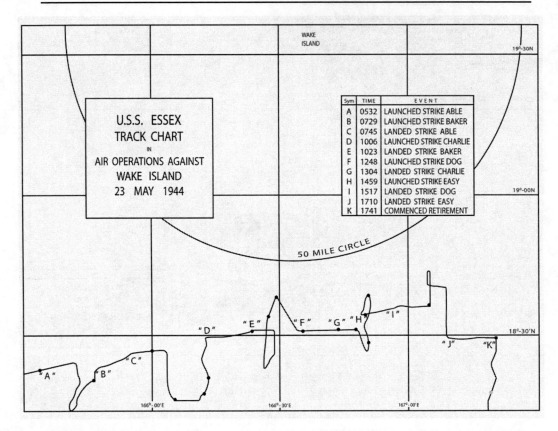

USS *Essex* Track Chart in Air Operations Against Wake Island, May 23, 1944. Redrawn image based on *Essex* (CV-9) Action Report, March 30, 1944 (National Archives and Records Administration, College Park, Maryland).

group struck Wake with the fighters strafing several barges and small craft in the harbor. The torpedo bombers had the most difficulty with the anti-aircraft guns, suffering three damaged planes. Two dive-bombers were also hit and one fighter. Fortunately, none of those aircrews was hurt.

At 1315 Ensign Bonner Arlander Davis, flying an F6F-3N, had completed his assignment providing air cover for the lifeguard submarine, and was making his first landing approach. He received a wave off from the LSO. He was past the carrier flight deck making his turn to port at 200 feet to start his downward leg for his second approach when his left wing dropped, hit the water and spun his plane into the sea. There was no sign of the pilot by the other planes, the *Essex* flight deck personnel or the destroyer *Bradford* that came up to the crash site to search.

The fourth strike was launched from the *Essex* at 1448 with 12 fighters, 6 torpedo bombers and 10 dive-bombers, as well the relief submarine cover of 2 F6F-3Ns. Lieutenant Commander Brewer again led this strike with the 28 *Essex'* planes and 12 from the *San Jacinto*. The highlight of this strike was a direct hit on an oil storage tank, leaving the air filled with heavy black smoke. Two CAG 15 torpedo bombers and four dive-bombers were hit by gunfire, but returned to land aboard.

The fifth and last mission against Wake Island, with McCampbell at the led, was launched at 1459 with a compliment of 10 fighters, 6 torpedo bombers, and 5 dive-bombers.

The anti-snooper patrol (ASP) with four fighters took off along with four CAP fighters and two F6F-3Ns as submarine air cover. Accompanied by ten planes from the *San Jacinto,* the strike group attacked the northern half of the island.

A few minutes after all the strike planes, the CAP, ASP, and submarine rescue cover aircraft were recovered aboard the *Essex* at 1736, the carrier set course away from Wake Island at 180° pushing through the sea at 18 knots. En route home the *Essex* spent a day being refueled by the fleet oiler USS *Cimarron*. The *Essex* and Task Group 58.6 made the 950-mile passage from Wake Island and sailed back into Majuro harbor on Friday, May 26, 1944.[23]

Air Group 15 had flown 146 sorties over Wake Island, with an additional 20 more sorties in defense of the Task Group. The squadrons had dropped 378 bombs (66.25 tons) and fired 98 rockets during the strikes. CAG 15 had destroyed 14 buildings, a 40-foot diameter steel fuel tank, a fuel storage building, an observation tower and damaged seven more buildings, the RDF generator building, an earth covered shelter and two bomber revetments.

USS *Essex* (CV-9) turns in formation with other Task Force 58 ships, May 27, 1944, during maneuvers prior to the Marianas operation. Note her deck load of Curtiss SB2C-1C "Helldiver" bombers and Grumman TBF " Avenger" torpedo planes. Turning astern are USS *Jacinto* (CVL-30) and USS *Wasp* (CV-18) (Photograph 80-G-373623 National Archives and Records Administration, College Park, Maryland).

Back at Majuro after the raids on Marcus and Wake, Graham summed up what was on his mind as an enlisted gunner in VB 15. He felt that in the squadron there was almost a campaign to treat the enlisted men poorly. By example he pointed out that when they lost or had stolen their gear they were just to submit a chit for replacement. To add insult to injury, those who reported losing gear were forced to go the captain's mast held by the Executive Officer.

Another insult included not issuing air crew wings for those who had flown combat missions over Marcus and Wake islands even though those who flew back in the states received them. The enlisted men also resented that while in port officers' ready rooms and wardrooms had air conditioning while their ready rooms and living quarters were terribly hot and stuffy.[24]

There were a number of observations and developments examined by Captain Ofstie as a result of the strikes by Task Group 58.6 at Marcus and Wake islands. The strikes had not been as effective as hoped since many of the facilities and shelters had been moved underground. It was recommended that under these circumstances, surface ship bombardment would be more effective than air dropped bombs. The use of night fighters to conduct pre-dawn attacks to prevent enemy aircraft from taking off was tested during the first day strike on Marcus Island. Though there was no enemy aircraft threat present, the tactic was recommended especially when followed by day fighter sweeps. It was also suggested that an appropriate bomb like the German "butterfly bomb"[25] be developed to interdict runways.

There was an identified need for standardization of night recovery (landing) procedures for night fighters, especially for carriers without the new night landing systems. Using the F6F as a fighter bomber as was used on the strikes of TG 58.6 required a longer takeoff distance to accommodate the added 400 gallons of fuel and the weight of a 500-pound bomb. This requirement complicated the spotting of the flight deck aircraft complement, and put more urgency on acquiring Type H Mark 4 high acceleration catapults and having two such catapults for each carrier.[26]

With their raids on Marcus and Wake islands completed, McCampbell's Carrier Air Group 15 had passed its combat initiation and was ready for a major Japanese engagement.

8

Marianas Operation
Forager Begins

"white beaches, swaying palms, and multi-hued aquamarine waters."[1]

As the *Essex* with Air Group 15 lay at anchor in Majuro harbor in late May 1944, Vice Admiral Spruance was assembling his forces to carry out the largest amphibious assault against the Japanese Empire yet attempted by the U.S. Navy. The target was the Marianas, including the islands of Saipan, Tinian, and Guam located some 1,250 miles south of Tokyo.

The decision to attack the Marianas had not come about quickly or without conflict among the Allied leadership. It had started on January 14, 1943, at the Casablanca Conference of the Combined Chiefs of Staff (CCS) when Admiral Ernest J. King, Commander in Chief, U.S. Fleet and Chief of Naval Operations, remarked that the "Marianas are the key of the situation because of their location on the Japanese line of communications."[2]

A major point of conflict arose between the U.S. Navy and the U.S. Army that would cloud the Pacific war atmosphere for months. Admiral King and the Navy felt that the drive toward Japan should move through Formosa (now Taiwan) from the Central Pacific, while General Douglas MacArthur, the former Army chief of staff and Philippine field marshal, passionately lobbied to retake the Philippines as he had promised in 1942.

The Trident Conference held in Washington on May 19, 1943, saw the CCS approve the high-level "Strategic Plan for the Defeat of Japan"[3] under which American forces would recapture the Philippines which was in General Douglas MacArthur's mind, as the Supreme Commander of Allied Forces in the Southwest Pacific Area, an honor bound requirement. MacArthur saw that the future efforts to invade Japan would be under his control, while Nimitz and the Navy would have a secondary role.

A number of factors evolved that came to work against MacArthur's grand plan of commanding a single thrust to drive to Japan's defeat. The major factor was the arrival of the new long-range bomber, the B-29 Superfortress, which was capable of bombing a target 1500 miles away with a bomb load of 10,000 pounds. From an island like Saipan or Tinian, the B-29s could pummel Japan. General Henry H. Arnold, Commanding General of the Army Air Forces, declared that such bombing "would have an immediate and marked effect upon the Japanese and if delivered in sufficient quantities, would undoubtedly go far to shorten the war."[4]

The successes of Nimitz' fast carrier and amphibious forces demonstrated that it was the world's most powerful naval striking force. Having taken the Gilbert and Marshall Islands, Nimitz was ready to take the Marianas and open up the second thrust toward

Japan. On October 25, the CCS recommended that the Central Pacific forces under Nimitz move from the Marshalls to attack and occupy the Marianas.

MacArthur reacted strongly against the proposal for the Marianas campaign and appealed first with the Joint Chiefs of Staff (JCS) with his plan delivered by his Chief of Staff at the December 3 Cairo meeting. MacArthur tried again to stop the proposal for the Marianas plan and switch the resources to his New Guinea-Mindanao campaign with a final appeal in the Washington meeting of the JCS in early February 1944.

To the General's disappointment, the directive on March 12, 1944, from the JCS to Admiral Nimitz and General MacArthur represented the final decision to move forward and occupy Saipan, Tinian, and Guam starting on June 15 "with the object of controlling the eastern approaches to the Philippines and Formosa, and establishing fleet and air bases."[5]

In 1889 the small Majuro Island in the Marshall Islands was described by Robert Louis Stevenson as the "pearl of the Pacific" because of its "white beaches, swaying palms, and multi-hued aquamarine waters."[6] But in June of 1944, Majuro lagoon, which covered 114 square miles, was also the resting place for 111 surface combatants of

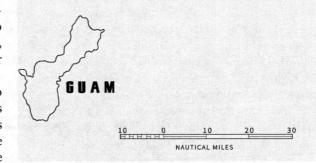

Map of Southern Marianas (redrawn image based on Henry I. Shaw, Jr., Bernard C. Nalty, Edwin T. Turnbladh, *History of U.S. Marine Corps Operations in World War II, Volume III: Central Pacific Drive*, p. 236, http://ibiblio.org/hyperwar/USMC/III/USMC-III-IV-1.html).

the U.S. Fast Carrier Task Force 58 which included fifteen carriers, seven battleships, eight heavy and thirteen light cruisers and sixty-eight destroyers. The fleet anchorage was a sight to behold, as the armada prepared to sail to combat. The lineup of carriers became known as "Murder's Row."[7] Of these 15 carriers, 14 had been commissioned after Pearl Harbor, a visible confirmation of the wartime power of the American industrial engine.[8]

As Nimitz was setting an aggressive offensive plan to take the Marianas, with Admiral Spruance preparing TF 58 and his amphibious invasion forces, the Japanese were trying to find a way to defend their empire. All they had seen was defeat after defeat. After losing at Midway, followed by another strategic loss at Guadalcanal, Admiral Yamamoto had decided to make an inspection tour in the South Pacific to bolster morale. Unfortunately, for the Japanese, U.S. Naval Intelligence decoded a Japanese radio intercept message on April 14, 1943, that read, "On April 18 CINC Combined Fleet will visit RXZ, R–, and RXP in accordance with the following schedule…."[9] Based on this opportunist intelligence, on the 18th an Army Air Force P-38 Lightning fighter of the 339th Fighter Squadron shot down Admiral Yamamoto's plane, killing the admiral.[10]

After six weeks Yamamoto was replaced as commander of the Combined Fleet by Admiral Mineichi Koga who moved to reorganize his forces. He moved his main body, known as the Mobile Fleet, to defend a new line that ran along the Marianas, the Caroline Islands and the Philippines. Behind this line represented the Inner Japanese Empire, which had to be defended at all cost. Koga's plan called for using some 500 carrier aircraft from the remaining carriers, coupled with the 400 to 500 land-based naval air force planes based in the Marianas and Palau.

On March 8, 1944, Koga issued Operation "Z"[11] aimed at destroying the Pacific Fleet anytime it entered the Philippine Sea, either from the Marianas, Palau or along the coast of Northern New Guinea. The plan presented detailed plans to build new ground defenses, new airfields, and reinforce troops in the Marianas and Carolinas with a battalion from fifteen different regiments in Manchuria.

The problem with the execution of Operation Z was getting the men and supplies to their appointed destinations. After finally solving the problem with torpedoes that did not detonate properly, Nimitz' submarine forces, under Vice Admiral Charles A. Lockwood, were setting new tonnage records. American submarines had been sinking Japanese ships at the rate of 200,000 tons per month since September 1943. Additionally, the carrier island raids of early 1944 had taken a toll on available Japanese aircraft.

On March 31 one of two Japanese flying boats carrying Admiral Koga from Palau to his new headquarters at Davao, Mindanao in the Philippines was lost, never to be seen again. Koga was replaced on May 5 by Admiral Soemu Toyoda who issued a revision of Operation Z called Operation "A-Go."[12]

When the Marshall's fell, the Japanese had established the Central Pacific Area Fleet under the infamous man who had led the attack on Pearl Harbor, Vice Admiral Chiuchi Nagumo. Working now for Admiral Toyoda, Nagumo was responsible for the defense of the Marianas, Bonins and Palaus yet did not have tactical control over the Japanese army troops under the command of Lieutenant General Hideyoshi Obata of the 31st Army. Both leaders agreed to coordinate together to defend the islands.

Heading up the Japanese Mobile Fleet from his headquarters at Tawi Tawi in the Philippines was 57-year-old Vice Admiral Jisaburo Ozawa. He was one of the key officers in the Imperial Japanese Navy (IJN), "a man with a scientific brain and a flair for trying new expedients, as well as a seaman's innate sense of what can be accomplished with ships. Although not an aviator, he was a strategist, and it was he who had initiated the offensive use of aircraft carriers."[13] Ozawa was now in command of 90 percent of the IJN Combined Fleet, which represented all surface units.

Admiral Ozawa and his staff were focused, even obsessed, on bringing his fleet to bear at the first opportunity to meet and destroy the American fleet. The question now was where would the enemy come from? Would it come from New Guinea in an attack on Palau or from the Marianas? The situation was confusing to Ozawa and the entire leadership of the IJN.

On May 27, 1944, MacArthur's forces invaded Biak Island, at the western end of New Guinea in the Schouten Islands. To Toyoda and many other Japanese leaders, the Biak invasion was proof that the primary thrust of Nimitz and his American fleet was with MacArthur in New Guinea. Admiral Toyoda reacted immediately and directed Ozawa to make preparations to attack the American fleet off New Guinea. Toyoda also established Operation Kon to transport 2,500 troop reinforcements to Biak, and soon directed his giant battleships *Yamato* and *Musashi* to bombard Biak at night.

Captain Mitsuo Fuchida, staff officer over Air Operations of the Combined Fleet, did not agree with Admiral Toyoda on where Nimitz would strike. He believed that the American fleet would strike in the Marianas. It was around this time that he devised Operation TAN to attack the Americans in the Marshalls with 27 torpedo planes and a similar number of dive-bombers. To firm up his plan, he sent two of the newest scout planes from Tinian on June 3 to refuel at Truk and then to another refueling island spot at Nauru.

The next day his friend and reconnaissance expert, Commander Takehito Chihaya, loaded aboard one of the scout planes and flew overnight to arrive at dawn on the fifth at Majuro Harbor. What he saw below him were a vast array of American warships, including at least 12 carriers. He took photos and flew back directly to Truk for refueling, and then off to Tinian. There he developed the photos and sent them on to Fuchida. On June 10 Admiral Ozawa received word by radio from Saipan that Nimitz' fleet was nearing the Marianas to attack. The order was given to the Mobile Fleet task force to head to the Marianas.[14]

The Marianas group is composed of 15 islands scattered along the 145th meridian, east longitude. The distance from Farallon de Pajaros at the northern extremity of the chain to Guam at its southern end is approximately 425 miles. Since the northern islands are little more than volcanic peaks that have burst through the surface of the Pacific, only the larger of the southern Marianas were of military value. Those islands that figured in American and Japanese plans were Saipan, Tinian, Rota and Guam.

By June 1944, the Japanese had made some progress on building new airfields in the Marianas. Guam had two airfields, with another two still under construction. Tinian had three airfields ready, and one underway. There were also airstrips on Rota and Pagan. On Saipan, an island only 12 miles long and less than half as wide, there were three airfields: the old Aslito airfield, an emergency airstrip at Charan Kanoa and the unfinished airfield at Marpi Point.

Significant Japanese troop reinforcements heading to the Marianas were lost as U.S. submarines successfully sank numerous troop ships and cargo vessels. None of the garrisons in the Marianas was fully manned, yet it was not the only obstacle facing the Japanese in preparation for the Allied attack.[15] General Obata's chief of staff summed it up when he said, "unless the units are supplied with cement, steel reinforcements for cement, barbed wire, lumber, etc., which cannot be obtained in these islands, no matter how many soldiers there are, they can do nothing in regard to fortification but sit around with their arms folded, and the situation is unbearable."[16]

The Allied plans for "Operation Forager"[17] called for landings at Saipan (Phase I), followed by landings at Guam (Phase II) and then at Tinian (Phase III). The invasion D-Day for Saipan was set for June 15. The Saipan invasion called for landing the battle hardened 2nd and 4th Marine Divisions on the 15th, with the 3rd Marine Division to invade Guam three days later. The 27th Infantry Division served as the floating reserve that would support the combat operations on either island. Artillery support on Saipan was assigned to the XXIV Corps Artillery under Brigadier General Arthur M. Harper, plus the artillery units from the 14th and 10th Marines.

As designated by Nimitz, Admiral Spruance of the Fifth Fleet was in overall command of Operation Forager, with the Joint Expeditionary Force (TF 51) under Vice Admiral Richmond Kelly Turner and the Fast Carrier Forces of Task Force 58 under the direction of Vice Admiral Marc A. Mitscher. While Turner was training his Saipan invasion force at Pearl Harbor and the other islands in Hawaii, and the Guam invaders at Guadalcanal, Mitscher was busy reorganizing his carrier force.

The *Essex,* with Air Group 15, was designated as Task Group 58.4, which included the lighter carrier *Langley* with 30 planes of Air Group 32 and the light carrier *Cowpens* with 26 planes of Air Group 25. Also part of TG 58.4 were light cruisers *Vincennes, Houston* and *Miami,* anti-aircraft light cruisers *Reno* and *San Diego,* and 14 destroyers. The TG Commander was Rear Admiral W.K. Harrill with his flag aboard the *Essex.*

Mitscher's other three carrier task groups of Fast Carrier Task Force 58 were TG 58.1 under Rear Admiral J.J. Clarke with carriers *Hornet, Yorktown, Belleau Wood* (CVL-24), and *Bataan* (CVL-29), TG 58.2 commanded by Rear Admiral Montgomery with *Bunker Hill* (CV-17), *Wasp* (CV-18), *Cabot* (CVL-28), and *Monterey* (CVL-26), and TG 58.3 under Rear Admiral Reeves with *Lexington* (CV-16), *Enterprise* (CV-6), *San Jacinto* (CVL-30), and *Princeton* (CVL-23). The supporting warships accompanying these task groups included 5 cruisers, 14 destroyers (TG 58.1), 2 battleships, 3 cruisers and 14 destroyers (TG 58.2) and 3 battleships and 16 destroyers (TG 58.3). Including Harrill's TG 58.4, the formidable task force heading to battle in the Marianas was composed of 15 carriers and 57 warships.

On May 31, Mitscher sent TG 58.4 to sea for two days of intensive training, which also included gunnery and night fighter practice. After returning to Majuro harbor, the *Essex* remained at anchor through June 5. On the same day as the Allied landings at Normandy, June 6, 1944, Task Force 58 with 111 ships, containing 96,618 men and almost a 1000 aircraft departed the Marshall Islands under gray skies in a light drizzle. The warships exited in a single file from the lagoon approximately every two minutes, taking nearly five hours to complete.

TF 58 was followed from Eniwetok, Kwajalein, Hawaii, and Guadalcanal by the Fifth Fleet Amphibious Force of 535 ships carrying some 127,571 Marine and Army troops. This armada included seven battleships, eleven cruisers with their destroyers, two escort carriers (jeep carrier), transports, hospital ships, store ships, oilers and escorts.

The deployment of this Pacific armada en route to the Marianas on the same day as another massive naval amphibious supported invasion on the other side of the globe across the English Channel, demonstrated the incredible military, logistic and production capability of the United States.[18]

En route to the Marianas, TF 58 refueled west of Eniwetok. The campaign objectives for the Fast Carrier Task Forces were to control the air in the Marianas, including "reduction of enemy air operating capacity in the Bonins; furnish air cover to approaching amphibious forces; bomb and bombard ashore defenses prior to and during the landings; furnish support aircraft as practicable during the occupation; and finally, serve as the covering force against any external Japanese threat."[19]

The specific missions assigned to TG 58.4 with the *Essex* were to:

    a. Destroy enemy aircraft and aircraft facilities at Saipan and Pagan on D-3 [refers to D-Day minus 3 days] and D-2 Days.

b. On D+1 and D+2 Days operate similarly against Iwo Jima, Bonin Islands, in tactical concentration with T.G. 58.1 (latter with Chichi Jima as target).

c. Conduct air patrols and searches, and furnish air support and photographic flights as called for.[20]

Commander McCampbell had prepared his Air Group 15 squadrons well for the upcoming combat operations. McCampbell wrote his own air group doctrine that augmented the overall standard fleet operational procedures. Unless pressed to launch with his wingman and fly directly to his target as sometimes required, McCampbell specified a "running rendezvous"[21] for coordinated strike missions when he would take off, then execute a half circle and slow his speed to allow the other strike planes to join up on him. If they were unable to join up, they would follow him from behind.

McCampbell preferred the full deck load launch rather than a full air group launch because it took too long to bring all the planes up the elevators, forcing the airborne planes to circle repeatedly above until all the air group planes had taken off. The deck load launch allowed the strike force to hit the target earlier.

McCampbell's combat doctrine specified that the fighters would go down to hit the target first to strafe and get the "enemy's heads down before the bombers"[22] attacked. The fighters would return to the rendezvous point and circle to protect the bombers and be ready for particular attacks as they developed.

USS *Essex* (CV-9) at sea, with an overload of aircraft on her flight deck, May 14, 1944. She is carrying at least 36 TBF, 14 F6F and 70 SB2C type planes, probably to build up fleet stocks for the Marianas Operation (Photograph 80-G-373580 National Archives and Records Administration, College Park, Maryland).

As Air Group Commander, McCampbell used his radio to direct attacks from above. He would go down to attack himself unless he was directing two deck loads of aircraft. His reasoning was that if he went down and got hit, he would have to return to the carrier.

The standard procedure for rendezvousing after the mission was completed was set. He and his fighters would gather at the predetermined rendezvous point and await the bombers. On the way back to the carrier, the fighters therefore provided protection to the bombers. About half way to the carrier, the fighters would power ahead and land first aboard the carriers, as the bombers neared the CAP protection. The VF-15 fighters landed quickly and had a better landing record than the bombers, which kept the flight deck clear. In fact, the F6Fs did not have a single landing accident during the entire cruise aboard the *Essex*.[23]

The dive-bombers and torpedo bombers followed the fighters aboard. The crews from all squadrons were debriefed after landing by their respective air intelligence officers. As Air Group Commander, McCampbell was debriefed by his own air intelligence officer. Before his debrief, McCampbell usually would go up to the air officer's level and observe his squadron planes land aboard. He would often talk with the Essex' Air Officer, Commander Stanley C. Strong. McCampbell gave Strong high marks and called him "...a very good air officer."[24]

June 11

With TF 58 nearing the Marianas, Mitscher directed that fighter sweeps be conducted from 180 miles from Saipan at all important targets on the afternoon of June 11 (D-4). Mitscher's staff had decided to begin their first Marianas Campaign attack in the afternoon rather than the usual early morning fighter sweeps to surprise the Japanese.

Essex Air Group 15 was assigned Marpi Point and Charan-Kanoa airfields and the seaplane base at Saipan. After the destroyers were refueled, the *Essex* headed to the launch point bearing 116° off 180 miles. At 1130 the carrier launched the CAP of 12 F6Fs and the ASP of 4 dive bombers.

The Saipan fighter sweep mission, led by Commander McCampbell, took off at 1300 with 15 fighters and 2 dive-bombers from *Essex*, as well as 12 fighters each from *Cowpens* and *Langley*. The two SB2C bombers were assigned to rescue duty having been equipped with extra life rafts and other survival gear to help any possible downed pilots. Seven of the F6Fs carried 350-pound bombs.

The lead fighters of the McCampbell's Saipan Sweep arrived at Saipan at 1400 and began to attack. The bomb-laden fighters headed down in dives from 12,000 to level out and bomb at 2,500 feet, before strafing the island from east to west. After the bombing runs, the 8 F6Fs circling above came down to strafe the enemy. The next hour and a half the fighters kept up the strafing action focused on the airfields and seaplane facilities on Saipan. During one attack around 1430, Lieutenant (junior grade) Leo Thomas Kenney's fighter was hit by anti-aircraft fire off Flores Point in Tanapag Harbor and ended up diving straight into the sea. His body was not recovered.

Commander Brewer led his VF-15 fighters in an attack on the seaplane ramp where three seaplanes were lined up on the harbor ramp. Brewer placed his bomb in the middle of the enemy seaplanes and destroyed all of them. He and Ensign R.E. Fowler had come out of the attack five miles out to sea and northwest of Marpi Point. There they saw a dark green Kawanishi flying boat (codenamed "Emily"[25]) sporting the red wing circles of the Japanese air force.

As they both approached to attack the Emily, they noticed three other fighters shooting at the enemy plane, but they proceeded anyway. Brewer hit the number two engine and left wing and Fowler hit the cockpit area. There was smoke and in about 20 seconds, the Emily turned over on one wing, with the engine in flames, and descended into the sea. Brewer then headed west toward the town of Garapan when he noticed three Japanese Zero fighters off in the distance. He hurried to intercept, but other friendly fighters had already downed the planes.[26]

Meanwhile, a half-hour into the battle, McCampbell was flying low, at an altitude of 10,000 feet, southwest of Saipan observing the action when a Zeke, a Mitsubishi A6M Zero,

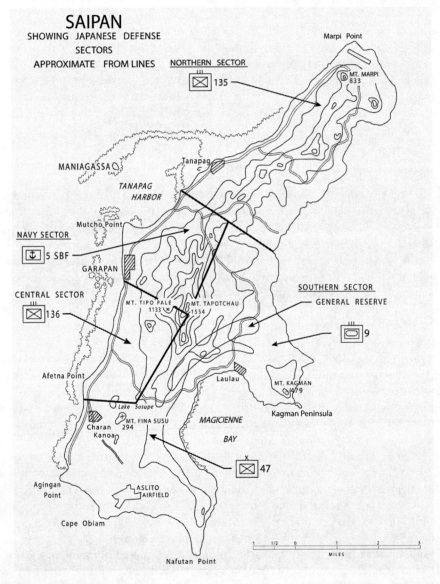

Map of Saipan, showing Japanese defense sectors (redrawn from Henry I. Shaw, Jr., Bernard C. Nalty, Edwin T. Turnbladh, *History of U.S, Marine Corps Operations in World War II, Volume III: Central Pacific Drive*, p. 238, http://ibiblio.org/hyperwar/USMC/III/USMC-III-IV-1.html).

closed in to attack our fighters from above. McCampbell turned in his direction and fired his guns at about 259 yards away. The Zeke winged over to his left as he followed him and fired another burst from the enemy from the rear position. The Zeke dipped one wing over as he was spiraling down to hit the water. One of his F6Fs was following the enemy plane down while firing his guns. The Zeke did not burn and sank immediately. No pilot was seen.[27]

It was McCampbell's first shoot down, and he was happy to discover that the F6F performed well against the Zero once he dropped his belly fuel tank. The action continued as Air Group 15 attacked Tanapag Harbor and Marpi Point. Lieutenant Commander James F. Rigg had just pulled up from a strafing run of the harbor when he came upon a Japanese seaplane fighter. He fired one burst and the seaplane went down. A Zero then came right at him as they both sped toward a head-on collision. The Zero's pilot pulled up at the last moment, revealing his underbelly, as Rigg fired. The Zero turned sharply to the right in flames and crashed into the sea.

Lieutenant Morris looked down to spot a Marvis flying boat taking off from Tanapag Harbor. Morris immediately dropped down to fire his guns. The Marvis reached 200 feet altitude, turned and went down on the reef. At the southern end of Saipan Lieutenant (junior grade) R.W. Rushing engaged in a dogfight with a Zero. Both fighters jockeyed for position as Rushing made a tight turn and let go with his guns. The reaction was immediate as the Zero fell away in flames.

The Zeros were not faring well at all as Ensign K.A. Flinn met and chased a Japanese fighter south of Saipan. With confidence that his fighter could outrun the F6F, the Zero pilot tried to escape by running away from the area. Flinn stayed close behind the Japanese and got on his tail firing his guns. The Zero burst into flames and soon crashed. Meanwhile, off the northern end of Tinian, Ensign D.E. Johnson, Jr., and Ensign G.H. Rader had engaged a single Zero. Johnson dove down and attacked the fighter from the front, while Rader assaulted from the rear. The Zero started to trail smoke, and quickly the enemy pilot bailed out before it crashed into the sea in flames.

After an hour and a half had passed on the sweep strike, the Air Group 15 planes headed back to the *Essex*, landing safely aboard at 1639. Two of the F6Fs had damage from Japanese anti-aircraft fire. McCampbell's fighters had gained invaluable experience engaging the Japanese Mitsubishi A6M Zero fighter (code-named Zeke). The F6F fighters had no problems keeping up and maneuvering against the Zero at all altitudes. This was a shock to the Japanese pilots who had always been told the Zero could outperform any American fighter. The major flaw with the Zero was its unarmored fuel tanks, which made it easy to catch fire. Four of the five Zeros shot down on the Air Group's fighter sweep operation went down in flames.

Except for the loss of VF-15 pilot Lieutenant (junior grade) Kenney to anti-aircraft fire, generally anti-aircraft fire had been light. The only threat to the Air Group was from Japanese aircraft, which turned out to be overrated. The Americans had destroyed five Zeros, one Tojo (Nakajima Ki-44 Shōki single-engine fighter), one Marvis and one Emily in the air, and on the surface/ground destroyed five Emilys and two Jakes (Aichi E13A naval reconnaissance floatplane), plus four Emilys and one Marvis damaged.[28]

June 12

The next morning, the *Essex* with TG 58.4 arrived at its launch point at bearing 45° out 95 miles off Saipan. Surface winds were 10–14 knots and over the target there were some clouds at 8,000 to 12,000 feet with occasional showers. On Saipan McCampbell's Air Group was focusing on hitting aviation facilities and planes on the airfields, and anti-aircraft guns at Marpi Point at the northern end. The night fighters took off at 0350, with 16 fighter sweep F6Fs off at 0400.

The Saipan strike group took off at night, launching at 0425 with 8 fighters, 15 dive-bombers and 8 torpedo bombers. This was the first night carrier launch for the Air Group 15 strike group. They were joined by 16 fighters and 9 torpedo bombers from the *Cowpens*. On the way McCampbell spotted the running lights of a Japanese vessel below and sent several fighters down to attack it. Immediately, the captain of the vessel turned off his lights, which foiled the American attack.

McCampbell's mission group reached Marpi Point just before dawn and began the attack. This day found the anti-aircraft fire light and of little effect. The fighters strafed anti-aircraft positions and facilities on the airfield, while the dive-bombers hit guns to the east of the field. The torpedo bombers cratered the runway at Marpi Point airfield. After strafing the airfield, the fighters strafed small cargo vessels off shore, creating damage to three small luggers and possibly sinking a small cargo ship (AK).

McCampbell's strike group returned to the *Essex* and *Cowpens*, and refueled, rearmed and launched at 0646 for an attack on the airfield and facilities on Pagan located 180 miles north of Saipan. The Japanese built an airfield on the narrow neck at the north end of Pagan. The island was controlled by a garrison of 3500 troops of the 9th Independent Mixed Regiment that had arrived in May of 1944 from Japan with some 800 IJN personnel and approximately 1,000 laborers.

This strike including 12 fighters, 13 dive-bombers and 8 torpedo bombers from Air Group 15, plus 8 fighters from the *Cowpens*. The strike group arrived at Pagan at 0815 as the fighters strafed the airstrip, barracks and buildings, while the dive-bombers began their 70° dive runs from 11,500 feet. The VB-15 bombers scored a direct hit on a large hangar and two adjacent shops on the south side of the field, leaving them engulfed in flames. One bomber destroyed a twin-engine plane that was just in front of the hangar.

The torpedo bombers began their dive runs from 9,000 feet carrying 100- and 500-pound fragmentation and incendiary bombs. They destroyed some four building, including two barracks on the north side of the airfield. Meanwhile, the fighters strafed and burned an enemy twin-engine bomber. They also sank two barges and two luggers in the harbor, and damaged and beached three other luggers.

A torpedo bomber piloted by Lieutenant (junior grade) John Chambers had his wing hit by anti-aircraft shells and was forced to make a water landing 25 miles from the *Essex*. The *Essex* launched two fighters at 0900 to cover the destroyer *Thatcher* on the rescue mission that recovered Chambers, his gunner and radio operator. The rest of McCampbell's Pagan strike group began landing aboard at 0916.[29]

As McCampbell's air group was refueling and rearming, word came that a task group scout plane had discovered a Japanese convoy of 20 ships or more bearing 248° at 99 miles from Pagan. The planned strike was canceled as the Air Group scrambled to launch on the convoy. With 16 fighters, 13 dive-bombers and 8 torpedo bombers, plus 12 fighters and 9 torpedo bombers from the *Cowpens*, McCampbell's strike group spotted the convoy at 1030. The convoy of transports, escorted by subchasers, a torpedo boat, patrol vessels and numerous fishing boats, were heading back towards Japan after resupplying Japanese garrisons in the Marianas.

Fighters orbited above the transport convey to provide protection against the possibility of air attacks from Japanese planes, but no enemy planes appeared. The captains of the Japanese ships tried to escape under cloud cover, but since they could not reach it, each ship took evasive action. It was no use. McCampbell's strike force was about to pounce.

The bombers attacked with a fury. Dive-bomber Lieutenant (junior grade) Turner was able to hit the stern of the largest transport in the middle of the convoy with a 500-pound bomb, damaging the propeller. The ship was dead in the water as the fighters strafed it. Later another pilot saw the ship sink. Another VB-15 pilot, Ensign Wilfred Bailey, landed his 500-pounder and a 100-pounder on each side of the bow of a small AK. It blew the bow off the ship, stopping it for the waiting fighters to strafe. The ship was not seen again, and was probably sunk.

Ensign Gunter of VB-15 and Lieutenant Sorensen of VT-15 attacked a medium cargo ship and sunk it. A dive-bomber also damaged two escort vessels. One was strafed and was seen dead in the water, while another one was set on fire forward and amidships.

The torpedo bombers had not had time to rearm with torpedoes before launching and were armed with bombs and rockets. After dropping his bombs, Ensign Otto Bleech of VT-15 attacked a medium 5400-ton AK using rockets. Two rockets hit at the water line and another two hit amidships. The entire ship was ablaze as the crew abandoned the vessel. After the fighters strafed it, the ship was not seen again, probably sunk.

Lieutenant Charles D. Webb of VT-15 placed two rockets on the stern of a small AK

A U.S. Navy Curtiss SB2C-1C Helldiver of Bombing Squadron 15 (VB-15) landing on the flight deck of the aircraft carrier USS *Essex* (CV-9) in 1944 (U.S. Navy National Museum of Naval Aviation photograph).

blowing two holes in the plating and causing a fire covering a 40 square foot area. The ship was not seen again. Webb took on another transport, leaving its stern in flames. His squadron mate, Ensign Harper, bombed another transport hitting its side.

With his strike group out of ammunition as the convoy with escorts was left in disarray, McCampbell took his covering fighters in for one last strafing run. As he departed the scene, he counted four ships dead in the water as the smaller vessels scrambled to evade. At 1353 McCampbell's strike landed aboard the *Essex*. Unfortunately, for Ensign John Storrs Foote and his gunner, the LSO waved off their dive-bomber and they crashed into the sea. They were successfully rescued.[30]

Back at 1100 another Pagan strike group had launched from the *Essex* with 10 fighters, 12 dive-bombers and 6 torpedo bombers. The attack was directed at the aircraft facilities where the fighters first strafed the Pagan RDF station and barracks. The dive-bombers hit the barracks at the RFD station, while the torpedo bombers cratered the runways. The strike group then attacked the small craft auxiliaries 10 miles west of Pagan. The fighters strafed 13 vessels leaving four burning and nine left dead in the water. The dive-bombers bombed the vessels scoring one sunk. The torpedo bombers used rockets against the craft, sinking three, and leaving five burning and four dead in the water. The Pagan strike landed at 1336.

McCampbell decided to send another strike against the convoy. This mission was led by Commander Brewer of VF-15 who took 12 fighters and 13 dive-bombers, with no other support from the *Cowpens*. They launched at 1500 heading to the last known location of the Japanese convoy. His strike group passed five enemy ships dead in the water from the early last strike.

Without stopping, Brewer and group continued on to find any remaining ships to attack. Once the convoy was discovered, he led his fighters down and dropped his belly fuel tank on a transport, which hit the deck and exploded into flames. Brewer pulled out while Ensign Bare and Ensign Slack strafed a Japanese destroyer. Just as they pulled up from the run, the warship exploded. It must have come from a fortuitous hit in the ships magazine. Some twelve VF-15 fighters had strafed the destroyer before she blew up.

All the enemy ships were under attack as Lieutenant (junior grade) Glass on a dive-bomber guide in run scored a direct hit with a 500-pounder in the stern of a small transport, leaving the ship listing 14°. His gunner, George Duncan, confirmed that debris was flying out from the stricken ship. Ensign Moore dropped his 500-pound bomb on another small transport on the starboard side, amidships and started a fire, leaving the ship listing on the starboard side.

A 500-pound bomb from a dive-bomber hit the fantail of a medium transport, the *Batavia Maru*, causing fires and the stern to go underwater. A prisoner of war later confirmed the sinking. Another 500-pounder from another VB-15 plane landed just off the port quarter of a small transport that had been hit during the first strike, and it was confirmed sunk by the gunner.

As he circled above preparing to lead his strike group home, Commander Brewer assessed that they had attacked some 12 ships, consisting of a destroyer, eight cargo vessels and three escorts. He reported that they had sunk the destroyer and two transports, leaving the remaining vessels damaged, except for two escorts. Brewer's convoy strike group landed aboard the *Essex* at 1815.

Later that day, a task group destroyer picked up seven Japanese and Korean survivors from the transports sinking, and took them to the *Essex*. They were interrogated by Admiral Harrill's staff, which confirmed one of the ships to be the *Batavia Maru*.[31]

June 13

The next morning, June 13 and D-2 Day, the *Essex* was positioned bearing 012° some 98 miles from Saipan. The first mission was launched at 0502 in average flying conditions to sweep the area for Japanese shipping. The strike group led by McCampbell consisted of 16 fighters, 13 dive-bombers and 8 torpedo bombers. The fighters formed a line in a spread formation to locate the convoy. On the way, one of the F6Fs belly fuel tanks developed an air lock and the fighter had to abort back to the carrier.

The sweep fighters continued and found an enemy ship at 0725. The last remaining cargo ship in the convoy, sized at 1,500 tons, was strafed by the fighters, as the dive and torpedo bombers attacked the target with bombs and rockets. VT-15 planes scored four hits on the ship, and it sank in four minutes. The only other ships located were a few hulks floating with lifelines seen over the sides, surrounded by scattered lifeboats and rafts bouncing on the waves.

As Ensign W. Fontaine from VB-15 was on his way back to the carrier, he spotted a Japanese bomber below him. He immediately made a run on the plane and reported it on the radio to the strike group. Commander McCampbell, who was flying at an altitude of 1,000 feet off the water, heard the alert and turned his head to the left. He noted,

> I turned left and saw the plane, a Helen [Nakajima Ki-49 army bomber], 200 feet above the water. He turned right, poured on the coal, and I chased him from astern. He was about two miles away. I caught up in two and a half minutes. My entire division [four planes] engaged him. I made first and last runs, in addition to one in the middle. The division overtook him at high speed, pulling out to the side. I pulled up above him to get positive identification and kill speed, then made two rear runs before losing enough speed to get on the third time and sit there until he blew up ... he blew up fifty feet off the water, no survivors. No visible fire from the Helen, possibly no rear gunner; looked like a brand new plane, very bright paint, possibly being ferried south. Saw gun in turret.[32]

This was McCampbell's second downed Japanese plane. The strike started landing aboard the *Essex* at 0930.

Back at 0813 Commander Brewer had launched from the *Essex* with 10 fighters, 10 dive-bomber and 8 torpedo bombers, along with 12 planes from the light carrier *Langley*. The strike force headed to Saipan. The fighters made strafing runs at Mutcho Point and on the tiny ten acre Maniagassa Island located 3,000 yards northwest of Tanapag Harbor looking for anti-aircraft guns and coastal defense gun positions. The dive-bombers also dropped their bombs on the same locations as the fighters. At Mutcho Point, the VT-15 planes bombed coastal gun positions

On the way back to the carrier, the fighters spotted three sampans in the West Cove of Anatahan Island, some 75 nautical miles north of Saipan. They strafed the sampans, sinking one and leaving two others afire. The torpedo bombers also strafed the sampans the fighters had hit earlier. Brewer's strike landed aboard the *Essex* at 1142.

Led by Lieutenant Commander Rigg of VB-15, the third strike that day on Saipan took off at 1130 with 11 Hellcats, 12 Helldivers and 8 Avengers. Earlier that morning, a planned 3-day bombardment of Saipan by Task Group 58.7 under the command of the fifty-six year old Kentuckian and hero of the Guadalcanal surface action, Vice Admiral Willis A. Lee, had begun. This force consisted of seven new fast battleships (none were more than three years old) with the mission to soften up Saipan in preparation for the upcoming Marine and Army landings.

As Rigg's attack group reached their target point at 13,000 feet altitude above Mutcho Point at 1245 in the afternoon, TG 58.7 was supposed to suspend their firing for six minutes to allow the air strike group to conduct their attack. Since the battleships seemed to be firing somewhat randomly, Lieutenant Commander Rigg took a chance and ordered the attack to proceed. The dive-bombers nosed over and descended to make their bomb runs from 5,000 feet as friendly 5-inch and 16-inch shells burst around them. Thankfully, there was weak anti-aircraft fire from the enemy gunners as they hit gun batteries at Mucho Point.

The battleships continued their bombardment plowing shells in fields, knocking down trees, pulverizing sugar cane and rice, while hitting few useful defensive targets on Saipan. Rigg's strike group survived the engagement unharmed and landed aboard the *Essex* at 1348.

The fourth strike under Lieutenant Commander Lambert of VT-15 headed out at 1330 and headed to attack anti-aircraft guns on the south shore of Saipan. The force included seven Avengers torpedo bombers from *Essex* and the *Langley,* escorted by twelve Hellcats. At the planned landing beach at Magicienne Bay, they bombed and strafed two gun positions. The attackers eliminated the anti-aircraft fire, but one torpedo bomber was hit in its wings, bomb bay and the gunner's position tunnel.

Meanwhile, Lieutenant Commander G.C. Duncan directed six fighters and six Helldivers to attack Japanese shipping at Pagan. They found and attacked a small AK transport at 1435 as the ship sailed on a course of 150° at 5 knots. The transport was hit on the "forward part of ship leaving it dead in water and burning. On the return leg the ship's bow was under the water and it had been abandoned. Another ship in company escaped."[33]

Duncan found another small, abandoned AK at 1540 dead in the water. Two bombs missed, but the ship was strafed. "There were no signs of life."[34] At 1625 another abandoned transport was discovered and strafed. At 1655 another small AK was seen already burning. A 250-pound bomb was dropped "under the stern and the ship left listing."[35] He found yet another AK at 1715 and dropped a 250-pound bomb, hitting "off the stern on the port side causing [the] ship to go into turns from which it was unable to extricate itself."[36] A Japanese convoy of three AKs and two escorts was located on a heading of 315° with speed at 10 knots. Unfortunately, the attack group was out of ammunition and no attack was made.

On their way home, Ensign K.B. West saw a Betty heading 180° at 8,000 feet above and behind two fighters manned by Lieutenant J.E. Barry, Jr., and wingman Ensign J.M. Power, Jr. The two *Essex* aviators reversed course and took off after the Betty. Some four minutes later, Ensign Power fired too early and out of range, which alerted the Japanese pilot, who immediately turned left and went into a dive. The Bettys' rear gunner fired first at Lieutenant Barry, damaging the leading edge of his F6F, disabling the hydraulic system and weakening the main spar of the aircraft. Barry continued downward with the enemy bomber, hitting the gunner. At 5,000 feet, the Betty was in flames and hit the water with no survivors.

When Lieutenant Barry arrived to land aboard the *Essex*, he learned that the wheel under the left wing was not down. With no other choice, he attempted to land with one wheel down, but the left wing dropped down and hit the deck, and skidded to a stop. The wing was so mangled that the plane was pushed over the side.

Also after 1330 the *Essex* launched six fighters and six bombers (in two plane sections) covering six sectors. Three sections found numerous small enemy shipping vessels near Saipan. They attacked and left the vessels burning or sunk.

At 1612 the *Essex* picked up a radar contact bearing 070 off 32 miles. Each carrier immediately launched four CAP fighters in response to the report. At 1628 and 1644 *Cowpens* CAP fighters shot down Japanese Bettys.[37]

Tawi Tawi, the headquarters of IJNs First Mobile Fleet, was the westernmost island of the Sula Archipelago positioned between Zamboanga Peninsula on Mindanao and the northeastern cape of Borneo. Meanwhile, on June 13, in reaction to the news of the first American air strikes on Saipan of June 11, Vice Admiral Ozawa sailed out of that anchorage with his Mobile Fleet heading toward the Philippine Sea and the Marianas. Unknown to the admiral, the submarine USS *Redfin* had observed the movement and reported it to Pearl Harbor.[38]

9

Iwo Jima

"If you do not join me in this job I will do it myself."[1]

There were no strikes on June 14 (D-1 day) as Admiral Harrill's TG 58.4 repositioned to rendezvous at 0541 some 130 miles on bearing 062° from Saipan with TG 50.17 for refueling operations. Also present was TG 58.1. The *Essex* was refueled by the USS *Kaskaskia* between 0700 and 1028. At 0900 a radar contact off 25 miles bearing 085° was detected. Just five minutes later, the contact, a Japanese Betty, was downed by a USS *Bataan* CAP fighter.

The *Essex* launched eight fighters for CAP duty and five Avengers for ASP at 1205. A conference was set aboard the *Essex* and at 1242 the carrier landed two aircraft from the *Hornet* and one Avenger from the *Lexington*. The commander of TG 58.1, Rear Admiral J.J. Clark, was the passenger aboard a *Hornet* VT-2 Avenger.

In the meeting Admiral Harrill voiced his concern over the upcoming operations in the Volcano and Bonin Islands. The admiral's chief of staff, Captain Herbert Regan, presented the case against the operations over concerns with fuel, weather, and the attack itself, though the key 'unstated' reason was mainly the distance from the Saipan amphibious landing. Admiral Clark was in "no mood to negotiate"[2] and after hearing the purported list of negatives declared, "If you do not join me in this job I will do it myself."[3]

An aggravating contribution to this command conflict had been caused by Mitscher who as CTG 58 had left the operation under joint command with Clark and Harrill. Admiral Harrill (Annapolis Class of 1914) should have been placed in charge of the operation since he was four years senior to Admiral Clark (Annapolis Class of 1918). Mitscher knew Clark was more aggressive, but also did not want to buck tradition, so he favored the poor policy of leaving the mission under joint command. Faced with Admiral Clark's challenge, Admiral Harrill was forced to keep TG 58.4 with the operation.

At 1356 the *Essex* landed replacement aircraft from the USS *Copahee*: one F6F, one Helldiver and one Avenger. Another two replacement F6Fs landed aboard at 1600 from *Cowpens*. The conference ended and at 1505 Admiral Clark took off from the *Essex* aboard one of the two *Hornet'* aircraft. The *Lexington* plane also launched. Following the conference, TG58.4 with *Essex* and TG 58.1 proceeded toward the Volcano and Bonin Islands to their assigned launch point for the next day's attack on Iwo Jima enemy air installations. The island and nearby Chichi Jima were "staging points"[4] for Japanese aircraft heading south to the Marianas.

Admiral Spruance was concerned that the TG 58.1 and 58.4 carriers were now some 700 miles to the northwest of Saipan just as the landing D-Day was about to take place, and ordered both task groups to return to Saipan on June 16 after they completed their planned raids.[5]

June 15 (D-Day)

The *Essex* and TG 58.4 arrived at their launch point bearing 084° off 130 miles from Iwo Jima just after noon, while TG 58.1 positioned northward off Chichi Jima. The weather was terrible "with high and low scattered clouds becoming broken to overcast at 1500 feet, frequent showers and squalls, surface wind SSE to S 16–24 Kts."[6]

At 1328 McCampbell launched a fighter sweep of twenty-two VF-15 F6Fs, while the *Yorktown* contributed sixteen more and the *Bataan* eight. The original plan was to avoid Japanese radar by coming in low, but the poor weather forced him to climb and attack from 8,000 feet. Unfortunately, they overshot the island and had to reverse course and return to Iwo Jima. While McCampbell's sweep maneuvered to attack, the Japanese were able to get a number of Zeros up to meet the American fighters.[7]

With his strike group at altitude, McCampbell saw a Zero heading his way on his left to attack. After much maneuvering in and out of clouds, wingman Lieutenant (jg) Rushing say a Zeke on McCampbell's tail. Rushing was about to engage the Zeke when the enemy fighter moved back up into the clouds. McCampbell considered whether he could turn back in the cloud, but then he noted a large splash in the water down below. He thought it was the Zeke, but two other pilots saw it as a belly tank. The Zeke continued to engage in the head-on attack, but McCampbell could not see his guns fire at him as he was forced to pull out to escape.[8]

Commander Brewer, who was southwest of the airfields, was flying at 6,000 feet when he encountered a Japanese fighter just below him. He dropped into a dive and descended to 1,500 feet and started firing at the enemy from 1,000 feet away using three-second bursts. At some 100 feet from the Zero, he saw it was on fire. Immediately the Japanese pilot bailed out and parachuted into the sea, as his fighter rolled over and crashed nose down.[9]

Just arriving on June 11, a new Japanese Air Group 301 was defending the island with two squadrons at Iwo Jima. Squadron (Hikotai) 316 made up largely of former floatplanes, had a rude awakening. Having launched eighteen A6M5s to counter McCampbell's sweep fighters, Lieutenant Shigeo Juni was killed along with sixteen of his fellow pilots. Likewise, for Squadron 401 from Group 341 lost ten of the thirteen planes that had taken off.

Lieutenant Commander George C. Duncan of VF-15 had been leading a four-plane formation strafing the airfields when they pulled up to made another one. At three miles east of Iwo Jima, his division ran into four Zekes at 5,000 feet. The enemy fighters tried to depart the scene, but Duncan led his fighters after the fleeing Zekes. Using their water injection systems, the F6Fs were able to catch up and come in close behind the Zekes. Duncan found the last enemy fighter in their formation and shot it down.

Duncan had shot down the first of the three Zeke fighters for VF-15 that day. He had been able to join VF-15 after he fooled his detailer that he was a fighter pilot. Actually, Duncan, an Annapolis graduate in the class of 1939 from Tacoma, Washington, had been shot up by the enemy leaving shell holes in his SOC floatplane in the Aleutians. Though not providing any documentary evidence, this floatplane pilot was reassigned to VF-15.[10]

During the day, Ensign Arthur Singer, Jr., was flying a photographic mission over Iwo Jima in his VF-15 F6F when he encountered enemy fighters. Singer sustained "multiple abrasions of the face from broken glass as a result of the action."[11]

After the dogfights with the Japanese fighters were quelled, the Hellcats dropped down to strafe and bomb the airfields, damaging or destroying enemy planes and facilities on the ground. The anti-aircraft fire was intense and well directed at the attackers as they came out between the clouds. Flak downed four planes at Iwo Jima, as well as two more lost over Chichi Jima and Haha Jima.

VF-15 Lieutenant (junior grade) Alfred Alexander Jones and his wingman, Lieutenant (junior grade) W.V. Henning, came down into a level strafing run at 800 feet at the south airfield on Iwo Jima, running straight down the runway toward the west. As they fired at anti-aircraft gunners, the gunners returned fire and hit Jones' F6F and wounded him in the leg. He went into a "smooth, slow"[12] roll and crashed into the sea just off shore. The aircraft did not catch fire, but immediately submerged into the sea. Meanwhile, enemy AA gunners hit VF-15 pilot Lieutenant George Ralph Crittenden too in his left leg, but he was able to get back to the *Essex* and land safely.

Some thirty minutes after the fighter sweep began, the strike led by Commander James Mini from the *Essex,* arrived with eight fighters, eighteen Helldivers and eleven torpedo bombers. They were accompanied by sixteen fighters and nine torpedo bombers from the *Langley*. The bombers in this strike were loaded with 100-, 250- and 500-pound bombs intended for the runways, aircraft and facilities on the airfields on Iwo Jima.

Right after takeoff from the *Essex* for the strike, the dive-bomber flown by Ensign Conrad W. Crellin lost power and could not sustain flight, and crashed on its starboard side as the "port wing snapped."[13] Crellin and his gunner, A.T. Graham, Jr., watched the "whole task force"[14] go by them as they managed to get aboard their life raft to be picked up by the last destroyer, the USS *Steerett*. Crellin and Graham were not returned to the *Essex* until June 17 using the breeches buoy "in return for ten gallons of ice cream for each aviator, the standard reward."[15] Graham wrote that while he was aboard the tin can he was seasick and could not eat without throwing up. Back aboard his carrier, he declared that he was happy to be sailing aboard a ship that does not continually rock back and forth.[16]

The flak, the worst that TG 58.4 had seen so far, was really heavy now over the airfields on Iwo Jima as the Japanese were fully alert after the fighter sweeps. Regardless, the dive-bombers plodded forward dropping their 500-pound bombs on the runways and buildings. Fragmentation bombs were used by the torpedo bombers to hit the parked Japanese aircraft. The Japanese planes were found grouped together: the Betty bombers, Zero fighters, the Hamp version Zeros with stubbed wings, observations planes, torpedo bombers, and transports.

As the last Helldiver to make a dive on Iwo Jima that day, anti-aircraft fire hit VB-15 Ensign Theodore Clement and his radioman/gunner, ARM2c Kenneth Leon Jackson. Their SB2C crashed on the island unobserved. VT-15 torpedo bombers had their problems pushing through the anti-aircraft fire too. Around 1645 Ensign Alexander Duncan McRae's Avenger was hit by "large caliber AA fire over the island…"[17] and crashed at the foot of Mount Suribachi, killing himself and his two crewmen; radioman ARM2c Leonard Cecil Lifset and gunner AMM3c Harold Ralph Dudley.

Ensign Theodore Weld Sterling, Jr., was forced to make a water landing in his Avenger off Iwo Jima. His oil pressure had dropped to zero after his plane was hit by anti-aircraft fire. He reported his situation to Lieutenant C.H. Sorensen, but shortly after Sterling with his crewmen, ARM2c Jack Henry Wendell Cooper and AOM3c Seymore Burton Gitelson, hit the water some ten miles southwest of Saipan. The three men scrambled out of the plane and boarded their life raft in heavy seas. The following day a rescue submarine could not locate them, and later search planes reported seeing no evidence of their life raft. Sterling, Cooper and Gitelson were never seen again.

On June 15, Task Group 58.4 destroyed fifty-four Japanese aircraft, with the Helldivers of VF-15 accounting for twenty-nine planes destroyed on the ground. The Hellcat sweeps for the two task groups had reported downing forty Japanese in dogfights, but actually, they had shot down twenty-seven. Overall, American carrier aircraft claimed eighty-six Japanese planes destroyed that day on the airfields, as many pilots made up to six passes.[18]

Meanwhile, as Task Groups 58.4 and 58.1 were striking airfields on Iwo Jima and the Bonins up north, the amphibious landings on Saipan on the morning of June 15 was first proceeded by a diversionary landing toward Tanapag Harbor some 6,000 yards north of the actual target beaches. The 24th Marines of the 4th Marine Division and the 1st Battalion of the 29th Marines loaded aboard their landing craft and headed toward shore with naval gunfire whizzing overhead. They came to within 5,000 yards of the shore when they turned around and motored back toward the transports.

At 0813 on the eleven target landing beaches the amphibious tractors (amtracks) started to move toward the shore. Marine Private Carl Matthews took the scene all in when "one of our tractors on our left received a direct hit and it disintegrated. Other shells were coming much too close to our own tractor. It was in that moment that I made the decision to do less looking and begin some serious praying. I glanced behind me and there were several mean and ugly Marines already on their knees."[19] Another Marine Private, Orvel Johnson, racing in his amtrac toward shore "heard the screaming shells, the horrendous explosions, saw the geysers of water and aerial bursts, the spray of flame, smoke and shrapnel."[20]

Back on D-1 day, seven battleships, eleven cruisers and twenty-six destroyers of General Turner's Joint Expeditionary Force coordinated with TG 58 to bombard the Japanese defenses on Saipan. The battleship *Tennessee* fired at the beach from 3,000 yards off Agingan Point, and at noon it moved up the coast to the north to fire at Afetna Point, which was the strategic center of the D-Day landing area. Meanwhile, the battleship *California* shelled Tanapag Harbor from the northern end of the landing beaches. Admiral Spruance watched the whole thing from his flagship, the cruiser *Indianapolis*.

At 0843 the first Marines hit the beaches to heavy automatic weapons fire. After twenty minutes, some 8,000 Marines were ashore, with 12,000 more on their way to land that day. Fighting was heavier on the southern beaches with the 4th Marine Division. It was worst at beach Blue Two. The 1st Battalion of the 25th Regiment was pinned down on the beach on Agingan Point around 0940 when the Japanese launched a counterattack. They called in air and naval gunfire, which helped but still received casualties from enemy artillery "from high ground not a half mile away."[21]

At nightfall of June 15, 20,000 Marine and Army assault troops were landed, but not without suffering 2,000 casualties, including several hundred dead. General Holland M. Smith was concerned that the invasion had been more difficult than expected. So concerned was Admiral Spruance that he postponed the planned invasion of Guam originally set for June 18. Securing Saipan would not take the planned three days, but would turn into a bloody three-week struggle.[22]

While the battle had raged on the Saipan beaches, the landings were essentially unopposed in the air. Just thirteen Japanese planes were downed, with the fighters from the *San Jacinto* claiming seven bogies. Of these Lieutenant Robert Maxwell shot down three that evening, becoming the first ace for VF-51. Late in the afternoon, Lieutenant Commander Evan P. Aurand downed a Judy some nine miles from the carrier, *Bunker Hill*. Chuck Harmer's *Enterprise* night fighters piloting Corsairs were able to down two enemy bogies that night.[23]

Meanwhile, as Operation Forager was raging in the Marianas, on June 15 the Mobile Fleet, heading to engage the Americans there, refueled at the entrance to the Guimaras

Straits between Negros and Panay. That same day at 0855 Vice Admiral Toyoda, from his flagship anchored in the Inland Sea, sent out his order to all flag and commanding officers: "On the morning of the 15th a strong enemy force began landing operations in the Saipan-Tinian area. The Combined Fleet will attack the enemy in the Marianas area and annihilate the invasion force. Activate AGo Operation for decisive battle."[24]

On the Saipan D-Day Admiral Lockwood had forty submarines deployed throughout the Pacific; from Japan's home islands to New Guinea and wolfpacks roaming the Philippines and the Bonin Islands. West of Saipan there were four submarines deployed in a north to south line, with two more off Guam. Late in the afternoon of June 15 off San Bernardino Straits between Samar and Luzon, Lieutenant Commander Robert Risser, Captain of the *Flying Fish,* saw three carriers, three battleships and numerous escorts. He trailed the enemy force until it was dark and reported what he had observed to Admiral Lockwood at Pearl. Low on fuel, Risser was forced to abandon the tracking and to head back toward his base in Australia.

Aboard the submarine *Seahorse,* some two hundred miles off Surigao Strait, Lieutenant Commander Slade D. Cutter, observed four large Japanese warships. After dark the *Seahorse* surfaced and Cutter sent his report concerning "plenty of battleships."[25] These Japanese battleships were part of the Kon Force that had been heading to Biak before the operation had been canceled and redirected to linkup with Ozawa's Mobile Fleet. Unknown to Cutter, the force he saw had included the sister monster superwagons, *Yamato* and *Musashi.* Unfortunately, the main motor brushes began to spark and the submarine had to the shut down the motor. They could only make fourteen knots, which killed any hope of catching the enemy warships.[26]

That same day, Admiral Spruance asked General MacArthur to extend the searches of his B-24 Liberators to their maximum range, which was 1200 miles from Wakde and Los Negros in the Admiralties, to find Ozawa. The combination of the B-24 air searches plus Mitscher's carrier-based aircraft sector searches should have resulted in the detection of the approaching enemy fleet, but that was not the case. The submarines of the Pacific Fleet were to take the well-deserved credit for this critical detection of the Mobile Fleet.[27]

June 16 (D+1)

Over the evening into the 15th the weather degraded even more, as the forecasters predicted a typhoon was coming into the Bonin and Volcano Islands. Air operations for the morning of June 16 were canceled. The two task groups moved south to a position bearing 165° at 120 miles off Iwo Jima.

The weather actually improved slightly around noon and both task groups launched strikes to Iwo Jima. Led by Commander McCampbell, at 1340 the *Essex* launched a fighter sweep with eleven F6Fs, and a strike with seven Hellcats, fourteen Helldivers and eight Avengers.

The Japanese had awakened to the poor weather and logically determined that the Americans would never send out strikes. McCampbell's fighter sweep strafed the airfields and reported that there were no operational Japanese planes remaining. The *Essex* Helldivers cratered the runways hitting parked planes, as well as destroying an ammunition dump and a fuel supply area. The torpedo bombers set the barracks on fire, as the strike fighters strafed two fuel dumps causing fires.

During the mission over Iwo Jima, Lieutenant John Randolph Ivey of VF-15 was hit by anti-aircraft fire in the face and lost his eye.

Thereafter he flew irrationally and in aimless directions and maneuvers, but finally was guided back to the disposition and within sight of the carrier. His wingman, Ens. G.E. Mellon … and his section leader, Lt(jg) G.R. Carr … stayed with him continually, attempting to direct the wounded pilot to bail out or land, but the damaged plane continued its purposeless maneuvers. The wingmen were directed to land aboard, where-upon the wounded pilot flew away from the disposition. He was tracked on the radar screen, and a combat air patrol was vectored out. Radar contact was later lost, and the combat patrol sighted an oil slick and dye marker presumed to have been the site of his eventual crash.[28]

The combined Iwo Jima air strikes from TG 58.4 and TG 58.1 on June 16 had launched a total of fifty-five planes, reporting some 60 Japanese planes hit on the ground. All the aircraft were landed by 1710 and both task groups headed south toward Saipan. Before proceeding, Admiral Clark ordered his carriers to refuel the smaller escort ships. This decision to conduct an underway replenishment was a shock to many considering the approaching extreme weather of a typhoon. Though the destroyers rocked back and forth in the heavy seas, as fuel lines and houses broke loose, the effort was completed. Finally, TG 58.1 was underway toward Saipan.[29]

Meanwhile back on in morning of June 16, Admiral Spruance held a conference aboard Vice Admiral Kelly Turner's flagship, the *Rocky Mount*, off Saipan. He was concerned that the Japanese appeared to have split into two groups based on the recent submarine reports. This development would complicate the situation. Spruance's primary fear was that Turner's invasion force, with the assault troops already ashore, would have difficulty defending its offshore position against a suicidal attack by IJN surface forces, while Ozawa lured Mitscher's carriers after his Mobile Fleet. As it would turn out, Spruance would be engaging a single fleet as various elements of Ozawa's force soon joined.

The results of the conference favored taking this as a major opportunity to destroy Ozawa's Mobile Fleet in a major sea battle. Turner would detach five heavy and three light cruisers with 21 destroyers to TF 58, leaving Turner's fire-support groups with seven battleships, three cruisers and five destroyers to protect the beaches on Saipan. To get night searches out to 600 miles from Saipan, Admiral Hoover at Eniwetok was ordered to provide six radar-equipped Martin PBMs the next day from PatRon Sixteen. Mitscher's carrier aircraft could only search out 325 to 350 miles.

After the conference, Spruance aboard his flagship *Indianapolis*, in company with the surface reinforcements from Turner's Expeditionary Force, steamed to join the carriers. At 1415 Admiral Spruance sent out his battle plan: "Our air will first knock out enemy carriers, then will attack enemy battleships and cruisers to slow or disable them. Battle line will destroy enemy fleet either by fleet action if the enemy elects to fight or by sinking slowed or crippled ships if enemy retreats. Action against the enemy must be pushed vigorously by all hands to ensure complete destruction of the fleet. Destroyers running short of fuel may be returned to Saipan if necessary for refueling."[30]

Vice Admiral Matome Ugaki, aboard his flagship *Yamato* in company with the *Musashi*, a light cruiser and six destroyers rendezvoused with the First Supply Force at 1000 on June 16. After refueling promptly, at 1650, Ugaki's force linked up with Ozawa's force as the oilers began refueling the ships of the Mobile Fleet.[31]

June 17 (D+2)

Back at 0510 on June 17, while en route to relieve *Flying Fish* off San Bernardino, the *Cavalla* located the two large oilers and three destroyers of the IJN Second Supply Force.

After reporting to Pearl, Admiral Lockwood ordered the *Cavalla* to track the oilers in the hope that they would lead them to the Mobile Fleet. The submarine was unable to keep up with the enemy fueling group and soon lost contact. Late that same evening at 2115, the *Cavalla* sighted "fifteen or more large combatants"[32] steaming at 19 to 20 knots heading due east.[33]

Meanwhile, the *Essex* and Task Group 58.4 continued south heading to their rendezvous with Task Force 58 off Saipan. After topping off the destroyers, in the afternoon at 1419 Lieutenant Commander James F. Rigg catapulted a strike from the *Essex* from a position 90 miles at bearing 272° to Pagan's airfield with fifteen fighters, eleven Helldivers and eight Avenger torpedo bombers. There also was a five-sector search launched at that time in two plane sections (an F6F and Helldiver) per sector. The search was out to the extreme 350-mile range looking for Ozawa's Mobile Fleet.

The strike reached Pagan around 1600, but found no enemy fighters in the air or active (not already damaged) ones on the runways. The fighters strafed the "RDF, radio station, buildings and barracks on W[est] shore causing damage and fires."[34] They also dropped 12-hour delay bombs on the runway to prevent the Japanese from using them. Ensign Singer and his wingman, Lieutenant James L. Bruce, strafed several small vessels in the harbor as the other fighters strafed any target of interest.

The Helldivers dropped 500-pound bombs to crater the runway. Some of these bombs were set with the 12-hour delay. The torpedo bombers used their rockets to hit the RDF station and their bombs to destroy the radio station, barracks and other buildings.

At 1653 the destroyer USS *Converse* transferred seven Japanese POWs to the *Essex*. These men were survivors rescued by the screening destroyers from the ships sunk from the Saipan-Yokohama convoy on 12–13 June. Later at 2240 the USS *Dyson* rescued five more survivors. As the Task Group passed through the waters, twelve additional survivors were picked up.

During the strike, two Avengers were damaged, but all planes returned with no casualties. Rigg's strike and the sector search planes returned to the *Essex*, landing aboard at 1728. The sector search mission yielded no Mobile Fleet targets.

As the *Essex* steamed south to the rendezvous point, the crew heard the Radio Tokyo propaganda report that 4150 Marines died and three waves of Marines were repelled on Saipan. They also reported that twenty-nine U.S. planes had been shot down over Iwo Jima and the Bonins.

There was other news that day. Word spread aboard the *Essex* that on the previous night, B-29s bombed Japan. The attack on the Imperial Iron and Steel Works at Yawata in northern Kyūshū came from 75 B-29s from the 20th Air Force flown from bases near Chengdu, China. Seven B-29s were lost in the strike. For TG 58.4 and Mitscher's entire Task Force 58, the most significant news was that the Japanese Fleet that had been reported to be 750 miles away coming from the Philippines yesterday morning was, on the morning of June 17, just 350 miles away.[35]

The refueling of Ozawa's Mobile Fleet was not complete until the evening of June 17 at 2000. The oilers from the Second Supply Force merged with the First Supply Force oilers as the combined six moved to a standby location.

By the evening of June 17, Ozawa was aware of the recent attacks on Iwo Jima and Chichi Jima, as well as the day's Pagan strike. He also knew the current status of fighting on Saipan, and realized that Mitscher's large carrier fleet would be off Saipan, with small carriers supporting the landings. Twenty-four hours earlier he had been notified of at least one American carrier group positioned off Guam.

What Ozawa did not know was that the land-based fighters of the First Air Fleet commanded by Vice Admiral Kakuji Kakuta had been significantly reduced in number by the various American attacks including at Iwo Jima. Ozawa's A-Go Plan had called for Kakuta to have some 500 land-based planes at Yap, Guam, Tinian and Palaus available to support his carrier force of some 450 planes. Kakuta had understated his losses in all his message traffic to Ozawa, and from this point forward his counts were going to diminish greatly.[36]

June 18 (D+3)

On the morning of June 18, TG 58.4 and TG 58.1 were approaching the other ships of Mitscher's TF 58. The *Essex* and TG 58.4 were operating from a location 225 miles west-southwest of Saipan. At 0533 the carrier launched a three sector search out to 325 miles with standard teams of one F6F fighter and one SB2c dive-bomber. At 0600 that day Ozawa's Mobile Fleet was approximately 420 nautical miles away.

Meanwhile that morning, the Japanese sent out their first reconnaissance missions with fourteen Kates and two Jake floatplanes searching eastward covering a compass radius from 350 to 110 degrees. These searches took them out to 425 miles. With both Ozawa's and Mitscher's scouts looking for each other's' fleets, there was every reason to believe that the planes would overlap and engage each other. That was exactly what happened.

Two scout planes radioed in that they had seen American planes, but three other planes were never heard from again by the Japanese. But Mitscher's sector search pilots knew what happened to them. Lieutenant (junior grade) Charles English Henderson III, nicknamed "Hotshot Charlie,"[37] from the *Enterprise* piloting his Avenger torpedo bomber downed a Jake floatplane from the right rear angle using just 17 rounds of his .50 caliber bullets.

At 0755 Lieutenant (junior grade) Raymond L. Turner from *Essex's* VB-15 was flying at 1,000 feet altitude in his Helldiver making his cross-leg turn at the limit of his 325-mile sector search when he saw an aircraft five miles ahead of him. He closed the distance and saw what he though was an enemy Jill, but it was actually a Kate, an older Nakajima torpedo plane used for recon. His sector search-mate, Ensign James E. Duffy, in his Hellcat escorted Turner as they came to within 500 yards of the enemy plane. Turner engaged from "below and behind while Duffy went wide, trapping the Nakajima"[38] in a squeeze. They both fired their .50 caliber rounds at the enemy bomber, knocking "chunks of aluminum"[39] off the aircraft, and starting fires. In seconds the Kate was in the sea.

Later at 0930, another *Essex* Air Group 15 sector search team with VB-15, Lieutenant (junior grade) William S. Rising and VF-15 Ensign Kenneth A. Finn, noticed a Betty bomber. Finn powered after the Mitsubishi plane in his Hellcat through low clouds. After four passes at the enemy plane, Finn set the port wing on fire. The Betty pilot immediately descended to attempt a water landing, but one wingtip hit a wave and caused the plane to cartwheel in a mass of "flames, smoke, spray and debris."[40] Finn had just claimed his second victory. At 1032 the sector search aircraft landed aboard the *Essex*. At 1158 the *Essex* finally rendezvoused with the other task groups of Mitscher's TF 58. As it turned out, no TF 58 aircraft located any of Ozawa's ships on June 18.[41]

10

The Great Marianas Turkey Shoot

"They were streaking past like a blizzard."[1]

In the midnight darkness on the morning of June 19, 1944, two opposing fleets steamed in their tactical formations anticipating the largest carrier-to-carrier battle in history. Vice Admiral Mitscher's Task Force 58 was 230 miles west-southwest of Saipan, while Vice Admiral Ozawa's A-Go Mobile Fleet was positioned some 300 miles farther to the southwest.

Admiral Ozawa's Mobile Fleet force consisted of 5 carriers, 4 light carriers, 5 battleships, 11 heavy cruisers, 2 light cruisers, 23 destroyers, 19 submarines, and a number of support vessels including oilers, ammunition ships, etc. Aboard his carriers were 440 planes, with approximately 630 land-based aircraft located in the Marianas and other air bases within range. Mitscher's TF 58 outnumbered Ozawa's combatant force 2:1 with 7 carriers, 8 light carriers, 7 battleships, 8 heavy cruisers, 13 light cruisers, 68 destroyers and 27 submarines, plus requisite support ships. His fast carriers carried some 900 planes, and aboard the light carriers were 200 more planes that could be devoted to other assignments.[2]

At 0415 that morning Ozawa's Mobile Fleet had formed its battle line for the promised engagement with Mitscher's TF 58. Up front on a northeastward course was Vice Admiral Takeo Kurita's Vanguard 'C' Force, which included Obayashi's Carrier Division Three (CarDiv 3) headed by Rear Admiral Sueo Obayashi with carriers *Chitose*, *Chiyoda* and *Zuiho*, and his screening force of four battleships (the world's largest, *Yamato* and *Musashi*, plus battleships *Kongo* and *Haruna*), nine heavy cruisers, and eight destroyers. Each of the carriers was steaming 10 kilometers apart.

Behind Kurita's force, some 100 miles back, was CarDiv One commanded by Ozawa himself with the carriers *Taiho*, *Shokaku*, and *Zuikaku*, screened by two heavy cruisers, one light cruiser, and seven destroyers. Steaming along with Ozawa was CarDiv Two with the *Junyo*, *Hiyo* and *Ryuho* commanded by Rear Admiral Takaji Joshima, with a screening force consisting of the battleship *Nagato*, heavy cruiser *Mogami* and eight destroyers.[3]

When the sun broke on the horizon at 0555, all four of the Fast Carrier groups were within sight of each other. Mitscher had positioned his strongest carrier groups, 58.1 (Admiral Clark), 58.3 (Admiral Reeves) and 58.2 (Admiral Montgomery), up front twelve miles apart on a line north to south running "perpendicular to the general wind direction."[4] This placement allowed each carrier to conduct carrier air operations without concern over other carrier groups.

Closest to the Japanese and fifteen miles ahead of the center, TG 58.3 with Mitscher's flagship *Lexington*, was Rear Admiral Lee's TG 58.7 with seven fast battleships, four heavy cruisers and fourteen destroyers. Considered the weakest carrier group, Admiral Harrill's TG 58.4 with *Essex* was twelve miles north of the Lee's battle line to provide air protection for all the carrier groups.[5]

The American approach to protect this most lethal offensive weapon system, the Fast Carrier Task Force, consisted of two defensive layers: radar-directed fighters on combat air patrols, and shipboard anti-aircraft guns. This defense methodology was not by happenstance, but had been determined by analytical research and scientific techniques. Each carrier was set in the center of a four-mile circle with its supporting force of cruisers and destroyers positioned to force enemy planes to fly through a hail of anti-aircraft fire. Since the maximum range for a heavy anti-aircraft gun was eight miles, it provided a dense pattern of flak.

The contribution to the war effort from the science and technology community was nothing if not extraordinary. Advances in the areas like VHF radio communication, aircraft and shipboard radar, and even ammunition, made a real difference. Mitscher's carriers had four-channel VHF radios, which helped to defeat voice frequency jamming by the Japanese. There was also the VHF deck-condition status code, which revealed a constant status of the flight deck activity in the launch and recovery cycle. For surface tracking and navigation on a screen display there was the new dead-reckoning tracer (DRT). Friendly aircraft could now be differentiated from enemy bogies using "friend or foe"[6] (IFF) transponders.[7]

There were three types of radars on American carriers during World War II: surface search, air search and gun (anti-aircraft) fire control. Surface search radars, like the SG-1 system aboard the *Essex*, had little significance for carriers that depended on their escort warships for surface protection. Critical to their offensive mission and defense for all carriers were air search and fire control radars. The *Essex* radar complement included two long-range search radars; the SK-1 (range 100 nautical miles) and the SC-2 (80 nautical miles). The SM low angle air/height finding radar was also aboard with a range of 50 nautical miles. For anti-aircraft (AA) fire control radar, the *Essex* included the L-band Mk-4 (range 40k yards) and the Mk-12 (range 45k yards), plus the X-band Mk-22 radar for low angle height finding targeting.[8]

Perhaps the greatest development in Navy ordnance during World War II was the variable timed (VT) fuse. As directed by the National Defense Research Committee as a top priority, PhD Merle A. Tuve led the project (known as "Section T")[9] at the John Hopkin's Applied Physics Laboratory (APL) to develop a fuse device that could survive the shock of being fired from a gun at 20,000 times the force of gravity. Funded by the Navy at the tune of $800,000, APL developed and tested a tiny radio transmitter positioned in the head of an anti-aircraft shell which sent out radio signals which reflected off an aircraft. When a reflected signal reached a specified noise level in the receiver vacuum tube, a large current was directed to an electrical detonator to explode a TNT charge in the nose of the shell at a lethal radius of thirty feet.

Combat analysis showed that it took approximately 500 rounds of VT shells to destroy an enemy plane, which was four times better than standard timed or impact fuses on the same projectiles. In the Pacific campaign, the VT fuse was so effective that the Secretary of the Navy, James V. Forrestal would later remark, "Without the protection this ingenious device has given the surface ships of our Fleet, our westward push could not have been so swift, and the cost in men and ships would have been immeasurably greater."[10]

A major factor in the success in defending Mitscher's TF 58 during the fleet action was the skilled work and dedication of the fighter direction officers (FDOs). The task force FDO was Lieutenant Joseph R. Eggert aboard the *Lexington* who made sure all Japanese raids were covered by enough Hellcats to intercept each Japanese raid, while ensuring there were adequate reserves to handle any following enemy raids. He accomplished this feat by maintaining voice contact with each of the four carrier group FDOs. Each of the task group FDOs controlled the overall intercepts for their carrier group, and allotted intercepting planes to the FDOs of each carrier until their missions were complete. The *Hornet* Action Report recorded the quality achieved for FDOs as they coordinated with fighters and fighter directors to achieve interceptions.

Designated as one of the most important positions in the Navy, the FDOs were hand-picked specialists trained at St. Simons Island, Georgia, or the Pacific Fleet Radar School in Hawaii. These graduates were teamed up with "radar operators, plotters and talkers"[11] and sent to the fleet carriers for work in the Combat Information Center (CIC). These men, usually seven in number, maintained the radar plot and controlled aircraft deployment in these small, cramped, but air-conditioned CIC compartments on the galley deck on the carrier's island.[12]

Back on June 18, a rendezvous was held between Mitscher and Lee to discuss the current situation, as well as previous direction from Admiral Spruance stating, "Task Force 58 must cover Saipan and our forces engaged in that operation."[13] Spruance was concerned that Ozawa could easily send part of his fleet to out flank Mitscher's task force and attack his forces off Saipan. His tactical plan was to "reduce the possibility of the enemy passing us in darkness"[14] by having TF 58 sail eastward at night and westward in daylight to engage Ozawa's Mobile Fleet.

After the meeting, at noon TF 58 headed in a southwesterly course until darkness at 2030 when the fleet reversed course to 080°. During the daylight hours the force had traveled just 115 miles westward due to continual turns into the wind to the east to launch or recover aircraft.

Intelligence reports received after 2030 that evening began to come forth that could affect the validity of Spruance's decision to maintain the eastward course that night. At 2200 Mitscher received a report from Nimitz that HF/DF intelligence had established a fix for Ozawa's fleet. Apparently, Ozawa had broken radio silence to coordinate with the land-based planes for the next days' operations at Guam and other islands. The fix placed the enemy fleet some 300 miles west-southwest of Mitscher's TF 58.

Around 2000 the submarine *Stingray,* skippered by Lieutenant Commander Sam C. Loomis, Jr., sent off a routine report indicating that he had a minor fire in the radio antenna. The report transmission had been jammed by the Japanese. Admiral Lockwood received the garbled and unreadable report from Loomis, but informed Spruance. Spruance's staff, which was aware of *Stingray's* patrol area, determined the submarines position as 175 mile East-Southeast of the reported Ozawa HF/DF fix. If *Stingray* had been trying to report the position of the Mobile Fleet (which it was not), it would have placed Ozawa much closer to TF 58.

At 2010 the submarine *Finback,* commanded by Lieutenant Commander James L. Jordan, saw two spotlights coming from over the horizon to the south. These were later determined to be searchlights to assist the Japanese planes to land aboard the Cardiv 3 carriers. The report was sent from the submarine, but it was not reported to Admiral Spruance until 0150 the next morning on June 19.[15]

With intelligence that seemed to confirm that TF 58 was continuing to steam away from Ozawa's Mobile Fleet, at 2325 by voice radio Mitscher proposed to Spruance that TF 58 reverse course to the west at 0130 June 19 to be in perfect position to strike at Ozawa at daybreak. Spruance responded to Mitscher's request at 38 minutes after midnight: "Change proposed does not appear advisable. Believe indications given by *Stingray* more accurate than that determined by direction-finder. If that is so, continuation as at present seems preferable. End run by other carrier groups remains possibility and must not be overlooked."[16] Time would soon reveal that Spruance's decision was the incorrect one.

The fog of war could have been cleared up if only unfortunate events had not occurred. Flying from Garapan Roads on a search mission 600 miles out in a westerly quadrant, the position of the enemy was confirmed by Lieutenant H.F. Arle piloting his Mariner PBM. His radio operator saw some forty ships only seventy-five miles away on his HF/DF plot. They reported the position of the Mobile Fleet, but the message was never received, and the location intelligence was not available until Arle landed. It was received by Mitscher seven and a half hours later.[17]

With a mission as a battle line carrier, Task Group 58.4 was operating in an area approximately 130 miles on a bearing 250° from Saipan. At 0531 the *Essex* launched its first CAP with 11 fighters and a standard 2-plane VF-VB sector search of three sectors.

Back at 0830 Ozawa had launched his Raid 1 consisting of 16 Zeke fighters, 45 Zekes loaded with bombs and 8 Jill torpedo bombers from Obayashi's van carriers. Admiral Lee's battleships picked up the force on radar at 1000 at 150 miles out. CAP 2 with VF-15's Lieutenant Commander Brewer with 12 F6Fs was catapulted off the flight deck of the *Essex* at 0910, followed 33 minutes later with the recovery of the first CAP and search planes. At 1013 the first Japanese raid was detected bearing 250° from the *Essex* at 118 miles. Since CAP 2 with 11 F6Fs and 8 fighters from the *Cowpens* were already airborne and on patrol for an hour, the Task Group FDO directed Brewer to intercept the raiding party.

At 1035 Brewer called out "Tallyho"[18] over the radio having sighted the Japanese raid 35 miles away. He recorded the enemy raiders as "Twenty-four rats, sixteen hawks, no fish at 18,000 feet"[19] (fighters, dive-bombers and no torpedo bombers). From 24,000 feet, Brewer decided to attack the formation leader, firing at him from 800 feet. The Judy D4Y exploded in flames. As the F6F came through the cloud of bombers, debris and flames, Brewer caught a glimpse of another plane and pulled up shooting at it. This second Judy came apart and soon hit the sea in flames.

Brewer then took off after another Zeke and, after catching him and firing at his wingroot, he downed the fighter. Another Zeke came in diving at him, but Brewer was able to get on his tail, fire bursts at the fighter as it made violent maneuvers to avoid them. After hitting the Zeke's fuselage, wings and cockpit, the enemy fighter caught fire and headed down in a spiral to its destruction.

Brewer's twenty-year-old wingman, Ensign Richard F. Fowler, had a good day too. Like a good wingman, Fowler flew on Brewer's right for the first two passes as Brewer downed his bombers. On the third pass, the wingman of the Zeke that Brewer had shot down made a turning dive placing him directly in front of Fowler's fighter. Fowler immediately fired his cannons and stayed on the tail of the Zeke until it started smoking, "fell off on a wing, and spiraled tightly"[20] to the sea. Now at 10,000 feet, he saw two Zekes in a Lufberry circle and engaged one of them, but he missed. The Zekes got on Fowler's tail, firing at him, as he dived down to 6,000 feet trying to escape. Thankfully, a fellow F6F joined in the action. The two Zekes turned toward the new F6F, while Fowler turned around and fired at one of the Zekes, causing the enemy fighter to lose part of its wing. The enemy pilot escaped the Zeke, but there was no parachute.

Off on his starboard, Fowler saw another Zeke, and he turned to engage. He got on his tail and fired until a part of its vertical stabilizer came off. The enemy fighter began to smoke until Fowler saw flames coming from the aft section of his engine. In seconds the Zeke splashed into the sea.

Then Fowler joined with two other F6Fs chasing a Hamp (stubby version of carrier-based Zero). The Hamp flew into a cloud, and he saw it come out of a cloud as he positioned his F6F on its tail. He splashed the Hamp, and saw two Judys, firing at one of them from above with his single working gun. Pieces of the Judy bomber came off, but somehow remained in formation. Fowler's guns were totally out of ammunition, forcing him to head home to the *Essex*.

Trailing Brewer and leading the second division of four VF-15 Hellcats, Lieutenant (junior grade) George R. Carr selected a target and fired at an enemy bomber that immediately exploded. Carr was not able to avoid the debris before executing a wingover, and in the process saw another bomber that was a "sitting duck high-side."[21] Carr fired and the second bomber was in flames to enter "a graveyard spiral from which it never recovered."[22]

A Hamp took up a tail position behind him and Carr went into a perpendicular dive as his airspeed hit 430 knots. He conducted a roll to the starboard to shake off the Hamp along with his wingman. He climbed up and found himself alone, except for a Japanese bomber speeding directly at him. Carr reacted and fired at the wingroot and engine as the bomber exploded.

Not finished yet, Carr pulled up and saw two more bombers just 2,000 feet higher than him flying on a parallel course. He fired some bursts at the first enemy plane and saw something leave the plane that could have been the pilot, but he skidded sideways to the left to position himself behind the second bomber. After Carr fired on the enemy bomber, it broke out in flames as he attempted to follow him down to no avail. By the time he had regained altitude, there were no more enemy targets left, so he headed back to the *Essex*.[23]

Of the 69 Japanese planes in Ozawa's Raid 1, 42 did not return. The credit for the successful intercepts went to *Essex* and the 8 Hellcats from *Cowpens*, 12 from the *Bunker Hill*, several from the *Princeton* and numerous fighters from the *Lexington* and *Enterprise*. Some Japanese planes did make it to the task groups, having evaded the intercepts. The picket destroyers *Yarnall* and *Stockham* were attacked west of the battleline, but escaped any damage.

Steaming at 22 knots, Admiral Lee had positioned his task group with the *Indiana* in the center, with the other six battleships, four cruisers and destroyers in a six-mile circle. The only direct hit from the Japanese attackers was on the *South Dakota*. An enemy 500-pound bomb landed on the superstructure deck, opened a hole in the ship, damaged the wiring and piping, disabled a 40mm gun and damaged the Admiral's and captain's cabins. Twenty-seven men were killed and twenty-three were wounded. The battleship was not damaged enough to impede its operations.[24]

The heavy cruiser *Minneapolis* had a bomb hit just off the fantail as observed by Lieutenant Rollo Ross on the battleship *Washington*:

> I thought "that was close." But as soon as the splash came down, smoke just came pouring out and completely obscured her. I figured they weren't so lucky after all, that it must have been a hit that ignited a hell of a fire. After the next emergency turn I was startled to see the *Minneapolis* still maneuvering in the formation and emerging from all that smoke. Then it became obvious what had happened. The shock of that near miss had ignited the smoke generator on her fantail.[25]

As Japanese Raid 1 was raging, at 0816 on June 19 Commander James W. Blanchard took his submarine *Albacore* down to avoid an enemy plane in the area. At periscope depth, he cruised until sighting a carrier, a cruiser and other vessels seven miles off and bearing 70°. Blanchard had positioned himself on Ozawa's CarDiv One as he let the first carrier pass. He was after the second carrier as he closed from five miles out to two miles away from his target. Suddenly, at just the worst possible moment, the *Albacore's* target data computer malfunctioned. He continued his vigilant focus on his periscope viewer as the enemy carrier steamed by at 27 knots. Fearing the ship would soon pass out of his effective range, he determined his firing solution visually and quickly sent out his spread of six torpedoes at 0909. Some ninety seconds later, he "went to deep submergence with three destroyers heading her way."[26] They had 27 seconds to wait to see if any of his torpedoes hit the mighty carrier. The Japanese destroyers put two dozen "ash cans"[27] close to the submarine but no serious leaks were detected in any of the nine watertight compartments.

There was one single explosion that coincided with the sixth torpedo. There would have been a second explosion except for the courageous act of Warrant Officer Sakio Komatsu. He had just become airborne in his Jill dive-bomber on his launch from the *Taiho* carrier heading on Raid 2 when he sighted the spread of torpedoes closing in on the carrier. Without any delay, Komatsu nosedived at the closest Mark 14 torpedo and, incredibly, was able to explode it when he impacted the water. Komatsu and his observer were killed.

The *Albacore's* torpedo blew a hole in the starboard side of the carrier next to the forward gasoline tanks. It jammed the lower portion of the forward plane elevator as gasoline, water and fuel oil filled the elevator well. There was no explosion and no fires broke out. The captain considered the damage as minor as the carrier continued forward, with its flight deck clear. After thirty minutes, the crew had placed wood planks over the elevator hole. Even Admiral Ozawa showed no concern about this single torpedo hit on his 33,000 ton flagship *Taiho*.

As the carrier cruised along at 26 knots, an inexperienced damage-control officer ordered that all the ventilating ducts throughout the ship be opened to run at full blast to blow out the fumes. The crew also began pumping the gasoline and volatile Tarakan petroleum oil in the elevator well overboard. As the fumes moved throughout the ship, at 1532 the men on the bridge saw the armored flight deck bulge upward as a gigantic explosion erupted, blowing out the sides of the hangar and hull to below the water level. Everyone in the engine room was killed. Flames were everywhere. Now with no power, the carrier began to sink by the head.

Ozawa was disheartened to the point that he considered going down with the ship. His old friend, Captain Toshikazu Ohmae, responded, "The battle is still going on and you should remain in command for the final victory."[28] Ozawa reconsidered and transferred via lifeboat with his staff and the Emperor's portrait to the destroyer *Wakatsuki*. Then at 1706 they boarded the cruiser *Haguro*. As they settled in, there was another tremendous explosion that caused the *Taiho* to tilt to the port, capsize and slip by the stern below the waves. Just 500 of the 2150 crewmembers survived the sinking.

Meanwhile, the *Albacore* escaped the depth charging, surfaced and reported back to Pearl Harbor that he had scored "probable damage."[29] When Blanchard sailed into Majuro, he reported in error that he had damaged a Shokaku-class ship. For this he was awarded a commendation ribbon. It was not until months later when a prisoner interrogation revealed that the *Taiho* had been sunk. Eventually Blanchard was awarded the Navy Cross for the sinking.

Sixty miles beyond *Albacore's* attack position at 1152, Lieutenant Commander Herman J. Kossler raised his periscope on the *Cavalla* and noted, "The picture was too good to be true! A large carrier with two cruisers ahead on the port bow and a destroyer about 1000 yards on the port beam!"[30] The Japanese carrier *Shokaku* was landing aircraft aboard as the *Cavalla* moved up undetected while taking three periscope sights all the way.

The only reason Kossler had not fired torpedoes yet was that there was some concern that the carrier could be a friendly Essex-class ship. With his staff reviewing the ONI recognition manual, Kossler raised the periscope and took another look. There it was; "There was the rising sun, big as hell."[31] He let the executive officer and gunnery officer confirm his sighting as Kossler communicated his firing observations to Lieutenant (junior grade) James "Jug"[32] Casler on the plot loading the data into the torpedo data computer (TDC) to determine the firing solution. With the carrier speed and course, the TDC calculated the gyro angles to the forward torpedo room to set the values into "fish."[33]

The six 3000-pound, alcohol-fueled, steam powered torpedoes-three Mark 14 and three Mark 23s-were fired at eight-second intervals. Kossler recorded the action: "This destroyer [*Urakaze*] hadn't sighted us as we headed in. I put the periscope up. We were 1000 yards. I got ready to fire six torpedoes in such a way that if our dope was good at least four would hit. After the fourth I looked over at the destroyer and it was still on my neck. I fired the fifth and sixth on the way down. I know the first three hit."[34]

The time was 1220 when the torpedoes hit the *Shokaku* traveling at 46 knots, igniting the 668 pounds of Torex. Most of the hits were forward of the amidships near the aviation gasoline tanks. The gas main exploded flooding the flight deck with burning fuel. The explosion blew the forward plane elevator three feet skyward, crashing back into the well. There was a major hole in the starboard hull, causing the ship to list as boilers flooded on that side and reducing speed.

Shokaku's Captain Matsubara ordered counterflooding on the port side, but the engineers overcompensated and the list moved to port. With most electrical panels destroyed, Japanese crew had problems getting the fuel pumped overboard, and had to resort to a bucket brigade. They were able to keep the carrier afloat for four hours, but at 1500 a bomb exploded on the hanger desk igniting trapped fuel vapors. The ship "settled by the bow"[35] as the flooding increased dramatically. In just a few minutes the *Shokaku* sank. Of the 1,263 men aboard the *Shokaku,* including 376 from Air Group 601, only Captain Matsubara and 569 other officers and men survived. The Japanese had lost two carriers within twenty-five miles of each other.

As the crew of the *Shokaku* was fighting to save their carrier, the *Cavalla* had dived deep turning full left rudder while changing course and rigging for silent running. For the next three hours three Japanese destroyers continually dropped depth charges on the *Cavalla* as they crisscrossed the area. When the enemy finally gave up, Kossler had counted 106 depth charges. He had sunk a carrier on his first command patrol.[36]

Back at 0900 Ozawa had launched Raid 2 from his own CarDiv One with 128 aircraft. There were fifty-three Judy dive-bombers with 550-pound bombs, twenty-seven Jill torpedo bombers and forty-eight Zeke escorts. Ozawa also launched from his flagship carrier a Yokosuka D4Y1-C reconnaissance plane loaded with aluminum chaff. Used to confuse radar, the British called this chaff "Window."[37]

An hour had passed since Raid 2 had formed up and reached Kurita's van force from the West when his own anti-aircraft gunners started firing at CarDiv Ones' aircraft. Two planes were downed and another eight were forced to abort.[38]

Raid 2 was picked up on *Essex's* radar screen at 1109 at 112 miles, bearing 250°. Fifteen minutes later the FDO vectored McCampbell's group of 12 F6Fs to intercept the attackers. At 1139 McCampbell radioed Tally-Ho at 60 miles reporting 30–40 Japanese planes at 18,000 feet. McCampbell focused on the Judys first. His last division of four fighters attacked and engaged with them while McCampbell led the rest of his force down to hit the Judys.

His F6Fs were much higher in altitude at 20,000 feet than the Judys by as much as 4,000 to 5,000 feet. McCampbell dived and attacked a tail-end Charlie hoping to shot him down and proceed to the other side of the enemy formation. But suddenly the Judy in front of him exploded forcing him to quickly climb to avoid debris.

McCampbell went across the enemy formation above and was able to select the lead plane. He fired just one of his guns since the other five barrels had burned out and downed the Judy. Then he dropped into a formation of Jills and shot one down. McCampbell shot at the lead Jill but only claimed it as probable. He then headed back to the *Essex*.[39]

Ensign Ralph E. Foltz, McCampbell's wingman, stayed with the CAG down on his first pass and shot down one Zeke. Suddenly, he found a Zeke on his tail, so he went to full power and using water injection was able to pull away from the enemy fighter. As he climbed to reach two F6Fs, oil began squirting onto his windshield obstructing his view. Apparently, the Zeke had hit his engine oil line. Foltz came immediately up on a Judy, as he fired his guns at it. The plane exploded and he flew through it. With his oil pressure moving radically, he took off back to the *Essex*.

Another of McCampbell's division leaders, Ensign Claude W. Plant, made his target a Zeke on his first high speed pass, and shot until flames appeared. He selected a second enemy fighter and downed him, burning all the way to the sea. Plant looked down and saw another F6F with a Zeke on his tail. Plant descended and got behind the fighter, firing the full length from tail to cockpit to the engine as the Zeke's stabilizer broke into pieces and the engine started to burn. The enemy pilot slumped over in his seat and his plane fell off on a wing in flames, spiraling to the water below.

Plant focused on one of two Zekes that was some 500 feet below him. He headed toward the enemy fighter as it immediately made a sharp left turn. Plant and his F6F were able to keep up with the attacker, firing his guns until the Zeke fell off in an erratic "falling-leaf pattern"[40] and hit the water flat.

Unfortunately, Plant was picked up by another Zeke that had positioned itself on his tail. He tried to shake off the attacker, but soon 7.7mm and 20mm rounds hit his Hellcat in the "empennage, fuselage, wings, cockpit, engine, propeller, and water injection tank."[41] As Plant could feel the enemy bullets hitting the armor plate behind his seat, another F6F came to his rescue and shot the Zeke off his tail. When Plant landed back aboard the *Essex*, the crew counted some 150 holes in his fighter.[42]

Flying high cover as a member of Lieutenant Milton's division, Ensign George W. Pigman stayed at altitude for a moment as his fellow division squadron mates descended. When he headed down to join them, Pigman came up on a Judy and started firing a prolonged burst of bullets until the enemy bomber broke apart and fell to the sea. Almost hit by an approaching Judy, Pigman caught the attacker in its unarmored belly, leaving it falling over on one wing and exploding. The next Judy he picked was below him as he fired a long burst at it. Flames finally appeared as the Judy made violent skids, and then descended slowly to a sea landing and sank.

Another VF-15 pilot, Ensign Power, had a successful engagement against the Japanese, but not without its near-death experiences. He had just downed a Zeke when he moved to take on another one. The enemy pilot headed straight at him as both planes fired continual bursts. Both planes had suffered hits in their wing roots. Suddenly the Zeke exploded, but Power's F6F continued to fly. Unfortunately, Power was hit in the leg by shrapnel from a 20mm shell that had exploded inside his plane. The wounded pilot took the F6F down to 1,500 feet, leveled off and headed back to the *Essex*.

From high cover, Ensign Albert C. Slack descended and downed a Zeke, but then had another one get on his tail, shooting him up. Thankfully, another F6F shot down the Zeke from his rear. They joined up and flew back to the *Essex* and trapped aboard. Ensign George

H. Rader had come with his VF-15 division to the engagement, but after he went into action with the Japanese, no one saw him again. McCampbell listed him as "missing in action."[43] By 1230 all the VF-15 *Essex* planes had returned except for Rader.[44]

The *Essex* shot down its share of enemy fighter aircraft, but other TF 58 carriers participated in intercepting Raid 2. Of the 128 Japanese planes that headed out on Raid 2, 97 did not return. Raid 3 from Ozawa carriers consisting of forty-seven planes was launched around 1300 in the afternoon and were intercepted by planes from the *Hornet* and *Yorktown*. The raid had been broken up without inflicting any damage to any of TF58 assets. A number of the Japanese planes had landed after their missions on Guam and Tinian.

Lieutenant Brodhead and his VB-15 dive-bombers had been able to put crater holes in the runaway at Orote Airfield on Guam, which made it difficult for Admiral Kakuta and his carrier planes in carrying out the Japanese shuttle plan. Some planes had to jettison their bombs to ensure they had enough gas to return home.

When he discovered that Japanese carrier planes from Ozawa's first three raids had landed at various island airfields, Mitscher took decisive action to stop the flow. At 1423 McCampbell was catapulted off the deck of the *Essex* along with 11 other VF-15 F6Fs to sweep Guam of enemy aircraft. The strike group climbed to 24,000 feet to ensure altitude advantage if there were enemy fighters around. En route McCampbell noticed numerous Japanese planes here and there heading toward Orote Field on Guam.

Coming in after a long trip from Truk to Guam was Lieutenant Commander Harutoshi Okamoto's Air Group 253 with thirteen Zekes. Meanwhile, McCampbell was first in to shot down a Zeke, but then two Zekes reversed their course and headed at him with their guns blazing. McCampbell's plane was hit, but his wingman, Ensign Royce L. Nall, got more than he did. Nall's elevators were all shot up and his engine was smoking from the 20mm and 7.7mm shells.

McCampbell tried to draw the two fighters away, but they continued to attack as Nall's F6F was unable to maintain speed. He weaved and slide to a position to confront the nearest Zeke. With his trigger firing bursts, the Zeke exploded, as the other Zeke broke off heading toward Orote Field. McCampbell stayed on his tail as the enemy fighter executed what he called "the most beautiful slow roll I had ever seen; it was so perfect there was no need for changing point of aim or discontinuance of fire."[45] Incredibly, the Zeke pilot survived his mistake and was able to make an emergency landing at Orote.

The CAG had lost track of Nall and found himself surrounded by Zeros. As he surveyed the situation, he saw two American seaplanes on the water picking up downed flyers as two friendly F4U fighters were circling overhead trying to keep the enemy planes away from the rescuers. McCampbell decided to join the attack by making runs on the Zeros, and warding off the fighters. Soon McCampbell was joined by other Hellcats including one of his divisions led by Lieutenant Commander George Duncan.

Another of McCampbells divisions, led by Lieutenant Commander George Duncan, followed McCampbell off the carrier, but never reached as far as Orote Field on Guam. His wingman, Ensign Wendell V. Twelves, noted that Duncan took them up to 6,000 feet to get us above the cloud base and higher than small arms fire could reach over the islands. They flew at 260 knots to get into the action.[46]

As Duncan's division reached Cabras Island, they notice two Zekes above them. Duncan directed Henning and White to make an attack on them. Just then Duncan and Twelves heard a "Mayday"[47] from the pilot of one of two Curtiss SOC Seagull floatplanes located about 100 yards off Rota Point on Guam being strafed by two Zeros. As they both responded to the call for help, they were jumped by two Zekes. Duncan and Twelves were able to escape from the attackers, as Duncan sent Twelves to help the Seagulls while he handled the two fighters.

Twelves remembered that he was leaning forward as a sort of crazy physical jester to move his aircraft to speed up. He knew he had to rush to affect the rescue of the Seagulls. Twelves saw a dozen or more planes engaged in combat, with a few smoking. The radio was full of combat chatter.[48]

At approximately 1615, Twelves saw parachutes in the water off Rota Point and located the two floatplanes taxiing away from the beach with men hanging onto the Seagulls' pontoons. Then Twelves spotted a Zeke turning to make another pass on the floatplanes and then he felt a sinking sensation as he realized that he was still too far away to fire on the Zeke before he strafed the friendlies.[49]

From 4,000 feet Twelves dived at the Zeke, as the enemy fighter passed in front of him. With his airspeed at 360 knots, "My guns were armed, my gunsight was on, and my speed was building up. I made a quick scan for the second Zeke and returned my attention to the one now in front of me."[50] The Zeke took off toward one of the Seagulls firing his two 7.7mm nose guns. The men in the water "ducked under [the water] for protection as the Seagull pilot turned in a circle to throw the enemy's aim off."[51] The bullets from the 20mm wing guns hit the water, sending white spray around the Seagull.

Focusing on the enemy Zeke, Twelves saw the Seagulls race past him as the Zeke loomed above them and then began to bank to the left. He had to pull three Gs to get a 45-degree deflection shot on the Zeke from 500 yards away. Using his gunsight, he set the lead and fired a three-second burst at 400 yards. The Zeke received hits and passed below him as he rolled left looking for another shot. The Zeke was on fire at 200 feet off the sea with his nose down as it hit the ocean and began cartwheeling along in flames.[52]

Suddenly, the second Zeke came in above him at the 12 o'clock position at 5,000–6,000 feet, moving from right to left at some 90-degrees. Twelves climbed in his Hellcat, but the Zeke, totally focused on the Seagulls, still did not see him coming in. He intended to use a high-side deflection shot from the rear and above the Zeke. He executed a wingover, and setting his gunsight at 1050 mils lead, pulled back on the throttle and fired. Parts of the Zeke were visible debris as dark smoke trailed as the fighter winged over and spiraled to the sea, disappearing.[53]

His engagement was not ended. Just then another Zeke was firing bullets at him from behind. Twelves rolled over to the left and pulled six Gs trying to turn away from the enemy fighter. He fired his cannon while nearly stalling out. He moved left and right to break the aim of the Zeke. His escape options were not good. He could not dive while so low, and did not see any clouds around. Then he noticed the firing had stopped. He looked around and saw another F6F firing at the Zeke to save him.[54]

The smoke from the Zeke turned to flames at 200 feet, and then began to cartwheel over the surface of the water, leaving "a beautiful trail of fire"[55] and finally coming to a rest and sinking into the sea. Ensign Twelves circled and saw the two damaged Seagulls with "the survivors sitting on the wings. Everyone on and in the airplanes was waving and cheering. I felt like cheering myself as I rocked my wings."[56]

Meanwhile, the leader of Duncan's second fighter section, Lieutenant (junior grade) William V. Henning, with Lieutenant (junior grade) Carleton White both fired on a Zero. The fighter exploded just in front of them. Henning then caught another Zero, positioned his F6F on its tail and began shooting. The enemy fighter dived for the deck, but Henning kept up racing after the bandit. He had come in too close as the Zero blew up, sending shrapnel everywhere including over his wings and fuselage.

McCampbell's Hellcats gathered at altitude and were soon joined by Duncan's division as they headed back for home. At 1724 McCampbell's fighter sweep landed aboard the *Essex*. Twenty-six minutes earlier the *Essex* had launched the second fighter sweep mission over Guam with seven F6Fs with Commander Brewer as mission leader. As they approached Guam, they were at 15,000 feet and at first did not see any Japanese aircraft in the air above Guam or Orote Field. At 1820 they did discover a lone Judy dive-bomber circling low and getting ready to land. Brewer's division pounced on the Judy and shot it down before it hit the ground.

Suddenly, sixteen Zeros that had been obscured by cloud cover dove down from 6,000 feet to attack Brewer's fighters now at low altitude on the deck. Each F6F leader was attacked by four Zeros. Only Brewer, his wingman, Ensign Thomas Tarr, and Lieutenant N.W. Overton and his wingman, Ensign G.E. Mellon, were in a position to turn and respond to the attackers. With no altitude reserve, they had to climb to meet the Zeros. Brewer shot down his attacker as it sped past him to crash. Ensign Tarr was able to follow his Zero to the ground and destruction. Lieutenant Overton downed two Zeros and got two more probables. Ensign Mellon shot down one Zero.

In the general melee, the Zeros and F6Fs engaging each other. Lieutenant (junior grade) Thorolf Thompson and Ensign David Johnson were primarily engaged in shooting Zeros off the tails of other F6Fs, but they did each down a Zero. Lieutenant Strane got a Judy. When it was all over, a total of eleven Zeros had been downed. During the action, an F6F was seen "to pull up above the fracas, start a wingover, then shudder and fall off, and crash."[57] That specific pilot was unknown, but as it turned out that Commander Brewer and Ensign Tarr had both been killed.

As darkness came around 1845, the Zeros disappeared. They were not on the runways or around Orote Field. At that point, no one knew that Commander Brewer had been killed. Overton and others called for him on the radio, but there was no answer. Overton called for the Hellcats to rendezvous, as they circled to look for Brewer. When their fuel was running low, the VF-15 pilots were forced to depart for home. The second fighter sweep trapped back aboard the *Essex* at 1915.[58]

After the long day of fighter engagements, VF-15 was awarded 68.5 Japanese planes shot down, the most ever scored in one day by any American fighter squadron in the war. McCampbell had claimed seven for the two missions, and Commander Brewer had earned five victories. On June 19, 1944, the fifteen Hellcat squadrons in Task Force 58 claimed 371 victories.[59]

As the evening of the 19th arrived and the results had been tallied, there were celebrations throughout the wardrooms and ready rooms of TF 58. There were some men who reflected on their lost friends. The battle had taken the lives of fourteen fighter pilots, thirteen airmen missing or killed, as well as thirty sailors. But on board the *Lexington* Lieutenant (junior grade) Zeigel Neff from Missouri, who had shot down four Japanese planes, declared, "It was just like an old-time turkey shoot."[60] The legend has it that the VF-16 skipper, Lieutenant Commander Paul D. Buie, heard Neff's comment and passed it on.[61]

Thus ended the greatest carrier-to-carrier air battle in World War II, "The Great Marianas Turkey Shoot."[62]

11

Ozawa's Retreat
and Protecting Saipan

"Give 'em hell, boys. Wish I were with you."[1]

With the aerial victory of June 19 now acknowledged, it was time for Admiral Spruance to decide whether Mitscher's Fast Carrier Task Force 58 would be allowed to pursue Ozawa's Mobile Fleet. At 1630 that day Spruance signaled his decision: "Desire to attack enemy tomorrow if we know his position with sufficient accuracy. If our patrol planes give us required information tonight, no searches should be necessary. If not, we must continue searches tomorrow to ensure adequate protection of Saipan. Point Option should be advanced to the westward as much as air operations permit."[2]

To cover Saipan while keeping Guam and Rota suppressed, Spruance had Mitscher direct TG 58.4 to stay behind and refuel. After having essentially headed east since dawn that day, Mitscher's other three carrier task groups finally turned due west at 2000 to chase after Ozawa. This delay of nearly four hours since Spruance had approved the operation had been required to allow the carriers to recover their planes. Finally, Mitscher's force of ninety men-of-war, with Lee's battleships out front, was searching for Ozawa's forty-eight combatant ships, as well as his fleet oilers.

Unfortunately, for Mitscher, Ozawa's Mobile Fleet had turned to the northwest two hours earlier at 1808. Catching up to the Mobile Fleet was not the only problem Mitscher faced. Finding the Japanese fleet had been an allusive goal since the operation began. It was seemingly incredible that the American fleet had so clearly failed at this most basic naval combat requirement.

Even more mystifying was why Admiral Mitscher did not order even one search mission out the night of June 19–20 to locate Ozawa's fleet since he knew he would require it the next morning to engage. Mitscher's chief of staff recalled that Mitscher had asked TG 58.3 commander, Admiral Reeves, about a night search, but at 2030 Reeves indicated that his search planes were having engine problems. The speculation was that Mitscher would leave the search duties to the PBMs from Garapan Roads to find the enemy fleet. As midnight came that Monday night, the Mobile Fleet was positioned 460 west of Guam heading toward the northwest at 18 knots, while Task Force 58 was some 325 miles astern speeding at 23 knots.[3]

June 20 (D+5)

The previous day the *Essex* had steamed toward the designated rendezvous point with the fleet oilers at bearing 70° some sixty miles off Saipan. At 0208 on the morning of June

99

20 the *Essex* catapult launched four F6F night fighters from VF(N)-77. Lieutenant (junior grade) J.C. Hogue and Ensign E. Roycraft were sent to cover Rota airfields, while Lieutenant Commander Robert M. Freeman and Ensign George L. Tarleton headed off to Agana and Orote Airfields on Guam.

Freeman and Tarleton launched first since they had to fly 144 miles to their targets on Guam. They climbed to 6,000 feet in the clear, moonless night. As they flew toward Guam, they looked over toward Saipan where they saw a sky full of starshells exploding and flares of yellow, red or green lighting up the land below. Orote Field was totally dark, but at Agana, the field had landing lights on, a clear sign that the Japanese expected incoming birds. As Freeman and Tarleton approached, the lights at the end of the field began flashing, which must have been a signal to the Japanese pilots. The VF-15 pilots took the downward leg and strafed the runway. The anti-aircraft guns opened up on them, so they headed out. It was then 0335 as the Japanese turned off the field lights.

From five miles off the F6Fs circled the field until the lights came back on. They did five minutes later. Then at 0350 a light was seen passing below them at 5,000 feet. Assuming it was the tail light of an enemy plane, Freeman made a pass at it. Suddenly the light went out and he could not see anything. He found himself at the opposite end of the field from his wingman. Freeman noted a light moving around the field. At the same time Tarleton radioed that he wanted to attack a plane he saw, which Freeman approved.

Some ten seconds later Freeman saw two blinking lights likewise moving around the field. He took off to the east side of the field and positioned himself behind the rear contact. Suddenly in visual range of the plane another plane at the rear of his contact turned on its wing and amber tail lights. Freeman moved in to take on the new enemy contact moving at 130 knots at 2000 feet.

Freeman got in the rear left quarter and started to fire his four inboard guns from 100 feet away. The shots hit the plane in the fuselage sending sparks out as an orange flame appeared on the Japanese plane on its right side. The plane, which Freeman identified as a Val, slowed down to 85 knots as it nosed over in his turn to the left. Freeman did all he could to reduce his speed, using flaps and reduced throttle. He reposited himself and fired from 50 yards back.[4]

Freeman saw bullets hitting the wing tips, tail and fuselage, and after he had fired some six bursts of three seconds duration, the Val went nose downward in a steep dive toward the sea. He did not see the Val hit the water in the darkness, but felt confident the plane could not have recovered.

It was now 0410 as Freeman circled the field looking for more targets, but found none. He then climbed to 8,000 feet and remained at the west end of the airfield until he was joined by Ensign Tarleton at 0445.

Ensign Tarleton had his own report of the action after seeing the lights in the landing pattern. He closed too fast and was forced to go around again to slow down. While on the southern side of the field he saw running lights at the north end of the field. He was unsure whether it was the same plane he had noticed when his was at high altitude. Running at 120 knots he started his attack run on the plane, dropping his flaps to end up some 200 feet behind and below the enemy. He fired a short burst but saw not hits. He assumed he was leading the target too much and decided to pull his nose up and fire a five-second burst. Tarleton's shots hit the enemy plane in the wings and belly, as it nosed over and crashed in the sea.

Ensign Tarleton was 100 feet off the deck after dropping his wing flaps. He decided to circle the field 2–3 times. Located at the northern end of the field, he noticed some lights at the southern end. The headed toward the enemy contact too fast and overran the plane. He desired to move his throttle back to reduce his speed, but feared his exhaust flame would be seen. Moving underneath the enemy plane he saw a second plane with its lights out some 300 feet ahead. Tarleton fired one burst and climbed sharply, firing another burst. The enemy plane rolled over and his nose dropped, leaving himself no way to recover his altitude. He saw the contact receive hits and as he moved under him, he suddenly saw a large flash on his left wing. He was not sure what it was.

He saw his altitude gage during the attack run and it read 50 feet. He circled the field three to four times, but with the lights out and nothing moving, he climbed.[5]

While Freeman and Tarleton were working their air action over Guam, Hogue and Roycraft were over Rota. The airfield was lighted, but there were no planes on the field. They saw no action at Rota. All four night fighters returned for a recovery aboard the *Essex* at 0550.

At 0418 McCampbell led a fighter sweep over airfields on Guam and Rota with 17 F6Fs from VF-15. As they reached the west coast of Guam at 25,000 feet, they observed four enemy planes "down on the deck."[6] McCampbell decided they were too far off to break formation and lose the altitude advantage, so they proceeded. There was not much going on over either Guam or Rota. On the way home, the sweep fighters again saw the four planes. Two F6Fs headed down to 18,000 feet to intercept the Zeros, but they took to the clouds for cover. The other two Zeros turned ready to engage, but one escaped into the clouds. The second fighter was hit by several passes from the F6Fs, and left "spinning into a cloud."[7]

The sweep fighters did strafe the installations at Orote Field. On the return trip to the *Essex,* they sighted a single cargo ship between Guam and the task group, and after leaving the ship in flames, they soon landed aboard at 0738.

Two replacement fighters from the *Breton* landed aboard the *Essex* at 0941, and then at 1023, the escort destroyer *Lansdowne* came alongside to deliver Rear Admiral Baker (CTU 58.4.3) and Admiral Wiltse (CTU 58.4.2) for a conference with Admiral Harrill. The visiting admirals re-embarked the *Lansdowne* at 1252.

The second fighter sweep of the day launched at 1422 from *Essex* with twenty F6Fs loaded with 500-pounders. Led by Lieutenant Collins, this mission was another pass at Guam and Rota, but with more action than the first sweep had encountered. Lieutenant J.E. Barry, Jr., took his division down at Orote Field to bomb the runways with 12-hour delay fuses. Just as they nosed over, four Hamps (carrier Zeros) jumped them. The enemy fighters were able to surround the last F6F plane on the formation flown by Ensign J.W. Power. The last anyone saw of Power was his plane taking off toward the clouds with a Hamp chasing him close on his tail.

The other fighters of Lieutenant Barry's division had just recovered when they were jumped by another four Zeros. Suddenly, to the surprise of the Japanese pilots, eight F6Fs descended on the Zeros. The enemy fled toward the clouds for cover, but Ensign A.C. Black was able to close on one Zero and fire. The enemy pilot pulled up to a stall, and then fell off in a spin to the water below. Lieutenant Collins fighter sweep tried to locate the other Zeros, but they were unable to find them lurking somewhere in the clouds. The sweep landed aboard at 1802 with one F6F and its pilot missing.[8]

As the *Essex* and TG 58.4 carried out their assignments for the 20th, the fleets of Ozawa and Mitscher hunted for each other. At 0530 Mitscher's three carrier groups were still 330 to 350 miles away heading northwest. At that time, Ozawa launched nine floatplanes from his van cruisers on a wide spectrum search to the east out 300 miles, but detected nothing. Three of the Jakes failed to return. An hour and fifteen minutes later Admiral

Obayashi launched carrier-based planes to search sectors 10° to 50° out to 350 miles and at 0713 one of them reported seeing two American carriers. Ozawa deemed these contacts as false and continued with his plan to refuel the fleet on that day and attack the following day. The searches had covered the sectors overlapped from 40° to 140° with no firm contract.

At 0930 the two Japanese oiler groups were positioned at their designated rendezvous point (15°20' N, long. 134°40' E lat.), but most of the combatant ships were not there. Ozawa's Mobile Fleet finally arrived at the refueling location around noon, but Ozawa did not give the order to begin fueling until 1230. Thirty minutes later he and his staff transferred to the carrier *Zuikaku* to receive better communications.

It was then that Ozawa learned the terrible news that he had lost some 330 carrier planes the previous day, leaving one hundred operational aircraft according to the Mobile Fleet Action Report (remaining aircraft CarDiv 1: 32, CarDiv 2: 46 and CarDiv 3: 22). Vice Admiral Kakuta, his land-based air commander, sent Ozawa an overly optimistic message that a good number of planes had made it to Guam and Rota. In fact, most of those planes were damaged.

While Mitscher morning air searches were still out on sector searches, Commander Earnest M. Snowden, the *Lexington's* CAG, approached Mitscher with the idea of taking a dozen Hellcats loaded with 500-pound bombs out to their absolute maximum range of 475 nautical miles to find and sink the damaged Zuikaku-class carrier as reported by the submarine *Cavalla*. Hours later Snowden and his search team were heading back to the *Lexington* with no contracts to report, landing at 1050.[9]

At 1330, the *Enterprise* catapulted four search teams out on their assigned ten-degree sectors. Each search team consisted of an escort F6F and two Avengers. One Avenger in each team flew at a low altitude of 700 feet to stay below the haze, while the Hellcat and the second Avenger flew higher on either side scanning the sky ahead through the cumulus clouds for signs of the enemy fleet.

There was nothing to report until Lieutenant (junior grade) Charlie Henderson's team on the southern-most sector spotted a submarine that quickly submerged. One of the center sector teams under the command of Lieutenant Robert S. Nelson saw a Kate flying on the opposite heading, but decided that it was not worth diverting from his search course to attack the plane.

Meanwhile, at 1420 Spruance sent this message to Mitscher, "Would like to continue pursuit of enemy to northwestward tonight if this afternoon's operations give any indication it will be profitable."[10] He also inquired about the fuel status of his force. Mitscher replied that the destroyers would be very low by the morning, but he would continue the search with the ships that had fuel and have the carriers fuel the destroyers as best they could.

At 1538, just as Lieutenant Nelson had reached the end of his 325-mile leg in his Avenger torpedo bomber, he looked out on his port side and noticed a ripple in the sea on the horizon. Just minutes later, in an adjoining team led by Lieutenant (junior grade) Robert R. Jones, wingman Lieutenant (junior grade) Edward Laster also spotted the tracks. These Naval Aviators saw what no American pilot had seen in the previous two years: a Japanese carrier task force.

After determining his position, at 1542 Nelson sent off his voice radio report as follows: "Enemy fleet sighted. Latitude 15–00, longitude 135–24. Course 270, speed 20."[11] He repeated his message three times. Jones' radioman, ARM1c Robert Grenier, sent his message via Morse code on continuous wave (CW): "Many ships, one carrier 134–12E 14–55N."[12] The two reports were 70 nautical miles apart and south of the actual track, but they were good enough to be attacked. Nelson's wingman, Lieutenant (junior grade) James S Moore, Jr., checked Nelson's plot and concurred with Jones' report that the first location was one degree easterly in longitude off. Nelson's radioman, ARM1c James Livingston, sent off the plot amplification.

Jones headed back to deliver his information in person, while Nelson went to take a closer look. He noted,

> My most vivid recollections of the search flight are [of] the Japanese carrier leaving a circular wake as it turned after we had been in view for four or five minutes ... double-checking the plot of our position. As we were returning after transmitting the contact report, I recall the sight of fighter pilot Ned Colgan's F6F as it swooped down and away in pursuit of the Japanese plane we spotted heading on an opposite course, possibly carrying a contact report of his own. The splash of the Jap plane ... was in a way anticlimactic.[13]

At 1615 the radio monitors aboard the Japanese heavy cruiser *Atago* in Rear Admiral Obayashi's CarDiv 3 heard Nelson's and Moore's contact reports and alerted Ozawa. Realizing that American air attacks were eminent, at 1645 Ozawa stopped the fueling operations and changed his course from west to northwest, steaming at 24 knots. Based on Nelson's confirmed contact location, Mitscher's task force was 275 miles away from the Mobile Fleet.

Mitscher had to make a quick decision because time was not on his side. He would have to launch attacks immediately since the sun would set by 1900 that evening. At 1553 he notified Spruance that he would make an all-out strike even though his planes would have to recover aboard the carriers in the dark.[14]

Mitscher's task force air operations officer, Commander William J. Widhelm, worked his plotting table over Ozawa's fleet contacts and finally turned to Mitscher and declared, "We can make it, but it's going to be tight."[15] Mitscher immediately responded, "Launch 'em."[16]

The TF 58 carrier squadrons scrambled to prepare the aircraft for the mission. Mitscher gave his aircrews his pep talk, "Give 'em hell, boys. Wish I were with you."[17] At 1610 the pilots and aircrewmen of the eleven carriers manned their planes for their preflight checks, as the carriers turned into the wind. Fourteen minutes later the three carrier groups started launching their 240 planes carrying 115 tons of ordnance. After some aircraft aborted, the resultant carrier strike consisted of 226 planes, including 95 Hellcats, 54 Avengers, and 77 dive-bombers.

The strike group made their course 290° true. Updated radio messages from the carriers came in to the formation leaders some twenty minutes after launch putting the Mobile Fleet at a scary 300 miles away from the launch point. The distance was un-nerving. The U.S. Navy had never launched a major strike mission at such a long distance.

At 260 miles out Bombing 14 from the *Wasp* spotted the Japanese refueling group, and against the advice of the Avenger leader of Bombing 10 from the *Enterprise*, Lieutenant Van Eason, the skipper of Bombing 14, Lieutenant Commander Jack Blitch, knew his planes were low on fuel and decided to engage the oilers. There were six Japanese oilers to attack, and after the attack was finished the *Wasp* planes had sunk two of them-*Seiyo Maru* and *Genyo Maru*. The *Wasp* group was attacked by at least six Zekes, losing one SB2C bomber and an F6F while claiming hits on two enemy fighters.

Two hours after their launch, making an average of 130–140 knots, the strike group found Ozawa's carriers some thirty-five miles west of the oilers. The cloud cover was five-tenths cover between 3,000 and 10,000 feet. As the American approached the carriers, Ozawa launched a CAP of 75 planes including forty Zekes and twenty-eight fighter-bombers. With visibility at 25 miles below the 3,000-foot cloud cover, from 1840 to 1900

Mitscher's air strike aircraft engaged the Japanese fighters and heavy flak from Ozawa's ships. The Americans lost twenty planes, including eight of the Helldivers. Mitscher's planes claimed twenty-six enemy planes downed, plus nineteen probable and thirty-one damaged. Though not reconciled against the American claims, the operational aircraft inventory of the Mobile Fleet after the battle as shown in the Operation A-Go flag log read, "Surviving carrier air power: 35 aircraft operational."[18] This did not include some dozen floatplanes.

During the engagement, four Japanese carriers had been hit by bombs, but these would ultimately survive. The carrier *Hiyo* was not so fortunate. Lieutenant George Brown took his VT-24 Avengers down to attack the carrier. Brown went around to the right and turned in to attack from the bow, while Lieutenants (junior grade) Benjamin C. Tate and Warren R. Omark went to port to attack from the starboard beam and quarter. The action was recorded:

> Brownie, Ben Tate and I fanned out to approach from different angles. The attack course took us over the outlying screen of destroyers, then cruisers, and finally the battleships. This screen had to be penetrated in order to reach the proper range for launching torpedoes against the carrier. The antiaircraft fire was very intense, and I took as much evasive action as I could. During the attack, Brownie's aircraft was hit by AA and caught fire. I think one of the remarkable stories of the war then took place. Brownie's crewmen, and, knowing their plane was afire and unable to reach Brownie on the intercom, they parachuted and witnesses the attack from the water. We came in at about four hundred feet from the water to get a satisfactory launch of our torpedoes and dropped them on converging courses, which presumably did not allow the enemy carrier to take effective evasive action.[19]

Hiyo's captain, Toshiyuki Yokoi, could not avoid the incoming torpedoes. One of the Mark 13 torpedoes hit the starboard quarter in the engine room and perhaps another on the other side. Her hull was breached, as seawater entered her spaces. With her steering gear mangled, she was crippled. Zekes pounced on the fleeing Avengers, but the attackers were able to escape. Brown's damaged Avenger was seen by Tate and Omark flying slow and quite low over the sea. Tate saw Brown hold up his bloodstained right arm. "I tried to keep him on my wing to guide him back. I called him on the radio but he didn't answer with anything understandable. I lost him in the dark."[20] Omark was the last to see Brown. "He acted stunned, like a football player who had been hit in the head. I turned on my lights to help him, but evidently his light system was shot because he didn't turn on his. I lost him in the dark about an hour later."[21]

Meanwhile, the fires on the *Hiyo* continued to spread from stem to stern as more explosions erupted. As the darkness came, the carrier was down by the bow with her propellers out of the water. Some two hours after the torpedo hits, violent explosions were felt and six minutes later the *Hiyo* disappeared below the waves.

Other ships sustained damage. The carrier *Zuikaku* was hit aft of the bridge. The carrier *Junyo* sustained a crushed stack and destroyed mast, and suspended flight operations. The carrier *Ryuho* received slight damage, while the battleship *Haruna* was hit by two bombs aft that warped her hull. The cruiser *Maya* was hit by a bomb that exploded close to her torpedo tubes causing fires.[22]

After the air battle, around 1900, Mitscher's 209 surviving strike aircraft headed home in the growing dark on a course 090° toward the task force, as pilots considered their fuel status. The distance from Ozawa's carriers varied between 240 to 298 miles from TF 58 carriers. Total darkness came at 1945.

To shorten the distance from his planes to their carriers, Mitscher's carriers sped toward the planes at 22 knots. He also directed that the carrier groups spread out a distance of fifteen miles apart. On the way home gas-short planes had to ditch or struggle to get as close as possible to the task force. At around seventy miles from the carriers, planes began to pick up the homing beacons on their YE-ZB receivers, adjusting their courses as necessary. The task force CICs began to see blips on their radar screens at 2015 showing planes coming from the west. Fifteen minutes later the carriers reversed the helm and turned into the wind coming from the east.[23]

At 2030 the returning planes were sighted in the sky to the west, and fifteen minutes later some of the aircraft were circling with their red and green lights flashing. Air Group 16 Commander, Ernest M. Snowden, approached Commander Wilhelm and said, "We gotta give these guys some lights."[24] Mitscher got down from his swivel chair, walked over to the flag plot table, sat down at the end, looked over at Captain Burke and said, "Turn on the lights."[25]

Risking possible Japanese submarine attacks, the searchlights beamed vertically from each task group flagship into the sky, as cruisers fired star shells upward to brighten the area. Carriers turned on their running lights, masthead truck lights and deck-edge glow lights. Carrier pilot Lieutenant Commander Robert A. Winston was to record, "The effect on the pilots left behind was magnetic. They stood open mouthed for the sheer audacity of asking the Japs to come and get us. Then a spontaneous cheer went up. To hell with the Japs around us. Our pilots were not to be expendable."[26]

Some of the pilots were trying to locate their own carrier, so Mitscher ordered, "Tell them to land on any carrier."[27] Pilots were desperate for a clear flight deck. Some pilots made landing approaches on cruisers and battleships, or on even destroyers' search light beams. Others made controlled water landings when their fuel ran out. LSOs with their illuminated wands or fluorescent paddles tried to keep some kind of order in the landing chaos. They tried to wave off planes when more than one was in final approach. There were, of course, many deck crashes of all types that night. Warren Omark of VT-24 had such a difficulty as he noticed another plane next to him coming in, but thankfully, the other plane turned at the last minute to give his Avenger a clear landing ahead.[28]

By 2252 all the TF 58 planes had landed, crashed or been shot down. Mitscher's action report revealed that 6 Hellcats, 10 Helldivers and 4 Avengers were lost in combat, while 17 Hellcats, 35 Helldivers and 28 Avengers were destroyed in deck crashes or ditchings in the area of the task force. In these lost planes were 100 pilots and 109 aircrewmen, but by daylight of June 21, there were 51 pilots and 50 airmen rescued from the sea. In the following days 33 pilots and 26 airmen were also recovered. That left the net loss total at 16 pilots and 33 airmen.

After the battle, Ozawa recovered his few remaining planes and at 2046 received orders from Admiral Toyoda to retire. The Mobile Fleet escaped with the 6 remaining carriers, 5 battleships, 13 cruisers and 28 destroyers, speeding away making 20 knots. At 0130 on the morning of June 21, the two fleets were 327 miles apart bearing 285° from Mitscher's force. TF 58 was making only 16 knots in order to retrieve airmen along the way. The only reason for searching for Ozawa at this point was to engage any stragglers that were found.

Special long-range night flying Avengers were launched between 0200 and 0300 from the *Bunker Hill* and the *Enterprise*, and they were able to track the Mobile Fleet until 0743, reporting the enemy heading to the northwest some 360 miles from TF 58. At 0600 each task group had launched a deckload of Hellcats loaded with 500-pound bombs to find the stragglers, but after completing their 300-mile sector searches, they found nothing. After more searching by ships and aircraft, at 1920 on June 21 Spruance issued orders to retire TF 58 from the chase. At that time, Ozawa's Mobile Fleet was 300 miles from Okinawa.[29]

Admiral Mitscher summed up the Battle of the Philippine Sea in his Action Report: "The enemy had escaped. He had been badly hurt by one aggressive carrier strike at the one time he was within range. His fleet was not sunk."[30]

12

Saipan Operations and Softening Up Guam

"a tribute to our collective worth to the nation"[1]

The *Essex* and Air Group 15 did not take part in the operation to catch Ozawa's Mobile Fleet retreating to Okinawa, but instead continued action against Guam, while providing air support to Saipan forces of Task Units 16.7.6 and 16.7.11. At 0523 on June 21 (D+6) from 128 miles off Saipan, Commander McCampbell launched 14 F6Fs, 7 torpedo bombers and 14 dive-bombers to Agana Airfield on Guam. There were no Japanese planes airborne at Agana, so the fighters strafed the antiaircraft batteries, as the bombers cratered the runway and taxiways at Agana.

With little action at Guam, McCampbell radioed the commander of the auxiliary carriers to see if he, Rear Admiral G.F. Bogan, wanted him to divert the strike to aid the forces at Saipan. The admiral declined the invitation and the strike continued, trapping back aboard the *Essex* at 0828.

A second strike was sent off from the *Essex* at 1201 for air support over Saipan. The mission with 12 Hellcats, 15 Helldivers and 7 Avengers was tasked to attack Marpi Point airfield. Earlier the Japanese had mounted several new three-inch anti-aircraft guns on the bluff, which proved to be enough trouble to cause Lieutenant Commander V.G. Lambert to divert seven of his torpedo bombers to hit the guns with rockets and bombs.[2]

The dive-bombers approached the target at 11,000 feet flying at 200 knots, before they pushed over from 9.000 feet on their attack runs. Ensign William Nolte dived with his Helldiver, but was hit by flak, started to spin and lost his right wing. Both Nolte and his gunner, Aviation Radioman 2nd Class William Lowe, were killed. As escort for Lowe, Ensign Spike Borley saw the whole thing. Nolte's cockpit had been hit by flak and the fighter lost a wing. It appeared that the pilot was killed but the gunner was trying desperately to get out of the plane. Tragically, the plane was spinning so fast on the way down to the sea, the gunner had no chance to exit.[3] Otto Graham wrote in his diary: "Took hits from ack-ack that knocked out our flaps. This was the most violent pull-out I've ever experienced."[4]

Beanbag Barney Barnitz and his Helldover gunner, Carl Shelter, were also hit by flak over the field, but were able to maintain control even with smoking seen from their plane. They limped to the task group, but had to make a water landing near the destroyer *Lansdowne*. They were picked up by the destroyer and returned to the *Essex* the following day.

After the mission, Lieutenant (junior grade) John Van Altena and his radioman, Aviation Radioman 2nd Class Ray Kataja, were sent to search the area along with other aircrews where Nolte and Lowe had gone down, but they were not located. They did find two rafts with survivors and they remained on station until a rescue destroyer arrived.

The loss of Nolte and Lowe hit Bombing 15 hard. Graham noted in his diary, "The effect on the enlisted ready room was indeed sobering, even to these guys who've heard the words before it was a blow. Lowe was extremely popular. There'll be a deep gap in the squadron by his loss. Irreplaceable. That's twenty men we've lost now in just over a month."[5]

Lieutenant (junior grade) Baynard Milton of VF-15 had his Hellcat severely damaged by flak. He had his landing gear shot away, which left a large hole in the wing. His right flap was partially destroyed and he was leaking hydraulic fluid into the cockpit. Somehow he managed to fly a hundred miles back to the *Essex*. With only one landing gear, his right landing gear collapsed on landing and the plane slid along the deck until it hit the island. Incredible a *Movietone News* camera was filming the action as the deck crew fled the area. Milton exited the fighter and walked away. The F6F was deemed beyond repair and was pushed over the side. The footage was seen throughout the 1950s and was used in the popular documentary film, *Victory at Sea*.[6]

June 22 (D+7)

This day the *Essex* operated 315 miles off Saipan covering the area with six sector search patrols, while a major portion of the Task Force 58 refueled. There were no Japanese aircraft engaged that day, but Lieutenant (junior grade) John P. Van Altena and his radioman, R.E. Kataja, spotted two life rafts containing two downed aircrews each. A rescue destroyer picked up the crews. By 1300 all search patrols had landed.

That same day Japanese Warrant Officer Yoshida, who had arrived on Guam three days before, recorded his thoughts in his diary. He said each day the situation was worse on Guam. The Japanese fighter units lost nearly all their aircraft in action in addition to enduring bombing from the Americans in daylight and at night. There were no time to repair the planes on Guam and by that time there were only two Zeros left. These two token aircraft were heavily guarded.[7]

During June 21–22 there was no sign of Japanese air activity in the Marianas, but in fact Admiral Kakuta had been positioning what he had left from around Tinian, Saipan and Guam, as well as from his major staging bases Iwo Jima and Chichi Jima. Receiving word that the runways at airfields at Guam and Tinian had been repaired, Kakuta began the redeployment of his planes.

June 23 (D+8)

With the *Essex* 105 miles from Saipan at bearing 283°, at 0530 McCampbell catapulted a twelve fighter sweep to Guam. There was not a particular expectation that the mission would be any different than the other routine sweeps they had conducted. Over Orote Airfield CAG 15 led his F6Fs to 22,000 feet as they circled to attack from "down sun"[8] which placed the sun directly in the eyes of the enemy.

As they circled, they caught the flashes of sun off metal below as seven or eight enemy planes were starting their engines. Some other planes were hidden in revetments covered by green and brown camouflage around the runways, but they were discovered as the sun glinted off their rotating propellers.

McCampbell had planned to take his group down for a strafing run on the field, but when several of the planes took off, he decided to continue to circle the airfield to see what developed. They lost track of the Japanese fighters in the morning shadows. Ground crews were placing smoke pots at the end of the runways to obscure the activity on that portion of the runway.

McCampbell headed for Agana Airfield to see what was cooking, but there was no activity. After turning back toward Orote Airfield, McCampbell saw a group of four planes in formation that turned out to be Zekes. With both the F6Fs and Zekes at 15,000 feet, suddenly the Japanese dived down to 2,000 feet and formed a Lufberry circle, a defensive maneuver. The CAG circled to form up his eight fighters, leaving four F6Fs high as cover, and attacked the Japanese in the Lufberry circle.

Just then, six Zekes came out of the sun to engage the eight American fighters, while the four F6Fs at altitude swooped down to attack the Zekes. For the next thirty minutes the skies over Orote Field were full of an aerial melee. McCampbell's attack run on a Zeke was made from the rear and above as the plane left the circle smoking and moving toward Orote Field. The target exploded and McCampbell moved back into the mix as the enemy count of planes increased to at least eight.

Again, McCampbell engaged another Zeke from behind as the fighter headed to the north and then came around toward the south to attack him. McCampbell fired some three bursts and the Zeke headed down to the sea. Ensign Plant had joined him in the attack too.

Then McCampbell pulled away and headed off at another Zeke at 1,000 feet in a dive. The target moved to the south at full power trying to get away, but McCampbell went to emergency power for about two minutes and caught him. A burst of the guns from a good way off sent the Zeke into a left wing over. Closing in, McCampbell slowed which allowed the Zeke to position under him from 500–800 feet below. He lost sight of the enemy fighter and moved back into the melee.

On approaching Orote Field at 4,000 feet altitude, McCampbell found himself with a Zeke on his tail. He radioed his fellow fighters to see if any of them could come in to get the Zeke off his tail. He noticed several friendlies come in his direction, but he did not see the Zeke again. Once at Orote Field McCampbell saw no enemy aircraft in the air, so he radioed his pilots to rendezvous at a place where a friendly parachute has been seen. After ten minutes circling the field, McCampbell and seven others returned to the *Essex*, landing at 0849.[9]

McCampbell's fighter sweep had shot down eleven fighters and three probables. Two F6Fs did not return. Lieutenant (junior grade) J.L. Bruce had bailed out and parachuted to the sea under the watchful eyes of Lieutenant (junior grade) W.A. Lundin circling above. Unfortunately, Bruce's life raft fell off the parachute braces on the way down, and his parachute quickly sank on entry. There was no sign of Bruce.

Several other pilots saw Lieutenant R.L. Stearns slumped over in his stick when his F6F was hit in the cockpit by a Zeke. Sterns plane was in a steep glide heading to Orote Field as his wing broke off and he crashed. His wingman, Ensign W.J. Clark, saw Stearns' fighter hit by a deflection shot as the Zeke dived across Clark's plane.

Ensign Stime had discovered a Zeke on McCampbell's tail and made a highside run on it. He saw the Zeke begin to smoke and soon hit the water. Stime also engaged another Zeke, fired his bursts and saw it crash in the side of a cliff. Flying with Stime was Ensign Pigman who was able to get on the tail of a Zeke and fire a long burst, sending the plane into the ground in a ball of flames. Lieutenant (junior grade) Rushing claimed one kill and a probable. Lieutenant Symmes hit one Zeke in the cockpit that crashed landed in pieces just short of Orote Field.[10]

At 0834 eleven fighters, twelve dive-bombers and eight torpedo bombers were launched to Ushi Point Field on Tinian. They met no air resistance, as the F6Fs carried out their strafing runs. The dive-bombers cratered the runway as VT-15 bombed the barracks and hangars northwest of the airfield. A gunner, J.W. Coppola, was wounded in the foot from shrapnel. They landed at 1219.

The third mission of the day was catapulted off at 1155 to Orote Field with fourteen Hellcats, twelve Helldivers and eight Avengers. With the fighters covering, the dive-bombers focused on the wooded areas where McCampbell had seen flashing propellers, but their bombs yielded no visible results. They also cratered the runways. One Helldiver saw two single-engine enemy planes at the end of the runway and bombed them to destruction. VT-15 dropped 2,000-pound bombs on the runway and 100-pound bombs on the parking area on the north side of the field. The *Essex* took them back aboard at 1458.

The last strike of the day was launched to Guam at 1444 led by Lieutenant Commander Jim Rigg, the acting commanding officer of VF-15 now that Commander Brewer had been killed. There were some 9 or 10 Zekes in the area of Guam staying high above. The F6Fs covered as the Helldivers started their runs on the field. Suddenly, four Zekes came out of the clouds pouncing on the bombers. The F6Fs got in behind the Zekes. Lieutenant Morris took the first Zeke and made three passes on it until it began to smoke. The Zeke headed straight down and hit the water, and disintegrated.

Lieutenant Carr was moving along at 6,000 feet with his wingman, Ensign Berree, when they were attacked by four Zekes. Carr was able to get on the tail of one fighter and followed it down from 6,000 to 1,000 feet firing periodic bursts. The enemy fighter never pulled up and crashed into the sea. Berree missed the fighter in his first pass, but he came around and fired two bursts from 200 yards at the wing roots of the Zeke. The enemy fighter started to smoke and went into a split-S turn, but was unable to finish it and hit the water to his destruction.

Lieutenant (junior grade) Crellin from VB-15 and his gunner, Otto Graham, flew this strike, and had the best view of the action around them. Graham was responsible for taking strike photos since they were the last of the fourteen Helldivers that attacked the field. As Crellin headed in at 14,000 feet, Graham was watching out the left side when a large flak burst exploded to his right that "scared the daylights out of me."[11] Two Zekes descended on their Helldiver when their F6F escorts hit them, and the two Japanese fighters exploded.

As they pulled off the target, Graham saw the contrails of another dogfight in the distance as the Japanese attacked the Helldivers from out of the clouds. He watched as Bert Morris hit the first of four Zekes that went after the bombers, sending it into the ocean off the beach, an action for which Morris would receive the Distinguished Flying Cross in September 1944. He saw George Carr get the second Zeke, sending it straight in while his wingman downed another one.

On the way back, when the bombers had dropped their bombs on the runway and revetments, the F6Fs in Morris's division saw a Zeke flying below them. This was no amateur Japanese pilot as he resisted the attacks from four American pilots. He banked and turned, and flew on his back on the deck at altitudes from 50 to 150 feet, and as Lieutenant Commander Rigg described, "He went through every stunt in the books (and some not in) and as far as is known, escaped unharmed."[12] The strike landed at 1709.

As the sun set, Warrant Officer Yoshida wrote in his diary that the 202nd Air Group had no aircraft left, though they did receive a few reinforcements that night from Yap.[13]

By the end of the day on June 23, 1944, Commander David McCampbell had shot down 10½ Japanese planes in combat.

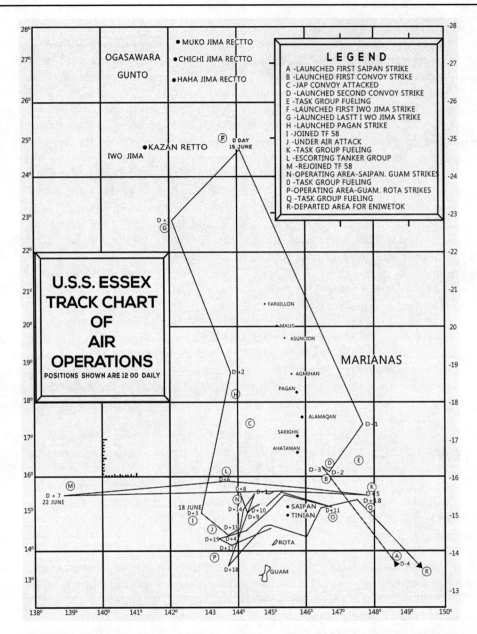

USS *Essex* Track Chart of Forager Operations. Redrawn image based on Action Report: Forager, June 6–July 6, 1944, Commanding Officer USS *Essex*, July 6, 1944 (National Archives and Records Administration, College Park, Maryland).

June 24 (D+9)

On June 24, the *Essex* lay on a bearing of 265° at 85 miles off Saipan. The flying conditions were average with "low broken clouds at 1800 and intermittent showers. Surface winds were E 8–12 Kts."[14] The target was Guam and the mission of the four strikes that day continued to be neutralizing its airfields of Japanese planes. The clouds were solid over the island and provided heavy showers.

McCampbell led the first strike off at 0527 to Orote Field with nineteen fighters, twelve Helldiver and eight Avengers. Though there had to be enemy fighters around based on the previous days' encounters, the Japanese planes were not visible. In fact, the Japanese were preparing for the defense of Guam, which they knew would come soon. The evidence began to show as reinforcements arrived. McCampbell's planes spotted a heavy transport ship in the harbor and a large barge loaded with at least 50 Japanese soldiers.

The fighters dived to strafe the barge, sinking it and leaving many dead soldiers in the water. The enemy transport was engaged by Avengers with 100-pound bombs and rockets. Lieutenant (junior grade) Bentz and Ensign Harry A. Goodwin were two of the VT-15 pilots that fired their rockets and machine guns at the ship. Four bombs and six rockets were seen hitting the deck of the transport. VB and VT bombers dropped bombs on the Orote runways, started a fuel fire and hit the revetment area to the north of the field.

Lieutenant Commander James Mini led the second mission (9 VF, 9 VB, 5 VT) off at 0829 to Agana Airfield. They encountered heavy anti-aircraft fire as they hit the field. Fighters stayed high for cover as the Helldivers bombed the runway and facility buildings. The Avengers dropped three 2000-pound bombs on the runways, and two on the revetments southwest of the field.

Lieutenant (junior grade) James W. Bernitz and his radioman, Carl Shetler, were forced to make a water landing as their Helldiver was hit by flak. They were later rescued by a destroyer.

Lieutenant Commander Duncan led the third strike off at 1130 (12 VF, 9 VB, 8 VT) to Orote Field. The mission mirrored the other strikes that day. A twin-engine bomber was reported destroyed on the ground, and rockets fired at a large transport missed their mark.

Ensign Singer had been sent to take oblique photos over Rota Island in their F6F-3P photoreconnaissance plane. On his run he was engaged by four Zekes coming at him in two sections. He immediately pulled up and fired at the wing root of one fighter. The Zeke was hit and exploded. The other Zekes turned to the right as Singer fired at a second plane, hitting it in the engine, which caught fire, sending it to a sea crash. Singer then dove down to the deck and escaped the last two Japanese fighters using full power. Though wounded in the face, he made it back to the *Essex*. The Air Intelligence Officer deemed the photos to be excellent.

The last strike of the day left at 1430 to Orote Field with 12 fighters, 6 Helldivers and 5 Avengers. More bombs were dropped on the runways, facilities and revetment area. Three Zekes were reported as damaged on the ground. The mission trapped at 1633.

Proving that the enemy still was able to shuttle and redeploy aircraft, that evening a Sally Japanese Army Air Force Ki-21 bomber landed at Orote Field from Iwo Jima. Japanese Warrant Officer Yoshida was able to convince the plane captain to fly the stranded pilots from the 202nd Air Group back to Yap. Suffering from malaria, Yoshida flew aboard the Sally that departed Guam the same evening to a hospital at Yap.[15]

The Japanese were indeed supplying reinforcements to Guam and Tinian. The key spot for air supply was from Iwo Jima where on June 24 there was a shortage of airfield ramp space as some 120 enemy planes were waiting to redeploy as the weather and the American sweeps allowed. The only problem with these aircraft were the men who flew them. Approximately 30 percent of the pilots had completed the full training regime and the rest had no experience in combat.[16]

June 25 (D+10)

The *Essex* was sitting 80 miles off Saipan in overcast skies as the morning CAPs were launch at 0541 and 0801. The only strike was catapulted at 1027 to Guam led by Lieutenant Commander Rigg. The mission methodology remained the same as before as the twelve fighters provided cover for his twelve Helldivers and five Avengers. There were planes on Orote Field as the dive-bombers destroyed six Zekes, with two more probables. The torpedo bombers had six rocket hits on a 7,000-ton freighter also hitting the fuel storage area at Apra Harbor.[17]

June 26 (D+11)

Task Group 58.4 rendezvoused with the fueling group this date bearing 30° and thirty miles from Saipan. There was no other air activity during the day except just after noon, two torpedo bombers from the *Enterprise* landed aboard the *Essex,* with one carrying Vice Admiral J.C. McCain.

June 27 (D+12)

Operating 155 miles off Saipan, the task group conducted neutralization strikes over Guam and Rota. The morning saw the carrier refueling the escort destroyers. The cruisers *Houston* and *Miami*, along with the destroyers of DESDIV 23, were on an anti-shipping sweep and bombardment mission. At 0900 eight F6Fs were launched to provide cover for the bombardment group, along with four VF/VT sector searches.

An Avenger with Vice Admiral McCain aboard was launched at 1004 with two F6F escorts to Aslito Field on Saipan. Later at 1530 McCampbell led sixteen Hellcats, ten Hell-divers and eight Avengers on a strike to Rota. The fighters strafed the airfield runway and revetment areas, while the Helldivers dropped bombs on the runway. Ensign Frederick Lightner dropped his 2000-pound bomb on the west side of the airstrip. The torpedo bombers attacked the shop area south of Rota Field, starting fires as they made their runs. The strike landed back aboard the *Essex* at 1753.[18]

That evening the *Essex* showed the movie *Kid Galahad*, the first movie that squadron mate Bert Morris stared in. McCampbell noted that the movie had been shown at least nine times, leaving significant kidding for Bert. It was so bad that Bert paid the mess steward who ran the projector to hide the movie until it could be traded away.[19]

June 28 (D+13)

On June 28 planes from *Essex* and *Cowpens* combined and attacked the airfields on the smaller islands, including on Pagan. The Pagan strike found no air activity, and the air-field looked nearly abandoned. The Avengers used rockets to damage the buildings in the town, having found all facilities destroyed at the target field.

June 29 (D+14)

That day the *Essex* launched a strike to Rota with eleven Helldivers without fighter support. Leaving at 0945, eight of the dive-bombers reached Rota Airfield and dropped their 1,000-pound bombs on the runway. Two night fighters were launched later at 1927 to

Rota where they encountered no air activity, making five strafing runs on the airfield and barracks.

At 1502 ComCruDiv 14, Rear Admiral Wilder D. Baker, came aboard the *Essex* from the destroyer *Ellet* to assume temporary duty as CTG 58.4 while Admiral Harrill was operated on for his acute appendicitis.

June 30 (D+15)–July 2 (D+17)

There were no strikes the last day of June as the *Essex* stood 140 miles west of Saipan. In the early morning of July 1, two night fighters conducted eight strafing runs on Rota Town and a mill. The next day the *Essex* provided CAP and ASP patrols, with no strike or intruder missions.[20]

July 3 (D+18)

At 0615 the *Essex* sighted the fueling group and by 0800 the task group was fueling, including the destroyers of DesRon 12. A Rota strike was launched at 0734 with 12 fighters, 13 Helldivers and 7 Avengers. Over the target, fighters strafed sugar mills at Rota Town, a small boat area and gun emplacements, as the torpedo bombers hit a sugar mill leaving it on fire. The dive-bombers destroyed a fuel dump and with their bombs started fire to three buildings.

The fueling operations were completed at 1245 and Task Group 58.4 set course for Eniwetok for rearmament and provisioning. The task group anchored at their destination on July 6 at 0930. Eniwetok, on the northern end of the Marshall Islands, was a new base with a larger anchorage than Majuro, and some 660 miles closer to Saipan (1017 miles). After the Americans had taken the atoll in February 1944, they started developing it as a major naval logistics base.[21]

At Eniwetok Admiral Harrill departed and was replaced by Rear Admiral Gerald F. Bogan on July 13. It seems that Harrill's departure was no great loss to many for he was criticized for his "vacillating"[22] before making a decision. Disrespectfully nicknamed "Whiskey"[23] McCampbell recalled his understanding of the admiral's departure. A week after the Marianas Turkey Shoot, Harrill developed a stomach ache. Captain Ofstie asked about the Admiral Harrill, with the chief surgeon responding that he might have appendicitis. Ofstie ordered the surgeon to take out Harrill's appendix to get rid of him. A few days later, hearing that Harrill was considering whether he would leave or stay aboard, Captain Ofstie ordered Harrill to be confined to the senior officer's room in sick bay. Eventually when they arrived at Eniwetok, Harrill decided to leave the ship and take shore duty back in the States. It seemed that nobody missed him.[24]

Task Group 58.4 reorganized with the carrier *Princeton* (CVL-23) replacing *Cowpens*. Task Group 58.4 now consisted of the flagship *Essex*, CVL *Langley*, CVL *Princeton*, three light cruisers, one anti-aircraft light cruiser, and seven destroyers. Air Group 27 aboard the *Princeton* was a welcome addition to the task group. It had done well on June 19 and became the most successful light carrier fighter squadron in the fleet with thirty victories.

The most significant thing that happened at Eniwetok for Air Group 15 was receiving the first new Grumman F6F-5. The key difference with this fighter over the F6F-3s was their new R-2800–10W engine, which made them so much faster than the F6F-3s. This created real problems during combat missions because the F6F-3s could not keep up with the new F6F-5s. McCampbell traded in for a new F6F-5, naming her the "Minsi II."[25] The new fighter had distinctive glossy sea blue paint, replacing the old "tri-color"[26] scheme with upper surfaces painted sea blue, and intermediate blue with the lower surfaces painted white.

VB-15 also received new replacement SB2C-3 Helldivers for the old worn out SB2C-1Cs. These new aircraft had four-bladed propellers, and a more powerful engine, the R-2600–20 Twin Cyclone. Now the takeoffs were not as harrowing as the old dips toward the sea off the ramp. Because the Hellcats could carry two 1,000-pound bombs, with the new ones also handling six 5-inch rockets, the number of Helldivers was reduced to 24 from 36. The extra pilots were transferred to VF-15 to assume fighter-bomber roles.

The replenishment of the *Essex* took four days of continuous loading, with the carrier taking on 285 tons of provisions and 420 tons of bombs and ammunition. The ship was unable to obtain all the fresh and frozen provisions it was entitled to and ended up 156 tons short on departure. The lack of adequate boat transportation made it difficult to get many of the small items required.

There were so many ships in the anchorage (several hundred), there was a real shortage of boats. With a crew of 3,000 officers and men, there were only two motor whaleboats available to transport men on liberty. With a borrowed LCVP and their two whaleboats, they were able to have shore leave for a few hours for 21 percent of the crew.

Air Group 15 was glad to see returning shipmates, Ensign Thomas A Woods and Radioman Archie McPherson, who had been shot down in their dive-bomber during the Marcus Island raids. A new arrival, Ensign Jack Taylor, had graduated from fighter training, but had missed the *Essex* sailing from Majuro by two days.[27]

Liberty at Eniwetok was not too bad, though some of the crew complained of the "forward area shore rations,"[28] with enlisted men only receiving two warm beers on the beach each day. AOM1/C Elmer Cordray wrote in his diary on July 11, "Went over on the beach here at Eniwetok swimming on a rotation party with Fergerson and Hoover. Water was swell. Ate dinner over there. Boy! Was it hot over there. Received two V-mails from Doris and a letter from the folks telling me about Ray Lamb's death."[29] McCampbell recalled, "We got ashore there once … they had set up a little bar on the beach; they called it an officers' club. You could get beer, and that's all; maybe pretzels."[30]

The initial phase of the Marianas Campaign for the *Essex* with Carrier Air Group 15 had started when the carrier had sailed out of Majuro in the Marshall's and came to an end when the carrier arrived at Eniwetok on July 6, 1944. During this first major engagement, Air Group 15 had flown a total of 1564 sorties, totaling 5216 flight hours. The distribution of sorties included 826 over enemy shore targets, 211 other offensive sorties involving Japanese shipping, interception and search missions, 508 defensive sorties guarding the Task Group, and 19 administrative sorties.

The *Essex* had dropped 2073 bombs on enemy targets, fired 217 rockets and shot 330,203 machine gun bullets at the enemy. The Air Group had shot down 104 Japanese aircraft, and destroyed 136 planes on the ground. McCampbell's team had lost 14 pilots and 7 aircrewmen killed or missing in action, as well as 2 pilots killed in accidents. They had lost 16 planes to enemy action and 7 aircraft due to operational events. Air Group 15 had utilized 387,700 gallons of aviation gasoline. During this phase, the *Essex* had sailed some 12,000 miles, while consuming a total of 1,735,000 gallons of fuel oil.[31]

The fighting on Saipan had been tough and deadly. Marine Captain David A. Kelleher, who had fought on Saipan from the very first day said in a letter, "David, my boy, the Marines will win this war yet. I have never experienced such a battle. I have never seen such skill in fighting. I have never seen anything more of a tribute to our collective worth to the nation than the ugly, smoking profile of Saipan ... and the way the Marines took it—confidently, carefully, proudly—was something no one here can ever know. This battle was transcendent."[32] Captain Kelleher died on July 25 on Tinian eleven days after he wrote this letter.[33]

On the morning of July 10, the official flag raising ceremony was held at Charan Kanoa, the sight of the first landing and the headquarters of General Holland Smith. Saipan had been taken, but not without the cost of many lives. Of the 46,426 Marines and 20,035 Army troops that took part in the operation, 3,426 were killed and 13,099 were wounded. Some 23,811 Japanese soldiers were buried on Saipan, with 1780 prisoners interned (included 921 Japanese). There were also 14,560 civilians interned by August 5.

General Holland Smith remarked, "I have always considered Saipan the decisive battle of the Pacific offensive's administrative Pearl Harbor ... the naval and military heart and brain of Japanese defense strategy."[34] The German naval attaché at Tokyo later remarked, "Saipan was really understood to be a matter of life and death. About that time they began telling the people the truth about the war."[35]

13

Supporting Landings
on Guam and Tinian

"the perfect amphibious operation in the Pacific War."[1]

On July 14, 1944, Task Group 58.4 sailed out of Eniwetok anchorage in company with Task Group 58.3. The course was set directly toward Guam, and by July 17, the *Essex* arrived within support range to take up a position 66 miles on a bearing 125° from Guam. With TG 58.4 now operating from the southeast of Guam, the other three task groups took up stations to the southwest, west and north of the island.

July 18

The initial mission for Task Group 58.4 was in support of pre-landing operations using "repeated deck load strikes coordinated with attacks of the other TG's, and in accordance with target assignments by CTG 53."[2] After topping off the destroyers, on July 18 the first strike was off the deck at 0745 to attack Japanese installations around Agat town. By 0945 Guam could be seen from the *Essex* just 28 miles away. There would be three more missions during the day, none with any Japanese air action.

McCampbell took one strike group out that day to destroy four coastal defense guns, but he was unable to locate them. The dive-bombers on this strike were led by Lieutenant Roger F. Noyes. They were directed to destroy positions at Banji Point on the west coast of Guam and on the Aluton and Yona Islands off the coast that could be used to fire on the landing troops on the day of the invasion, planned for July 21. In this case, photo interpreters had discovered some machine gun installations, but Noyes and his pilots could not find them. Without definite targets, they decided to conduct area bombing with their 100-, 250- and 500-pound bombs.

The Avengers attacked Bangi Point and the islands, and with their rockets and 100-pound bombs, they hit any building they found in Agat town. During the next strike, the fighters strafed trenches running from Agat town to Faepi Point, hit buildings and destroyed a bridge. The bombers dropped bombs and strafed on what they thought were light anti-aircraft guns near Bangi Point. The general word at the intelligence debrief was that the island was devastated.

On the second strike Ensign Otto Bleech in his Avenger was hit by an anti-aircraft shell in his wing fuel tank. He jettisoned his bombs, closed his bomb bay doors and saw his oil pressure drop to zero. His hydraulic systems went dead, and his radio was out. The engine slowed down and then froze up.

Bleech alerted his two crewmen and had the radioman come up into the second cockpit and brace against the armor plating facing aft. Bleech then made a perfect dead stick water landing at 75 miles per hour. They all evacuated the plane and loaded into the life raft in ten seconds, and fifteen seconds later watched their damaged Avenger sink out of sight. Thankfully, they were rescued and made it back to the *Essex* that day.

In an accident, an ammunition box fell during a flight and tore a hole in the vertical fin of a Helldiver. The pilot was able to make it back aboard.

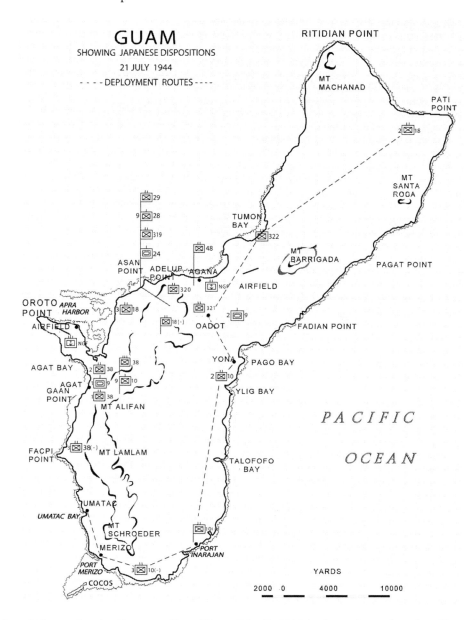

Map of Guam, showing Japanese dispositions, July 21, 1944 (redrawn image based on Henry I. Shaw, Jr., Bernard C. Nalty, Edwin T. Turnbladh, *History of U.S, Marine Corps Operations in World War II, Volume III: Central Pacific Drive*, p. 445, ibiblio.org/hyperwar/USMC/III/USMC-III-IV-1.html).

July 19

Early the next morning DesDiv 23, with destroyers *Lardner*, *Lansdowne* and *McCalla*, joined the task group. The *Lansdowne* was fueled before 0726, with the first strike off about an hour later. Air Group 15 conducted four more strikes over Guam. The planes had continued problems finding any worthwhile targets as they tried to hit pillboxes, mobile artillery and even trucks. In what could be called saturation bombing, they dropped bombs on suspected locations of gun positions and trenches around Bangi Point. Struggling to find any targets, some sorties came back with bombs, which had to be jettisoned before landing aboard. The last strike came aboard at 1643.[3]

July 20

On July 20, from 95 miles off Guam at bearing 125°, the *Essex* launched five harassment strikes over Guam attacking road junctions, culverts and narrow bridges. These targets were selected, as were those on the previous days, in an effort to destroy anything that would aid the Japanese forces in holding back the approaching American attack to take back Guam.

Though the Japanese air threat was non-existent over the targets, even the generally light anti-aircraft fire could still prove deadly. During the second strike of the day to hit bridges and the east shore road, VB-15 attacked beach defenses on southeastern Guam. An SB2C piloted by Lieutenant Niles Raymond Siebert was hit as he winged over to dive on a bridge. At 4,000 feet the Helldivers' left wing was blown off and the plane spun in and exploded on impact, killing Siebert and his Aviation Radioman, 1st Class Leon G. Murray.[4]

John Bridgers had roomed almost two years with Lieutenant Niles Raymond Siebert in a Quonset hut at Creed's Field, in tents at New Caledonia and Guadalcanal, and in sea cabins on the *Saratoga*, *Hornet* and *Essex*. Bridgers recalled that his death was like losing a brother.[5]

July 21 (W-Day)

On July 21 the landings on Guam began under the overall command of Rear Admiral Richard Conolly with his Southern Attack Force (Task Force 53). Conolly also served as TG 53.1 as commander of the Northern Attack Group. The Southern Attack Group TG 53.2 was commanded by Rear Admiral Reifsnider. The Marine forces were under the command of Major General Roy S. Geiger.

The invasion had been originally planned for June 18, but was postponed by the appearance of Ozawa's Mobile Fleet and by the fierce fighting on Saipan. Guam was the most important of the Marianas since it had been an American possession for forty years before the war. The local Chamorros of Guam had suffered under Japanese rule. The new rulers changed the name to Omiya Jima, allowed only Japanese to be spoken, closed schools and churches, rationed food, and employed them into forced labor to build Japanese airfields and put many of them in concentration camps.

Under Admiral Conolly as TG 53.1, the first landings hit the beach on Blue Beach on the Asan Beaches in the Northern Sector at 0829 with 20,328 men of the 3rd Marine Division. In the Southern Sector, landings took place on the beach in Agat Bay by 9,886 men of the 1st Provisional Marine Brigade. The Agat Bay beach was located between Agat Town and Bangi Point, overlooked by the high cliffs of Orote Peninsula and two islets, Neye and Yona.[6]

McCampbell led the first strike off at 0625 to the beaches at Asan, Agat and Orote. The fighters strafed the entire area between Agat town and Bangi Point, and dropped anti-personnel bombs. The Helldivers also strafed and bombed the beaches, while the Avengers focused on the wooded areas above the beaches, firing rockets into the trees where Japanese troops might be located.

There was no anti-aircraft activity during the first strike or the second. The second mission, attacking guns, an observation post and a bridge, came in low and dropped delayed action bombs to avoid potential concussions. The third and last strike of the day attacked the southernmost village on Guam, Merizo, and the caves and guns at Talofofo Bay, landing back aboard the *Essex* at 1325.

Though pre-invasion missions were predetermined strikes on assigned targets, most of the support operations once the troops had landed were called in strikes in which the Air Support Commander would direct attacks from planes on station nearby and available for action. Became of the need to be flexible in selection of weapons for call strikes, the planes had to be adaptable for rockets, fixed guns for strafing, incendiary and fragmentation bombs, and for a variety of weights of general purpose bombs with instantaneous and delay fuses.

July 22

At 0648 on July 22, the task group rendezvoused with fueling group TU 50.17 some 135 miles SE of Guam. The *Essex* launched several CAP and ASP patrols, and took on fuel from the fleet oiler *Tapahannock* from 1353 to 1730. During the evening, the *Essex* moved to Tinian, and was positioned bearing 115° some 86 miles off the island. The mission was to protect the landing forces ready to invade Tinian.[7]

On this same day, a mission from Isely Field on Saipan by Army Air Force pilots over Tinian tested a new and deadly weapon developed by a team of Harvard University chemists led by Louis Fieser. These first thirty bombs dropped in the Pacific Theater were filled with napalm containing a mixture of jellied gasoline and "coprecipitated aluminum salts of naphthenic and palmitc acids,"[8] creating a sticky incendiary substance that burned off vegetation and killed troops. The test was "inconclusive and variations on the mixture were later made."[9]

July 23

Commander McCampbell took the first strike on July 23 with ninety-two planes from the *Essex* and *Langley*. They attacked artillery and AA positions, pillboxes, a radio station and villages where Japanese troops were expected to be found. They also hit railroad tracks that wined through the sugar cane fields to the mill.

Twenty-seven Helldivers from VB-15, led by their squadron commander Mini, attacked through low clouds and were forced to glide their bombs in rather than their usual dive-bombing attack scheme, increasing their chances of being hit by anti-aircraft fire. Ensign Frederick C. Talbot's plane was hit and he had to land at Isely Field on Saipan to get it repaired. Lieutenant (junior grade) Clifford Russell Jordan and his gunner, ARM2c Stanley N. Whitby, were dropping their bombs on gun emplacements when they were hit by an AA shell that exploded, sending shrapnel into the engine and fuselage. It also shattered Jordan's right leg and hit him in the right arm.

In severe pain, Jordan was able to level off his Avenger as he headed out to sea. They were smoking and losing altitude, forcing Jordan to make a water landing. They bounced off a wave and hit the second wave straight on, which threw the pilot into the gun sight, knocking him out. With seawater rapidly filling the plane, Whitby got out of his harness, exited his rear cockpit, moved forward on the wing, unfastened Jordan's seat belt and dragged his unconscious pilot out of his cockpit.

After inflating Jordan's Mae West life preserver, Whitby pushed his pilot off the wing and into the sea, and jumped in. The tail of their Helldiver came up just before sinking. This activity had taken just thirty seconds. Fortunately, Navy UDT frogmen were clearing mines nearby and brought their boat over to rescue the two aviators. The frogmen took the flyers to the nearest ship, the USS *Tennessee* (BB-43) that had been shelling the beach. After the twenty-minute boat ride, Jordan and Whitby were taken aboard where doctors in sickbay determined that Lieutenant Jordan needed to be transferred to a hospital ship, the USS *Hope*. Whitby was transferred to a destroyer the next day.

On the return flight from strike one, Ensign A.G. Slack's F6F lost power on final approach to the *Essex* and had to make a water landing nearby. He was rescued by a destroyer. There was AA damage to three Avengers over Tinian, which was repaired after they landed aboard.

The second strike of the day launched at 1400, likewise, with *Essex* and *Langley* planes. They again were called on to hit suspected targets that yielded no visible results. The third strike at 1544 attacked and destroyed a sugar mill and attacked Tinian town. There were no buildings standing at the end of the day in the town.[10]

July 24 (J-Day)

This was the invasion day for the island of Tinian. Though the island was only 10.5 miles long, with a maximum width of five miles, it was deemed to be an outstanding location to launch the new B-29 to bomb Japan. There was already a first-class airfield with two 4,700 feet runways, with three more under construction. There was also enough level land to expand as required.

The general concept and operational plan for the Tinian landing was developed by Vice Admiral Richmond K. Turner's staff en route to the Marianas from Pearl Harbor. Approved by Lieutenant General Holland M. Smith, the plan called for the Northern (Saipan) Attack Force (TF 52) to deploy from the shore of Saipan to land on the shore at the northern part of Tinian. The ground troops for the invasion were commanded Major General Harry Schmidt USMC, with Major General Clifton B. Cates heading up the 4th Marine Division and Major General Thomas E. Watson commanding the 2nd Marine Division. From aboard the *Rocky Mount*, General Schmidt issued the Northern Troops and Landing Force (NTLF) Operation Plan 30–44e on July 13.[11]

In the rainy early evening before the landing, the assault troops of the 4th Marine Division loaded into 37 LSTs at the pier at Tanapag Harbor on Saipan and at 1800 moved out to their line of departure some 3,000 yards off the designated White Beaches on the western side of Tinian. Later, in the darkness at 0330 on July 24, the 2nd Marine Division loaded aboard their transports at anchor off Charan Kanoa, Saipan.

A short time before sunrise the transports moved out on their secret mission to a position four miles offshore from Tinian Town with their escorts, the battleship *Colorado*, light cruiser *Cleveland* and destroyers *Remey*, *Norman Scott*, *Wadleigh*, and *Monssen*. At 0612 the captain of the transport *Calvert* lowered his landing craft and embarked the Marines. At 0630 all of *Calvert*'s twenty-two boats were loaded and ready to head into

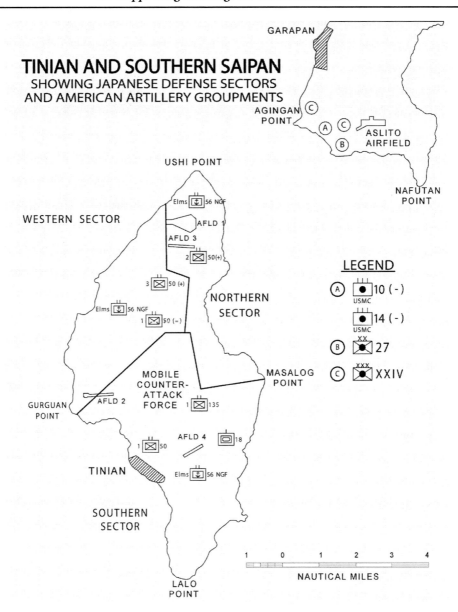

Map of Tinian and Southern Saipan, showing Japanese defense sectors and American Artillery Groupments (redrawn image based on Henry I. Shaw, Jr., Bernard C. Nalty, Edwin T. Turnbladh, *History of U.S, Marine Corps Operations in World War II, Volume III: Central Pacific Drive*, p. 357, ibiblio.org/hyperwar/USMC/III/USMC-III-IV-1.html).

shore. Navy aircraft by 0700 were bombing and strafing the Tinian Town area as the Marines on each of the transports climbed down the cargo nets to their landing craft.

At 0730 the *Calvert*'s coxswains drove their landing craft toward the shore under naval gunfire, but had to turn the boats around and reform for a second run-in due to friendly naval gunfire. A second run was started which came to within 400 yards of the beach before turning around and heading back to the *Calvert*. All the troops and landing craft were recovered by 1000, and the transports sailed to the White Beaches an hour later.

While the feint landing had fooled the Japanese, unfortunately for the American escort warships, air reconnaissance photos had failed to notice three Japanese 6-inch naval guns located behind Sunharon Harbor. When the *Colorado* moved to within 3,200 yards of Tinian Town at 0740, she sustained 22 direct hits in fifteen minutes which killed 43 sailors and wounded another 176. The destroyer *Norman Scott* was hit by six shells and suffered the loss of 19 men killed and 47 injured. Both ships were able to sail back to Saipan under their own power.

While units of the 2nd Marine Division were carrying out the Tinian Town feint, the 4th Marine Division sent in the first wave of 24 LVTs to White Beach 1 at 0730. Meanwhile, the remaining 16 LVTs headed in abreast the first wave toward White Beach 2. The beaches were unusually narrow compared to most amphibious landings, being less than 200 yards wide. The Marines encountered light Japanese resistance upon landing and they were able to make the beach secure and beyond as planned by days end.[12]

From 58 miles off Tinian at 0529 that day the *Essex* Air Group 15 launched to join up with *Princeton*'s aviators to provide a full strike ahead of the landings on the beaches and Japanese targets like the ammunition dump and village. The second mission under direction of the Air Support Commander hit gun positions on the cliffs and woods above the beaches. After the mission, on approaching the *Essex* to land, Ensign David H. Johnson, Jr., was waved off because his wheels were not down, and as he began to turn, the F6F stalled, rolled onto its back and crashed into the sea in a nose-down configuration. He never came up.

The third mission of the day over Tinian was focused on close support of the troops during which TG 15 planes hit mortar positions, pillboxes and trucks. The Japanese had done an excellent job camouflaging their gear, making it extremely difficult for even low flying attackers to identify targets. On one low-flying run down at 300 feet by an Avenger attacking with rockets and bombs, the pilot saw two coastal guns that were camouflaged to blend perfectly with the surrounding cliff location.

There were also two call strikes that day to Guam and Rota. The Helldivers were assigned to find and destroy hidden gun positions on Guam, but had little success until Lieutenant Frank West found a gun and was able to make a direct hit on it. He also dropped bombs on a railway junction, destroying the tracks and switches.[13]

July 25

The next day Task Group 58.4 took over supporting the Marianas while the other three task groups sailed to missions out of the area. On bearing 090° from Guam off 100 miles, the *Essex* launched twelve Helldivers on the first call strike of the day at 0529 to attack. They were joined with Avengers and fighters from the *Langley* and *Princeton* to attack troop barracks, as well as the main roads south and east of Agana. The second call strike launched at 0900 to hit guns in revetments on Orote Point.

The third call strike to Guam with twelve Helldivers (with planes from *Langley* and *Princeton*) turned out to be a long one. They launched at 1228 and were assigned to Sumay and the nearby area. On the return home, all the planes were very low on fuel after surviving a 4.5-hour mission. Lieutenant Henry H. Kramer in his Helldiver touched down on the *Essex* flight deck, but since his hook would not come down, he was waved off. On the second try the LSO felt his approach was too ragged and gave him another wave off. On his third approach he ran out of gas and ditched. He and his gunner were rescued by a destroyer.

The fourth call strike mission of the day was made by eight Avengers conducting area bombing on Guam, landing aboard at 1827.

July 26

The day started 110 miles off Guam bearing 090° with another call strike at 0530 to hit any troop concentrations on Neye Island using eight Helldivers. Intelligence was concerned that the Japanese might be planning an attack from Rota, so they directed the Task Group to hit the Rota airstrip. The *Essex* sent ten fighters off at 1300 with other planes from *Langley* and *Princeton* to drop half their bombs on the runway with 12-hour delay fuses, and the other half with instant fuses. They attacked in pairs, with each pair consisting of an F6F and Helldiver. The mission landed aboard the *Essex* at 1553.

July 27

On this day the task group carriers supported ground troops during two strikes. The first strike was along a ridge southeast of Agana and at a quarry where the enemy had guns. Ensign J.C. Crowley's Avenger was hit at Agana Field by an anti-aircraft shell that blew off six inches of his left elevator, and broke his windshield covering the .30 caliber machine gun. The gunner was hit by flying glass.

While another Avenger was over the airfield, turret gunner William G. Peppel saw a Japanese aircraft hidden by the trees. The pilot made a run on it and fired two rockets, but apparently missed his target. It appeared that the plane was moved by one of the rocket explosions so they made another run and fired shots from their turret gun, which set the aircraft afire. The *Essex* planes landed back aboard the carrier at 1002.

On the second strike to Rota, launching at 1259, all but one of the planes hit railways leading to the airfield, as well as nearby buildings and warehouses. Ensign Lewis R. Timberlake Jr., and his crew were not so lucky. On takeoff the torpedo bomber lost manifold pressure at 150 feet altitude as the engine began to cut out and then it stalled. The plane made a flat water landing at 70 knots. The turret gunner, Goren, immediately got on the wing and made his way to the radio compartment hatch to see the water rising quickly around his injured and half-conscious radio operator, ARM2c James D. McAllister. He opened the hatch, unbuckled his safety belt and pulled him out of the water.

Ensign Timberlake, also injured, inflated the Mae West as Goren held McAllister. They got McAllison into the life raft and the three of them waited until they were rescued by a Dumbo (air-sea rescue version of a B-17). The wounded radioman had a compound fracture of the left leg. Timberlake suffered a "laceration of upper mid-lip with contusion to upper jaw and teeth."[14]

Seven minutes after the last of three patrols landed at 1820, the *Essex* left the task group and sailed for Saipan escorted by destroyers *Stanly* and *Ausburne*.

July 28

At 0617 the next morning, the *Essex* and her two escorts anchored at Tanapag Harbor, Saipan. Replenishment bombs and other ammunition were loaded aboard the *Essex* until 1757 when the carrier sailed with escorts *Ausburne* and *McCalla* to rejoin Task Group 58.4.

July 29

The *Essex* rendezvoused with the task group 51 miles on a bearing 80° from Guam and refueled with Task Unit 50.17. That day two strikes were sent out to hit supply areas, gun positions, pillboxes and troop concentrations on the Orote Peninsula, including the nearby Orote airfield.[15]

July 30–31

On July 30, Task Force 58 reorganized as they rendezvoused 115 miles off Guam. TG 58.4 saw the *Princeton* depart for Eniwetok, and reformed with the *Essex, Langley,* battleships *Iowa, Indiana, Alabama,* and *New Jersey* and cruiser *San Diego,* DesDivs 103 and 104. The light carrier *Belleau Wood* and the battleship *Washington* joined them later. There were no strikes on the 30th or 31st.

From August 1 through August 8 the *Essex* Carrier Air Group 15 flew air support strikes over Guam as called by the Air Support Commander. There was an average of three strikes per day during that period, of which Commander McCampbell flew occasional missions. In his last combat report on the Guam/Tinian Campaign, McCampbell wrote of the poor pilot morale as a result of those "tiresome"[16] support missions that had seemly no visible evidence of success.

Grumman F6F Hellcat fighter undergoing maintenance on board USS *Essex* (CV-9) anchored off Saipan on July 30, 1944. This plane is "Minsi II," belonging to the *Essex* Air Group Commander, David McCampbell, USN (Official U.S. Navy Photograph # 80-G-373647, National Archives collection).

At 1458 on August 7, Captain C.W. Weber relieved newly promoted Rear Admiral R.A. Ofstie as the *Essex* Commanding Officer. At 1501 on August 10, 1944, the *Essex* with Task Group 58.4 departed Guam and set a course to Eniwetok. They reached their destination and anchored on August 13.

During the operational period of 31 days between July 14 and August 13, Air Group 15 had flown 1063 sorties against shore targets, 421 sorties defending the task group, 205 training and administrative sorties, for a grand total of 1689 sorties. They had dropped 2800 bombs and fired 592 rockets. No enemy planes were shot down, and one confirmed plane was destroyed on the ground. The losses were two aviators killed in action, and four lost in operational accidents. The *Essex* had traveled 11,636 miles using 1,680,990 gallons of fuel. The aircraft had consumed 348,800 gallons of aviation gasoline.[17]

On August 1, eight days after the landings of J-Day, as the Marines reached the cliffs overlooking Marpo and Lao Points, General Harry Schmitt announced that Tinian had been secured. In fact, some Japanese soldiers were holed up in caves and continued to fight for another three months.

Of the garrison of 8,039 on Tinian, the Japanese lost 5,542 killed, 2,265 missing and 252 captured. Of the 41,364 Americans engaged in the fight for Tinian, the Marines lost 326 killed and 1,593 wounded. Some 13,000 Japanese civilians were interned on Tinian, but as many as 4,000 had been killed by suicide or murdered by Japanese soldiers and during combat activities.

General Holland Smith declared Tinian to be "the perfect amphibious operation in the Pacific War."[18] Spruance called it "The most brilliantly conceived and executed amphibious operation in World War II."[19] As soon as the airfield had been secured, some 15,000 Seabees began construction of six 7,900-foot runways. The Army Air Force's B-29 Superfortress began bombing Japanese targets beginning October 28, 1944, with the first mission over the mainland of Japan on November 24. On August 6, 1945, the B-29 *Enola Gay* took off from the North Field runway on Tinian, flew six hours and then dropped an atomic bomb on Hiroshima, Japan, that killed 30 percent of the city's population.[20]

On August 10 at 1130 General Geiger declared that organized resistance on Guam had ceased. At that moment, Admiral Nimitz with General Vandegrift was flying in over Saipan, and Admiral Spruance, with Lieutenant General Holland M. Smith, were sailing into Apra Harbor on the western side of Guam aboard the cruiser *Indianapolis.* As it turned out, the announcement was somewhat premature, for it was not until the afternoon of the 12th that Japanese General Hideyoshi Obata's last command post was taken near Mount Mataguac. The General and his troops were all killed or committed suicide.

According to General Smith's *Report on Forager* dated September 1, 1944, there were 10,693 Japanese killed on Guam, and only 98 prisoners taken. On the three-week battle, the American forces lost 1,290 killed, with the 3rd Marine Division losing the most men with 679. There were 145 more missing in action and 5,648 wounded in action.

On August 12, 1944, the islands of Saipan, Tinian and Guam were under American control. Operation Forager and the Marianas Campaign were at an end.[21]

14

Stalemate II:
Palau, Southern Philippines

"As if in a daze we saw them catch fire and burn."[1]

During the two-week rest period for Task Force 58 at Eniwetok, Nimitz discussed the fleet reorganization with Mitscher, which would occur on August 26. The Fifth Fleet became the Third Fleet, with Admiral William F. Halsey, Jr., relieving Admiral Spruance. Mitscher's Task Force 58 changed to Task Force 38. The task groups were reformed with changes in carrier assignments as follows:

TG 38.1   *Hornet, Cowpens, Wasp* and *Monterey*
TG 38.2   *Bunker Hill, Intrepid, Cabot* and *Independence*
TG 38.3   *Essex, Lexington, Langley, Princeton*
TG 38.4   *Enterprise, Franklin, Belleau Wood* and *San Jacinto*

As part of the reorganization, on August 12, 1944, Rear Admiral Frederick C. Sherman relieved Rear Admiral Alfred E. Montgomery as Commander of Task Group 38.3 (Com-CarDivONE). Admiral Sherman had paid his dues as an experienced and a highly decorated officer. After the sinking of the *Lexington* in the Battle of the Coral Sea in May 1942, he was promoted to Rear Admiral and served as Assistant Chief of Staff for the COMINCH, Admiral Ernest King. By October 1942, he was back at sea in the Pacific as Commander of Carrier Task Force 16, and soon took over Carrier Division Two. He led his carrier forces on a series of raids in the South and Central Pacific, damaging or destroying 46 Japanese ships and some 350 planes from November 1943 to February 1944. Though he was honored with three Navy Crosses, he was known to have an abrasive personality that hurt his career.[2] Admiral John Towers assessed him as being, "Self-interest. Very unpopular with aviators because of intolerance. Able but not for high command because of personality absolutely precludes establishment of wholehearted loyalty."[3]

The updating of Pacific War Strategy regarding the Philippines was generally firmed up in the Washington Planning Conferences of February–March 1944, which resulted in actions planned for post–Marianas operations. The Joint Chiefs of Staff desired the estab-lishment of a line from the Palau Islands to Yap, Ulithi, Morotai and Halmahera. General MacArthur's Southwest Pacific Forces, under Vice Admiral T.C. Kinkaid, would handle Morotai and Halmahera, while Vice Admiral Halsey's Western Pacific Task Forces of the Third Fleet would have responsibility for Peleliu Island, Yap and Ulithi.

Back on May 29, 1944, Vice Admiral Halsey, as Commander of the Third Fleet, had been directed to begin planning and preparations to take the Palau group. The Western

Caroline Islands were important to gain control of the remaining link between the Central and the Southwest Pacific Force, which would give the Allies a "direct line of advance westward to the eastern approaches of the Philippines and the Formosa-China coasts."[4] Taking the Palau Island and Ulithi was important as the forward base for naval operations to invade the Philippines. The operation plan was first called "Stalemate,"[5] but after the Saipan operations had taken so long to complete, the original order was canceled and a new plan, Stalemate II, was issued on July 7. Stalemate II called for a D-day of September 15, with initial simultaneous landings on Peleliu Island in the Palua group, and on Morotai Island some 480 miles to the southwest.[6]

While at Eniwetok, McCampbell received the replacement Hellcat for the troubled Minsi II. After a full checkout, it was named the "Minsi III"[7] which he would fly for the rest of his deployment aboard the *Essex*.

On the evening before leaving, Admiral Sherman met with McCampbell and congratulated him for his success as a fighter pilot. As the meeting closed, Sherman reminded him that his job was not being a fighter pilot, but was to command an air group with total responsibly for carrier air operations and target coordination on the missions he led. Sherman clearly stated that there was to be no more "Zero fever,"[8] although he could defend himself or his fellow airmen in his group if attacked. McCampbell responded with a compliant, "Aye, aye, sir."[9]

Palau Islands

After two weeks of replenishing Task Force 38 ships in preparation for the upcoming operations, on August 29 Mitscher streamed out of Eniwetok with Task Groups 38.1, 38.2, and 38.3 and set a course to the Palaus some 700 miles southwest of Guam. Task Group 38.1 sailed northwest for three days of strikes at the Chichi Jima in the Bonins, and to the south at Yap, Ulithi, Ngulu and then at the Palaus.

The *Essex* sailed at 0817 from Eniwetok in the Marshall Islands as Rear Admiral Sherman's flagship for Task Group 38.3 in company with carriers *Lexington*, *Langley*, *Princeton*; AA cruiser *Reno*, and nine destroyers of DesRon 55. The course was set toward the fueling rendezvous at sea prior to attacks against the Palau Islands in accordance with Operation Order ComCarDivONE No. 1–44 dated August 25, 1944.

On September 2 with high and scattered cumulus clouds above and infrequent rain showers, the task group rendezvoused with the Task Groups 30.7 and 30.8 fleet oilers approximately 1,000 miles southeast of Palau Islands and began fueling on a southeasterly course. The next morning the oilers departed as fueling was completed. TG 38.3 set course for the initial launching position and was joined by CruDiv 13 consisting of *Santa Fe*, *Mobile*, and *Birmingham* with four destroyers of DesDiv 100.

On September 6 (D-9 Day) the task group topped off the destroyers and prepared to launch their first strikes from 265 miles southeast of the Palau Islands. Commander McCampbell led a major fighter sweep over the Palau Islands with ninety-six planes from TG 38.3 plus planes from carriers *Intrepid*, *Bunker Hill*, *Wasp* and *Hornet*. The focus of the sweep was on the airfields on Babelthuap and Ngesebus Islands. The *Essex*'s sixteen F6Fs launched at 1259 and strafed and bombed the runways and buildings, while the *Lexington* fighters dropped napalm.[10]

Operating from 65 miles south of Palau Islands on September 7, TG 38.3 conducted five strikes over Palau after a fighter sweep sent off at 0529, led by Commander J.F. Rigg as the new Commander Officer of VF-15. The strikes that day were at Peleliu at the airfield and facilities, as well as anti-aircraft gun positions. There was no air opposition on any of the missions.

The air group commander from the *Lexington* took out a strike force, which included *Essex* dive and torpedo bombers. McCampbell also led one strike out. During all the raids, it seemed to the attackers that the Japanese were only mildly engaged. The Task Group planes destroyed or damaged some enemy planes on the ground, but they did not come up to fight.

After one raid, there was a mishap when an *Essex* Avenger pilot apparently misjudged the closing distances and nearly hit the tail of another TBF plane while forming up to return to the carrier. The last strike of the day cratered the runways, destroyed a radio station and hit several buildings. A total of 419 planes from the *Essex* and *Lexington* attacked Peleliu that day.

The following day there were three strikes over Palau from the *Essex* from 68 miles southwest of the islands. The first raid launched at 0645 with twenty F6Fs, eleven Helldivers and nine Avengers to attack targets at Peleliu and Babelthuap. The group hit all manner of targets including fuel dumps, warehouses, barracks and other buildings. A Helldivers gunner, Claude Joseph LaBorde, was the only wounded aircrewman, hit by 40mm shrapnel.

Commander Mini took the second strike off at 1043 to Peleliu, but en route he saw the beaches were clouded up. He decided to divert to attack Angaur Island where they encountered heavy anti-aircraft fire.

On the third strike of the day, as Lieutenant Henry H. Kramer in his F6F fighter-bomber released his bombs on anti-aircraft gun positions on Koror Island and began to pull up out of the dive, a fellow pilot saw a fire under his port wing. He called on the radio to warn Kramer. In response, Kramer jettisoned his belly fuel tank, but the fire spread to cover the wing, and was heading up to the cockpit. Kramer opened his cockpit canopy, but before he exited the fighter-bomber, he "did a wingover and went into a spin."[11] With flames spreading, the plane hit the water just off shore. Kramer was killed in the action, with no body recovered.

Over the western beaches at Peleliu, Lieutenant W.H. Harper and Lieutenant G.B. Webb were bombing and firing rockets in their Avengers, when they were hit by AA fire from the beach. Harper's plane caught fire, but he was able to make a water landing and get his crew into the life raft. Lieutenant Webb's plane headed south in a trail of smoke. Another pilot saw Webb jump out of the plane, but his two crewmen were still in the plane when it hit the water at a 15° angle as the right wing broke off. There were no survivors with the plane, but Lieutenant (junior grade) Axman dropped a life raft to Webb from his own TBF. Webb was later picked up by a lifeguard submarine.

A lifeguard submarine was fired on by the Japanese as it cruised off the coast helping to rescue pilots. The *Essex* sent Ensign C.W. Plant and Ensign Len S. Hamblin to provide fighter air cover over the submarine in a rescue. After the rescue, they were released to fly north to investigate oil slicks off Babelthuap. With nothing to report, they proceeded to strafe AA positions on Balelthuap, Koror and Malakai Islands. At about 1405 on an attack run, Ensign Hamblin was hit by AA fire and crashed into the sea. Ensign Plant circled the crash area until he was low on fuel, but saw no sign of Hamblin.[12]

With their missions completed, in the afternoon of the September 8, the *Essex* and the rest of Task Force 38 set a course to Mindanao in the southern Philippines for their next strikes. McCampbell later recalled that they didn't get much done at Palau because the Japanese were dug in, their planes were not on the fields, and the only action left was to strafe and bomb AA guns and a few buildings.[13]

Mindanao, Philippines

With the Palaus softened up for the scheduled invasion on September 15, the Allied strategy called for an invasion of Mindanao, the southernmost major island of the Philippines, in mid to late October 1944. The Japanese plan to defend the inner perimeter of their empire required the army to hold the Philippines, while the IJN strengthened their forces on Formosa for an anticipated naval engagement in the East China Sea or, perhaps, back in the Philippine Sea. Holding Formosa was critical because it allowed the Japanese to get reinforcements to the front lines from Japan. By this point in the war, the Japanese Army Air Force had already reinforced the southern Philippines.

The immediate plans for Mitscher's Task Carrier Forces was to prepare for the Mindanao invasion by clearing the Japanese from the air, destroy airfield installations and shipping, in that order. The *Essex* with TG 38.3 steamed at high speed to a pre-dawn launch position 50 miles off the northeast coast of Mindanao.

The first mission off that morning of September 9 for Air Group 15 was a fighter sweep over northeastern Mindanao led by Lieutenant Commander Rigg with sixteen Hellcats. As they came in, they spotted two Japanese Sally bombers. Rigg, with Lieutenant Bert Morris and Lieutenant R.W. Davis Jr., downed both Sallys. It was later discovered that the two enemy aircraft downed were actually Mitsubishi Ki-57-II transport variants of the Sally, known as the Topsy.

Rigg's fighters came in to escort the first strike from the *Essex* over the Lumbia and Cagayan airfields. *Lexington's* Air Group 19 and Air Group 15 attackers both arrived at Lumbia Field at 0715, to the complete surprise of the Japanese. The Helldivers and Avengers bombed and several minutes later Commander Mini saw ten Japanese planes on fire at Lumbia Airfield and another five burning at Cagayan Airfield.

The attackers hit fuel dumps, barracks and a massive tent being used to service planes. The bombers then departed the airfields and discovered a Japanese convoy of some thirty-five coastal freighters, trawlers and luggars off Mindanao at Bislig Bay loaded with fuel, ammunition and miscellaneous cargo. The fighters along with the bombers were able to sink a number of ships and left the other vessels burning.

McCampbell took out the second fighter sweep at 0600 over the five airfields including Del Monte and Lumbia. They encountered only two aircraft, a Mavis flying boat and two Sonia dive-bombers out on morning patrol. Lieutenant Baynard Milton shot down the Mavis and Ensign Plant nailed one of the Sonias.

After hitting the airfields, McCampbell took the sweep out to attack the previously discovered convoy at Bislig Bay again. They were able to leave additional ships and smaller vessels in flames. While on Lieutenant John Edmund Barry, Jr.'s attack run on a medium cargo trawler in the convoy ten miles north of Sanco Point, he strafed the vessel, causing a massive explosion that reached a height of 2,000 feet and blew the tail off Barry's F6F. The fighter somersaulted into the sea. Ensign W.R. Johnson observed the accident and reported that there was no evidence of the pilot. Lieutenant Barry's body was never recovered.

Lieutenant Commander Lambert of VT-15 led the second strike launching at 0858 with twelve fighters, eleven Helldivers and six Avengers to attack Del Monte Airfield and shipping in the vicinity. The bombers and fighters sank an escort ship off Cagayan Light, one cargo ship off Sipaca Point, as well as a large landing barge loaded with some 150 troops off Salay. Helldivers discovered a cargo ship and soon left it beached and in flames.

The fighters found no enemy aircraft, so they attacked the burning convoy while strafing any survivors. On his last pass over the convoy, Lieutenant Commander George C. Duncan, who led the fighters, opened his canopy and fired all his .38 caliber bullets at the enemy.

Aviation Radioman 2nd Class John Miller, flying in Lieutenant (junior grade) Calvin Platt's Helldiver, described the second strike that day on September 9 in his diary. The target for the morning was some Japanese installations on Mindanao Island in the Philippines. The planes in his Division Six launched at 0900 on their second mission along with Lieutenant Bridgers' Division Two with a total of twelve Helldivers. The total mission strike aircraft of SB2Cs, TBMs and F6Fs had 600 planes. They flew 120 miles over high mountains controlled by friendly Philippine guerrilla groups. If they were hit, they were told to bail out near the fires and smoke maintained by these guerrillas.

The strike group headed to a Japanese airfield on the other side of the island to attack Del Monte Field, Lumbia and the wharves and shipping at Surigao. They achieved complete surprise and destroyed aircraft on the ground, hangars and oil storage tanks, in addition to sinking a big tanker in the harbor.[14]

During the second strike mission on a strafing run, Helldiver pilot Lieutenant (junior grade) Scott Matthews and his gunner, Aviation Radioman 2nd Class Robert Kruger, were hit with heavy antiaircraft fire that started a fire in the starboard wing. The fire slowly went out leaving a large hole in the wing with significant internal damage. Matthews radioed his situation and fellow pilot John Bridgers came to escort him home after receiving permission from Commander Mini.

While Commander Mini took the rest of his squadron northwest and back toward the *Essex*, Matthews and Bridgers headed to the lifeguard submarine location in the Sula Sea west of Mindanao. Thirty minutes later Matthews and Bridgers arrived at the designated location, but there was no rescue submarine. Using the subs callsign "Lullaby Lane,"[15] Bridgers called the submarine several times, but received no response. Bridgers and Matthews discussed the situation and they decided to try getting Mathews' plane back to the *Essex*.

Matthews and Kruger threw everything they could out of the plane in an attempt to lighten it, including the machine guns. Flying configured as to achieve maximum range with minimum speed, they flew across the island while Matthews continued to leak hydraulic fluid. At dusk, Matthews and Bridgers arrived over the fleet, but since the Helldiver had lost the remaining hydraulic fluid, Matthews could not control his flaps or landing gear. He ditched astern of a plane guard destroyer as Bridgers circled overhead.

Once Matthews and Kruger were safely out of the Helldiver, Bridgers landed aboard the *Essex* to the cheers of the ships' crew and air group personnel. Bridgers noted that later, as he was leaving the wardroom, he was approached by the CAG and dressed down. He had been on the bridge when he had landed and was chewed out by the *Essex* captain because the ship was forced to maintain a straight-line course waiting for him to circle Mathews.

Bridgers explained that he had been with Mathews a long time and needed to see if he was ok. McCampbell replied that he couldn't have done anything anyway, and that the whole fleet was taking care of Mathews. Though McCampbell was angry, Bridgers was awarded the Distinguished Flying Cross for aiding his fellow aviator.[16]

McCampbell's fighters returned aboard before noon to replenish their fuel and ammunition. CAG 15 then led the third strike of the day with twenty fighters, eleven dive-bombers and six torpedo bombers. The mission target was Cagayan Bay, but on the way Lambert contacted McCampbell alerting him that all the shipping there had been sunk or was burning. CAG diverted the group to Surigao Strait, on the southern side of Leyte Island, where they hit dock facilities. The only Japanese aircraft found was a Mavis. Lieutenant Commander G.R. Crittenden and his wingman, Ensign W.R. Johnson climbed up and attacked the plane, with Crittenden getting the credit for the shot-down.[17]

As the night came, the Japanese assessed their losses. They recorded that some 300 American aircraft had attacked (actually the *Essex* alone launched 143 sorties) and that at Cagayan and Lumbia airfields outside Davao they had lost 70 planes, as well as a radar facility destroyed at San Agustin. A Japanese Air Force captain noted that morning at the Cagayan South airfield had the main Korean base force and leading units of the 66th Squadron present. He revealed that ten American bombers came in to attack the field at 0800 from 9,000 feet. These bombers rolled over and came down in a straight line to hit their planes and seaplanes moored at the base. The Japanese saw their aircraft burned and destroyed in front of them.[18]

The *Essex* Action Report noted that "maps prepared aboard the *Essex* proved adequate for cross-country navigation, pilots had difficulty in locating certain airfields (being totally unable to find a few) or identifying some of those which were located and attacked."[19] McCampbell complained about the lack of available maps during the Mindanao attacks. The only maps they had were from National Geographic. One recon mission over northern Mindanao called for attacks on six airfields that were not even on the chart. McCampbell briefed fighter pilots to go into an airfield with one division per airfield, and to count the number of planes and estimate the number they destroyed in their attack. McCampbell briefed that he did not know all the airfield were and regardless the divisions were to strafe or engage in air combat as necessary, He said to follow him, and he would select the airfield and targets to hit as they came up. He was confusing to them, but they complied.[20]

On September 10 at 0603, a contingent of twelve fighters on a fighter sweep led by Lieutenant Commander Rigg launched from the *Essex* to join a strike group led by the *Lexington's* CAG, Commander Theodore Hugh "Pedro"[21] Winters. The mission was to hit airfields in northern Mindanao at Macalajar Bay, Del Monte, Cagayan and Lumbia.

After strafing the airfield at Macalajar Bay, the fighters engaged a Japanese patrol plane, but Rigg was focusing his attention on his wingman, Ensign H.M. Foshee, who had been hit in his engine by AA fire over the field. With his engine failing, Foshee was able to limp out to sea far enough to be eligible to be picked up by the lifeguard submarine. Foshee ditched his plane as Lieutenant Overton reported his position to the rescue submarine and maintained cover over him until help arrived.

West of Del Monte Airfield, Rigg saw a Japanese Nakajima J1N1 Gekko twin-engine night fighter, known by the Allies as an Irving. The enemy fighter thought the fighters were friendly and wobbled his wings as a greeting. Quickly, the Japanese pilot discovered his error, and dived to escape the oncoming fighters and jettisoned his two 500-pound bombs. The F6F of Lieutenant (junior grade) George R. Carr overtook the Irving fighter and began firing.

Meanwhile, at 0730 both Lieutenant Richard W. Davis, Jr., and Ensign Howard C. Green attempted to engage the enemy plane, but they came too close together and suffered a violent collision with each other. Ensign Green's aircraft burst into flames and continued to burn all the way down to the crash one mile west of Del Monte Camp. Lieutenant Davis's fighter did not burn, but his cockpit was destroyed and the engine of his F6F fell out of the plane before crashing. No bodies were found, and they were both declared dead.

After firing several bursts, Lieutenant (junior grade) Carr shot down the Irving. A short while later over Macajalar Bay, Rigg spotted the second Irving fighter. To assist him, having lost Foshee as his wingman, Carr called in help from Lieutenant Strane's section. With nine Hellcats now approaching him, the Japanese pilot turned into Rigg and started firing at him. Rigg was able to fire a few bursts into the attacker as he sped past. Having no other safe direction to fly toward, the Irving turned back toward Rigg. Rigg reacted immediately, pulled up and around, and got on the fighters' tail. Rigg fired and hit the left engine, which broke out into flames. He hit the cockpit area, which sent the fighter into a vertical turn to the right from 200 feet before the starboard wing hit the water. The fighter cartwheeled across the sea surface, stopped abruptly and sank.

Just a few minutes after the fighter sweep had launched, the first strike from the *Essex* was catapulted with eleven fighters, seven Helldivers and five Avengers to attack the airfields. Lieutenant A. Singer found an enemy patrol plane and shot it down. After making a successful water landing, two Japanese survivors were able to exit the plane. The American fighters strafed the enemy airmen, which had become all too common on both side as the war continued.

Led by Lieutenant John Brodhead, the Helldivers mission was to hit shipping, but they did not find any around Cagayan and surrounding areas. Lieutenant (junior grade) Calvin Platt was hit by AA in his bomb bay, which caught on fire. He was able to open his bomb bay doors, jettisoned his bombs, and then dived. Platt was able to put out the fire, and headed back to the *Essex* for what was a safe landing. While the Helldivers bombed Cagayan Field, the Avengers used rockets and bombs to hit Del Monte Airfield and barracks. The strike landed aboard the *Essex* at 2149.

At 0834 Commander McCampbell led the second strike from the *Essex* with a dozen Hellcats, six Helldivers and two Avengers. The target was Surigao where they found the crated runways from the previous day's attack, and no Japanese air activity. Lieutenant Bert Morris took eight fighters to sweep Cagayan and Lumbia Airfields, where they found camouflaged fuel dumps in what looked like a wooded area. McCampbell's strike was back home to land at 1216.[22]

The *Essex* Second Action Report read, "After all visible planes and shipping in the northern Mindadao area had been either destroyed or thoroughly damage and after the fuel storage and docks at Surigao had been burned out, orders were received to withdraw immediately after the last strike on 10 September."[23] Thus, in the early afternoon, the *Essex* with Task Group 38.3 set an easterly course to the designated refueling position with elements of Task Group 30.8.[24]

15

Stalemate II:
First Visayas, Manila Strikes
and Second Visayas

"Get him off my tail."[1]

The morning of September 11, the *Essex* and Task Group 38.3 rendezvoused with Task Groups 30.7 and 30.8 some 300 miles east of Mindanao, and refueled on a course to the northwest. The carrier also took on replacement aircraft and new combat aircrews from the 7,800-ton escort carrier, *Nassau*. Late in the afternoon the battleships *Alabama*, *Indiana*, *Massachusetts*, *Washington*, and seven destroyers joined with the task group. The total strength of TG 38.3 included the carriers *Essex*, *Lexington*, *Langley* and *Princeton*, four battleships, the cruisers *Santa Fe*, *Birmingham*, *Mobile*, and *Reno* (CL-AA) and eighteen destroyers. The course was set to the initial strikes against the Central Philippines.

The Visayan Islands makes up the Central Philippines and includes the major islands of Panay, Negros, Cebu, Bohol, Leyte, Samar and Masbate. At 0800 on September 12 eight *Essex* fighters launched and soon joined with eight more fighters from the *Lexington* to sweep the airfields on the islands of Cebu, Mactan and Negros.

Over Cebu at 0915, the F6Fs dived down to 10,000 feet to sweep the airfield. The Japanese fighters on the runways and aprons, and taxiways were preparing to takeoff with their propellers turning. Lieutenant Commander Rigg's fighters were able to destroy most of the enemy planes as they strafed the enemy on their first pass. Two more passes hitting the aprons and taxiways took care of the remaining planes. The *Lexington* fighters had been flying cover when they came down to attack.

Meanwhile, five miles away from Cebu Airfield at Mactan Island's Open Airfield, the Japanese were getting airborne. Soon the sky was filled with enemy planes coming in to attack the American fighters. Rigg saw two Oscar fighters taking off at Mactan. He headed down to intercept as one enemy Oscar had just retracted its landing gear. Rigg fired and sent the plane looping and into the ground at the south end of the runway. Two other Oscars were flying together when Rigg shot one down, as the other one got away over the jungle.[2]

Continuing on, Rigg spotted another Oscar taking off back at Cebu Airfield. As the Japanese fighter lifted off the runway, Rigg used his six .50 caliber guns to cut the aircraft fuselage in half, aft of the cockpit, destroying the plane. Lieutenant Commander Rigg called it, "A beautiful sight."[3] The air battle was still not over even as he turned for home. Another Oscar was discovered flying at a low altitude between buildings in Cebu Town. Rigg attacked and downed the plane in the harbor at the end of the street.

Rigg found two *Lexington* fighters from VF-19 and joined with them. Another Oscar appeared, but they were unable to shot it down before the skilled Japanese pilot evaded them with a series of aerobatic maneuvers. The F6Fs returned to their respective carriers and landed.

Ensign Claude Plant, Jr., arrived at Cebu Airfield at 1030 and witnessed Rigg shooting down an Oscar. Soon Rigg heard a radio call from Plant pleading for help to "get him off my tail."[4] Rigg and several fellow pilots saw Plant being pursued by an Oscar and proceeded to swoop down to support their colleague. Rigg fired from long range to let the Japanese pilot know he was near, and the enemy pilot broke off and headed off. It was too late. Plant's F6F had fire coming from the port wing root before it exploded and crashed on Mactan Island, south of Open Airfield.

While leading his VF-15 section on an attack over Cebu Airfield, Lieutenant (junior grade) William V. Henning saw a Zero climbing from the runway on a course to the west. He and his wingman, Ensign L.R. Self, took off after the enemy fighter starting first with a climb and then getting in for a tail run on the fighter. The Zero turned in towards Self, who fired, leaving the fighter to burst into flames. Self immediately pulled up while Henning dived under the Zero to avoid a collision. Suddenly the Zero exploded which threw Henning's F6F some hundred feet in the air in pieces. Self never saw Henning again as his fighter had also been caught up in the Zero's explosion.

McCampbell took off with the first strike from the *Essex* just after Rigg's fighter sweep was launched around 0800. His strike to the Cebu Harbor area consisted of seventy planes including the *Essex* force of fifteen Hellcats, ten Helldivers and eight Avengers. The bombers attacked all the buildings and aircraft facilities at the two airfields as well as cargo ships, tankers and oil storage tanks previously owned by Texas Oil Company, Shell Oil and Asiatic Petroleum. The Helldivers used 100-pound anti-personnel bombs and 1,000-pounders, while the Avengers dropped 500-pound general-purpose bombs and fired rockets. The bombers sank two cargo ships in Cebu Harbor, sank a barge and damaged a sub-chaser leaving it listing and on fire. They hit piers, set fire to oil storage tanks, shot up the airfield hangars and barracks and destroyed small planes.

The Avengers attacked Mactan Airfield flying at low level with bombs and rockets. At approximately 1000 over Cebu Town, Ensign Thomas C. Maxwell crashed in the dock area in his Avenger, as observed by ARM2c Charles F. Loehr. Maxwell's aircrew, AMM1c William A. Shankle and ARM2c Bernard I. Schwartz, were also killed in the crash. Ensign Jesse C. Huggins was wounded with multiple abrasions on his right hand from flying debris when his torpedo bomber was hit near the second cockpit by a .40mm shell burst.

Both Rigg's fighter sweep and McCampbell's first strike started landing back aboard the *Essex* at 1115. After the debriefing, the air intelligence officers reviewed the photos and damage from the missions over the two islands. A decision was made to send another strike over the area to eliminate any remaining ships and port facilities, as well as working over the airfields yet again.

The *Essex* Air Group 15 contributed half of the seventy-two planes on this second strike to the Cebu and Mactan Islands, while the *Lexington* supplied the other half. When they arrived over the targets around 1345, there were still columns of smoke rising up to 10,000 feet from the previous attacks, with skies filled with haze.

The F6Fs strafed the area. Lieutenant Overton used rockets from his F6F to score direct hits on a ship in Cebu Harbor. Meanwhile, the Helldivers hit Shell Island storage facilities. Several of these dive-bombers were diverted to a tanker which they hit and set afire. The Avengers targeted the harbor shipping to attack a 5,000-ton cargo vessel, a smaller cargo ship and some coastal vessels. Though a majority of the bombs missed their targets, Lieutenant R.D. Cosgrove landed one of his three 500-pound bombs on one ship which soon was partially submerged.

Others had their successes too. Lieutenant (junior grade) Jerome C. Crumley sank a vessel that featured a crane aboard, and using his rockets hit several sampans. Lieutenant (junior grade) H.D. Jolly fired two rockets into a coastal vessel, causing a fire. Lieutenant (junior grade) Artman discovered some luggers north of Cebu Rock and scored a hit on one and several near misses on two of the six ships. The second strike landed back aboard the *Essex* at 1412 and revealed that there were no Japanese aircraft encountered in the air or detected on the airfields.

Launching at 1356, McCampbell led an eighty plane strike from the *Essex*, *Lexington* and *Langley* to the southeast coast of Negros Island and Siquijor Island. The Japanese targets were plentiful, including ships and smaller vessels off shore. The Hellcats strafed the airfields including Dumagusto Field at Negros. Over Dumagusto the Avengers joined in. There Lieutenant C.H. Sorensen in his torpedo bomber found a number of single engine enemy planes under the cover of trees in the vicinity of the runway. The Avengers dropped some sixty-five 100-pound bombs and claimed they destroyed twenty-five of them. Photos revealed that eleven were burning when the attackers departed. The third strike landed at 1754.[5]

September 12 had been a fruitful day for Air Group 15. Lieutenant Commander Rigg had downed five aircraft, becoming one of those "Ace-in-a-Day"[6] pilots. Commander McCampbell had shot down four. Ensign Self, Lieutenant Carr and Ensign W.R. Johnson had downed three each. Lieutenant Commander Duncan nailed two Japanese planes, and eight other *Essex* pilots had shot down at least one plane. Seven of the eight fighters launched from the *Essex* on the morning fighter sweep had downed at least one enemy aircraft. In all the *Essex* Carrier Air Group 15 downed twenty-seven Japanese planes that day.

The American air attacks in the southern and central Philippines had devastated the Japanese. Essentially the air and naval bases on Mindanao and at Cebu were now useless. The Japanese were left with very few scout planes to conduct air searches and the radar had been knocked out.

The attack on Cebu on September 11 had affected the Manapua Squadron (13th Air Group fighter squadron Number 30) and the Furaburika Squadron (Fighter Squadron Number 31). Both Japanese fighter squadrons had their aircraft fueled, armed and fitted with their long-range gas tanks as they waited for intelligence on the location of the American carriers. At approximately 0915 the Japanese army airfield and Cebu naval facilities had been attacked without warning.

The leader of the Furaburika Squadron recalled the events that day. He called the attack a perfect ambush. As the American fighters came in the Japanese pilots tried to jettison their long-range fuel tanks and take off to engage. Many of their fighters were shot down before they could reach the end of the runway. Their Navy fighters were destroyed on the runway. Some of their planes reached altitude, but were overwhelmed by the American force of fighters and bombers. Two four-plane divisions of the Furaburika Squadron were able to strike the American planes, but none survived.

By late afternoon of the September 11, the surviving planes from the two Japanese squadrons headed to Sarabiya Airfield in the Bacolod area at a major Japanese Army Air Facility. The two Japanese squadrons had lost fifty percent of their fighters on that day, and the shipping losses were determined to be 70,000 tons.[7]

On September 13, Commander McCampbell led a fighter sweep off at 0604 with twelve

F6Fs from the *Essex* and another twelve from the *Lexington's* VF-19. Since the Japanese had moved all their surviving aircraft northward, McCampbell's fighters encountered no enemy planes over Cebu Island. The *Lexington* fighters stayed to protect their scheduled bomber strike, while the VF-15 fighters with McCampbell headed to northern Negros Island. They approached at high altitude, then dropped down to 6,000 feet to observe the Bacolod air complex.

As McCampbell scanned below, he saw some twenty enemy planes parked in revetments and camouflaged locations, and a twin-engine Betty bomber taking off from the airfield. Another Betty was poised to begin its roll down the runway. Realizing he was too far away to engage, he alerted Lieutenant (junior grade) Lundin's and Lieutenant Commander Duncan's sections to attack. Lundin fired first at the airborne Betty on his first pass, while his other pilots likewise came in to engage. McCampbell's group made three passes before the Betty finally burst into flames and crashed into sea.

Meanwhile, Lieutenant Commander Duncan and his group took on the second Betty, which was soon downed in flames a mile south of the field. While all of this action took place, McCampbell's third group of fighters remained up at 6,000 feet as air cover. The fighters then focused on strafing the airfield for some twenty minutes until 0730 when the strike friendlies arrived.

Now positioned north of the Bacolod air complex, McCampbell took his twelve F6Fs up to 7,000 feet to have a look. There, off ten miles west of the field, were Japanese aircraft coming in.[8]

McCampbell reported that his group were flying at 8,000 feet at 1300 when they saw an Oscar just below them. The enemy plane had seen them and made a turn toward the group in an attempt at a head-on attack. The Oscar pulled away to the right and McCampbell closed and fired a deflection shot. The enemy plane was hit in the wing root on the right and spiraled into the sea.

With his fighters gathered behind him, McCampbell climbed to 8,000–9,000 feet when they caught a look at two Kates ahead and high at the 10 o'clock position. The American fighters turned toward them and gained altitude. McCampbell positioned himself off to the left of the Kates. When one came down past him, he fired a short burst at it, and then another which created a flame in his right wing root. In seconds the Kate was covered in flames as it went into the water. McCampbell saw another of his group shoot down the second Kate.

Lieutenant Rushing was not with McCampbell throughout the engagement with the Kates, and happened to see one friendly F6F flown by Ensign Brex smoking and in bad shape. While Rushing was in company with Brex, the damaged fighter was forced to land on Negros Island. The pilot was seen getting out of his F6F, waving and was apparently uninjured.[9]

Ensign Brex had been hit by a Japanese fighter and had his prop seize up, forcing the dead stick landing. After the landing Filipinos surrounded his plane with rifles, bows and arrows. From his dog tags they realized that Brex was an American and bandaged his wounds. They removed the machine guns and ammunition from the F6F and then burned the plane before marching off to a nearby village. Brex remained in the general area of his crash landing for some forty days. He then began a trek to a contact point designated by the local guerrillas. Brex arrived at a radio communications center on November 6, where he was able to make contact with the U.S. Army Air Force 5th Fighter Command. They sent a Dumbo amphibious plane on November 17 to pick him up. He was then taken to Morotai and then Manus where he received orders to ComAirPac at Pearl Harbor. On November 29, 1944, Ensign Brex rejoined VF-15.

With Lieutenant Rush separated from McCampbell, Ensign McGraw moved up to play wingman. Before long a Japanese Nate (bi-plane fighter trainer) appeared at their altitude. CAG had never seen one of these planes, but it was logical to find one at Bacolod, an army training center. McCampbell wrote that after he had been involved in several head-on attacks by the Nate, he was able to turn inside his turn and get his shots into him, sending the plane to a sea crash in flames.

Having engaged without his wingman, McCampbell radioed for a rendezvous at a point 10 miles south of Bacolod A/D (aerodrome). While he waited for his wingman to arrive, he was attacked by a Nate that just came up in front of him. The CAG chased him but not before he lost the Nate in the clouds. His observations were that a Nate could maneuver better than a Zeke, and could climb better than an F6F at 110–120 knots.[10]

McCampbell then returned to the rendezvous location to hopefully join with squadron mates, but he found five Nates gathered there at 12,000 feet altitude. McCampbell revealed that even though he was alone and at a lower altitude, he was confident that he could rush into the cloud cover to escape if necessary. The enemy lead plane spotted him and headed toward him.

McCampbell rocked his wings back in forth to fool the Japanese, but eventually the entire enemy group headed his way. He quickly led the planes down in front of the F6Fs below him. A major melee occurred as flaming planes were everywhere. McCampbell fired his guns at a Nate as it dived smoking into the clouds.

Awhile later the friendly F6F group rendezvoused and climbed up to 12,000 feet to chase another Nate which also escaped into the clouds. With fuel running low, McCampbell's fighter group returned to the *Essex* without any problems.[11]

As well as Bacolod, the fighter sweep had covered attacks to the north at Talisay (under construction), Silay and Tanza. The *Essex* fighters had encountered some forty Japanese planes, of which most were army fighters with a few Navy Zeros. The air battle lasted for forty-five minutes and resulted in twenty-one enemy planes destroyed.

The second Betty bomber was downed by Lieutenant Commander Duncan, as well as an Oscar and a Nate. He was chasing after another Nate when he came to realize that he was being drawn away from the other fighter sweep attackers. He was getting low on gas, and disengaged. Meanwhile, Lieutenant Bert Morris went after a Zero and shot it down. Lieutenant Lundin was able to claim half of the credit for downing the first Betty, and he too downed an Oscar.

Before he had provided cover for Ensign Brex, Lieutenant Rushing had downed two Oscars. Ensign Bare did not down any planes in the attack, but on his way home to the *Essex* he attacked a Nate at 6,000 feet along with Lieutenant Flinn and Lieutenant Morris. The Nate had come in front of the Bare's F6Fs and he fired, and the fighter exploded.

Ensign Twelves spotted Japanese fighters when he came into the area at around 0730. Some Nates were nearby as he and his mates climbed up to engage. When Twelves reached altitude, he saw even more Nates. One rolled over and he executed a wing over and was able to get behind it. He fired and hit the plane as the pilot went into a spiral and pulled out. Twelves fired bursts as the fighter continued to spiral, and soon the Nate crashed into the sea.

Not finished, Twelves headed up to get altitude and encountered another Nate heading into the clouds. He followed the fighter into the cloud and fired at the Nate every time he saw it. Finally the Nate caught fire, lost control and crashed into a hill. Twelves almost ran into another Nate as he recovered at 3,000 feet. He fired two bursts causing the Nate to smoke, then did a wingover and raced into the clouds. Twelves wanted to follow, but his wingman was having trouble with a Nate on his tail. Twelves got in firing position before the Nate firing at his wingman, first a short burst and the Nate exploded. Just then Twelves heard knocks behind him on his seat armor plating as his F6F lost the hydraulic system. He headed to the clouds as his wingman went after the attacking Nate.

After Lieutenant Morris and Ensign Flinn encountered their first Nates, they pulled up and saw another fighter some 1,500 feet above them. Morris fired first and started the enemy fighter to smoke. Flinn then fired a long burst at the engine and it caught fire. He came above the Nate and saw the pilot slumped over his controls just before it went into a "graveyard spiral"[12] to hit the water.

Morris and Flinn then saw a single Zero chasing after several F6Fs before it pulled out. The fighters were having trouble catching up with the Zero, so Morris and Flinn dived down and attacked. Morris fired and the Zero exploded. Then Morris and Flinn noticed that another Nate had come so close in front of Ensign Bare and Ensign Davis that they did not have time to fire their guns. The Morris-Flinn team took over. Morris fired a burst head-on with the Nate, while Flinn turned left and got behind the enemy fighter and fired. The Nate lost its cowling and broke out in flames. The Japanese pilot was trying to bail out as the fighter entered the clouds, out of sight.

That day Ensign Davis, Ensign McGraw and Ensign Self all claimed victories (probables). Self had forced one Nate to crash land on Bacolod Airfield.

The sixty-eight plane strike (33 from the *Essex*) that day from the *Essex*, *Lexington* and *Princeton* saw action too. The group had arrived at 0745 over Bacolod. Lieutenant Strane had escorted the bombers in and shot down on Japanese fighter, while his wingman, Ensign Jim Duffy, got one too. Section leader Lieutenant R.L. Hall and his wingman, Ensign Fowler, also downed one fighter each.

The bombers struck the airfield and building, as the Avengers flew down the runway dropping 500-pound bombs and strafing all that moved. On the way home near Manapla Airfield, ten Japanese fighters followed the strike Helldivers to the fleet, but they did not attack. The strike landed back aboard the *Essex* at 0922. The mission photos were analyzed and they showed that only eleven enemy aircraft remained on Bacolod Airfield. As it turned out the Japanese aircraft had been routed into Fabrica and Saravia Airdromes.

The next and second strike was launched from the *Essex* at 0855 with twelve Hellcats, nine Helldivers and seven Avengers to the Saravia Field area on Negros Island. The Air Group 15 planes were part of a strike led by the *Lexington* Air Group 19. The strike force arrived at 1030 with only one plane (observation plane) in the air over Fabrica Airfield. The Hellcats strafed the airfields at Fabrica and Saravia first, destroying numerous planes on the ground. Some of the planes caught fire and others did not. Fighters also hit Japanese army trucks at San Pablo on Leyte Island.

Dive-bombers hit Saravia Airdrome where some thirty twin-engine bombers were attacked. The AA was heavier than usual as the American bombed. Lieutenant (junior grade) Clyde Gardner dropped his bomb some ten feet away from a twin-engine bomber creating a spectacular explosion. Lieutenant (junior grade) Alfred DeCasaro bombed a four-plane revetment, destroying at least two planes.[13]

VB-15 pilot, Lieutenant (junior grade) Richard Glass, released his bombs and then strafed the area. He set one plane on fire and his gunner/radioman, ARM2c George Arthur Duncan, got another. Suddenly, Duncan was hit by shrapnel in his abdomen, back and both arms as he continued to fire. Pilot Glass realized his gunner was hurt, pulled out and headed home. Unfortunately, Duncan was dead when they landed back aboard the *Essex*.

Lieutenant Philip Eugene Golden in his Helldiver bombed and strafed at low altitude over Saravia Field around 1105 when it was hit by AA in the port aileron, which was ripped off. This caused the plane to slew to the right, crash on its right wing, cartwheel and then burn. Golden's gunner/radioman, ARM2c John Daniel Downey, was also killed in the crash. Lieutenant John David Bridgers felt he had a part in the death of Lieutenant Golden because he had ordered that when the Helldivers had completed their dive bombing they should "put those heavy 20mm cannon we'd been hauling around to some use"[14] by strafing as they departed.[15]

The third strike of fifteen fighters, eight dive-bombers and five torpedo bombers catapulted off the *Essex* at 1158 led by Lieutenant Commander Duncan. They were joined by planes from the *Lexington* and the *Princeton* on another mission to northern Negros at Fabrica, Saravia and Manapua. They saw the damage and fires from the previous attackers as they approached. One Helldiver pilot reported that he was flying through something that looked like grey confetti. It turned out to be smoke from the fires below.

The fourth strike of the day launched at 1401 with twenty-five *Essex* planes and joined with *Lexington* planes to attack Cebu and Mactan Islands. They encountered severe squalls on the way and turned north to find another target. They found some small vessels in the Visayans and attacked them. The strike force returned and landed at 1721 after a rather unproductive mission.[16]

During the strikes of September 12–13, the twelve carriers of Task Force 38 had shot down 173 Japanese aircraft, destroyed some 305 more on the airfields, sank 59 ships, damaged a like number of vessels, and destroyed ground facilities everywhere they attacked. All this was accomplished with the loss of only eight U.S. planes in combat. Not one American ship was damaged.

Cruising off the Philippines on September 13 aboard his Third Fleet fast battleship and flagship, the *New Jersey*, Admiral Halsey reflected on the situation in the central and southern Philippines. All during that week the air combat reports from his carriers had noted light Japanese resistance and his fleet had rarely encountered attacks from land-based enemy planes. A rescued pilot who had been shot down over Leyte Island had reported that there were significantly fewer Japanese troops than Americans had estimated.[17] Halsey began to suspect that the central Philippines was "a hollow shell, with weak defenses and skinny facilities. In my opinion, this was the vulnerable belly of the imperial dragon.... I began to wonder whether I dared recommend that MacArthur shift to Leyte the invasion which he had planned for Mindanao, and advance the date well ahead of the scheduled November 15.... I sat in a corner of the bridge and thought it over."[18]

So it was that on the early morning on Wednesday the 13th Halsey directed his Chief-of-Staff, Rear Admiral R.B. Carney, to send his urgent message to Nimitz stating, "Am firmly convinced Palau not now needed to support occupation of the Philippines"[19] and recommending that plans for the seizure of Morotai and the Palaus be abandoned, that the ground forces earmarked for these purposes be diverted to MacArthur for his use in the Philippines, and that the invasion of Leyte be undertaken at the earliest date.

Admiral Nimitz considered Halsey's recommendations for two hours, but decided that it was too late to recall the invasion replying, "Carry out ... Stalemate as planned."[20] This fateful decision in the Battle of Peleliu resulted in 6,526 casualties with 1,252 killed in the 1st Marine Division, and 3,278 casualties and 542 killed in the Army 81st Infantry Division.

Nimitz did immediately send a message to the Joint Chiefs of Staff who were meeting in Quebec at the Octagon Conference with President Roosevelt and Prime Minister Winston Churchill. The Joint Chiefs, in consultation with MacArthur and Nimitz, decided on September 14 to bring forward the Leyte landings by two months to October 20, 1944. Halsey continued to disagree with Nimitz's decision for the rest of his life.[21]

The Japanese situation in the Philippines was perilous after the disastrous America raids of September 12–13. Late on the evening of the 12th, the 22nd and 30th Air Groups moved to Clark Field near Manila, along with the 2nd Air Division. The next morning the 13th Air Group was informed that it would now be responsible for the southern air defenses, with the Furaburika Squadron designated as primary.

But as the September 13 action had ended, the 13th Air Group reassessed the damages and loss they had suffered. The Bacolod complex was in ruin and only sixteen planes remained. They had suffered eighty-seven planes destroyed and shot down six American planes. The Japanese decided to make more changes. The 10th Air Group moved from Puerto Princesa on Palawan, out west of the Philippines, up to Luzon at Clark Field. Likewise, the 45th Squadron and the 27th Squadron also headed to Clark Field. Now the southern Philippines and the Visayas were void of Japanese air defense coverage.

At 0606 on September 14 McCampbell led a fighter sweep off the *Essex* with ten F6Fs to attack the Visayas, including Tiring, Saravia, Mandurriao and Fabrica airfields. No Japanese aircraft were encountered in the air, but they found twenty-five planes on the ground at Santa Barbara Airfield and strafed them. The sweep made five runs, but only nine enemy planes burned. Apparently, there was no gas in the other planes they hit. Before leaving the Iloilo area, the fighters strafed the harbor, catching some small vessels on fire. The sweep moved to northern Negros to attack Saravia Airfield and destroy twenty-two planes, and on to Fabrica Airfield for another sixteen.

Lieutenant Commander Rigg led the second strike off after McCampbell's sweep fighters catapulted with twenty-eight planes. Their seventeen fighters rolled in first against facilities at Santa Barbara on Panay, seeing the still smoking planes hit previously by McCampbell's sweep. The *Essex* bombers joined up with like aircraft from the *Lexington* and *Langley* to attack at Iloilo, then broke out to attack Santa Barbara. The Avengers bombed the barracks on the west side of the field, as well as the repair shops on the north side. There was little left for them to attack. Both the sweep and strike planes landed back around 1024.

The second strike with twenty-four planes was launched at 0900 to the Iloilo area, but found few worthy targets. A third strike took off at 1249 to north Negros Island with the same results as the other missions. The only excitement that mission encountered was returning to the location of Ensign Brex's crash. Lieutenant Commander Duncan and Lieutenant Carr escorted Lieutenant Broadhead of VB-15 squadron to the spot where the Helldiver pilot dropped cartons of cigarettes, money and medical supplies by parachute over a clearing. Soon some one-hundred Filipinos came out into the open to wave and spread out on the ground an American flag.

The afternoon of the 14th the *Essex* and Task Force 38.3 departed the Visayas area and steamed to a rendezvous point at 05–40 N, 134–40 E planned for the 16th. On September 16 they arrived to refuel with Task Group 30.8, take on eight new aircraft, receive replacement flight crews, and load supplies. On the 17th at dusk the *Essex* was positioned off Palaus to support the Marine landings at Pelelui when a lone Japanese patrol plane headed toward the carrier. The plane turned back from thirty-five miles out.[22]

Manila

With no Japanese air threat over the Palaus Islands, on September 19 Task Group 38.3 fueled with TG 38.1 and TG 38.2 and steamed to the initial launch point for strikes against

Manila, Luzon. On the evening of September 20, Graham wrote in his diary that they had been briefed about the planned attacks for the next day. They would attack Clark and Nichols fields that morning, and repeat an attack in the afternoon. Afterward they would attack the Visayans sporting an estimated 500 Japanese planes. The bombers would carry torpedoes expected to engage two enemy battleships, four light cruisers, nine destroyers. They all wanted to attack Manila, but more than anything they hoped this might be the last operational mission for the Air Group.[23]

Celebrating the possibility that this might be their last campaign, that night Graham and his buddies drank moonshine the torpedomen had made from torpedo alcohol. Soon the ready rooms were full of the sounds of "…bawdy verses about the other's accomplishments."[24]

That same evening of September 20, the Japanese air command planned to execute a surprise attack on the Americans. They had a force of approximately 300 army air force aircraft to accomplish it, under the command of Lieutenant General Tominaga of 4th Air Army. The number of IJN planes available was significantly lower since the defense of the Philippines was considered the responsibility of the army. The IJN had just begun to deploy units to the area primarily to the 5th Base Air Force under Vice Admiral Teraoka. On the 20th Tominaga had conducted an inspection visit to Clark base airfields to inspire the squadrons to do their duty.[25]

Before dawn on September 21, the *Essex* arrived off Cape San Ildefonso, Luzon. The action started that very day as Commander McCampbell led the first strike off at 0805 with thirty-six planes from the *Essex,* plus another thirty-six aircraft from the *Lexington.* The target was the Nichols Field in the Clark Airfield complex and nearby Las Pinas Field. McCampbell and eleven fellow pilots were flying the new F6F-5 fighters with six rockets loaded on launchers attached under the wings. McCampbell's Minsi III now sported seventeen Japanese flags on his fuselage just below the cockpit. The Helldivers were loaded with 1,000-pound bombs to crater the runways and 250-pound fragmentation bombs for use against personnel and aircraft. The Avenger torpedo bombers carried four 500-pound bombs in the bomb bay and eight rockets under the wings.

En route to the target they spotted three Tojos (Nakajima type 2 fighter) and a single Tony (Kawasaki type 3 fighter). The Tojos were off in the distance, but the Tony was close. A number of F6Fs headed down to engage over Las Pinas Field. Returning to the designated rendezvous point, Ensign H.R. Berree and Ensign G.W. Pigman noticed a Tony on the tail of one of their fellow F6Fs. Firing long bursts, Berree and Pigman closed on the Tony, forcing it to pull up to escape them using a tight wingover followed by evasion techniques. The bullets from both Ensigns' guns began to hit in the cockpit and wing root areas. The enemy pilot must have been injured as his plane went out of control and soon crashed into Laguna de Bay.[26]

As the fighters made their attacks, Commander Mini took his Helldivers on the first air attack on Manila. They carried "window"[27] (aluminum strings that deflected AA gunners' radar), which appeared to be effective as the AA bursts were generally behind the planes. Diving from 13,000 feet, the Helldivers came through a haze generated by Japanese smudge pots they had scattered around the city and surrounding hillsides. The aircrews had been concerned that Manila would be heavily defended by anti-aircraft guns installations, but with the window and the poor performance of the Japanese AA gunners, the Helldivers carried out their bombing successfully and returned aboard the *Essex* at 1100 with no real damage.

Lieutenant Commander Lambert led the Avengers to attack Nichols Field. They came in at 12,000 feet and began glides down to 7,000 feet to attack planes, hangars at the northern end of the field and shops. One pilot dropped bombs on a revetment at the southern end of the field, and another saw two Topies (Mitsubishi transports) parked in another revetment, but he apparently missed his targets.

At 0900, just as McCampbell's strike had reached Nichols Field, a second strike was launched from the *Essex* with thirty-five planes led by Lieutenant Commander Rigg. They joined the strike led by the *Lexington's* CAG, Commander Pedro Winters, back to Manila. Lieutenant Rogers Noyes, with his Aviation Radioman 1st Class Paul Sheehan, led the VB-15 Helldivers to the target, but his radio failed and he relinquished the group to Lieutenant Richard Mills. The attack was going well until a Zero was able to get on the tail of Ensign M.G. Livesay's dive-bomber. Promptly a covering F6F came down from altitude to shot down the enemy fighter in a single pass. Livesay flew back to the *Essex* undamaged. The Helldivers had destroyed a fuel dump, as well as caused added damage to a hangar at Nichols Field. Some six parked planes also were hit. The attackers were trapped aboard at 1209.

McCampbell led the third strike off the *Essex* at 1338 with twelve F6Fs, twelve Helldivers and nine Avengers. Joined by planes from the *Lexington*, they headed to attack a Japanese convoy on the west coast of Luzon sixty miles north of Subic Bay near Salvador Island and some ten miles off shore. The lead ship of the convoy, a destroyer, was speeding at fifteen knots in a column of ships following it including a large cargo ship, two smaller cargo ships, a large ship (probable tanker), and two escort destroyers.

McCampbell's twenty-four fighters led the attack with rockets and 350-pound depth bombs. The lead destroyer received a direct hit from Lieutenant (junior grade) M.M. Gunter, Jr., as four other F6Fs got near misses. The Japanese destroyer lost way, stopped dead in the water and began to list. The ship was claimed as a probable sinking. Meanwhile, McCampbell was able to get four rocket hits on one of the smaller cargo ships. Lieutenant Richard Glass scored a direct hit with a bomb on the stern of another cargo ship, leaving it dead in the water.

Helldiver pilot, Lieutenant (junior grade) John Storrs Foote, got a direct bomb hit on the second large ship, while several of Commander Mini's other Helldiver pilots also got hits. Though the destroyer and escorts threw up heavy AA fire, no planes received major damage.

Led by Bob Cosgrove, ten Avenger torpedo bombers from VT-15 carried torpedoes as they circled the southern end of the convoy, and then attacked from the west toward the east. They dropped their torpedoes at 400 feet and some down at 250 feet. One Avenger reached a speed of 250 knots on his run in and dropped his torpedoes from 1,000 to 1,200 yards out.

The results of the attacks were poor, with Lieutenant (junior grade) S.M. Holladay getting a hit on the port bow of one ship, as three other pilots launched their torpedoes at the same ship with no hits. One of the torpedoes passed under the ship with no result and the other two just disappeared. Though somewhat disappointed, McCampbell did see the ship's crew abandon it and soon only the superstructure was above water. Holladay's torpedo and one Helldivers' 1,000-pound bomb had done the trick.

Another ship in the convoy was attacked by five torpedo bombers. Only one torpedo ran straight and normal, but it missed astern. The other four torpedoes porpoised. The old Mark 13 torpedoes from a World War I design, now equipped with a new ring and stabilizer still did not work well even with perfect air drops.

The third strike recovered aboard the *Essex* at 1646. Back at 1430 the fourth strike of the day catapulted off the *Essex* with twenty-eight planes to join up with *Lexington's* Commander Pedro Winters led aircraft to make a second attack on the enemy convoy. Lieutenant Commander Rigg led the *Essex* component. The F6Fs scored hits with ten rockets, while the destroyer and escorts fired their AA guns. The Helldivers and Avengers carried bombs this mission, sinking several ships that had been seriously damaged from the first attacks and left others smoking. Two small luggers nearby were also sunk. The mission aircraft landed back aboard the *Essex* at 1824.

This mission saw no Japanese aircraft encountered. The previous convoy strike led my McCampbell had seen a formation of eight Japanese fighters over Luzon, but they made no attempt to attack the American sixty-plane strikes from the *Essex* and *Lexington*.[28]

On September 22 at 0625, McCampbell launched from the *Essex* with thirty-four planes on a course to Manila and Nichols Field with another thirty-six planes from the *Lexington*. The F6F-5s were armed with rockets, with the remaining F6F-3s carrying one 500-pound bomb. The Helldivers carried 1,000-pound bombs, and the Avengers were armed with 500-pound bombs in place of the poor performing torpedoes.

After takeoff one of the *Essex*' Helldivers could not retract its wheels, forcing it to abort and land back on the carrier. The strike planes continued to Manila at 13,000 feet and arrived on scene an hour later. This time the force encountered barrage balloons from the ships in the harbor, but they were of no impact on the strike team.

Lieutenant Roger F. Noyes led the Helldivers down on their first dive-bombing attack on fuel tanks between the inner harbor and Earnshaw's Docks that were owned by the Honolulu Iron Works. The hits on the fuel tanks set them on fire, sending smoke into the sky up thousands of feet. The tanks began to explode which started fires around the dock area.

Lieutenant William S. Burns took the torpedo bombers in to hit the aircraft shops to the west of the north-south runway at Nichols Field. They made a direct hit on one hangar, as well as two shops and crated the runway. The AA fire was heavy, but the window allowed the planes to attack with no hits.

VF-15 Division leader Lieutenant Morris, with wingman Ensign R.L. Davis, and Section leader, Lieutenant (junior grade) Bare, with his wingman, Ensign Flinn, spotted a Japanese I-boat fleet submarine tied up at the dock in the inner harbor and attacked with their rockets. Davis recorded, "We were loaded with six 5-inch rockets each. Our dive started at 15,000 feet and we were supposed to fire the rockets between 1,000 and 1,500 feet to be effective. Just as I passed through 2,000 feet, Bert yelled that there were barrage balloons. It was too late to do anything but salvo the rockets and weave our way out of there."[29] Photos from the strike confirmed serious damage to the submarine, sitting in a large oil slick.

On the way home, flying at 12,000 feet behind his fighters to inspect the mission damage, McCampbell saw a twin-engine Japanese Navy light P1Y1 bomber code-named Frances at 20,000 feet over Manila Bay. He immediately took his division up to engage the bomber. It took some ten minutes to reach 18,000 feet and still the bomber was three miles ahead of him. Suddenly the enemy pilot reversed course and headed toward McCampbell's four F6Fs. Realizing for the first time that he was being chased, the Frances pilot put on his power to evade the American fighters.

The F6Fs went to emergency power and soon caught up with the Frances. McCampbell was still armed with his air to ground rockets, which were not designed to fire at aircraft. He decided to try it anyway, and he fired two 5-inch rockets at the enemy plane. One of his rockets hit the starboard stabilizer and knocked off the top one-third of it, but did not explode. The Japanese pilot continued to attempt to evade McCampbell by fishtailing, but CAG-15 was able to get on his tail, firing at the right engine and wing root area where the fuel tanks were. The enemy bomber caught fire, the right wing broke away from the fuselage, and the right engine dislodged and tore away, as parts fell off the plane. It continued to descend to crash in Manila Bay.

CAG-19, Commander T.H. Winters, from the *Lexington* took the second strike of the day out, which included fifteen F6Fs, nine Helldivers and seven Avengers from the *Essex*. Lieutenant Commander Rigg provided the fighter escort for the strike. The attack force hit the port facilities and piers in Manila Harbor and three Japanese cargo ships anchored in the harbor. The Helldivers and Avengers hit the harbor targets and damaged the ships, but none were sunk.

On the way home, the fighters spotted ten Japanese fighters at 10,000 and 12,000 feet practicing dogfighting. The enemy fighters did not attack, except for one Tony, which made a single pass at the American formation. As he came in, Lieutenant Crittenden and his wingman, Ensign Slack, turned into the fighter and faced head-on with it at 4,000 feet. Crittenden fired one burst at the fighter as it rolled over to make its run. The Tony began smoking and broke off the attack. Crittenden did not follow the fighter down, but claimed a probable downing.

As the strike headed back across Luzon to the carriers off the east coast, over central Luzon they ran across another five Tonys. When Rigg's fighters turned to intercept them, the Tonys hurried away. The *Essex* strike force landed aboard at 1037. It was the last strike of the day.

That evening a Japanese Ki-51 Sonia from Japanese Captain Yiko Nitsuko's 2nd Scout Squadron discovered the carriers of Task Force 38 off Cape Engano at the northern end of Luzon. The Japanese command sent every plane they had to attack the American carriers, but they failed to locate them since the TF was then heading south toward the Visayas. The *Essex* and Task Group 38.3 were indeed steaming south to the designated fueling point set for September 23.

The evening found the Japanese assessing their situation. When the *Essex* attacked Manila, there were thirty ships in the harbor. The attacks had reduced the number by seventeen plus one destroyer that were sunk or burned. One 10,000-ton cargo ship was sunk as well as an 8,000-ton ship. Three other large ships were damaged severely. The sky was so hazy and filled with smoke and explosions by the end of the day, that they described the atmosphere as "ghostly."[30]

Japanese Convoy Tama 27 of six ships, including two of them at 5,000-tons each, which was discovered by the *Essex* sailing north off the western shore of Luzon was reported by the Japanese to have been totally destroyed.[31]

Task Group 38.3 fueled on September 23 and then steamed to their destination at dawn the 24th off the northeast coast of Samar Island. The Second Visayas operation was in preparation for the upcoming landing on Leyte Island scheduled for October 20. This primary focus of the second Visayas strikes was shipping and harbor installations.

At 0600 on September 24, the *Essex* launched 18 fighters and dive-bombers that joined in the largest coordinated attack yet from the Task Force 38 carriers. In addition to the *Essex* planes, there were twelve dive-bombers from the *Lexington*, twenty-four fighters from the *Princeton* and the *Langley*, as well as thirty-two fighters from the four carriers of Admiral McCain's Task Group 38.1.

As the attack fighters engaged the Japanese ships and harbor areas around Coron Bay, they encountered heavy anti-aircraft fire from both ground targets and ships. There were so many available friendly American in the strike, an air group coordinator assigned targets. The *Essex* was assigned two cargo ships to attack located in the northern cove of Basuanga

Island. They only received near misses, with no sinking. The *Lexington* force attacked its four assigned targets in the same cove, with similar results. The Japanese later reported that six of their ships were heavily damaged in Coron Bay.

Also launched at 0600 that morning from the *Essex* was a strike led by McCampbell to Cebu and Mactan with eleven fighters and six torpedo bombers, plus twelve *Lexington* fighters and eight dive-bombers. The fighters led the way for the torpedo bombers as they strafed the targets. The six Avengers were each armed with a 2,000-pound blockbuster bomb and rockets.

A cargo ship was attacked by two torpedo bomber pilots between Mactan Island and Cebu. They both missed the ship, but Lieutenant (junior grade) J.C. Huggins and Lieutenant (junior grade) E.F. Lightner were successful in scoring two bomb hits on a 3,000-ton freighter to the south of Cebu. The ship sank immediately as a result of four thousand pounds of explosive material. Another spectacular bombing success was executed by Lieutenant (junior grade) J. Smyth who scored a direct hit on a pier that opened up a large hole, and destroyed the surrounding cranes and dock facilities.

Meanwhile over Cebu Harbor, McCampbell saw two Japanese Mitsubishi F1M2 "Pete"[32] seaplanes (bi-planes) and dived toward them from 12,000 feet with his wingman, Lieutenant Rushing, and his fighter team to engage. They came through clouds, lost the seaplanes for a moment, but picked them up again at low altitude. The seaplanes were flying at 500 feet heading to the south. Their primary mission was to search for American submarines and drop their depth charges.

McCampbell and his wingman attacked the two seaplanes, which immediately split off in different directions to evade the gunfire and maneuver back to their base. McCampbell and Lieutenant (junior grade) Roy L. Nall were able to get on the tail on one of the seaplanes, while Rushing engaged the second seaplane. Both of the enemy seaplanes were hit, caught fire, and crashed into the sea. McCampbell's strike group landed aboard the *Essex* at 1003.

Another strike was sent off to Cebu and Mactan Island at 0859 from the *Essex* with eleven fighters, eleven Helldivers and four Avengers. They were also joined by *Lexington* planes. They hit the harbor piers and warehouses with machinegun fire and 2,000-pound bombs, sinking one 100-foot lugger, damaging five other luggers, and damaging a tanker positioned at the Philippine Refining Company dock. They hit a coconut oil refinery and several other buildings near the pier and on departure, left the area smoking as the buildings burned.

While over Cebu Harbor flying his F6F at around 1230, Ensign Henry Clayton Gaver was hit by AA fire on a strafing run and began trailing heavy white smoke. Gaver notified his division leader, Lieutenant (junior grade) Arthur Singer, that he had lost his engine and would have to make a water landing. Singer saw Gaver fly low just a few feet over the surface when his wing dropped down and hit the water. The plane somersaulted and burst into flames. Singer and other squadron mates circled, but saw "no evidence of survival."[33]

At 1111 a radar contact noted a bogey. Though *Lexington* had the CAP fighters aloft, the *Essex* assumed Fighter Direction Control at 1144 because of poor radar performance on the *Lexington*. The CAP was vectored from 340° out 31 miles to 285° out 110 miles to locate a Japanese Mitsubishi Ki-46 "Dinah"[34] twin-engine reconnaissance aircraft flying at 220 knots toward the task group. At 1202 the enemy plane was downed by the CAP fighters.

At 1258, the third strike with twenty-five planes was launched from the *Essex* and joined with aircraft from the *Lexington* for another attack on Cebu and Mactan Islands. The attackers hit all available targets not destroyed in the previous strikes. At the same time, Lieutenant Morris led a fighter sweep of eight F6F-5s over Panay Island. No enemy aircraft were seen, but they did make attacks on several coastal vessels near Iloilo Island and Antayan Island. Both the strike and sweep missions landed at 1751.

After the days' missions had been completed at sunset, Task Group 38.3 along with TGs 38.1 and 38.2 departed the Visayas and headed to a planned fueling rendezvous northwest of Palau with Task Group 30.8 on September 26. From there the task groups steamed through Kossol Passage in the Palaus and dropped anchor between berths 3, 9 and 10 at 0730 on September 27. During the period September 28–30, bombs and other ammunition was being loaded aboard the *Essex* during daylight hours and then the carrier moved out to Kossol Passage.

Ensign Gaver's body washed up on shore at Cebu and was recovered by Filipinos, who buried him in the Maniawa Municipal Cemetery.[35]

The Stalemate II Operation was now at an end. The entire operation during which Task Force 38 devastated the Palaus and the Philippines was a considerable success. Mitscher's fast carriers had destroyed 893 Japanese airborne and parked planes, and sank 224,000 tons of shipping.

The contribution of the *Essex* and Commander McCampbell's Carrier Air Group Fifteen to that operation from August 29 to September 27, 1944, was remarkable. CAG-15 flew 1,071 combat mission sorties, 240 defensive sorties over the task group, 32 rescue CAP sorties over Lifeguard Submarines, 200 training sorties, and one administrative flight. The Air Group shot down 66 enemy planes, destroyed 166 enemy planes on the ground, sank 10 confirmed Japanese ships, claimed another 5 probable ships sank, with 14 other ships over 100 tons damaged, plus numerous smaller vessels under 1,000 tons.

To accomplish these results Air Group 15 dropped 2,107 bombs, fired 466 rockets, dropped nine torpedoes. The Air Group lost ten pilots and four aircrewmen killed or missing in action, and two pilots and four aircrewmen wounded. Fifteen planes were lost in combat and two were lost to operational accidents.

The *Essex* steamed 12,965 miles during Stalemate II and used 2,052,065 gallons. The carrier also supplied 270,354 gallons of fuel to five destroyers at sea. The Carrier Air Group consumed 335,800 gallons of aviation gasoline.[36]

16

Okinawa Jima, Nansei Shoto

"burning, beached and sunk vessels"[1]

From Kossol Passage, Rear Admiral Sherman, aboard his flagship *Essex,* proceeded with Task Group 38.3 on the evening of October 1 to the southeast toward the new fleet anchorage at Ulithi Atoll. Ulithi was symbolically unique because it was on the same longitudinal meridian as Tokyo, Japan. The *Essex* and TG 38.3 arrived at Ulithi Atoll to anchor on October 2, 1944, and began receiving replacement aircraft and aircrews, as well as ammunition and supplies in preparation for their next mission. In his diary Otto Graham wrote of the discouraged gunners of VB-15 who sadly discovered that the cherished rumor of being relieved so they could return home turned out not to be true. It didn't help that the leisure time ashore found their refreshments limited to two warm beers per day and Spam sandwiches.[2]

Food aboard the *Essex* by that time had not been fresh since way back in May when they had departed Hawaii on their combat tour. Since there were no refrigerated supply ships, and all fresh food was usually consumed by six weeks, all they ate was from cans. Ensign C.A. Borley of VF-15 complained of breakfast of reconstituted eggs, canned beets, and canned asparagus. The bread was hard and had weevils in it just like the ships in the 1700s. Their dinners consisted of beets, asparagus and Spam.[3]

The heaviest weather they had ever run into moved into the area, sending Sherman's TG 38.3 and Bogan's 38.2 out of Ulithi for protection from a violent typhoon that lasted some three days. The *Essex* anchored back at Ulithi at berth 147 on October 4–5.

Having completed his Stalemate II Operation successfully, and reduced any significant threat from the Japanese air forces in the Philippines, Halsey released orders to neutralize the air capability north of the Philippines in the Okinawa area and Formosa. This would help to reduce the potential of major resupply of air assets ferrying through from Japan to the Philippines in coming landing operations in the Philippines.[4]

Aboard the *Essex,* Admiral Sherman's Task Group 38.3 with the Task Force 38 Commander, Vice Admiral Mitscher, in his flagship *Lexington,* departed Ulithi in the afternoon of October 6 in rough waters at the trailing end of a typhoon centered up north. Just after darkness on October 7, the entire Fast Carrier Task Force 38 rendezvoused 375 miles west of the Marianas in clearing weather, but filled with heavy seas and deep swells. The entire next day was consumed in refueling operations with the nine oilers of the fueling group.

In an attempt to deceive the Japanese as to Halsey's intentions, Rear Admiral Allan E. "Hoke"[5] Smith was ordered to take his task group, made up of heavy cruisers *Chester, Pensacola,* the *Salt Lake City* with six destroyers, to Marcus Island, arriving at 0815 on October 9. There, the task group bombarded the island from dawn to dusk that day. To enhance the effect and increase the illusion of an upcoming landing, Smith created significant attention by dispersing smoke puffs from over the horizon, using floating dummy radar targets and deploying pyrotechnics.

Just after the dramatic bombardment action had started at 0845, a Japanese patrol plane out of Kanoya in southern Kyushu was shot down halfway between Okina Daito and Iwo Jima by an American patrol bomber out of Tinian. The Japanese pilot did not report his engagement with the American bomber. When the Japanese plane did not return from its patrol, the commandant of the Sasebo Naval District surmised that his plane had been shot down by American carrier aircraft. Now unsure whether the American carriers were in the Bonins or north of the Philippines as far as Kyushu or the Ryukus, he alerted the naval commands in both areas of potential enemy action. At this point in time, Task Force 38 was actually 225 miles southwest of the shot down.[6]

After the refueling, the *Essex* set out on a course to the Nampo Islands (Okinawa Jima). On the evening of the 9th, Admiral Sherman ordered Task Group 38.3 to run in at high speed to the Ryukyus Island chain that ran a hundred miles south from the Japanese home island of Kyushu to a hundred miles north of Formosa (Taiwan). These islands were known to the Japanese as the Nansei Shoto (Southwest Archipelago).

All of the assets of Mitscher's Task Force 38, with its seventeen carriers and over 1,000 planes, was now ready to engage the Japanese in Okinawa and Formosa. Of concern at the time was the lack of intelligence regarding the Ryukus area, except that the main Japanese bases were on the largest island in the chain, Okinawa. Mitscher's Task Force 38 was heading into unknown territory. This was also the closest Air Group 15 would ever get to Japan during World War II.

Positioned at 125 miles southeast of Okinawa, McCampbell, with his wingman, Lieutenant Rushing, launched at 0543 from the *Essex* to lead the attacks on Central Okinawa and Kuma Shima Island consisting of a fighter sweep and two strikes by bombers and fighters. Lieutenant Commander Riggs led fourteen fighters off the carrier after McCampbell catapulted and they were joined by sixteen VF-19 fighters from the *Lexington*. On their way to the target at Yontan Air Base, they saw no airborne enemy planes. When they made their runs on the airfield, they fired at some dozen Japanese planes on the runways ready for takeoff. They hit several, causing explosions and left the airfield with some burning.

Rigg's fighters proceeded to Yontan South Air Base and strafed with limited effect due to the well-constructed aircraft revetments. They were able to destroy a fuel truck and a coastal steamer. Meanwhile, McCampbell and Rushing were busy strafing the shipping at Okinawa. They discovered four cargos ships, attacking the largest 6,000-ton ship first with machine guns and rockets. They scored two rocket hits. They were able to hit the stern of the second ship, causing its depth charges to explode. They went after the last two cargo ships and damaged them. Thirty minutes later, they noted that the second ship was dead in the water, the third ship was leaking oil and the fourth ship lay dead in the water in the bay at Nago Wan.

The first strike of thirty-two Hellcats from the *Essex*, *Lexington* and *Princeton*, accompanied by twenty-seven Helldivers and twenty-seven Avengers from the three carriers attacked the Yontan airfields and destroyed barracks, shops and hangars, as well as cratering the runways.

While the first sweep and strike were a complete surprise to the Japanese, by the time the second strike arrived over Okinawa, after having launched at 0745, the enemy fighters were taking off. Lieutenant Morris took his twelve fighters from the *Essex* to attack shipping at Nago Wan using 500-pound bombs. They sank one 8,000-ton freighter, three small freighters and did some damage to two more small freighters. One of the explosions created an incredible visual display when a direct hit on the ammunition on one ship that was moored with another ship, blew up both of them.

It was at this time that Japanese planes arrived on the scene. They included a variety of aircraft from Zeros to bi-plane training craft. Lieutenant Morris took on a Tony, as he descended to attack on the tail of the enemy plane. He downed the plane, ending in a sea crash. Lieutenant (junior grade) Milton saw another Tony in the act of taking off. He fired several bursts of gunfire and sent it crashing into the trees beyond the runway. Lieutenant Berree with his wingman found an Oscar (Nakajima army fighter) flying low heading for the American bombers that were in the process of tearing up the port facilities and shipping in the harbor. Berree fired his shells and watched the enemy plane nose over and crash in the sea. As Berree and his wingman made their way toward the airfield, they ran into a Nate army trainer and shot it down.

Ensign Borley's division discovered five Japanese planes below them. Borley engaged a Zero as it banked to the right and out of his sight. The enemy pilot made a major misstate by making a full circle break, and came around to meet Borley again. This time Borley got in his cannon bursts and sent the Zero to a fiery crash into the water.

Ensign Flinn and his division spotted four Japanese planes flying in formation as they had just taken off. Flinn was able to down one Tony as it tried to make a forced landing. The enemy plane never made land and it crashed into the sea short of the runway. Another Tony was shot down by Ensign Pigman as he fired into the wing root of the enemy plane and saw the plane cartwheel on the airfield, scattering parts as it went.

Off his wing, at the 9 o'clock position, Ensign Frazelle with his section leader saw an Oscar and both immediately fired at it. Their shells apparently missed the enemy plane, so Frazelle moved behind the plane and fired a long burst. The Oscar began to smoke as flames appeared. It crashed on its back in the water.

The attacks kept coming as Lieutenant Nall led his division against incoming Japanese aircraft trying to get at the bombers. His primary mission had been to take photos, but the need to protect the bombers was critical. Meanwhile, Commander Mini took his dive-bombers to attack a beached ship, but they only scored near misses.

McCampbell, who had seen numerous barges and small vessels in the channel between Okinawa and the island of Yahagi Shima, directed the Avengers, led by Lieutenant C.H. Sorensen, to attack the area. Sorensen took the torpedo bombers on glide runs in from south to north. He bombed and destroyed an oil barge camouflaged with tree branches and netting. Lieutenant Goodwin hit the bow of another barge, and on his next run hit a third one. Lieutenant William S. Burns bombed a lugger causing a fire.

As the second strike headed home (to a 1038 landing), a third strike launched from the *Essex* with thirty-three planes at 1017. They joined up with planes from the other two carriers and headed again to Yontan Air Base to hit hangars, barracks and facilities, as well as small vessels around the island. More planes were hit on the ground, but none were detected in the skies over Yontan. On their strike tour, they saw the results of the previous attacks that left "burning, beached and sunk vessels,"[7] destroyed planes and airfield destruction.

Lieutenant E.W. Overton led the fourth and last strike of the day off the *Essex* at 1223 with thirty-nine planes to attack Yontan Air Base. On the way to the target, the air coordinator redirected the mission to attack Yontan South Air Base. Lieutenant Singer was one of two pilots sent to take photos of the enemy airbase. As he returned, he looked down to see an airfield on little Le Shima off the Okinawa coast crowded with twin-engine Nakajima

"Frans"[8] bombers and some other planes. The bombers were circling to land. Singer, in his F6F-5, dived in a turn and fired at the first bomber about to land and shot it down in flames to the ground. He cut his engine to slow down in an attempt to shot at the second bomber in the line, but he overran it. He took off after another bomber turning left to evade him. He fired and shot his second Fran down as it exploded with such force that it caused his Hellcat to shake.

Singer was at 1,500 feet and began climbing to look for the rest of the evading planes. He spotted a Sally flying boat heading north at low altitude over the water. He fired his guns, but the port guns were jammed and caused him to miss the Sally. The Sally turned back toward the Le Shima airfield as Singer continued to fire his guns as best he could. He saw the Sally lose parts of the plane as it tried to land, had its landing gear folded up, sending the plane into a skid down the runway and finally to stop "nosed up."[9]

Singer then pulled up and spotted another Fran going for the clouds off Okinawa. He gave chase as he attempted to reset his guns. The Fran suddenly came out of the clouds in front of him as Singer fired bursts from his three working guns. The Fran caught fire aft of the engine and went into a dive, spiraling down to a water crash. Singer surveyed the area, but saw no more planes to attack, and began to head home with four kills.

The *Essex* had suffered two wounded casualties in the combat action of October 10. ARM2c Stanley Clarence Peterson of VT-15 suffered multiple wounds on his face, shoulder and arms from 7.7mm anti-aircraft bullets during a dive on the second strike. ARM Charles Lossie Rowland of VB-15 suffered bullet wounds on his left arm and, after landing back aboard the *Essex*, the doctors determined that his left arm had to be amputated above the elbow. On the third strike an Avenger made a water landing after takeoff, but the three crewmembers were rescued by a plane-guard destroyer. In total, Task Force 38 lost twenty-one planes, but thankfully only five pilots and four airmen.

The attacks of October 10 at Okinawa had been an undisputed success. Task Force 38 carriers flew 1396 sorties and had claimed over 111 Japanese aircraft destroyed. The *Essex* pilots claimed 23 planes, including Singer's four kills. The Japanese records showed that 30 Navy planes were shot down or destroyed on the ground, and 15 Army planes. The new Yontan Air Base was annihilated and shipping losses were heavy. The Japanese reported four major ships sunk, including a 10,000 freighter, the submarine tender *Jinggyo*, 13 torpedo boats, 2 special midget attack submarines and 22 small naval vessels.[10]

17

Battle of Formosa

"nothing but so many eggs thrown at the stone wall of the indomitable enemy formation"[1]

Once the attacks had begun over Okinawa on October 10, Admiral Toyoda, the Commander-in-Chief of the Japanese Combined Fleet, received word at Shinchiku in northern Formosa on his way back to Tokyo from a command inspection trip to the Philippines to lift morale. Back at Toyoda's Combined Fleet HQ at Hyoshi, near Tokyo, his Chief of Staff, Rear Admiral Kusaka, heard the news and at 0925 sent out alerts to the Japanese Navy's base air forces for SHO-1 (Leyte) and SHO-2 (Formosa). Five minutes later, he issued orders to Vice Admiral Fukudome, the Commander of the Sixth Base Air Force at Takao on Formosa, "to attack and destroy the enemy."[2] On Formosa, Fukudome had about 230 operational fighters to engage the American forces, and was convinced that his forces could defend their position that was so close to their Home Islands.[3]

On October 11, the *Essex* refueled 375 miles east of Formosa along with other carriers of TF 38. Before the strikes began on Formosa, Halsey had plans to attack Aparri Field on the northern coast of Luzon. On the morning of October 11, carriers from Admiral McCain's TG 38.1 and Admiral Davison's TG 38.4 fueled with eleven oilers. At 1240 the carriers launched a 61-plane strike at Aparri Field from 323 miles. The strike was unopposed and resulted in destroying ten to twelve twin-engine Japanese planes on the ground, two hangars, two shops and an ammunition dump. The loss was seven planes from the task groups.[4] Halsey later acknowledged that the raid was a mistake, and said, "I should have struck Formosa first."[5]

The attack plan for Formosa designated specific geographic area responsibilities to the Task Groups. Admiral Bogin's TG 38.1 was given the responsibility for the north end of the island, Admiral Sherman's TG 38.3 had the central area, Admiral Davison's TG 38.4 had the Takao area and Admiral McCain's TG 38.2 was assigned the south end. The attack plan suffered from poor intelligence availability. Early intelligence reports indicated that there were only five airfields derived from "dim reproductions of photographs taken from high altitudes"[6] and cloudy conditions, but combat photos showed some sixteen airfields. Air Group 15 pilots had a problem identifying their mission targets and often reported bombing on unknown airfields.[7]

Ensign C.A. Borley remembered the only intelligence materials for the Formosa pre-strike briefing session consisted of photographs taken by submarines which were useless. They were told that there were some 300 enemy planes on the island located across as many as twenty-four airfields.[8]

He described his thoughts as he climbed into his F6F-5. It was dark with no lights and the sea was roaring. None of them had received any night-flying training. When they took

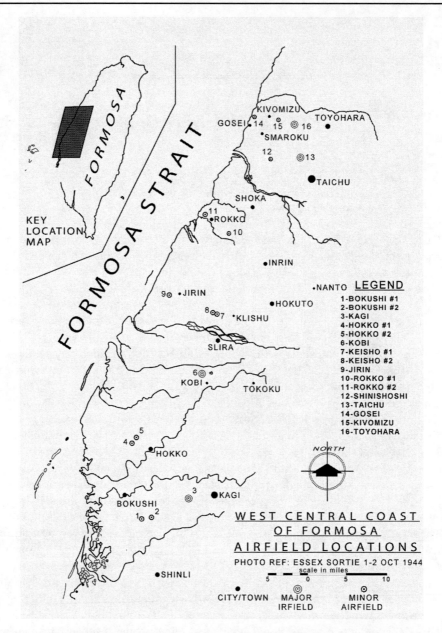

Rough sketch map of West Central Coast of Formosa Airfield locations (redrawn image based on Action Report—USS *Essex*, The Battle of Formosa, October 12–14, 1944, Commanding Officer USS *Essex*, November 21, 1944, National Archives and Records Administration, College Park, Maryland).

off they would have to go on instruments, rendezvous in darkness, and go to their targets which they knew nothing about. It looked pretty grim.[9]

Twenty minutes after launch his VF-15 squadron mate, Lieutenant (junior grade) Norman R. Berree, had to abort the mission due to a fuel pump problem, Borley thought, "I really wanted to find a mechanical fault with my airplane, but unfortunately everything was working perfectly."[10]

After completing fueling operations, the *Essex* with TG 38.3 steamed to the launch location 75 miles east of the southern tip of Formosa. At 0600 on October 12 McCampbell launched with three other F6Fs as the target coordinator for attacks on the west coast of Formosa and in the Pescadores Islands, located some 25 miles off the west coast of Formosa. Just after McCampbell's section launched, Lieutenant Commander Riggs led sixteen fighters from the *Essex* off on the fighter sweep, to be joined by another sixteen F6Fs from the *Lexington* at 19,000 feet over Central Formosa.

As they arrived over the target area, the Japanese fighters came over to intercept flying at 23,000 feet. Both the *Essex* and *Lexington* fighters had to climb to reach the enemy planes. The American fighters came in to attack in four-plane formations, and then split off in two-plane sections, but the Japanese followed no such formation discipline.[11] Rigg noted, "At no time was there noticed a single friendly VF alone, unless he was joining up on other F6Fs; the Enemy Aircraft did not follow this procedure, consequently it was easy to pick them out and off."[12]

A general melee ensued between F6Fs and Zeros or other enemy fighters between 15,000 and 25,000 feet. At these altitudes the F6F performed well and could outmaneuver the Zero and a Tojo (Army Ki-44 Zero).[13] At an altitude of 8,000 feet or below, the Zero had some advantage in maneuverability over the F6F. During the engagement, some enemy planes curiously dropped phosphorus bombs on the American fighters, but they never were able to hit an F6F.

The melee action was so fast that keeping track of the number of planes downed was near impossible. Rigg fired the first shots of the engagement when he attacked a Zero after swooping down from 19,000 feet. His wingman fired his guns and finished the fighter off as it flamed down. On passes firing at other Japanese planes, Rigg saw them begin to smoke, but could not follow them to see if they eventually crashed. Attacking another Zero, he was able to see the fighter catch fire and crash after several bursts from his guns.

A Japanese Tojo flew a head-on attack at Lieutenant Commander Duncan with the obvious intention of ramming him. Both planes fired at each other, as Duncan pulled up just in time. The enemy fighter caught fire and descended to crash. Another Tojo was attacked by Lieutenant Carr when the pilot dropped his wheels to increase drag and slow his plane down. Carr saw the plane begin to smoke, as a *Lexington* fighter sent more bullets into the aircraft, finalizing with a crash. Carr was credited with half a kill.

The action continued. Under the watchful eyes of Lieutenant (junior grade) R.P. Fush, a Zero made an attack run on some F6Fs. Fush took after the plane and downed it. Then he found a Tojo and hit the engine, causing the plane to spiral to a crash. Several F6Fs were chasing an evading Zero when it turned straight on toward Lieutenant Twelves and fired, hitting his cockpit, engine and in the wings. Twelves's plotting board on his knee was hit by one bullet and another one hit his cylinder head temperature gauge on his instrument panel. It was not looking good as the Japanese fighter fired more bullets into Twelves's wings, ailerons, propeller blade, stabilizer and rudder. Thankfully, the Zero turned across in front of Twelves's windshield and received one burst that started a fire. Knowing that his attack was over, the Japanese pilot bailed out and soon his parachute was opened.

While engaged in dogfights, a new Japanese Mitsubishi J2M Raiden Navy Interceptor Fighter called a Jack was discovered flying in formation. The plane was fast, and had outstanding climb capabilities. As a formation of four of these planes attempted to get into proper attack position on Twelves's division, one of them broke off and headed toward Twelves. The Jack could out climb the F6Fs even at an altitude of 18,000 feet. The F6Fs stayed in formation and then Twelves got in a burst after their first run and downed a plane.

Combat action saw Lieutenant (junior grade) J.P. Altena and Lieutenant (junior grade) M.M. Gunter, Jr., down two Tojos each. Lieutenant (junior grade) W.S. Deming, Jr., climbed to meet a group of Tojos at 18,000 feet and shot one down. A Tojo was following an F6F that had broken formation when Ensign Hoey came to his rescue and shot him off the American's tail. The Japanese pilot attempted to ram Hoey, but his engine stopped and he crashed.

Ensign Pigman was leading his division as they climbed to engage a group of Tojos. Pigman was able to get on the tail of one Tojo and shot it down. The Japanese pilot was able to bail out. Then Pigman rejoined his division when he saw a Zero below him. He fired and the enemy plane exploded. He fired at yet another Zero, but it continued to stay in formation and Pigman did not see the result of his action.

Ensign Borley might have dreaded the mission, but he was surely focused on shooting down Japanese planes. Climbing from 17,000 feet Borley saw a Tojo some 3,000 feet below him. He conducted a "high-side run"[14] on the plane and opened up firing when he got in range. At 15,000 feet, he scored hits on the Tojo in the cockpit and the wings as the plane began to smoke. Flames were seen coming from the cowling, as he enemy fighter headed straight down to a water crash.

Ensign Borley came out of his dive at 14,000 feet and began to climb when he spied a Zero on an opposite course to his. Using an overhead run in, Borley's bullets hit the Zero, sending it into a slow spiral in flames, and down to a crash and explosion. Then, he noticed a group of fellow F6Fs flying at 8,000 feet and joined up with them. Several Oscars were spotted 500 feet below them, flying on a parallel course. Borley picked out one Oscar and sped towards it. The enemy pilot saw him approach over his shoulder when Borley began to send bullets his way. The Oscar rolled over and the pilot bailed out to the surprise of Borley.

Borley was not finished yet. Now at 7,000 feet, he saw another Oscar heading toward land. Borley increased his speed following the enemy plane at 280 knots and started firing at around 800 feet. The Oscar was hit, caught fire, entered a shallow dive and crashed on land. He again rejoined his division.

Flying at 19,000 feet Ensign P. Bugg engaged and shot down a Tojo. The Japanese pilot bailed out, but his parachute did not deploy as he dropped to his death in the sea below. Ensign J.C. Taylor was flying in formation with his section leader when they saw two Tojos on the tail of an F6F below them. The section leader took one and Taylor headed off after the other, shooting it down. He climbed up to 20,000 feet and found three more Tojos down at 12,000 feet. Taylor dived and shot one down.

Finally, the Japanese broke off the engagement. The fighter sweep team headed over to attack Keishu Airdrome where they discovered fighters firing up their engines in preparation for takeoff. At low altitude, the sweep F6Fs strafed all the enemy fighters and attacked some other enemy planes hidden in their revetments. Lieutenant Commander Rigg noted some dozen burning planes on the runways and in the revetments.

In the attack at Keishu, Lieutenant John Van Altena's fighter was hit by AA fire. On his trip back to the *Essex*, he was forced to ditch in the sea. Ensign Charles Adam Dorn, his wingman, circled the area and saw that Van Altena was in his life raft. Dorn continued to circle until Van Altena was rescued by a lifeguard submarine, and then he headed back toward the carrier. Unfortunately, Ensign Dorn was short of fuel and unable to make the *Essex,* and had to make a water landing twenty miles short of the carrier. He was listed as missing, and never seen again. He had given his life for a fellow squadron pilot.[15]

Ensign Borley with his section leader were with some other sixteen planes returning to the carrier when they spotted Japanese aircraft taking off from an airfield outside Kaohsiung. Our planes headed down to strafe them. Borley attacked the antiaircraft gun position as his F6F was hit in the engine and caught fire. He was traveling around 400 miles an hour when the engine stopped, so he decided to glide to the ocean some four to five miles ahead. He was forced to fly directly over Kaohsiung just below 2,000 feet being shot at as he went. He reached the sea and was about a half mile from the shore getting ready to ditch when his fighter stalled at 135 mile an hour and hit the water from 100-foot altitude.

The F6F broke in half and sank quickly. By the time he exited the cockpit, he was underwater. He swam up to the surface and saw the planes' tail go below the waves. He decided to get out of his parachute and raft to avoid detection and stayed with only his Mae West. Meanwhile antiaircraft shrapnel fire at him from the shore was raining down on him. Although he was unaware of it at the time, he was in the center of a minefield.[16]

Borley knew he was so close to the shore that he might attract attention, so he began swimming toward the open sea. As he feared, after thirty minutes a Japanese sampan came in his direction. Borley deflated his yellow Mae West half way and tried to stay as low as he could to the water's surface. The men in the sampan saw him and moved toward him. Borley took his .38 caliber revolver out of its holster knowing that it might not work after being in salt water.

As the boat came closer, Borley fired his gun, which knocked one man out of the sampan. He then fired three more shots and the second man went down, falling overboard. The boat veered away from Borley as he continued swimming out to sea. Thankfully, the Japanese did not find him before a lone F6F flew over and spotted Borley's yellow life jacket, and waggling its wings. Nothing happened until later in the afternoon when two F6Fs flew over and dropped a life raft.[17] Eventually a Japanese patrol boat headed out of the harbor, and it was strafed by four of the squadron Hellcats. Borley broke open his dye marker to be seen. One of the fighters came down by dropping its landing gear and deploying his flaps, and then opened his canopy and threw down a raft. Borley scrambled aboard the raft and began to paddle.[18]

Still Borley was not picked up, and he spent the night of October 12 huddled in the life raft. The next day came as he drifted further away from shore. During the day several friendly planes flew over and waggled their wings, but the day ended with no rescue. The night came as the weather became rougher. The third day came, but he saw only sea birds, a few fish and open sky. The morning of the fourth day came as a flying fish landed in his raft. He tried to eat the raw fish, but it only took him one bite to decide that he was not hungry enough to partake. Finally, in mid-afternoon of the fifth day, the submarine *Sawfish* spotted the yellow raft and came alongside to rescue Ensign Borley. He was taken back to Pearl Harbor to wait the return of the VF-15.

Just after the *Essex* fighter sweep had taken off that morning of October 12, the first strike was launched with seven Hellcats, nine Helldivers and seven Avengers, and was joined by a like number of aircraft from the *Lexington* and *Langley*. Coupled with the poor target intelligence, the bombing strike encountered thick cloud cover over the western mountains, which complicated the task of finding airfields. McCampbell was trying to determine the location of the bomber strike target airfield, Kobi Air Base, even as his fighter control frequencies were being jammed by the Japanese. He decided to attack the largest airfield that he assumed was Kobi.

The fighters dived down, strafed and fired rockets at all the planes found at Kobi, including twin-engine G4M Betty bombers. After the attack run, McCampbell and the other fighters climbed to cover the American bombers heading in. Commander Mini directed the Helldivers to their designated target at Toyohara Air Base, but the fog was so thick, he had to divert his bombers to Kobi.

The Avengers, led by Lieutenant (junior grade) R.L. Bentz, took his six torpedo bombers (one had turned back with an engine problem) to Toyohara, but also had to abandon his primary target in favor of Kobi. The mission had specified that they attack hangars and buildings, so they complied and destroyed two hangars, three small buildings and a revetment. As they completed their attack run, they discovered that there were some one-hundred enemy aircraft on the air base they had overlooked.

The next mission off the *Essex* at 0653 was a search to the north covering from 50° to 80° out to 275 miles. The search sectors were undertaken by the usual two-plane Hellcat-Helldiver teams. Of the three teams, only one search team found a target: the X-shaped airfield on Miyako Shima in the Okinawa area. Their missions landed back at 1138.

The second strike mission that day, with seventy-five planes from the *Essex*, *Lexington* and *Langley*, took off at 0814, and was led by the *Lexington* CAG, Commander Pedro Winters. The mission targets were Boko Harbor and the Pescadores Islands. The harbor was full of ships as the strike force attacked. Lieutenant Commander Lambert led the *Essex* planes in and used delayed-fuse bombs hitting under the bow to sink one ship. The attack group strafed an airfield, and sank one flying boat. Several destroyer escorts were damaged and they sank a 10,000-ton freighter, a 3,000-ton tanker, one 750-ton ship and a 500-ton ship, along with several smaller vessels.

The bomber strike moved south of the harbor and ran into heavy flak from AA fire. Ensign H.C. Copeland in his Avenger was hit in the engine and lost three cylinders. He was able to make it off the land and ditched near the end of Formosa. He and his crewmen, R.J. Bradley and W.C. Poppel, evacuated the bomber and scrambled into their life raft. Soon they saw a small 1,200-ton Japanese freighter change direction and head toward them.

Lieutenant (junior grade) Symmes saw what was happening and came down to drop a life raft with a note to the pilot telling him what was going on. Symmes then began a series of attack runs on the freighter, and sank the ship. But the threat to the downed crew was not over. The survivors of the enemy freighter were able to get a powerboat off the ship and headed again toward the *Essex* flyers. With his wingman circling over the raft, Symmes strafed the powerboat and sank it. He then headed out to sea to search for the life-guard submarine and led it back to the rescue location. After the Avenger crew was safely aboard the submarine, Symmes and his wingman headed home. On the way, they strafed another small freighter.[19]

McCampbell, with his wingman, returned from his target coordinator duties and trapped aboard the *Essex* at 1135. He later recalled the action at Formosa and noted that even as they shot down most of what they sent down, they continued to replenish planes lost at the hands of the Americans to the island.

Formosa had 7,000 to 8,000-foot mountains along most of the length of the island, which caused McCampbell to consider whether to take his air group either to the south or north end or come over to attack in the middle of the island and fly over the mountains. Often, they ran into clouds at 5,000 to 6,000 feet, so his flights went through the overcast to avoid the risk presented by the mountains.

Lieutenant Commander Mini was concerned that his bombing squadron had never been trained to travel in formation through clouds on instruments. McCampbell responded by suggesting that he send up a few planes first and have them radio back to provide which altitude the cloud cover ended. He suggested that the leader of each section go on instruments while his wingman followed him on his wing. The torpedo planes all came up successfully as predicted.[20]

For McCampbell's Pescadores mission, he said he did not see much air action there. There was a shipyard that they strafed and in the dry dock there was a cruiser that they bombed and strafed. McCampbell noted they sunk three or four commercial ships. He remembered one at the entrance to the harbor that the bombers hit, which caused a massive explosion of most likely of gasoline or ammunition.[21]

The third strike of the day, accompanied by a fighter sweep, launched from the *Essex* at 1125 with seventeen Hellcats, ten Helldivers and seven Avengers to attack Toyohara Airfield. The target airfield was still covered with clouds, so the mission was diverted to Rokko Airfield Number 1. They discovered the field by accident since it was not on their maps. The strike force attacked the airfield still under construction and destroyed most of the building and facilities. The strike group with fighter sweep landed back at 1503.

The fourth strike of the day took off at 1355 from the *Essex* with sixteen F6Fs, eleven Helldivers and five Avengers. They joined with planes from the *Lexington* led by their CAG Commander Winters, the designated Target Coordinator. The target was Nikosho Airfield where they strafed and bombed several ships offshore.

On October 12, Task Group 38, with all four carrier groups, had flown 1378 sorties. It was a bad day for the Japanese. Admiral Fukudome recorded that when the air combat started he clapped his hands in elation that his fighters were winning the battle and declared, "Well done! Tremendous success!"[22] But soon he noted in shock that the falling aircraft were his Japanese planes and recorded, "Our fighters were nothing but so many eggs thrown at the stone wall of the indomitable enemy formation."[23]

The Japanese suffered severe damage of their ground facilities, including the complete destruction of Fukudome's headquarters. They had lost one-third of their fighters on the first American strike, and had only 60 remaining when the second wave attacked. By the third wave, there were no Japanese fighters to intercept the American strike. Task Group 38 suffered the loss of 48 aircraft on the first day.

Search missions to find the American carriers reported in the afternoon that they had spotted three groups of American carriers to the east of Formosa. In retaliation for the raids, at around 1400 as heavy weather moved in from a typhoon, fifty-five Tenzan torpedo bombers (Jills) of the Japanese "T"[24] Force took off from several air bases in a plan of attack called the "Milky Way Plan."[25] From 1900 to 2220 the Japanese bombers tried to get through the screening American surface combatants, but none were able to get through to the carriers. Reports vary, but Vice Admiral Fukudome admitted that he lost 42 planes in the raids, which accomplished nothing.[26]

Task Force 38 was located the Friday morning of October 13 some 70 miles, bearing 110° from Seikoo Roadstead, Formosa. At 0514 Lieutenant Commander Rigg led the sixteen Hellcats of the fighter sweep off the deck of the *Essex* and ascended at a rate of 500 feet per minute to an altitude of 12,000 feet to rendezvous with another sixteen F6Fs from the *Lexington*. The sweep was observed as it passed overhead by Ensign Borley who was still in his raft. The group headed to north and west Formosa in search of targets. They were quite disappointed to find only three Japanese planes that promptly ducked back into the clouds to avoid action.

The first strike was sent to attack Ansan Naval Base in the Pescadores under the command of Commander Winters. McCampbell launched with the VF-15 fighters as the mission Target Coordinator, with Lieutenant Morris leading the *Essex* F6Fs. The weather had turned worse than in the morning fighter sweep. The strike force ran into heavy cloud cover over the harbor with a ceiling from 1,500 and 8,000 feet.

Lieutenant Morris spotted a destroyer in a graving yard (an excavated drydock with a lock) and "skip-bombed"[27] it with two fragmentation bombs, hitting the ship's sides. Enemy AA fire opened up on the fighters as they strafed the area and dropped their bombs. A battleship was also bombed in the graving yard. The Helldivers and Avengers were likewise hampered by the cloud cover and trying to see an opening in the cover. In the process, Lieutenant (junior grade) Earl Clifford Mallette's Helldiver was hit during his dive run on a fuel storage tank west of Boka City by an anti-aircraft shell in the engine cowling. He managed to level off and jettison his bombs in preparation for a water landing. He flew low at some sixty feet off the water and at high speed with his aircraft smoking, when suddenly the plane rotated on its back as its right wing touched the water, sending the plane cartwheeling to a crash. The event was seen by and Lieutenant Roger Noyes and ARM1c Paul Harold Sheehan, who noted "that only an oil slick was visible in the vicinity of the crash."[28] He saw no evidence of survival as an enemy destroyer approached the area. Malette and his radioman, ARM2c Stanley Nelson Whitby, were declared dead, killed in action.

Meanwhile, Lieutenant (junior grade) M.P. Deputy took over as torpedo squadron strike leader when Lieutenant R.D. Cosgrove's radio went out. Deputy took his eight Avengers toward a hole in the clouds, but only four made it through. With the four that made it, Deputy and team make glide attacks on the naval base dropping their incendiary bombs and starting fires. The other four found another hole in the clouds and decided to attack Chomosui Airfield instead, starting fire to a hangar.

The second strike with seven Hellcats, ten Helldivers and eight Avengers had launched at 0932 from the *Essex* on a mission to bomb the Bukai Dam at Lake Jitsugetsutan on Formosa. The concrete dam was the primary power source for the island. McCampbell headed from the Pescadores to meet the strike on Formosa, but he was too late. The strike leader of the torpedo bombers misidentified the target and ended up bombing a small dam on Lake Kanan of no importance, and causing no discernable damage. Four torpedoes were launched at the dam, but only two were observed on runs toward the sloped surface. They hit the earth-filled dam, but did not explode. A 2,000-pound general-purpose bomb was also dropped on the dam, but caused no visible destruction. The attack event was deemed a failed experiment.

The Helldivers were tasked to attack the two powerplants and penstocks on Lake Jitsugetsutan, but, likewise, having failed to locate the correct target, they bombed a sugar-alcohol refinery at the town of Mato. The strike force returned home and trapped at 1338.

In the early afternoon, Halsey called for a fighter sweep to the airfields on Miyako Shima Islands and Ishigaki Shima, located north of Formosa in the Nansei Shoto island chain. The mission, led by Lieutenant Commander Duncan, took off from the *Essex* at 1316 with ten fighters, and was joined by fighters from the *Cabot*. The F6Fs strafed the planes, but none of them burned.

While over Miyako Shima at around 1600, newly promoted Lieutenant (junior grade) Kenneth Ashton Flinn, ran into trouble. His Hellcat was hit by AA fire and he was forced to make a water landing just off the beach. Unfortunately, for Flinn, he had landed in just six feet of water and his fighter was visible from the shore. Flinn exited his cockpit and stood on the wing to wave at his fellow pilots that came in to make low passes over him. After the F6Fs had to leave with their fuel running low, the Japanese took Flinn as prisoner. Tragically, after the war Flinn's fate was discovered. He had been tortured in the first days after his capture, and then beheaded.

On the way back to the carrier, Duncan's fighter team was attacked by Zekes, but they were rescued by Hellcats from *Princeton's* VF-17 squadron. The fighter sweep landed back aboard at 1708. The third and last strike of the day had also launched at 1316 from the *Essex*. The planes joined with aircraft from the *Lexington* and *Princeton* to make up a strike force of seventy-two aircraft. The mission target was Kagi Airfield on Formosa where a number of enemy planes had been sighted during the morning. The strike force strafed and bombed the airfield, destroying a large number of Japanese planes on the ground, as well as destroying a hangar and some buildings.[29]

By the 13th, Halsey had all but decided that his forces had accomplished their mission at Okinawa and Formosa, and planned to withdraw his fleet south to the Philippines. The Japanese had continued to send "snooper"[30] sorties at Mitscher's carriers throughout the day. In the evening, the *Essex* and the other ships of Admiral Sherman's TG 38.3 fought off the enemy planes successfully. Most of the intruders were shot down by antiaircraft weapons from the screening combatants or by combat air patrols. Two Betty bombers and one Judy torpedo bomber were shot down by the *Essex* CAP. The *Essex* was not directly attacked that evening.

Just after sundown at 1835, while Admiral John S. McCain's TG 38.1 was still recovering planes from the last day's missions, eight Japanese Jill torpedo bombers came in low and evaded radar detection to attack the force. Six of the bombers were downed by anti-aircraft fire, but a single Jill bomber dropped its aerial torpedo and hit the *Canberra* (CA-70) heavy cruiser in the starboard stern below the armor belt and between number 3 and 4 firerooms, killing twenty-three sailors instantly. The ship came to a dead stop with no propulsion, as 4500 tons of water flooded the number 1 and 2 engine rooms.

The usual approach in handling such a damaged ship was to have the crew evacuate to other warships and to scuttle the ship, but Admiral Halsey decided to tow it to safety at Ulithi. Ten minutes after the *Canberra* was hit, the cruiser *Wichita* received a message from Admiral McCain to "stand by to take under tow."[31] At 1905 CruDiv 13 and DesDiv 100 left their formation to go to the aid of the *Canberra*. The *Wichita* reached the *Canberra* at 1928 and began transferring the towline. By 2154 the *Canberra* was under tow making headway.

The task created a major challenge for Task Force 38. The crippled *Canberra* was only ninety miles off Formosa. In order to cover the *Canberra* towing operation, Halsey engaged the support of the XX Bomber Command of the Army Air Force, which sent 109 B-29s the next day from southern China to bomb southern Formosa in the Takao area. The B-29s arrived at 1230 and bombed for two hours, attacking shipping, airfields and dropping an amazing 650 tons of bombs on the Okayama Aircraft Assembly Plant.

With the support of General H.H. Arnold, the Commanding General of the Army Air Force, the Joint Chiefs of Staff insisted that the B-29s provide as much bombing of Formosa as was possible. Though providing fuel for the bombers in China was about as difficult as it got, the 20th Bomber Command was able to send two more B-29 missions to Formosa on the 16th and 17th. During the three days of Formosa attacks, the 20th Bomber Command dropped 1290 tons of bombs during their 232 sorties.

Halsey also directed Mitscher to conduct carrier air attacks over Formosa on October 14. Three carrier task groups were tasked for action, with Admiral Sherman's TG 38.3 assigned to the central sector. With the *Essex* positioned 100 miles east of Formosa, Commander McCampbell led the fighter sweep and strike force off at 0613 with eighty-three planes from the *Essex*, *Lexington*, *Princeton* and *Langley* to hit airfields in the Shinchiku area.

The *Essex* planes attacked three airfields and destroyed some hangars, building and only a few planes. The reason for the lack of Japanese air coverage was that their losses had been heavy the first two days from the TF 38 attacks and that many of remaining planes had been transferred to southern Kyushi. McCampbell's *Essex* components of the fighter sweep and strike group landed back aboard the *Essex* at 1001. The *Essex* set a course to the fueling rendezvous around noon.

While TGs 38.1, 38.2 and 38.3 had attacked Formosa, Admiral Davison's TG 38.4 launched several attacks on the Aparri and Laoag airfields in northern Luzon, but only destroyed a few enemy aircraft on the ground.

Meanwhile that day, the Japanese 6th Base Air Force had assembled 430 aircraft to attack the American carriers. The general attack force departed that morning from bases in southern Kyushi en route to refuel at Okinawa. After receiving intelligence that the carriers had been located sixty miles southwest of Ishigaki Island, the attack force took off to engage.

At 1510 the *Essex* saw its first serious attack by one bogey on radar located 12 miles out and closing. The carrier went to general quarters as the Japanese attacker approached in the clouds above the *Essex*. Finally, spotters saw the Judy (an Aichi Navy dive-bomber) and the carriers and screening ships fired a massive barrage of anti-aircraft fire. The dive-bomber came out of his dive at 1,500 feet, but decided to escape the fury of the defenders. The Judy later dropped one bomb on the *Lexington,* but it missed and was shot down.

The Japanese attacks on all of the task group carriers continued all afternoon, into the evening and beyond in to the following morning of October 15. The first wave of around 100 planes hit between 1400 and 1500, while the second wave consisted of a dozen scout planes, 110 fighter-bombers and 100 torpedo and heavy bombers. The T Force attacked with about twenty-five planes.

In the afternoon of October 14, three Japanese snooper planes were shot down by CAP planes of TG 38.3. Just after 1700, the *Essex* radar picked up two sets of five bogeys each approaching the carrier. At ten miles out, the bogeys began orbiting. At that moment another group of seven Jills were sighted just five miles away. The first two Jills headed in as the 5-inch anti-aircraft guns opened up. Closer in at some 2 miles out the 40mm guns were fired, and at even closer range the 20mm guns opened up on the intruders.

At 1710, *Essex's* Captain Weber ordered general quarters. Several seconds passed and then the first Japanese torpedo was launched at the starboard beam of the carrier. Weber issued an emergency turn to starboard and the torpedo passed underneath the stern. Six more enemy torpedoes were fired at the *Essex* during the following minutes. The lookouts saw four of them miss the carrier. After three minutes had passed the action was ended, as four Japanese torpedo bombers were smoking and crashed into the sea. The other attackers departed back toward their bases.

Meanwhile, in response to the days' attacks of October 14 from the three carrier groups, the Japanese sent out a group of from 11 to 16 torpedo-carrying Frans at dusk to attack Admiral McCain's TG 38.4. At 1845 a torpedo struck the light cruiser *Houston* (CL-81) and "detonated against the bottom amidships, midway between the centerline keel and the starboard bilge keel while the vessel was listing to port during a high speed right turn."[32] All her engineering spaces were flooded and power was lost. Dead in the water now some 150 miles bearing 104° from southern Formosa, she had been damaged even worse that the *Canberra* had been the previous day.

The *Houston* looked like it was about to break apart, so the destroyers immediately rushed to take off the crew. The *Houston's* Captain W.W. Behrens received conflicting reports from his various damage control stations and told Admiral McCain at 1933 that he planned to abandon ship. Later at 2020 Captain Behrens changed his mind in favor of getting a tow and saving the ship. Admiral McCain then ordered Captain E.E. Herrmann of the heavy cruiser *Boston* to undertake towing operations. By 2320 the towing hawser was attached and towing began.

Rear Admiral Laurance T. DuBose commanding Task Force 30.3, with his cruisers *Santa Fe*, *Birmingham* and *Mobile*, accompanied by eight destroyers, was ordered to take charge of towing the two cruisers. The task was given the informal name of CripDiv I. Halsey also detached light carriers *Cowpens* and *Cabot* to provide air cover for the crippled ships.

Admiral Halsey was concerned that covering the towing operations of the *Canberra* and *Houston* might jeopardize the upcoming strikes planned for Luzon and the Visayas set for October 16. Working with his experienced staff, he decided that they could protect the crippled ships and continue with key strikes on Leyte, Cebu and Negros.

Though the *Canberra* and *Houston* were the only American ships that had received more than superficial damage, the reports from the returning Japanese pilots from the American carrier attacks told only of fantastic successes, including the sinking of nine carriers. The Japanese Imperial Navy communiqué reported the sinking of 17 American ships and the destruction of 112 planes, but the public saw even more fantasy stats in the newspaper headlines declaring the sinking of more than 50 ships and 1,000 planes.

In fact, the actual results of the three-day Formosa air battles for CTG 38 was over 550 Japanese planes destroyed. *The War College Analysis I,* report on page 122 noted that CTG 38 claimed 655 destroyed including those from near the task force. The Japanese admitted they lost 495 planes, so the best estimate was somewhere between 550 and 600 enemy planes destroyed.

Air Group 15 of the *Essex* reported flying 334 sorties during the period of October 12–14, 1944, with 280 over land and shipping targets. They claimed 23 planes shot down in the air, 67 destroyed on the ground and six ships sunk.[33]

On October 15 the *Essex* and TG 38.3 conducted fueling operations with TG 30.8 (Fleet Oiler and Transport Carrier Group) some 350 miles southeast of Formosa. During the day, Admiral Fukudome sent three Japanese strikes against CripDiv I. The first strike from the 6th Base Air Force with 100 planes from Shinchiku did not find the American carriers. The second one from Okinawa attacked Admiral McCain's TG 38.1 and was badly hurt. The third one from Formosa in the afternoon returned to base when the strike commander's plane had engine trouble.

At 0920 on the October 16 a Japanese reconnaissance plane sighted the slow sailing CripDiv I ships. A strike of 99 carrier aircraft was launched from Kyushu to find and destroy any crippled American ships. For some unknown reason the strike was canceled. At 1000 another attack group of 107 planes took off from Formosa, and found the carriers at 1315 crossing the entrance to Luzon Straits. Fighters from the *Cabot* and *Cowpens* engaged more than half of the Japanese planes and shot down 41. Three enemy planes got through the screening ships. With the five-inch guns disabled by a power failure, one Fran dropped his torpedo at an altitude of 75 feet and 3,000 yards astern of the *Houston*. It struck the towed cruiser in the stern and blew the hangar hatch 150 feet into the air, while knocking twenty men overboard. The Fran flew parallel to the ship for some 200 yards before it was shot down by anti-aircraft fire. A few minutes later a Kate headed toward the *Santa Fe* and dropped a torpedo, but the American cruiser evaded the torpedo and shot down the Kate.

The *Houston's* fleet tug, *Pawnee*, continued to tow the crippled cruiser, as the *Santa Fe* came up to inquire of the status. Admiral DuBose called out using a bullhorn to Captain

Behrens, "Is your case hopeless?"[34] Berens replied, "Not hopeless but grave."[35] All but 300 men were taken off the *Houston*, while the remaining crew tried to restore enough power to pump 6300 tons of saltwater out of the crippled cruiser. No ship with that much flooding had ever survived, but she did.

Over Radio Tokyo, the reporters spoke of the destruction of CripDiv I and the last remnants of Task Force 38. Halsey decided to take advantage of the Japanese delusion and positioned Admiral Sherman's TG 38.3 with the *Essex* between Japan and CripDiv I in the hope of intercepting the unwary Japanese forces with the *Canberra* and *Houston* "bait."[36]

During the day Vice Admiral Shima's Second Striking Force with heavy cruisers *Nachi* and *Ashigara*, a light cruiser and a division of destroyers sailed from the Inland Sea and headed south to find and attack CripDiv I. While they were refueling their screening ships on the morning of October 16 east of Okinawa, Admiral Shima was attacked by two planes from the light carrier *Bunker Hill*. His force drove off the American attackers, but thirty minutes later Shima's force reversed course to the north to retire. He had estimated that there must be more "remnants"[37] than he had been led to believe in the area. Later in the afternoon, Admiral Fukudome sent a message to Shima advising him that there were "more than six carriers"[38] operating east of Formosa.

American radio intelligence was alerted on the 16th that Shima's Second Strike Force was in the area and Admiral McCain set up pie-shaped search areas to find and destroy the ships. The *Essex* was assigned a 50-degree sector to be search out to 300 miles. Air Group 15 sent out five teams with each made up of a dive-bomber and two fighters. One team with Lieutenants Matthews and Berree, and Ensign Craig shot down a Japanese dive-bomber and damaged a Nakajima two-engine P1Y Navy bomber before it outran them and escaped. A second search team with Lieutenants McCutcheon and Milton, and Ensign Pigman shot down a Nakajima bomber. The *Essex* search teams did not locate Admiral Shima's cruiser group.

During the Formosa campaign between October 11–16 Task Force 38 had severely diminished the Japanese air resources, but it had also cost the lives of sixty-four pilots and crewmen, as well as the loss of 76 planes in combat and 13 in other operational events.[39]

Rear Admiral Matsuda, a Japanese carrier flag officer, later recalled that before the 10th they

> had a satisfactory number of instructors and also a considerable amount of fuel; after that loss, gaso-line and instructors ran short and got worse and worse by degrees.... Also, the mechanics and engi-neers who kept planes in operation were left on islands. As islands fell, pilots came home; but maintenance men did not, and gradually skilled mechanics ran short.... And of course the skilled men producing planes got lower and lower in standards so that the output of planes was inferior.[40]

The Japanese were basking in the glory of their own delusion of the defeat of Halsey's Task Force 38. The outrageous claims of American losses led to mass celebrations endorsed by the Emperor of Japan for the "Glorious Victory of Taiwan."[41] Just after noon on October 17, Halsey sent his response to the Japanese claims in a message to Nimitz, which was released to the public on October 19, 1944: "Admiral Nimitz has received from Admiral Halsey the comforting assurance that he is now retiring toward the enemy following the salvage of all the Third Fleet ships recently reported sunk by Radio Tokyo."[42]

18

Battle of Leyte Gulf

"Jesus Christ, the whole Jap fleet's down here!"[1]

It was heralded by numerous superlatives descriptions; "the greatest naval engagement ever fought"; "the largest naval battle in history"[2]; "the greatest naval battle of the Second World War"[3]; and more. The Battle of Leyte Gulf was certainly all of these. Never has a naval battle involved so many facets. It involved the largest number of ships, covered a geographical area of 100,000 square miles, included nearly 200,000 participants, and used all the elements of naval warfare—air, surface, submarine and amphibious. The battle was composed of four separate, yet interrelated battles occurring in three different seas, separated by up to 500 miles.[4]

Back on October 10, the first group of MacArthur's Expeditionary Force ships began their northward advance some 1,250 miles from Hollandia, Dutch New Guinea, toward a position called "Point Fin"[5] off the coast of Leyte Gulf. This was the designated position that all units of the Force must transit to conduct the planned landings at Leyte Island set for October 20, 1944.

Reporting to General MacArthur, as Supreme Commander Southwest Pacific Area, was Vice Admiral Thomas C. Kinkaid, the Commander of the Seventh Fleet and the designated Commander of the Central Philippines Attack Force. Also reporting to MacArthur was Lieutenant General Walter Krueger, the Commanding General Sixth Army and designated the Commander of the Expeditionary Force.

The Central Philippines Attack Force consisted of 738 ships, and adding Halsey's Task Force 38 with 18 fleet carriers, 6 battleships, 17 cruisers and 64 destroyers, this was one the most powerful naval forces ever assembled.[6]

Admiral Davison's TG 38.4 fueled on October 16 and continued with attacks on Luzon for the next three days. Admiral McCain's TG 38.1, likewise, fueled on the 16th and then steamed with Admiral Bogan's TG 38.2 and Admiral Sherman's TG 38.3 on the 17th toward the Philippines. The *Essex* refueled on the 18th.

At 0630 on October 17, the 136-foot motor minesweepers of Commander Wayne R. Loud's Minesweeping and Hydrographic Group began sweeping the channel approach to Suluan Island. They were followed in by Rear Admiral Struble's Dinagat Attack Group of eight destroyer transports and miscellaneous craft carrying 500 men of the U.S. Army's 6th Ranger Infantry Battalion under Lieutenant Colonel H.A. Mucci. At 0650 the Japanese lookouts spotted the attack force and alerted the garrison commander, who immediately notified his superiors.[7]

At 0749 on that day, word reached Admiral Toyoda of the landing. In a combined meeting of the Army and Navy staff the next day, Admiral Toyoda's staff told the attendees that the *Sho Ichi Go* (meaning Operation Victory One) order had already gone out. The Army was advised that it was to be an "all or nothing"[8] operation in which the IJN would defeat the American invasion force in the Philippines, "or die trying."[9]

General Kenyro Sato, chief of the Military Affairs Bureau of the War Ministry, protested the use of the fleet in an improbable action in the Philippines, and thereby leaving the home islands open to an invasion. He responded in a voice filled with emotion, "The Combined Fleet belongs not only to the navy but to the state. Only the existence of the fleet will make the enemy cautious. So please, gentlemen, be prudent."[10]

The head of the Navy's Operations Section, Rear Admiral Tasuku Nakazawa, responded by explaining that the Philippines might be the last chance the IJN had to die with honor. With tears in his eyes he said, "Please give the Combined Fleet the chance to bloom as flowers of death. This is the navy's earnest request."[11] General Sato relented and a few hours later, the Emperor gave his approval to the execution of *Sho Ichi Go*. Admiral Toyoda issued the execute order at 1110 on October 18.[12]

The Japanese plan called for attacks on the Americans in the Philippines from four naval fleets. Just after midnight at 0100 on the 18th, the 1st Diversion Attack Force commanded by Vice Admiral Takeo Kurita sailed to the east from its base of operations at Lingga Anchorage near Singapore. His fleet arrived at Brunei Bay in northwest Borneo on October 20. After fueling and replenishing for two days, his fleet split into two naval forces and sailed at 0805. The Central Force with Admiral Kurita was the strongest force with the mammoth battleships *Musashi* and *Yamato*, the older battleships *Haruna*, *Nagato*, and *Kongô*; the heavy cruisers *Atago*, *Maya*, *Takao*, *Chôkai*, *Myôkô*, *Haguro*, *Kumano*, *Suzuya*, *Tone*, and *Chikuma*; the light cruisers *Noshiro* and *Yahagi*; and fifteen destroyers. This force sailed toward the northeast and up the west coast of Palawan Island, and then turned eastward across the waters of central Philippines to San Bernardino Strait.

The other force from Kurita's split, known as the Southern Force, sailed from Brunei Bay eastward through the Sulu Sea to make its way through the Surigao Strait between the islands of Mundanao and Leyte islands. This force was commanded by Vice Admiral Shoji Nishimura and consisted of the old battleships *Fuso* and *Yamashiro*, the heavy cruiser *Mogami*, and four destroyers. Departing from Bako, the principal port in the Pescadores, on October 21 and steaming south off western Luzon was the Second Striking Force to join with the Southern Force. It was commanded by Vice Admiral Kiyohide Shima with the heavy cruisers *Nachi* (Flag) and *Ashigara*, the light cruiser *Abukuma*, and four destroyers. This force refueled in the Calamian Islands and arrived late to join Nishimura's force, and follow them into Surigao Strait.

Sailing from the Hashirashima anchorage near Kure in the Inland Sea of Japan on the afternoon of October 20, was Vice Admiral Jisaburo Ozawa's Northern Force. This force consisted of the fleet carrier *Zuikaku*, light carriers *Zuihô*, *Chitose*, and *Chiyoda*, converted battleship-carriers *Hyûga* and *Ise*, light cruisers *Ôyodo* and *Tama*, and 5 destroyers, plus a screening force of the light cruiser *Isuzu* and four destroyers. His carrier force had only 116 aircraft aboard. On the evening of October 22, Ozawa turned south toward Luzon. His force was considered a decoy force to draw the American naval forces to the north, while the other Japanese naval attack forces came from the west on either side of Leyte Gulf to converge and destroy the amphibious landing force and ships in a pincer movement.

In addition to the naval surface forces, the Japanese tasked all available submarines off Formosa to head south to the eastern approaches to Philippines. On October 23, the surviving aircraft of the Second Air Fleet began arriving on the island of Luzon.[13]

At 2300 on October 19, MacArthur's invasion force was at Point Fin some 17 miles from Desolation Point on Dinagat Island beginning to transit into Leyte Gulf to position themselves seven miles off the beaches by 0800 the next morning. At dawn of October 20, 1944, the bombardment of the beaches began and by 0700 the battleships *Mississippi, Maryland,* and *West Virginia* began to fire their heavy shells, as other fire support destroyers joined in. The last 45 minutes before H-hour only naval gunfire and rocket barrages were directed at the beach, with no planes allowed.

The landing craft were formed up by the coxswains who starting their runs into the beaches around 0945. At 1000, H-hour, most of the first wave of the landing craft was on the beach at the four designated points along the western shore of Leyte Gulf. Thirty minutes earlier another landing took place at Panaon Strait to the southward. Aircraft came back in to provide close air support once the landings were in progress.

MacArthur and his staff watched the landing from the bridge of the light cruiser *Nashville.* MacArthur had an early lunch in his cabin and then as was reported by the press correspondents:

> MacArthur appeared on deck in fresh, smooth-pressed suntans, be-braided hat, and sun glasses, and let himself down a ladder into a barge. He took a position in the stern, directly behind and above Philippines' President Osmena, Resident Commissioner Romulo, Chief of Staff Sutherland, and Air Commander Kenney, looking all the time a picture of composure and dignified good humor. He smiled broadly and said to Sutherland, "Well, believe it or not, we're here." When the landing barge grounded and the forward end flapped down, MacArthur stepped calmly into knee-deep water and, with Kenney, Sutherland, and other officers around him, waded impressively ashore. The party inspected the beach, walked inland about 200 yards and studied the damage done by the bombardment.
>
> Back on the beach MacArthur delivered his liberation speech. He was genuinely moved; his hands shook and his voice took on the timbre of deep emotion. "People of the Philippines, I have returned...." He walked down the beach, sat down under a palm, chatted awhile with President Osmena. He was introduced to Major General Irving of the 24th Division. Then he went back to the *Nashville.* Douglas MacArthur had returned.[14]

The landing had been lightly opposed by air and land gunfire. A few LSTs had been hit causing seventy-five casualties. The light cruiser *Honolulu* was hit by an aerial torpedo, the heavy cruiser HMAS *Australia* was struck by a suicide plane on the bridge and the escort carrier *Sangamon* was damaged by a 550-pound bomb. By the end of the A-day plus one, 103,000 troops from the Army XXIV Corps and the X Corps had landed safely on Leyte. The ramps belonging to 151 LSTs were open on the beaches, while 58 transports, 221 LCTs, 79 LCI and hundreds of other vessels had been employed in Leyte Gulf. The landings were a success.[15]

On October 21 at dawn, the *Essex* launched a fighter sweep led by Commander McCampbell to San Jose Airfield on Mindoro Island. En route to the target, McCampbell sighted an enemy freighter anchored in the harbor and alerted the strike force following him. As he flew over Tablas Island scanning the area for the airfield, his fighter team spotted and then attacked two Nate bi-planes. The official report recorded, "two Nates, both of which were quickly disposed of...."[16] McCampbell claimed one Nate and Lieutenant Rushing had the other. Then McCampbell sighted a twin-engine scout plane, chased it, and downed it too.

The other pilots in McCampbell's sweep were engaged in action as well. Lieutenant Crittenden and Lieutenant (junior grade) A.C. Slack shot down a Sally heavy bomber. Slack found a Nate and downed it too. Then Ensign Minor A. Craig located a Mitsubishi reconnaissance plane called the Dinah and shot it down. Soon the escorting fighters and bombers from the air strike that trailed McCampbell's sweep fighters came in to attack. They had been joined by *Lexington* aircraft to attack shipping and air bases in the western Visayan Islands. The first target was the freighter McCampbell had contacted them about off Romblon Island. Several fighters descended to strafe the ship, leaving it burning as they departed.

Meanwhile, Lieutenant Brodhead took his Helldivers armed with 1,000-pound bombs in to attack shipping targets in Coron Bay. Assigned to engage two cargo ships, the strike leader, Commander Winters, they sank one ship and damaged the second on. As they were flying out, they spotted and strafed a small cargo ship.

As the fighters passed over a southern Luzon Island, they saw an airfield at Legespi. They strafed some of the "real"[17] aircraft on the ground and were able to exclude the "dummy"[18] planes they saw. On the chance there were

Commander David McCampbell standing in his full flight gear. Note the flag markings showing 21 downed Japanese planes (U.S. Navy photograph).

other enemy aircraft in the area, they radioed what they found to the *Essex*.

The next strike force of forty-three planes launched from the *Essex*. After a Hellcat and a Helldiver had to return for problems, the remaining forty-one planes attacked four airfields, but according to Commander Mini's action report, the raid was unsatisfactory. Mini explained that the mission was to attack Naga Airfield in southern Luzon. When there were no valued targets discovered, the group was split up, with eight Helldivers attacking Legespi air field (inflicting damage to two buildings), and 5 Helldivers attacking an apparent non-operational single airstrip on Iahuy Island (destroying a metal hangar and small fuel dump). One VB Helldiver with non-working dive flaps joined with VT torpedo bombers and attacked Antayan air field (damaging a barracks building).[19]

On October 22, the aircrews of the *Essex* were inactive, which mirrored the fairly low air activity levels of both the Japanese and American forces. There were some fifty TF 38 carrier sorties to hit Cebu, as well as some 50 medium and 50 heavy land-based bombers that struck a variety of targets. Though some intelligence was coming in about the Leyte Gulf landings by this time, the Japanese official records revealed that the high command were still perplexed regarding the low level of American carrier activity. They did not fully understand that Halsey's carriers were waiting for the arrival of the IJN.[20]

Of major concern for Halsey and Mitscher regarding the TF 38 carrier groups was the condition of the men after so many months of constant attacks. Mitscher remarked, "... probably 10,000 men have never put a foot on shore during the period of ten months. No other force in the world had been subjected to such a period of constant operation without rest and rehabilitation."[21] Reports from the ship's medical officers from the crew contained many references to fatigue. Mitscher worried that the slow reactions from these crews could reach a level where "they are not completely effective against attack."[22] With this situation in mind and seeing no significant Japanese reaction to the initial Leyte landings, at 2230 on October 22 Halsey sent orders to Vice Admiral McCain to detach TG 38.1 and sail to Ulithi for rest and replenishment.[23]

The submarines *Darter*, under Commander David H. McClintock, and the *Dace*, captained by Commander Bladen D. Claggett, had been patrolling the Palawan Passage since they left their base at Mios Woendi Island just east of Biak, Indonesia back on October 1. At 0116 on October 23 at the southern entrance to the Passage, as both submarines commanders were speaking to each other by megaphone while surfaced a few yards apart, the *Darter* picked up a radar contact 30,000 yards off. McClintock yelled to Claggett, "We have a radar contact! Let's go!"[24]

The two submarines closed at flank speed and saw what they believed to be eleven heavy ships and six destroyers steaming in two columns. In fact, the Japanese force consisted of ten heavy cruisers and five battleships in three columns with two light cruisers and 12 to 14 destroyers screening the force. The *Darter* broke radio silence and sent a contact report to Rear Admiral Christie, which was relayed to Halsey at 0620 on October 23. The American submarines had located Kurita's Central Force.

At 0532, the *Darter* fired all of its ten bow torpedo tubes from 980 yards at Admiral Kurita's flagship, the heavy cruiser *Atago* at the head of the port column. She sank eighteen minutes later. Then McClintock swung his submarine around to the left and fired his four stern tubes at the cruiser *Takao* at 1550 yards. Two of the *Darter's* torpedoes blew off her rudder and two propellers, while flooding three of her boiler rooms. The *Takao* was crippled, but eventually hobbled home to Brunei, never to return to the war. Meanwhile, the *Dace* fired her four torpedoes at the third ship in the starboard column, the heavy cruiser *Maya*. The ship exploded and sank.[25]

In light of the action of the *Darter* and *Dace* in locating and attacking Kurita's task force, Halsey directed his three carrier task groups to search the inland seas the morning of October 24 with each task group assigned a specific search arc out 300 miles. Each search team of one Helldiver and two Hellcats was responsible for searching a 10-degree arc, while other fighters were stationed at 100-mile intervals from the carriers to relay radio reports.

Meanwhile, at dawn of October 23, as the Japanese naval forces approached, Mitscher's carrier task groups rendezvoused with the tankers to refuel 280 miles northwest of Samar Island. After fueling was complete, Mitscher's Task Force 38 split up and headed to their assigned combat areas. Admiral Davison's TG 38.4 moved closest to the Seventh Fleet's landing forces, due east of Leyte Gulf. Admiral Bogan's TG 38.2 took up a position north of Davison's force, east of San Bernardino Strait. Admiral Sherman's 38.3 with the *Essex* moved to a position even further to the northwest and east of the main Philippine Island, Luzon.[26]

In compliance to Halsey's orders from the previous day, at 0610 on October 24 from 75 miles east of Polillo Island (located 18 miles off the eastern coast of Luzon) the *Essex* launched sector searches covering an arc from 225° to 245° out to 300 miles. The sixteen-plane mission with eight Helldivers and eight Hellcats was led by Lieutenant Commander

G.E. Duncan. Two minutes later the first of an eighteen-plane fighter sweep took off from the *Essex* to hit the Manila area airfields.

Curiously, the *Essex* fighter sweep found no airborne Japanese planes over Manila. But this was not the case for the search fighters. On the way out, Lieutenant (junior grade) R.P. Fush spotted a Lily (Kawasaki 99 light bomber) some 1,000 feet below him over Malvar Airfield. He descended and came in behind the bomber to shoot it down.

Off the coast, the *Essex* F6F pilots discovered a Japanese cruiser steaming alone and attacked it with bombs and machine gun fire. Lieutenant Commander Duncan hit the cruiser with his bomb, leaving the ship moving forward, but with oil streaming behind it. Heading back from the search, Ensign L.R. Self found two Zeros taking off from Malvar Airfield. Self selected one of the fighters as he dived, firing his guns. The fighter was hit in the cockpit and dropped to the ground, where its port wing hit the ground and was torn off, as the plane broke out in flames. The enemy pilot attempted to exit the burning plane, but Duncan continued to fire and killed him in his cockpit. He slumped over and burned with the plane. Duncan also shot down the second Zero when it reached 300 feet. The pilot was able to get out of the fighter, but the parachute did not deploy until he hit the ground.

As Lieutenant John C.C. Symmes's search group got near the Manila area, Ensign Jerome L. Lathrop spotted a Jill (Nakajima single-engine torpedo bomber), jettisoned his 500-pound bomb, attacked it, and shot it down. An hour later, between Cabra and Lubang Islands, Symmes found two Bettys and one Irving. As the Irving turned toward him, he alerted his wingman and told the other pilots to take on the Bettys while he jettisoned his bomb and went on the offensive. The Irving turned off to the right as Symmes sped to chase him down. He fired several bursts and downed the bomber.

Lieutenant G.E. Mellon went after one of the Bettys and shot it down. The enemy pilot made a descent water landing, but the plane sank and no heads were seen. Lieutenant (junior grade) R.N. Stime, Jr., downed the other Betty and, likewise, the pilot attempted a water landing, but it did not succeed. The wing of the Betty hit the sea, cartwheeled and broke up. No survivors were noted. Still loaded with his 500-pound bomb, Mellon and his fellow pilots discovered the cruiser *Takao* sitting dead in the water. Mellon made a run in and dropped his bomb, but had a near miss while the rest of the *Essex* search fighters strafed the ship.[27]

Meanwhile, that same morning just before 0600, Lieutenant (junior grade) Max Adams from Bombing Eighteen taxied his Helldiver into position on the wooden flight deck of the carrier *Intrepid*, the flagship of Admiral Bogan's TG 38.2. Adams launched a few minutes later and headed southwest off Samar Island to cover "sector three"[28] of his designated search area accompanied by four Hellcats. About half way across the Sibuyan Sea, two of the Hellcats broke off to loiter and relay by radio any contact reports.

Adams flew over Tablas Strait and, as he approached the southern tip of Mindoro Island on the western side of the Strait, he noticed several contacts on his radar screen off twenty-five miles. He immediately radioed his two Hellcat escorts and they all three headed south to investigate. Flying at 9,000 feet, they saw the tiny wakes of ships below them, beginning to make a turn. They descended to get a closer look and shortly a fighter in Adam's group radioed with call sign "Five Fox Lucky"[29] to the relay Hellcats the message, "13DD, 4BB, 8CA off southern tip Mindoro, course 050, speed 10 to 12 knots. No train or transports."[30]

At 0812, the battleship *Yamato* spotted a plane from Adams' group. Ten minutes later Halsey received the contact report in his flagship *New Jersey* in Admiral Bogan's TG 38.2 off San Bernardino Strait. Having confirmed the intension of Kurita's force to steam toward

Leyte and fully aware that the enemy fleet represented a major threat to the Leyte forces, Halsey took immediate action and sent orders directly to Sherman and Davison, bypassing Mitscher, to concentrate on Bogan's middle group, which was located the closest to the enemy, and to launch air strikes. He then directed Admiral McCain's TG 38.1, now some 600 miles east of Samar Island on its way to Ulithi, to put about and rendezvous with Captain Acuff's mobile tankers the next morning at 15° N, long 130° E.[31]

At 0837 Vice Admiral Halsey reacted to the report to make an urgent call via TBS radio ("Talk-Between-Ships"[32] was a very high frequency shipborne radio equipment of medium power used for ships tactically maneuvering) using the collective call sign for all the carrier task groups of his Fast Carrier Task Force 38 declaring, "Strike! Repeat: Strike! Good luck!"[33]

Three minutes before Halsey's voice order was broadcasted to the task group admirals, Commander McCampbell and his wingman, Lieutenant (junior grade) Rushing, with five other F6F pilots, had just spotted a group of sixty Japanese planes coming to attack Task Group 38.3. While McCampbell and Rushing climbed to attack the enemy fighters, beginning their legendary exploits by the downing of fifteen planes between them (*see Chapter 1*), Lieutenant Crittenden led the other four *Essex* F6Fs of the second division down from 18,000 feet to engage the enemy strike of torpedo bombers below. He shot down five bombers while others scored their kills. Lieutenant (junior grade) W.A. Lundin downed a bomber and a Zero, Lieutenant E.B. West shot down two Zeros and Ensign McGraw destroyed a bomber.

Somehow Lieutenant Strane got separated from the other fighters, and did not see any aircraft to attack until later when he spotted a single Zero heading back towards Manila. Flying at 9,000 feet, he found the fighter just above clouds at 5,500 feet and was concerned that the enemy pilot would descend into the clouds before he could engage.

Thankfully, the Zero pilot did not see his F6F as Strane swooped down, got on his tail and fired on it. His bullets hit and the stabilizer and parts of the Zero's wing began to fly off. The Japanese pilot decided to bail out and soon his parachute deposited him in the sea below. A destroyer came toward the downed enemy pilot to pick him up, but Strane did not observe it.[34]

Just after 0930, while McCampbell and his other six Hellcats were shooting down Japanese fighters and bombers like there was no tomorrow, a Japanese Judy (Yokosuka D4Y Suisei) bomber pilot was following behind a group of American Hellcats returning to land aboard the light carrier *Princeton*. The Judy came out of the low clouds and headed in toward the carrier totally undetected until lookouts saw it. Alerted, the *Princeton* turned her rudder hard over as the 20- and 40-mm anti-aircraft guns opened up on the intruder.

The Japanese bomber continued in and dropped its 550-pound armor-piercing bomb, which hit the center of the flight deck forward of the aft elevator. The bomb penetrated the flight deck and the hangar deck and exploded below in the ships' bakery. Observing from the bridge above, the commanding officer of the *Princeton*, Captain William H. Buracker, was not initially so concerned and noted, "I saw the hole, which was small, and visualized slapping on a patch in a hurry and resuming operations."[35] But the explosion tore open the hangar deck as flames reached six torpedo bombers being refueled and rearmed. The aviation fuel exploded and detonated the torpedo warheads, creating a burning hell.

Landing just as the explosions erupted below the flight deck, VF-27 pilot Ensign Paul Drury recalled, "I knew there was no way we were going to get airborne under those circumstances and I didn't think it was too likely that anyone was about to steal my plane."[36]

The situation deteriorated and at 1010 Captain Buracker set condition Salvage Control I, which directed that only 490 of the crew of 1,570 men remain aboard. Destroyers took the crew off and away from the carrier. When the ammunition in the ready-service lockers began to explode, condition Salvage Condition II was set which left only the damage control men aboard.

By 1330, the fires had been isolated to the aft magazine and the ship was on an even keel. The light cruiser *Birmingham* had been directed to approach close aboard the *Princeton* to help fight the fires and prepare to tow the carrier. The crew of the *Birmingham* continued firefighting and attempting to get towlines over to the carrier for two hours, when suddenly at 1530 a terrifying explosion blew up a major section of the stern of the *Princeton*, sending shrapnel of every shape and size across the exposed decks of the *Birmingham*. The gruesome event cost the lives of 229 men, wounded 236, and left 4 missing. The decks looked like a slaughterhouse, covered with blood.

The stern explosion had made the survival of the *Princeton* impossible. At 1600, Captain Buracker ordered to abandon ship, and thirty-eight minutes later he was the last man to leave the carrier. After the destroyer *Irwin's* torpedoes missed with six attempts from damaged tubes, the destroyer *Reno* was ordered by Rear Admiral Sherman to, "Destroy Princeton...."[37] The destroyer fired its torpedoes and at 1750 the 600-foot *Princeton* sank below the waves of the Sibuyan Sea. The carrier lost 108 killed and 190 were wounded, but 1,361 survived.[38]

At 1050, Lieutenant Morris launched with a CAP of seven other F6Fs from the *Essex*. One of the fighters had engine trouble and had to return to the carrier. Morris and his team flew cover over the task group as smoke poured up from the damaged *Princeton* below them. Three of the Hellcats were vectored out to engage a new group of thirty Japanese planes coming in. When they saw the American fighters approach, the dive-bombers and torpedo planes turned away while the fighters formed into a Lufberry circle.

Morris led his division of four Hellcats to the attack while four enemy bombers broke off and headed to the deck. The Japanese fighters split into two-plane sections as Morris picked one out to engage. He came in from above and made a run on the Zero firing bursts that hit the intruder. The enemy plane caught fire and crashed. In the meantime, his wingman headed off after one of the four bombers, downed it, and then rejoined Morris.

Morris made a run on a pair of Zeros that were heading his way. Morris's bullets missed the fighters and as he turned, the Zeros followed him and fired, scoring hits on his F6F. Morris escaped into a nearby cloud and after he was inside, he made a full circle and exited the cloud the same place he had entered. He found the Zeros had gone to the spot on the other side of the cloud where they expected the Hellcat to exit. Morris got on the tail of one of the fighters and shot it down.

The enemy hits on his fighter began to have their effect. Morris's engine started to cough and hydraulic fluid was leaking. He broke off and headed home toward the *Essex*. Meanwhile, Lieutenant (junior grade) J.B. Bare was making high runs on the Lufberry circle. When he noted a Zero on the tail of a Hellcat, he made a run causing the Zero to break off. Attacking another Zero from the rear, Bare saw the fighter fall away into a spin and smoke all the way to a water crash.

As the Japanese fighters moved southward, Bare observed a fellow Hellcat moving toward a group of three Zeros. The Zeros split out allowing the Hellcat to get tail position on one of them. Bare also got a rear position just as one of the Zeros executed a wingover to sit behind another F6F. Bare downed the Zero, but soon was engaged by a pair of Zeros. Bare turned into one of the fighters and shot his way out.

Lieutenant Twelves attacked a straggler Jill torpedo bomber and fired on it, causing a huge explosion. Twelves assumed he must have had hit a torpedo to create such a blast. As two Zeros descend to attack him, he powered up and climbed to join Lieutenant Morris above. They both made runs from high and Twelves was able to down two Zeros in the action.

The majority of the Japanese Zeros were continuing to maintain the Lufberry circle. Twelves tried to wait from on high to spot a weak point, but the hits suffered from his earlier action with the Zeros had damaged his oil lines. When one line opened and sprayed oil on his windshield, Twelves decided to depart with another F6F leading him back to the *Essex*.

Other *Essex* fighters continued to fly CAP above the task group as more Japanese bombers approached. Lieutenant (junior grade) N.B. Voorhest attacked an Aichi dive-bomber getting ready to start a dive run from 19,000 feet. He climbed up to attack as the Judy headed into a low dive and a water crash. Ensign W.R. Johnson spotted a torpedo bomber out to one side and followed it down as it dived, downing it just above the waves.

A twin-engine heavy Nakajima bomber was chased by Lieutenant (junior grade) W.N. Anderson at 2,000 feet altitude as he fired into the wing root and starboard engine. The bomber hit the water at an angle and exploded.

The entire morning of October 24 had the *Essex* on alert for enemy air attacks, and they seemed never to end. At 1015, a twin-engine Betty bomber was able to penetrate the CAP and attack the *Langley*. It was followed by an F6F and continued on until the anti-aircraft flak hit him and he crashed between the *Essex* and *Langley*. The following Hellcat nearly got fired on too, but he banked and wiggled his wings.

Twenty minutes later another raid came in fast with five bombers. Two were downed and the other three were chased off before they could drop their weapons. At 1100 yet another raid approached the *Essex*. While Admiral Sherman's Task Group 38.3 had been consumed in defending against the Japanese air attackers and trying to save the *Princeton*, Admiral Bogan's TG 38.2 and Admiral Davison's TG 38.4 were sending hundreds of planes on strikes as ordered by Halsey at 0837 that morning.

Led by Commander James H. Mini, the *Essex* launched its first strike of eight Hellcats, twenty Helldivers and sixteen Avengers at 1053 and joined up with the same number and type of aircraft from the *Lexington*. The overall strike, commanded by the *Lexington* CAG-19, Commander T.H. Winters, Jr., headed across Luzon and ran into low overcast limiting visibility to five miles. The enemy task group was located at 1330.[39]

Lieutenant Commander John Bridgers, the newly promoted skipper of VB-15, recalled that for the mission that they flew westward through heavy cumulus clouds when the strike group became separated. They moved across the southern tip of Luzon Island and out into the inland waters. No ships were seen. Commander Mini directed a division of the fighter cover to scout to the south under Lieutenant Baynard Milton. Soon a message was received from him that the whole Japanese fleet must be down there.

The entire group headed south at 15,000 feet and above the scattered clouds. As they approached enemy fired colored bursts of radar-directed AA fire up through the clouds. Commander Mini radioed that he was ready to attack a battleship directly in front and below him, and directed Bridgers to move east and concentrate fire on a second battleship that he knew would be visible when he came to the edge of the cloud bank.[40]

Mini took a division of Avengers with him, leaving the others with Bridgers. "Suddenly, from beneath the clouds, steamed a dreadnought of vast proportions, the largest I had ever seen."[41] It was the *Musashi*.

The *Musashi* battleship fired up multiple streams of tracers at the attacking planes, with larger AA guns sending up colored bursts of smoke filling the sky. The other Japanese screening ships fired at the Americans too. Bridgers radioed that they were beginning their high-speed approach to alert the torpedo squadron leader to begin their attack at sea level. The bombers started their power glide down to 12,000 while keeping the *Musashi* on their port side. Bridgers signaled the Helldivers to attack, while he began his stern-to-bow attack run with his wingman, Warren Parrish, in company on his port wing. He increased his angle of attack and opened his flaps.

Suddenly his Helldiver went into a skid which he could not control. All he could do was skid along the length of the ship and hope he could drop his bomb near the ship. He had never encountered this type problem. During the dive Bridgers saw the battleship train their main battery of heavy guns toward the torpedo planes that were heading in low. When the guns fired the entire ship was lost in a cloud of smoke, which was most frightening to the attackers.

Bridgers released his bomb at 2,500 feet, and then closed his dive brakes and glided at low altitude above the waves. When he was able to turn, he could see the battleship was undamaged. Out of range, he started making gentle S turns to allow his division to rejoin with him and climb to altitude.[42]

Lieutenant (junior grade) Warren Parrish, contrary to Bridgers, made a perfectly controlled vertical dive and released his bomb amidships scoring a hit on the *Musashi*, and departed at such a low altitude that his propeller sent up salt spray. He had to climb to avoid a Japanese destroyer that sent 20mm and 37mm anti-aircraft shells at him. Parrish later earned a Navy Cross for his attack on the 67,000-ton super battleship. Lieutenant (junior grade) Matthews also hit the *Musashi* with his 1,000-pound bomb.

As they headed home, Bridgers noted that none of other planes were to be seen, including the skipper's dive bombers, or fighters or torpedo planes. As for his dive control problem, his gunner, Bob Cribb, told him that the dive brakes only worked on one side, which created the violent skidding they experienced.[43]

While the Helldivers were attacking the *Musashi*, Lambert split his group of Avengers into two sections, sending one down the port side and the other with him down the starboard side of the battleship. Lambert recorded: "Coming in through the most intense and accurate AA yet experienced, the squadron made three hits [Musashi reported four hits] on one battleship, two hits on another battleship, and two hits each on two different heavy cruisers. In this action, two planes were lost, but the pilot and turret gunner of one plane, Lieutenant (j.g.) W. F. Axtman and J.T. O'Donnell, were rescued by friendly forces after watching the entire action from their rubber boat."[44]

Bob Cosgrove had led the Avengers down the port side and scored one hit, while his gunner, Loyce Deen, was hit by shrapnel in his right foot. Meanwhile, in Avenger pilot Jerome Crumley's crew, gunner David Miller had been replaced by a photographer to record the attack from the turret with two 16mm movie cameras. The pilot and radioman, Eugene Shannon, had briefed the photographer to buckle up, but he did not in order to have free range of movement to position the cameras. During the attack run-in the flak caused the plane to bounce around, and finally sending a camera into Shannon's compartment. The camera opened up, sending 500 feet of film into the space as Shannon recalled,

All of the sudden, I was surrounded by 16mm film, which was like trying to get out of a spider's web. The more I tried, the more tied up I got! We're bouncing around, flak is going off to either side, shrapnel is flying through the airplane, and there I am, struggling to get free of this movie film! I finally got free just as we dropped the torpedo and pulled up really sharp. I looked out the window and we were maybe fifty feet above the bow of the biggest battleship I ever saw, and I was staring right at these Japanese officers in white uniforms on the bridge.[45]

The attacks on the *Musashi* by the *Essex* Helldivers had scored two hits on the starboard amidships near turret number three aft, which caused casualties in the anti-aircraft gun crews. Two other bombs hit turret number one on the port side. Lambert's Avengers sent four torpedoes into the battleship, sealing her fate. Two hit on the starboard bow, flooding the storerooms, while the third one hit on the port side forward of turret number one. The fourth torpedo struck on the port side amidships. As the last *Essex* planes left the scene around 1315, the *Musashi* damage control crews attempted to control the flooding, but the ship was some thirteen feet by the bow and its speed had dropped to 20 knots.

Commander Mini, and his wingman, Lieutenant (junior grade) Lauren E. Nelson, as well as Lieutenant (junior grade) Fontaine scored hits on the battleship *Nagato*, while Lieutenant (junior grade) Kelley bombed an *Atago*-class cruiser. In the action, Commander Mini had been hit in the *Nagato* attack and wingman Nelson escorted him back home to the *Essex*. Mini was unable to lower his landing gear, and ditched next to the destroyer *Morrison*. Both he and Aviation Radioman 1st Class Arne Frobom were rescued.[46]

At 1259, the *Essex* launched its second and last strike of eight Hellcats and twelve Helldivers to again attack the big ships in Sibuyan Sea. They arrived over Kurita's force at 1359 when Lieutenant Noyes took his Helldivers in to bomb the *Musashi*, *Nagato* and heavy cruiser *Chokai*. Barney Barnitz's bomb hit the *Musashi* first, followed by Crellin, Hall, Talbot, Platt and Gardner. When Barnitz came out of his dive, Lieutenant (junior grade) Conrad Crellin and his gunner, Aviation Radioman 3rd Class Carl Shelter, were hit by *Musashi's* anti-aircraft fire. It was deadly. The Helldivers' left wing fuel tank caught fire as the plane flipped over on its back at 500 feet altitude. They crashed into the sea in an inverted position at 200 miles per hour, instantly killing both of them.

Admiral Kurita's Central Force had been under attack for many hours. A total of 259 planes from Task Force 38 carriers had unleashed their weapons on the Japanese. The six and final attack on the *Musashi* had seen the battleship receive seven more hits, causing the ship to list 6° to port from flooding. The main steering engine soon went out and the ship was dead in the water. The *Musashi* had taken 19 torpedoes and 17 bomb hits. The heavy cruiser *Myoko* was badly damaged and had turned back to return to Borneo.[47]

At 1530, Admiral Kurita ordered his fleet to head west, and out of range of the American attackers. Thirty minutes later he sent the following message of explanation to Admiral Toyoda:

> Originally the main strength of [my] force had intended to force its way through San Bernardino Strait about one hour after sundown, coordinating it moves with air action. However, the enemy made more than 250 sorties against us between 0830 and 1530, the number of planes involved and their fierceness mounting with every wave. Our air forces, on the other hand, were not able to obtain even expected results, causing our losses to mount steadily. Under these circumstances, it was deemed that were we to force our way through, we would merely make ourselves meat for the enemy, with very little chances of success. It was therefore concluded that the best course open to us was temporarily to retire beyond the reach of enemy planes.[48]

The American air strikes against Kurita's Central Force had ended for the day, to his surprise since it was still daylight. Knowing his mission was to attack Leyte Gulf the next day coordinating with the Southern Force with Admirals Shima and Nishimura coming through the Surigao Strait, at 1715 he ordered the force to reverse course across the Sibuyan Sea and head to San Bernardino Strait.

On the way, Kurita's force passed the dying *Musashi* as the sun moved lower on the horizon. Thirty minutes later at 1930, as the force moved out of sight, the *Musashi* rolled slowly to port and within minutes, she was capsized with her massive propellers extending high in the darkening sky. After a momentary pause and a great underwater explosion, the battleship sank taking 1,023 of its 2,399-man crew with her to the bottom. The Battle of the Sibuyan Sea was at an end.[49]

Earlier, just after 0600 of the 24th the *Enterprise* had launched two groups of fighters and bombers to the southwest. The fighters were armed with their .50 caliber ammunition and four five-inch rockets while the bombers carried two 500-pound bombs. The group crossed the islands of Bohol, Cebu and Negros and then headed out into the Sulu Sea. At 0820 they saw seven ships in formation heading northward at 15 knots. Close inspection revealed two battleships (*Fuso* and *Yamashiro*), a heavy cruiser (*Mogami*) and four destroyers. They had identified Vice Admiral Nishimura's Force "C" in the Sulu Sea 75 miles southeast of the Cagayan Islands on a course toward Surigao Strait. When the *Enterprise* strike group had departed the scene, they had exploded a bomb on the stern of the battleship *Fuso*, and made a direct hit on the forward gun mount of the destroyer *Shigure*. The enemy force steamed ahead.

Vice Admiral Shima's Striking Force, which had departed Coron Bay at 0400 that morning sailing south, was spotted by a V Army Air Force bomber at 1155 near the Cagayan Islands. His force consisted of the heavy cruisers *Nachi* and *Ashigara*, light cruiser *Abukuma* and four destroyers.[50]

By noon that day, both Admiral Halsey and Admiral Kinkaid were aware of three of the forces that posed a threat to Leyte Gulf. Now that it appeared that the most powerful of the three enemy naval forces under Kurita had suffered at the hands of his carrier task groups, his attention was focused on the question that his Air Operations Officer, Captain Doug Moulton, declared in no uncertain terms as he pounded his fist on the chart table, "Where in hell are those goddam Nip carriers?"[51]

At 0830, and again at 1145 that morning of October 24, Vice Admiral Ozawa had received word that his search planes had made contact with Task Force 38 forces. At 1145, he launched his first strike from 150 miles north of Task Group 38.3 with 40 fighters, 28 dive-bombers, 6 torpedo planes and 2 reconnaissance aircraft. The strike pilots, having little flying experience, had been briefed to land on friendly airfields on Luzon after the strike.

At 1245 Lieutenant John Monsarrat, the *Langley's* fighter director, noticed some sixty bogeys in the northeast sector of his radar screen. It was Ozawa's strike force coming in from 105 miles out. Since the flagship *Essex* was coordinating fighter direction for the task group, they ordered Monsarrat to intercept the strike with four *Langley* fighters. He complied and sent four F6Fs to climb and intercept the enemy on a bearing of 035°. Knowing he needed more interceptors, Monsarrat asked the *Essex* for help, and soon another eight fighters had joined the CAP intercept. As the lead fighter pilot of the *Langley* called, "Tally-ho indicating the enemy planes were in sight,"[52] Monsarrat responded, "Help is on the way."[53]

The Japanese 76-plane strike had no real impact on the Americans. Half the Japanese planes were shot down and the others retired back to Luzon. Only a few Japanese fighters were ever in gunfire range of TG 38.3 ships. During debrief sessions some of the American pilots noticed the fighters had tailhooks.[54]

At 1405, Admiral Sherman's TG was finally able to launch search planes to the north. At 1640 Sherman's Hellcats spotted Ozawa's force 190 miles to the north. The contact report accurately described the ships present. Sherman was a happy man and later recalled, "The carrier forces to the north were our meat; they were close enough so that they could not get away if we headed to the northward.... As the sun went down the situation was entirely to my liking and I felt we had a chance to completely wipe out a major group of the enemy fleet including the precious carriers which he [the enemy] could ill afford to lose."[55]

Meanwhile, at 1935 Kurita's Central Force was located by a night F6F(N) pilot from the *Independence* heading 120° at 12 knots towards Tacao or Masbate Passes, which were the two entrances to San Bernardino Strait. A contact report was radioed to the carrier at 1958 and relayed to Admiral Halsey at 2006, and then to Admiral Kinkaid at 2024.[56]

Halsey had to make a critical decision at this point regarding his next move. Should he send his surface forces and carriers against Kurita or focus all his TF 38 resources at destroying Ozawa's Northern Force? Another option was to split his forces to both targets. His fateful decision was revealed at 2024 when he sent a message to Kinkaid, "Strike reports indicate enemy [Kurita's Central Force] heavily damaged. Am proceeding north with 3 groups to attack enemy carrier force at dawn."[57]

Admiral Kinkaid misinterpreted his message to mean that Halsey was taking his carriers north, while leaving behind at San Bernardino Strait Vice Admiral Lee's Task Group 34, consisting of four battleships, two heavy and three light cruisers and nineteen destroyers. The misunderstanding was based on an earlier message entitled "Battle Plan"[58] sent by Halsey at 1512 to TF 38 ships and to Nimitz that directed the formation of Lee's TG 34 force. Kinkaid, who was not even an information addressee on the earlier message, had intercepted the message and was now comforted by the information of the last message from Halsey. Kinkaid later recalled, "This division of gunships was exactly correct in the circumstances."[59] In fact, not even a few token destroyers were guarding San Bernardino Strait. This was the most unfortunate mistake Admiral Halsey ever made.[60]

Halsey had listened to his staff officers, who did not all agree with his decision to leave the strait unguarded, and then put his finger on the location of Ozawa's Northern Force on the chart plot and said, "We will run north at top speed and put those carriers out for keeps."[61] He added, "It preserved my fleet's integrity, it left the initiative with me, and it promised the greatest possibility of surprise."[62]

At 2022 Halsey ordered Bogan's TG 38.2 and Davison's TG 38.4 to steam north at 25 knots to join Sherman's TG 38.3 and attack Ozawa. At midnight these three fast carrier task groups, Lee's TG 34, the other battleships and cruisers of TF 38 surface forces with Halsey aboard his flagship *New Jersey*-a total force of 65 ships-were racing north. This was just what Ozawa's "decoy force"[63] of 17 ships had planned for and had now accomplished. Meanwhile, at 0035 on the early morning of October 25, Kurita's Central Force had completed transiting San Bernardino Strait and sailed into the Philippine Sea.[64]

The morning of October 25, 1944, saw Ozawa's Northern Force steaming south from 100 miles northeast of Task Force 38 when his radar operators picked up blips from American search planes. He immediately turned around and sailed north for 40 miles until he was located.

After he finished breakfast, Lieutenant John D. Bridgers and his fellow pilots of VB-15 gathered in the ready room. Bridgers later recalled,

A new plan of attack had been devised. During the night, our battleships and some of the cruisers and destroyers had been withdrawn from the fast carrier task force and reassembled as a surface force. These ships were then stationed about a hundred miles north of the carriers, the idea being that we would try to disable their ships by aerial bombardment and leave them for the surface force to sink with their more accurate gunfire. On this day, we were armed with semi-armor-piercing bombs, sharp nosed like a shell for penetration and armed by a delayed-action fuse. They would penetrate and detonate deep in the ship's bowels. We manned our planes under a still-black sky and started our engines with no lights showing.[65]

What came to be known as the Battle of Cape Engaño was about to begun east of that cape. At 0555 on the morning of October 25, the *Essex* launched its first strike from 350 miles northeast of Luzon against Ozawa's Northern Force with fourteen Hellcats, fifteen Helldivers and twelve Avengers. Four fighters were separated from the CAP to search for the exact position of the enemy force, which was sighted at 0710 by Lieutenant (junior grade) Homer Voorhest of VB-15 who was flying an F6F. He found two battleships, four carriers, five cruisers, and six destroyers. The leader of the search, Lieutenant Collins, had remained high and watched the Japanese fleet until his fuel ran low.

The first air strike of 110 planes from the *Essex*, *Lexington* and *Langley* was led by Commander McCampbell as target coordinator for TG 38.3. His group had been orbiting some fifty miles from the Japanese, waiting for the enemy contact report. When he received it, the strike headed in. He and wingman Rushing stayed high as he send down ten F6Fs loaded with 500-pound bombs. They dropped their bombs and strafed as they went.

As they came in, one Japanese carrier had already launched twenty Zeros. Lieutenant Strane saw half a dozen Zeros at 9,000 feet ready to attack the American bombers. He took his fighters in to attack the enemy fighters, and scored his first Zero shot down on his initial bursts. On seeing two Zeros firing at his wingman diving to the left, Strane maneuvered to down both of the enemy fighters.

Before he knew it, he was engaged in a fight with a group of Zeros. He turned into one Zero, fired his guns and saw flames and smoke erupting, but before he could see the plane crash, another Zero came at him head on from above firing its 20mm shells. Strane attempt to get away, but he was hit in his engine, which failed, as flames erupted.

He used his radio to give his position before bailing out from 2,500 feet. His parachute caught on the rim of his cockpit for a few seconds and then it released and he was free. As two Zeros circled him, he waited until the last moment to pull his ripcord. The parachute opened and he made a single swing until he hit the water. He went down, swallowing some salt water, and then came up and got into his life raft. Strane fired some flare cartridges from his "Very pistol,"[66] but was unable to get anyone's attention in the bright sun. He waited it out, hoping for a rescue, and watched as the battle raged above him. He was later picked up by a destroyer at dusk looking for the enemy fleet.[67]

From above the Helldivers, Lieutenant (junior grade) Charles White in his F6F met three Zeros in the attack. White pulled up and fired head-on at one of the enemy fighters. The Zero immediately broke out in flames, as a wing detached and crashed. He then descended to gain speed and saw another Zero in front of him. White fired and the Zero began to break apart, went into a spin and crashed. As he was ascending, Lieutenant (junior grade) Ralph E. Foltz reacted to seeing a Zero and almost went into a spin by turning so sharply. He was able to get control and shot down a Zero.

Lieutenant Singer downed one Zero and headed after another one. As his wingman chased after four Zeros, a fighter was able to get on Singer's tail firing at him. Singer made a quick right turn but could not lose the Zero as another one came in. He was able to fire a deflection shot at the second Zero as it began to smoke. With the first Zero still on his rear, Singer dived from 7,000 to 3,000 feet and pulled out to the right. Though his windshield was fogged up, he was able to see at the edge of his windshield that the Zero was heading directly at him. Singer fired and the Zero blew up.

As McCampbell began assigning groups of planes to targets, Lieutenant Bridgers, leading his VB-15 Helldivers, got his target from McCampbell, "He directed me to take a carrier [the light carrier *Chitose*] that was rejoining the formation from the starboard quarter. It was returning from turning into the wind to launch aircraft. I began my high-speed approach from the usual 12,000 feet and did what was called a 'bursting fart break-up.' I did a mild wingover across my wingman, Warren Parrish."[68] Bridgers made his dive and leveled out with ease.

> Starting my line-up on the bow as my aiming point, I carried my attack down to 1,500 feet before I released my bombs and was low over the water before I leveled out. I found myself completely surrounded by enemy ships and had not noticed the intense AA fire until then. I weaved between the ships, maintaining whatever distance possible from each ship. I took a moment to kick my plane up on one wing and saw two splashes close aboard the carrier's port side and smoke coming up through its flight deck.

Bridgers' Helldivers had dropped twelve 1,000-pound bombs on the carrier and scored eight hits. As they departed, the *Chitose* was burning and listing to one side. McCampbell saw that the attacks were successful and redirected the torpedo bombers, led by Lieutenant Commander Lambert, to attack one of the battleships on the starboard side of the enemy formation. Four of Avengers were already into their glide in runs and released their torpedoes, scoring two hits into the enemy carrier. The carrier later sank at 0937.

Lambert split his attack force on each side to attack the battleship. Lieutenant J.G. Higgins, Lieutenant (junior grade) L.G. Muskin and Ensign Kenneth B. Horton both scored hits. Lieutenant (junior grade) H.D. Jolly, Ensign D.J. Ward and Lieutenant (junior grade) J. Smyth dropped their torpedoes toward the *Ise*-class battleship. Lieutenant Charles W. Sorensen and Lieutenant (junior grade) L.R. Timberlake release their torpedoes against another carrier, with one hitting amidships. While Lambert and Lieutenant (junior grade) S.M. Holladay were running in toward the battleship, an enemy carrier turned across their tracks. Both of them released their torpedoes and claimed hits.[69]

The fleet carrier *Zuikaku* had taken one torpedo from either an *Intrepid* or *San Jacinto* plane, which disabled her communications and caused the ship to list six degrees. The steering was left so difficult that Ozawa moved his flag to the light cruiser *Oyodo*. The destroyer *Akitsuki* sank immediately.

Before the first strike had landed back aboard their carriers, at approximately 0835 the second strike was already launched. The second strike, consisting of 18 Avengers, 6 Helldivers and 12 Hellcats from the *Lexington*, *Langley* and Davison's TGs *Franklin*, came in between 0945 and 1000. The "enemy force presented a picture of wild confusion"[70] as the planes from the *Lexington* and *Franklin* scored bomb hits on the light carrier *Chiyoda*. She was "set heavily afire, causing flooding and a sharp list."[71] The bomb that hit her at 1018 disabled her engines. The converted battleship *Hyuga* attempted to get her in tow, but was unsuccessful. The light cruiser *Isuzu* and destroyer *Maki* were called in to take the crew off the stricken carrier, but they failed, leaving *Chiyoda* abandoned for now.

Planes from the *Franklin* and *Langley* attacked stragglers including a destroyer, the light cruiser *Tama* and *Hyuga*. Aircraft from the *San Jacinto* and *Belleau Wood* took on the light cruisers and hit the *Tama*. Air coordinator McCampbell had to return to the *Essex* for fuel, but Lieutenant C.O. Roberts from the *Belleau Wood* fighter squadron watched the Northern Fleet formation settle between 1100 and 1200. He reported the 14 enemy ship locations to the third strike. Based on Robert's information, the orders were to focus the strike on Ozawa's main body to the north bearing 351° at 102 miles from the *Lexington*.[72]

The third launch catapulted off between 1145 and 1200, and reached their targets by 1310. *Lexington's* Commander T. Hugh Winters served as air coordinator on this 98-plane strike. Led by Lieutenant Commander Duncan, the *Essex* had contributed twelve Hellcats, fourteen Helldivers and ten Avengers to the third strike. With Commander Mini floating in his raft, Lieutenant Roger Noyes was in charge of the *Essex* Helldivers.

With the enemy carriers retreating to the north, leaving their cripples and remaining surface ships behind, the third strike went after undamaged ships. The *Essex* bombers were assigned to attack the carrier *Zuiho* located on the western side of the Japanese force. Six planes attacked the carrier, as it turned around toward the southeast to avoid the bombs. Four Avengers were also assigned to go after the carrier. The *Essex* attackers along with other TG planes hit the carrier.

Nine *Essex* Helldivers attacked the *Zuikaku*, the pride of the Pearl Harbor attack. The carrier, which had been hit by previous attacks from others, tried to avoid the attack. Lieutenant H.A. Goodwin and Ensign A.R. Hodges managed to drop 2,000-pound bombs in the center of the flight deck of the carrier. Aircrew gunners saw flames coming out of the bomb holes as the planes pulled out. The *Zuikaku* rolled over and sank at 1414.

On pulling up from the attack, Noyes was hit by heavy anti-aircraft fire with his bomb bay still open. Fires started on both his wings as he went into a vertical bank to the right. He almost hit the water, but was able to pull out. Incredibly, his fires went out from the dive and he limped back to the *Essex* damaged as he was holding a reduced 125 knot speed. The AA shells had cut the control cables to the port aileron, making it difficult to keep level and on course. His hydraulic system was a mess and prevented him from closing the bomb bay doors or using flaps. After making a good landing, the air officer decided to have the deck crew push it over the side. The rest of the *Essex* planes from the third strike landed aboard at 1439.

The fourth strike group launched around 1315 and was over their targets at 1445. The *Essex* was not part of this strike. The focus was on the Main Body now located 30 miles ahead of the rest. The planes from the *Lexington* and *Langley* claimed hits from their bombs and torpedoes against the *Ise* battleship, but were unable to sink the stubborn ship primarily because of its fierce anti-aircraft fire. The crippled *Zuiho* was hit by 27 planes from strike aircraft and went below the waves at 1526.

At 1512 the *Essex* launched fourteen Hellcats and Helldivers, plus ten Avengers on the fifth and last strike of the day. They joined with planes from the *Lexington*, *Langley* and the *Enterprise* on the 96-plane strike, led by Commander Malcolm T. Wordell of the *Langley* air group. At this time, the remaining Northern Force consisted of the two 30,000-ton battleships, *Ise* and *Hyuga*, three light cruisers *Isuzu*, *Oyodo* and *Tama*, and eight destroyers. Three enemy carriers were sunk and the fourth one, *Chiyoda,* was crippled and dead in the water.

Wordell sent the strike bombers to attack the two battleships, while Rear Admiral Laurence T. DuBose's force of four cruisers and twelve destroyers raced at 25 knots, bearing 010°, to sink the remaining carrier and enemy surface ships. At 1640, the *Chiyoda* was a mass of flames from the 8-inch shells from the four cruisers. At 1647 the carrier rolled over and sank.

The fighters strafed the battleships and other surface ships, while eight of the fifteen Helldivers scored hits. Japanese reports later reported that the *Hyuza* had received one direct hit and that the *Ise* had not received any hits. There was no doubt that the Japanese battleships were tough to sink. A year later Admiral Ozawa's chief of staff, Captain Ohmae, witnessed the attacks and remarked, "I saw all this bombing and thought the American pilot is not so good."[73] At 1804, the *Essex* planes landed back aboard their carrier. During the evening the *Essex* set a fueling rendezvous for October 26 at a point some 300 miles east of San Bernardino Strait.[74]

While Halsey and Mitscher were busy focusing on and attacking the Northern Force off Cape Engaño, the action around Leyte Gulf was heavy. Back at 2230 on October 24, the Battle of Surigao Strait began. Admiral Kinkaid and Rear Admiral J.B. Oldendorf over ComCruDiv 4 established the battle plan that promised the death of the Japanese Southern Force. They had the assets to do it with 6 battleships, 8 cruisers, 28 destroyers and 76 PT boats.

The battle began with PT boats engaging Vice Admiral Nishimura of the Southern Force. When the PT boat attack phase of the battle had ended at 0213 on October 25, thirty of the thirty-nine boats had come under enemy fire, firing 34 torpedoes, but hitting only the light cruiser *Abukuma* of Admiral Shima's force. The destroyers began their attacks from Captain Coward's Destroyer Squadron 54 at 0230, followed at 0351 when all the cruisers opened fire. Two minutes later the battleships began firing their salvos.

Nishimura's force was being hammered to such an extent that at 0419 his flagship, the battleship *Yamashiro,* capsized and sank with the admiral and most of her crew. Coming in to the strait some 40 miles behind Nishimura's force, Admiral Shima's force finally entered the battle in a column of two heavy cruisers and four destroyers with the hope of aiding his comrade. Anxious to engage, his radar screen revealed two enemy ships bearing 025° off 13,000 yards. He ordered both cruisers to attack with torpedoes at 0424. They fired eight torpedoes at the target. Unfortunately, the targets had actually been the two Hibuson Islands off at twice the distance. This was the only contribution to the battle by Admiral Shima's force, as he reversed course and retreated.

When the surface action had ended around 0500 the morning of the 25th, the surviving Japanese ships of what was left of the Southern Force were in full retreat. The battleships *Fuso* and *Yamashiro* had been sunk in the center of the strait, as well as two destroyers. After pursuit from Oldendorf's warships and air attacks from Rear Admiral Thomas L. Sprague's escort carriers, by November 5 the only Japanese ships that were afloat that had entered Surigao Strait were the heavy cruiser *Ashigao* and five destroyers.[75]

After a meeting held by Admiral Kinkaid with his staff "to check for errors of omission"[76] ended around 0400, Kinkaid's operations officer, Captain Richard H. Cruzen, asked his boss, "Admiral, I can think of only one other thing. We have never directly asked Halsey if TF 34 is guarding San Bernardino Strait."[77] Kinkaid agreed and at 0412 he sent a message to Halsey asking for confirmation. Halsey was surprised by the message he received at 0648 and responded to the negative at 0705.

At 0822, Kinkaid asked for fast carrier and fast battleships support from Halsey to counter Kurita's force coming in to attack them off Samar. Halsey felt Kinkaid had all he needed to engage Kurita and recalled, "I figured that the eighteen little carriers had enough planes to protect themselves until Oldendorf could bring up his heavy ships."[78] In his mind, he could only send McCain's TG 38.1 to rescue Kinkaid and that TG was over 300 miles from Leyte Gulf. He continued to be driven by the urge and total passion to destroy Ozawa's entire Northern Force.

At Pearl Harbor Admiral Nimitz had assumed that Halsey had left Admiral Lee's TG 34 in place at San Bernardino Strait. In Washington Admiral King paced the floor and cursed Halsey in a rage in the company of his visitor, Rear Admiral Joseph James "Jocko" Clark. Halsey received a message from Nimitz that infuriated him. The message had been padded as normal by a cryptographer's to say, "Turkey Trots to Water. From Cincpac. Where is, repeat, where is Task Force 34. The world wonders."[79] At 1000 Halsey's communication's signalman unfortunately decrypted the message by dropping only the first phase, leaving a rather insulting query for Halsey to ponder.

Halsey went ballistic, grabbed his cap, threw it on the floor and began cursing until his Chief of Staff, Admiral Robert B. Mick Carney, calmed him down. Now Halsey had to support Kinkaid, but he took an hour before taking action. At 1055, Halsey ordered Admiral Lee's TG 34 and Admiral Bogan's TG 38.2 south.[80]

Meanwhile, after Kurita's Central Force had exited San Bernardino Strait into the Philippine Sea at 0035, it sailed southward down the eastern coast of Samar Island for 125–150 miles in six hours undetected. Admiral Kurita's force consisted of the battleships *Yamato*, *Nagato*, *Kongō*, and *Haruna*; heavy cruisers *Chōkai*, *Haguro*, *Kumano*, *Suzuya*, *Chikuma*, *Tone*; light cruisers *Yahagi*, and *Noshiro*; and 11 destroyers.

The American force designated by Admiral Kinkaid to counter Kurita's Central Force were three task units, with voice radio call signs Taffy 1, Taffy 2 and Taffy 3, of Rear Admiral Thomas L. Sprague's 7th Fleet Escort Carrier Task Group 77.4. Each TU was operating from 30 to 50 miles apart. Closest to Kurita's Force sailing west off Samar Island was Rear Admiral Clifton F. Sprague's TU 77.4.3 (Taffy 3) with escort carriers *Fanshaw Bay*, *St. Lo*, *White Plains*, *Kalinin Bay*, *Kitkun Bay* and *Gambier Bay*, plus 3 destroyers (DD) and 4 destroyer escorts (DE).

In the center off the entrance of Leyte Gulf was Rear Admiral Felix Stump's TU 77.4.2 (Taffy 2) consisting of escort carriers *Natoma Bay*, *Manila Bay*, *Marcus Island*, *Kadashan Bay*, *Savo Island*, and *Ommaney Bay*, plus 3 DDs and 4 DEs. To the south off Mindanao Island was Rear Admiral Thomas L. Sprague's TU 77.4.1 (Taffy 1) with escort carriers *Sangamon*, *Suwannee*, *Santee*, and *Petrof Bay,* and plus 3 DDs and 4 DEs.

Admiral Kinkaid had ordered three daybreak searches including one to cover the northern sectors between 340° to 30°, but the aircraft had not launched by 0658 from the escort carrier *Ommaney Bay*, and that was too late.

The Battle off Samar started at 0658 when Kurita's battleship *Yamato* fired 18-inch shells from 15 miles over the horizon at Taffy 3. This was the first time in history that American ships had come under attack from such large shells. The first salvo landed 300 yards off the starboard bow of the *White Plains* just as it was beginning to launch aircraft. One shell exploded underwater, knocked men off their feet, and even made a fighter jump ahead off its chock and cut three feet off of the wing of an adjoining fighter. It was incredible.[81]

Seeing the impact of the salvos, Admiral Sprague knew, "it did not appear that any of our ships could survive another five minutes of the heavy-caliber fire being received, and some counteraction was urgently and immediately required. The task unit was surrounded by the ultimate of desperate circumstances."[82] He ordered his screening destroyers to lay a smoke screen.

With his escort carriers under attack from heavy warships, Sprague broadcasted in plain language an appeal for help, giving the position, bearing and distance to the enemy force. This message was received by Admiral Kinkaid at 0724 aboard his flagship *Wasatch* and was the first information he had that Kurita was in the Philippine Sea.

At 0716, Admiral Clifton Sprague ordered his three destroyers to engage the heavy ships of Kurita's Force. Destroyers *Hoel* and *Johnston*, with destroyer escort *Roberts*, reversed courses and conducted a half salvo torpedo attack against the Japanese battleships at a range of just under 10,000 yards. Then they delivered the other half salvo at about 7,000 yards against enemy cruisers. After having fought in what was, according to Admiral Kinkaid, "one of the most gallant and heroic acts of the war,"[83] the three ships were sunk.[84]

Within ten minutes of the first Japanese salvos, the escort carriers of Taffy 2 had been in launching as fast as they could to assist Taffy 3. Initially the issue was that Taffy 2 had to recall the routine missions they had launched earlier to Leyte Gulf. These planes had to be rearmed with torpedoes or 500-pound bombs first. Admiral Stump's Taffy 2 was able to launch three strikes with a total of 36 fighters and 43 torpedo bombers within an hour and one half.[85]

After receiving continual air attacks and the brave destroyer attacks, the Japanese force turned away momentarily. After the various escort carriers had launched their aircraft, they did their best to head south away from Kurita's Force. Despite heroic efforts to evade the gunfire from the enemy cruisers, the *Gambier Bay* capsized and sank at 0907. The *Saint Lo* was hit by a smoking Zeke kamikaze at 1051 that crashed through the flight deck and exploded in her torpedo and bomb magazine. With flames from bow to stern, she sank at 1125.

At 0911, Kurita issued an order to break off action, "Rendezvous, my course north, speed 20."[86] His objective was to close in and reform his dispersed fleet before heading into Leyte Gulf. From this point at 0911 until 1236, he maneuvered aimless to avoid unrelenting air attacks. The more he delayed his attack on Leyte, the less likely he was to continue. His mind was clouded by a number of thoughts.

Since earlier that morning at 0425, he was aware that his Southern Force had been defeated at Surigao Strait. Kinkaid's plain language messages that had been intercepted by the Japanese communications center at Owada, Honshu and relayed to Kurita, had significantly influenced him. At 0940 Kinkaid had reported, "Being attacked by four battleships, light cruisers and other ships. Request dispatch of fast battleships and a fast carrier air strike,"[87] and at 1120 the message was, "We are still being attacked, proceed to a point 300 miles southeast of entrance to Leyte Gulf and await orders."[88]

Kurita got word of the use of carrier planes rotating between Tacloban Airfield and the carriers, and developed an opinion that carrier and Army planes could soon be combining to attack his force. He had not heard any intelligence regarding the actions of Halsey's TF 38 or that of Ozawa's decoy force, which also increased the threat to his remaining force.

With the great strain of all his thoughts regarding the threats that he faced, and without sleeping for three days, at 1230 Admiral Kurita, without conferring with his staff, decided to turn around and steam for San Bernardino Strait on a course of 015° at speeds of 15 to 20 knots. At 1236, Kurita sent the following message to Toyoda: "First Striking Force has abandoned penetration of Leyte anchorage. Is proceeding north searching for enemy task force. Will engage decisively, then pass through San Bernardino Strait."[89]

Since refueling operations had completed at 0940, Vice Admiral McCain's TG 38.1 had been racing to intercept Kurita at 30 knots. At 1030, a 96-planes strike began launching from the *Hornet*, *Wasp* and *Hancock*. Kurita was still 340 miles from the TG. At 1310 the strike leader from the *Wasp* located the enemy force steaming north at 24 knots. Flak was intense as the aircraft attacked. There were few claimed hits and no significant damage reported. Nine of McCain's TG planes landed on Leyte airstrips while eleven were reported missing at days end.

The second strike launched at 1245 from the *Hancock* and *Hornet* consisted of twenty Hellcats, twenty Helldivers and thirteen Avengers. The vectors provided by the escort carriers seemed to confuse the strike team and it was unable to make a coordinated attack at 1500. The results of both strikes was four claims-four hits on the *Yamato*, four on one of the *Kongo*-class battleships, one on the *Nagato*, five on an unidentified battleship and other hits on several cruisers and destroyers.

In the afternoon Taffy 2 escort carriers launched two strikes against Kurita, but eventually the torpedoes and armor-piercing bombs were expended. The last attack occurred at 1723 off the northeastern tip of Samar Island. At 2140 that evening, a plane from the carrier *Independence* spotted Admiral Kurita's Central Force entering San Bernardino Straits in a single column. He had lost three heavy cruisers-*Suzuya*, *Chikuma* and *Chōkai*. The last naval battle of the war had ended for the Japanese.[90]

At midnight, Halsey was steaming at 28 knots toward the strait just 40 miles away. He was too late by two hours. His opportunity to engage Kurita's battleships with his fast battleships had passed. The irony was that he and his fast battleships had spent the previous day speeding 300 miles north off Luzon Island to finish off the Ozawa's Northern Force, but just as he came within 42 miles of the crippled enemy fleet, Halsey had to reverse course and steam back 300 miles to the strait. His fast battleships didn't fire a shot at either Japanese force. In Halsey's mind, it was one of his greatest disappointments of the war.[91]

The American losses off Samar were heavy. Escort carriers *Gambier Bay* and *St. Lo*, destroyers *Johnston* and *Hoel*, the destroyer escort *Samuel B. Roberts* were sunk. Seven escort carriers, the destroyer *Heermann* and the destroyer escort *Dennis* were all seriously damaged in the battle. The battle had cost the lives of 1130 men killed or missing, and 913 wounded.[92]

19

Last CAG-15 Strikes

"I had to give them hell."[1]

The *Essex* and Task Group 38.3 fueled on October 26. The following day, three divisional four-plane groups were sent on a fighter sweep over the Manila area all the way to Coron Bay to assess the status of the Japanese air defenses. The first division, led by Lieutenant Morris, covered the sector from 250° to 260° out to 300 miles. The team flew along the 250° bearing and then back on the 260° line. Over Legespi Airfield they encountered six enemy planes which they strafed. A cargo vessel was spotted off Burias Island and was attacked with rockets and gunfire. Nearby they found and strafed two destroyers.

The next search was led by Lieutenant Twelves covering sector 260° to 270° over Manila Bay. They discovered several cargo and naval ships in the bay and attacked them. Lieutenant Deming saw a Fran bomber near Cavite and shot it down. Twelves was at low altitude strafing a cargo ship when he spotted a twin-engine Betty. He engaged and it exploded at 500 feet above the water. Ensign Self encountered a Kate and attacked, sending it nose down and into the bay with its torpedo still attached. The search division was on the way home, but swung by Legaspi Airfield to strafe the planes already hit by Morris's division.

The third divisional search team headed by Lieutenant White covered the 270° to 280° sector. They discovered a PT boat west of Cantanduanos Island. Descending to take a close look, they noticed the boat did not have the large white star on the desk to identify it as a friendly, but it did have stars on the hull, so they did not engage. To add more confusion the PT boat fired on the planes with .50 caliber guns, but no one was hit.

Over southern Luzon, they saw two Betty bombers at 1,500 feet. Section leader Ensign J.H. Duffy shot one down as Ensign D.H. Gonya downed the other one. On the way back to the *Essex* early with engine trouble, an F6F pilot saw a submarine crash dive below him. Since he was on the edge of a "safe zone"[2] he radioed the carrier for instructions. It took several minutes to get the order to engage, which gave the submarine plenty of time to escape below the waves. He dropped a bomb but it had no useful effect.

Because the searches were long-range, McCampbell sent out up four F6Fs to serve as communications relay teams as had been used before. He had picked these assignments for pilots that were showing signs of fatigue, in the hope that they would not encounter combat. Lieutenant Crittenden and his wingman circled out at 100 miles and after their on-station period, they recovered aboard the *Essex* without incident. Unfortunately, this was not the case for the other team.

Just as Lieutenant (junior grade) Thomas T. Thompson and Lieutenant (junior grade) Keith B. West had arrived on-station 200 miles out, they encountered s group of at least a dozen Zekes. They radioed the plea "Hey Rube,"[3] dropped their belly tanks, and headed directly at the enemy formation while dropping their bombs as they went. As they came closer, they saw that the Zekes were escorting Judy dive-bombers and Jill torpedo bombers flying below them.

Thomson climbed and took on the led fighter head-on. Flames broke out on the Zeke and it fell off and crashed. Thomson then turned toward the wingman of the Zeke and fired his guns. He hit the fighter's engine as smoke trailed and he turned away. By this time, Thompson had climbed above the formation and dove down to attack three enemy fighters. One Zeke caught fire in the engine from a long burst of his gunfire, so he used his excess speed to climb again. He descended to meet another Zeke and attacked head-on firing his guns. The Zeke burst into flames as the pilot bailed out.

Six more Zekes came in to engage Thompson, and he continued for the next ten minutes or so to repeat his climb and attack routine. Meanwhile, Ensign West was able to stay with his leader through the action and got some hits too. He had engaged four Zekes and scored one confirmed kill when the Japanese pilot bailed out.

Seeing their fighter escorts dissolve into flames around them, the Japanese Judys and Jills jettisoned their bombs and torpedoes and reversed course homeward. While Thomson and West were congratulating themselves, a lone Zeke came out of a cloud and make a pass on West. The fighter's bullet glanced off his armored glass windshield, and hit an oil line, turning his windshield black. West radioed Thomson and they disengaged to return to the carrier. Thomson circled around West warding off half a dozen planes. One Kawasaki army fighter got on West's tail, but he was able to escape using his water injection to power ahead.

Lieutenant (junior grade) West made it home and trapped aboard the Lexington, while Thomson landed aboard the Essex. Thomson claimed two Zekes downed and West one, but beyond that achievement, they had turned back an entire attack group through their brave and heroic action on that day.[4]

Back at 2135 on the evening of October 26, Halsey sent the fol-

Commander David McCampbell in the cockpit of his F6F "Hellcat" fighter on board USS Essex (CV-9) on October 30, 1944. The Japanese flags represent his thirty "kills" by that date, nine of which were made in one action on October 24, 1944, during the Battle of Leyte Gulf (Official U.S. Navy Photograph # 80-G-373673, National Archives and Records Administration, College Park, Maryland, collection).

lowing dispatch to General MacArthur: "For General MacArthur. After 17 days of battle my fast carriers are unable to provide extended support for Leyte but 2 groups are available 27 October. The pilots are exhausted, and the carriers are low in provisions, bombs and torpedoes. When will land-based air take over at Leyte?"[5]

Halsey ordered Sherman's TG 38.3 back to Ulithi. The *Essex* and TG 38.3 departed to Ulithi on October 28. En route, the men of Air Group 15 were informed that they would be relieved for return to the United States as soon as Air Group 4 arrived at Ulithi. The *Essex* sailed into Ulithi anchorage at 0630 on October 30. That day bombs, ammunition and provisions were loaded aboard. The next day saw more of the same came aboard, as well as replacement pilots. The *Essex* was also refueled. On November 1, thirty new fighters were loaded on the carrier.[6]

Back on October 27 Admiral Onishi had organized five Japanese suicide squadrons (kamikaze forces): the Chuyu (Loyalty and Bravery), Giretsu (Nobility of Soul), Seichu (Sincere Loyalty), Shisei (Devotion) and Yamato (Historic Japan). While the *Essex* crews were resting and the equipment and supplies were being loaded at Ulithi, these kamikaze forces took action.[7]

On the 29th, the *Intrepid* was hit by a single kamikaze that killed ten men and wounded six. On the next day, the *Franklin* was hit by five kamikazes, that put a 40-foot hole in the flight deck, destroyed 33 planes, killed 56 men and injured 14. That same day the *Belleau Wood* was hit with 12 planes lost and 146 casualties. On November 1, destroyers *Claxton* and *Ammen* were hit, and the destroyer *Abner Read* was sunk by these suicide killers.[8]

The Japanese were regrouping to engage the Americans again in the Philippines. The tactical situation at Leyte had changed as the Japanese had landed troops on the western shore of Leyte at Ormoc Bay. Fresh planes from Formosa and Kyushu had been sent to the Philippines including the old familiar Bacolod Air Complex.

Halsey had organized Task Force 38 on October 30 by relieving Vice Admiral Mitscher with Vice Admiral John S. McCain, and giving TG 38.1 to Rear Admiral A.E. Montgomery. At 1630 on November 1, the *Essex* sailed toward Manus Island in the Admiralty Group, but changed course later to return to the Philippines. On November 3, the *Essex* fueled and spent the next day steaming at high speed toward the central Philippines. That day steaming with TG 38.3, Captain Ralph C. Alexander's light cruiser *Reno* was hit by a torpedo from Japanese submarine I-41, and retired back to Ulithi escorted by four destroyers. She was nine feet down by the stern and two feet down by the bow as the fleet tug *Zuni* had to take her in tow.

On November 5, Admiral Nimitz gave Halsey approval to strike Luzon, and requested General MacArthur "to release the forces of the Third Fleet as soon as the situation permitted."[9] At 0615 that day TGs 38.1, 38.2 and Sherman's TG 38.3 arrived off Polillo Islands to begin attacks. TG 38.3 was assigned the area between 14° N. and 15° N. including the shipping in Manila Bay.

At dawn on that day, Lieutenant Commander Rigg led a fifty-two Hellcat fighter sweep to the Manila area launched from the *Essex, Ticonderoga, Langley* and *Lexington*. Over Nichols Field, they saw Japanese fighters on the deck and headed in to attack. Lieutenant Overton discovered two Nakajima army fighters known as Oscars below him being chased by two other F6Fs. One of the Oscars pulled up, as Overton engaged. He fired and shot it down as it crashed and exploded. After completing a strafing pass, Lieutenant Bare took on a lone Luly Kawasaki army bomber. He made several passes and finally downed the bomber.[10]

As the fighter sweep departed the area, McCampbell's strike group of eighty-eight planes from the four carriers came in. The CAG-15 commander was serving as target coordinator on this mission. The escort F6Fs protected the bombers as they strafed and fired rockets. The bombers dropped their bombs on the hangars, buildings, runways and parked planes. Though few enemy planes were around, McCampbell found a Val Aichi D3A bomber over Subic Bay that had come in from the clouds to engage him. The bomber was initially able to evade him by staying low, but soon McCampbell was on his usual tail position. He fired a short burst and the engine stopped on the Val, forcing it to make a water landing. The bomber immediately sank with no observed survivors.

Soon McCampbell located a pair of Zeros coming straight at him. Being at a higher altitude than the Zeros, McCampbell and wingman Rushing were able to roll over and end up behind them. They both continued to fire at the Japanese fighters. McCampbell gun barrels burned out and he was left to shot down his Zero with his outboard port gun. Rushing shot down his Zero too, but had only two guns left. They saw eight to ten Zeros in the areas, but could not engage with few guns working. With this days' two planes downed, McCampbell's total of Japanese planes shot down was now 32.

McCampbell stayed in the area to await the second strike. The seventy-three plane strike from the four carriers arrived and continued to attack Nichols Field infrastructure. After the strike departed the area, the second division of four F6Fs was "jumped"[11] by six Japanese Army fighters. The *Essex* fighters turned in formation and shot down two of the intruders during the first pass, sending the other fighters scattering.

Meanwhile, Lieutenant Strane shot down an Oscar and Lieutenant Duffy downed a Nick (Kawasaki heavy army fighter). The Avengers did a bang up job that mission hitting parked aircraft. Lieutenants Bentz, Goodwin and Deputy made a run down the east-west runway dropping bombs in a perfect row of twin-engine bombers. A major group of enemy planes on the south end of the field were bombed and strafed by Lieutenants Crumley and Chaffe.

As a result of McCampbell's report that there were a number of Zeros around the Manila area, another fighter sweep was launched with Lieutenant Commander Duncan as leader from the *Essex*. Seven F6Fs were launched, but one had to turn back when his canopy would not close. A second fighter fell out of formation to head back to the carrier when its oxygen ran out. Incredibly when they reached Clark Field, a Zero hit another of his F6Fs and disabled the canopy, forcing him to disengage and return home.

Duncan, with his four remaining Hellcats continued with the sweep. They saw two Tojos (Nakajima Army fighters) and came down on them to attack. They had overrun the Tojos and the enemy fighters pulled up and split one to the right and one to the left to face Duncan and his wingman head-on. Duncan fired a burst, but then a Zero came into him on his port quarter, pulling up and turning off to the right. Duncan had fired a few shots into the Zero and it exploded into flames. Duncan's wingman, Lieutenant Bertschi, shot down one of the Tojos.

Lieutenant Twelves was surveying the area around Clark Field after the Helldivers had bombed, when two Tojos came at his division. As Twelves turned into them, another pair of Tojos sped out of the clouds on the prowl. Then four Zeros joined the fight. Twelves used a "deflection shot"[12] to down one Zero. As he watched the enemy fighter fall, his aircraft was hit as tracers came over the wings. His wingman had fallen back when his engine started losing power. Twelves was now being engaged by five Zeros. He fired at one Zero climbing 3,000 feet above him.

The Zero dived on him as Twelves turned his way and fired. Soon the Zero flamed downward as Twelves struggled to get out of a spin he had entered. After three spins, he came out, to be immediately attacked by the Zero's wingman. Twelves used water injection for more powers as he used his flaps. He had made one turn and executed a snap roll. The Zero pilot went into a slow roll to reposition himself as Twelves powered ahead to escape the scene.

Twelves wingman, Ensign Self, was continuing to have engine trouble, and could get only two-thirds power. He spotted four Tonys coming in to engage him. He was able to down one plane and somehow jinked and evaded to get to a low cumulus cloud. He stayed in the clouds for several minutes and when he exited, the Japanese were gone. Relieved, he headed home to the *Essex*.

As Ensign Bertschi was flying on Lieutenant Commander Duncan's wing, he looked up and saw two Tojos come at them. They both fired and split up to engage. Duncan shot one down and Bertschi downed the other Tojo. Duncan and Bertschi were forced to fight off several Japanese groups before heading for home.

On debrief, pilots reported a larger number of enemy ships in Manila Bay than usual. Admiral Sherman ordered a strike on that shipping and at 1100 that morning of November 5, a ninety-eight plane strike with Hellcats, Helldivers and Avengers launched to Manila Bay. The mission was to sink two destroyers and a cruiser. The F6Fs led the strike group and engaged four Zeros they encountered. The fighters descended, strafed and bombed the cruiser and destroyers. There were no bomb hits, but the rockets did hit the destroyers.

The Helldivers led by Lieutenant Brodhead dropped their 1,000-pound bombs, making three hits out of seven on the cruisers. The real action came with Lieutenant Commander Lambert's Avengers when six of them made their runs. Lambert's torpedo just missed the stern of the cruiser, identified as the heavy cruiser *Nachi*. The cruiser had evaded successfully four of the torpedoes, but two "fish"[13] hit the *Nachi* as she went dead in the water and settled by the stern. She was sinking as the Avengers departed.

After finishing his lunch, at 1300 McCampbell led a seventy-two plane strike against the shipping in Manila Bay from the *Essex*, *Lexington* and *Ticonderoga*. Lieutenant Commander Rigg led the Hellcats, while Lieutenant John D. Bridgers led the Helldivers. The target for the dive-bombers was a light cruiser, but they could not find it as they ran into low hanging clouds. They went after a destroyer as an alternative as it cruised through the Manila Harbor breakwater into Manila Bay. Seven dive-bombers made their runs on the destroyer, but only scored near misses.

The *Essex* Avengers were assigned to attack the light cruiser that McCampbell had spotted between Cavite and the Manila breakwater. Lieutenant Cosgrove was the only pilot to locate the cruiser and he headed in to attack. As he approached, the 37mm anti-aircraft fire was heavy, and his gunner, L.E. Dean, was killed by it. His radioman, Digby Denzek, crawled up into the turret to check on Dean, and discovered that he had been decapitated by the shell. Cosgrove was able to drop his torpedo, but was unable to see if it hit the target.

Cosgrove's Avenger had been damaged in its controls and the wing had a large hole in it. He was able to recover aboard the *Essex*. The decision was made that the damage was too extreme to get the dead gunner out of the wreckage. Just then the squawk box announced that ship was called to general quarters with a kamikaze attack inbound. The Avenger was pushed over the stern after the chaplain performed burial at sea over the American flag draped over the turret. This was the first time in the war that an airman was buried in his aircraft. The film of the event was later shown publically in the 1950s in the documentary film series *Victory at Sea*.[14]

After his return from the strike, Lieutenant Crittenden and seven other F6F fighters launched on an emergency CAP to fight off the approaching flight of kamikaze planes. Crittenden shot down one Judy, and three Zekes were downed by others in the Task Group. One Zeke was able to make it through the CAP and hit the *Lexington* in the flagship's island, killing 50 and wounding 137 men. Damage control teams put out the fires, and the carrier was operational within twenty minutes. Another kamikaze got through and headed for the *Essex,* but it was shot down by alert anti-aircraft gunners.

At 0230 the next morning of November 6, the *Essex* launched two night fighters- Lieutenant J.C. Hogue and Ensign K.M. Roberts-on a mission to disrupt pre-dawn flight operations in the Manila area. Loaded with their 250-pound bombs, they flew to the northern tip of Polillo Island and changed course toward Manila. Approaching at seventy-five miles from their target, they turned off their IFF signal.

Hogue made his first run in, dropping his bombs on the runway at Nichols Field, and then joined Roberts in strafing the field. Ensign Roberts saw a plane taxi across the field and dropped his bomb. They continued to strafe in the darkness, and then headed over to Neilson Field to continue their strafing action. They spotted some twenty twin-engine bombers parked near the runway. Hogue made several strafing runs scoring hits on a number of enemy aircraft. Suddenly, his F6F was illuminated by ten searchlights that were able to follow him until he descended to 100 feet off the deck.

The two fighters joined up over Laguna de Bay and made a course homeward. As they proceeded, they saw lights come on at Manaluyong Airfield just five miles away from Neilson Field. They noted a white light moving along the runway, which indicated a plane was taking off. Ensign Robert headed down and met the twin-engine plane just as it became airborne and beginning to turn to the left. He got on the tail position and fired a burst. The Japanese bomber suddenly exploded, forcing him to fly through the planes' debris. Damage was done to both of Robert's wings, ailerons and elevator surfaces. The Japanese bomber hit the ground and started a grass fire as the two fighters cleared the area. Hogue and Roberts somehow got separated on the way back and landed separately.[15]

As Hogue and Roberts had flown back to the *Essex,* they passed the outgoing fighter sweep of forty-eight F6Fs led by Lieutenant Commander Duncan from Admiral Sherman's four carriers on their way to hit Manila. Duncan's four-plane division engaged two Betty bombers taking off from Clark Field and shot them down. Duncan found and fired at a Mitsubishi P1Y1 Frances just as it was going airborne. The Frances looped and cartwheeled down the runway before exploding in flames.

Commander McCampbell launched at 0610 on the first strike mission of the day to attack shipping in Manila Bay. The weather was terrible from a typhoon moving across the East China Sea north of the Philippines. The winds were high, the clouds were low and below them was a thick haze that made visibility poor. The trick was to find the enemy through holes in the clouds to descend through.

The first attack came from Lieutenant Overton's fighters that claimed hits on a patrol boat in the center of the harbor. The nine Helldivers led by Lieutenant Bridgers had to use a glide bombing technique to engage anything they saw. Cosgrove led the Avengers in loaded with bombs, not torpedoes. Lieutenant Goodwin was able to claim hits on a transport vessel that was anchored outside the breakwater, while the other torpedo planes had near misses on several ships.

On his attack run, Lieutenant William Rising's Helldiver was hit by anti-aircraft fire. He continued across the harbor and over the Bataan Peninsula, and turned to the west. Overton followed him out and, at a location twenty-six miles off Sampoloc Point, Rising executed a water landing. Overton marked the spot and notified the rescue submarine.

Later on, two Helldivers from the *Essex* had been sent to located Rising and his gunner, Aviation Radioman 3rd Class John Ward Montgomery. They were found resting in their raft waving. The Helldivers dropped extra life rafts and supplies and headed off. The rescue submarine was only twenty-one minutes away from the survivors.

Shortly past noon, Commander McCampbell, as target director, led a seventy-eight plane strike on shipping in Port Silanguin, in southern Luzon and further away from the typhoon weather. The F6Fs strafed the cargo ships and small vessels in the harbor while the Helldivers and Avengers continued to use glide bombing to deliver they bombs on the targets. They claimed to have sunk two ships with a possible third, as well a causing damage to other vessels.

Lieutenant Overton led another fighter sweep over Manila to hit Clark Field. They claimed destroying a least a dozen Betty bombers. These planes were new and had been ferried in from Japan with their shiny chrome fuselages having had no time to get camouflage paint applied. The Japanese had moved their planes away from the runaways and camouflaged them using netting.

A division of fighters went to check on Rising and Montgomery and found them still in their raft. The fighters called the lifeguard submarine captain and received confirmation that the submarine would rescue them in fifteen minutes. On the way home, Ensign W.B. Riffle ran out of gas and ditched a mile from the destroyer screen. He was picked up a few minutes later. One fighter returned, but his aircraft had been so damaged by AA fire in the engine, wings and hydraulic system that the air officer ordered it pushed over the side.

After all carriers had recovered their planes on the evening November 6, Admiral Sherman ordered them to retire from the battle zone to their assigned fueling location some 450 miles east of Manila. The *Essex* fueled on November 7 as the aircrews rested.[16]

On November 8, the *Essex* patrolled 600 miles northeast of central Philippines in a "strategic support"[17] role, which meant that she was required to be ready for action at short notice. The next days' news came that Nimitz had ordered Halsey to release the carrier *Bunker Hill* and Air Group 15. The *Essex* changed course toward Guam as the word spread that they would be relieved on November 11 in Guam and sail back home in the *Bunker Hill*.[18]

Ever since October 23, the Japanese had been sending in troop reinforcement convoys from Manila called almost daily to Ormoc Bay on the western side of Leyte using high-speed naval transports escorted by destroyers. As mid–November approached, the Japanese had landed an estimated 45,000 troops and 10,000 tons of supplies on the west coast. These troop reinforcements were twice the number of Japanese troops in the area when the Americans landed on Leyte.

Though the Army Air Force had attacked these convoys, they had not been able to stop the reinforcements. MacArthur requested Halsey's carrier support, and he directed Admiral Sherman, who was in temporary command of Task Force 38, to reverse course and speed to central Philippines. Thus ended the euphoric joy felt by the men of Air Group 15 as their relief plans were put on hold. ARM3c A.T. Graham of VB-15 recorded in his diary, "Bitter day, indeed. It's days like today that makes General Sherman right as rain about war being hell. Scheduled condition two and searches tomorrow. We're supposed to be off Leyte at dawn."[19] On the evening of November 10, the *Essex* reversed course and steamed toward Leyte.

At 0600 on November 11, Admiral Sherman's TF 38 and TG 38.3 were 200 miles east of San Bernardino Strait. Early morning searches were launched from the *Essex* with four teams of two F6F fighters each to Sibuyan, Visayan and Camotes Seas. Lieutenant Carr was near Ormoc Bay when he spotted Japanese transports, five destroyers, and one destroyer escort. The destroyers formed around the transports, widened outward and put out a smokescreen to hide the convoy. Carr radioed the carrier and stayed to give movement updates as the enemy sailed in. Five Zeros came nearby but did not engage.

Lieutenant Demmings team didn't find the convoy, but did attack small craft before looking over Legaspi Airfield. Over the field, he was hit by anti-aircraft fire and had to ditch at Albay Gulf. He was picked up by friendly native Filipinos in a canoe. Meanwhile, Lieutenant J.J. Collins and Lieutenant (junior grade) Hal Thompson searched over northwest Leyte when they encountered what they thought were three silver P-47 Army fighters swaging their wings as if friendlies. On closer inspection Collins saw the red "meatballs"[20] on their wings, and after they dropped their wingtanks, they identified them as Oscars.

The enemy Oscars ascended and turned left, as Collins and Thompson chased them after dropping their belly tanks. The F6F pilots lowered their propeller pitch, turned on their water injection and low blower, and climbed to engage the Oscars. Collins went left toward the lead Oscar and saw the plane fill his windscreen before firing his guns at 1,500 feet. Using a full deflection shot and then a 60° deflection shot, he hit the Oscar in the wing roots, before it went into a spin to the water.

The two remaining Oscars continued to engage Collins and Thompson when three more Oscars arrived. One came in on Collins' tail a hundred yards behind him. Then Collins turned left while Thompson turned right, as the Oscar flew between them. An Oscar made a high-side run on Collins, as the American shot it down in flames. Both Collins and Thompson began to weave back and forth. Collins took on one Oscar with a deflection shot and sent the fighter away with his engine smoking.

Collins noticed that Thompson's F6F was smoking from the right wing root and had begun to nose over at 8,500 feet. One Oscar came at Collins as he evaded and shot back hitting the fighters' fuselage before it flew away. Another Oscar engaged Thompson as he continued to descend. At 3,000 feet Thompson's plane was nearly vertical as it sped downward to crash into the sea and sink.

From his rear view mirror, Collins saw two Oscars on his tail as he turned on his water injection to power over to the closest clouds off two miles away. Collins was speeding at 320 knots and entered the clouds. As he came out, the Oscars were thankfully gone. He flew back to the *Essex* alone.

Lieutenant (junior grade) R.N. Stime, Jr. was part of the third CAP of the day when he was vectored to engage a bogey coming in at 6,000 feet. The Judy dive-bomber was being chased by four F6Fs, but the Japanese bomber had outrun them until he jinked and slowed down. Each of the fighters hit the plane, but Stime got the last shots that downed the bomber near an *Essex* plane guard destroyer.

On the morning of the 11th, the Japanese TA convoy of six transports escorted by five destroyers was sailing at 7.5 knots toward the Ormoc anchorage, expecting to land around noon. At 0842 McCampbell launched from the *Essex* to lead the largest bomber strike that TG 38.3 had ever made, consisting of forty Helldivers, thirty-two Avengers and forty Hellcats. The mission was to attack the transports to prevent them from landing their troops.

McCampbell and his planes arrived at 1030 as the convoy was coming around Apale Point into Ormoc Bay. Immediately the convoy sped up and scattered while putting out smokescreens. McCampbell estimated they Japanese ships were just five miles from the anchorage. Although he did not know it, the first four of the transports that he saw were carrying 6,000 troops, as well as ammunition and supplies for three months.

McCampbell and his division of three others planes circled at 14,000 feet as the CAG directed his planes in the attack on the ships. Suddenly an Oscar came nearby and McCampbell chased the intruder. After three minutes, he caught up with the enemy plane and opened fire, hitting the engine that began smoking. The fighter pilot was stubborn and began to weave and jink to get away, but McCampbell stayed with him firing at the best moments. Finally, the plane flew toward the ground and exploded. This was McCampbell 33rd downed plane.

Meanwhile, the twelve *Essex* F6Fs under the direction of Lieutenant Commander Rigg were escorting the bombers to their targets. They did not see any enemy fighters so they strafed and dropped their 500-pound bombs on three of the four transports in the convoy. The Helldivers were dropping their bombs at the same time. McCampbell had directed Commander Mini and the Helldivers from *Essex* to make their strike runs first on the transports. From 15,000 feet they dived to attack. The first division sank a transport on the first run, and McCampbell hurried to send the other Hellcats to the other transports. The second division made four hits on the second transport and three hits on the third ship.

The anti-aircraft fire was heavy as Lieutenant (junior grade) John S. Foote's bomber was hit in the bomb bay starting a fire. Foote pulled up gaining some altitude until the plane nosed over and headed to the water. Just thirty feet off the water, Aviation Radioman 2nd Class Norm Schmidt jumped out of the Helldiver, but his parachute did not open and he landed on his back. The plane crashed and exploded. No one ever saw either of them again as the action continued.

Ensign Avery and his gunner, Otto Graham, were two planes behind Foote as they dived on the third transport, dropping their bombs and scoring hits. As they came out of the run and began their climb at low altitude over the water, their Hellcat was hit in the engine. One of the planes' wings dipped over, caught a wave and sent the plane cartwheeling across the water. It finally went into the sea. They were both killed.

The next Helldiver in line behind Avery's was Ensign Mel Livesay with Aviation Radioman 2nd Class Chuck Swihart. At 2,500 feet, Livesay dropped their bomb and as he pulled out at 2,000 feet, their plane was hit with violent anti-aircraft fire that shot off their left wing. They went into a spiral until the plane's parts hit the water. Next in line to be hit was Lieutenant (junior grade) David R. Hall and his gunner Aviation Radioman 3rd Class Oscar Adams. Though they were hit, Hall was able to make a water landing. He and Adams scrambled into a life raft and were picked up later that afternoon by an OS2U Kingfisher, and taken back to the *Essex*.

Lieutenant J.W. Barney Barnitz felt his Helldiver taking shell hits from AA fire in the area where his gunner, Neal Steinkemeyer, sat. Steinkemeyer confirmed he was wounded in the hand and legs and needed immediate attention. Barnitz flew to the Taclobam Airfield on Leyte Island which had earlier been recovered from the Japanese where Steinkemeyer received care at the U.S. Army base hospital. Then Barnitz took off and flew back to the *Essex* with damaged flight instruments.

Yet another Helldiver crew met the fate of the others, flying behind Barnitz. Lieutenant (junior grade) Bob Brice and his gunner, Aviation Radioman 2nd Class Lou Penza, were hit in the fuselage and left wing. Brice was able to get the plane back to the *Essex*, but had to make a water landing behind the plane guard destroyer when their landing gear would not come down. The two men were able to evacuate the Helldiver before it sank, and were picked up.[21]

While the Helldivers were being shot up by Japanese gunners, Lieutenant Commander Lambert's eighteen Avengers, again loaded with bombs, were attacking with glide runs. They were able to claim hits on the second and third transport and near hits on the fourth one. After their attacked, they headed to the rendezvous point to join up with the Helldivers and fighters to head back to the carriers.

As the planes were arriving at the rendezvous point, they were met by Oscars. The Hellcats came to intercept the intruders. Lieutenant (junior grade) Ralph Foltz with his wingman, Ensign Frazelle, had just completed his post-attack photographic runs when he saw an Oscar at 8,000 feet. They climbed and fired shots into the Oscar, making it smoke. Just then, his plane was hit by gunfire from a second Oscar attacking him. Foltz turned into him and they went head-on at each other. Firing, he pulled up at the last second, as the Oscar flew beneath him. The Oscar then caught fire, nosed over and headed to the sea below to crash.

Frazelle had stayed with Foltz until he noticed another Oscar heading in. He got on the tail of the enemy fighter and continued to fire at it until it entered a cloud. Frazelle stayed above the cloud and when the Oscar exited, he got on its tail and fired until the plane rotated on its back and descended straight to a water crash from 2,000 feet.

Meanwhile, Lieutenant Baynard Milton had shot down another Oscar. Lieutenant (junior grade) Nall was attacked by two fighters and was able to down one of them, while Lieutenant (junior grade) Berree got the other kill. Ensign Smith was having trouble with his F6F cockpit heater that was causing his windshield to fog up. He opened up his hood to help clear the fog after completing his bombing run and was engaged by an Oscar. He turned in toward the fighter and began firing as the other pilot flew in front of him. Smith fired a deflection shot and was surprised to see the fighter roll over and dive to a water crash. Ensign Lemley found an Oscar and shot it down. Unfortunately, for Ensign Erickson, he was attacked by two Oscars and was shot down. He baled out outside Ormoc Bay and was later picked up by a destroyer.

The attack on the Japanese convoy had involved 347 carrier aircraft from Admiral Sherman's task groups. The Japanese lost the destroyers *Shimakaze, Hamanami, Naganami,* and *Wakatsuki,* and the four transports. Thousands of pounds of supplies were lost and only 2,000 troops landed.

The *Essex* flight crews came back from the mission with the bad news of seven planes shot down and six men killed. It was the worse casualty report for a single mission of the war for CAG 15. The gunners of VB-15 gathered on the flight deck and discussed the results of the mission. They decided to refuse to fly under such dangerous conditions. These men had expected to be relieved by another air group and here they were being killed in such heavy one mission.

They took their complaint to Commander Mini who knew this revolt could turn into a court-martial offense punishable by death as "cowardice in the face of the enemy."[22] He consulted with Commander McCampbell who told Mini, "Tell them they are not going to fly any more, then take away their flight papers."[23] Without flight papers they would lose their 10 percent flight pay bonus. They would not be able to return with the air group. Commander Mini announced McCampbell's decision and said the Helldivers would fly on their missions anyway with the back seats empty. The gunners reversed their position and decided they would continue to fly. The revolt had ended.[24]

On November 12, the *Essex* fueled with the other ships of TG 38.3 some 280 miles northeast of Samar Island. The next morning, November 13, as mission director McCampbell led the first strike of the day with planes from the *Essex, Ticonderoga* and *Langley* to Manila Bay to target shipping that could reinforce Leyte and Luzon.

The strike arrived at 0830 with McCampbell's fighters in the lead. There was no enemy air opposition over the targets as the Helldivers "peeled off" from 15,000 feet and dropped their bombs on the cargo ships below at 2,500 feet. Leading his fifteen Helldivers into the attack, it was Commander Mini who scored the first hit on a 10,000-ton cargo ship, along with Lieutenant (junior grade) T.A. Woods and Lieutenant (junior grade) L.E. Nelson. They sank the ship.

Lieutenants (junior grade) W.P. Kelly and R.L. Turner sank another 10,000-ton cargo ship, while Lieutenant J.W. Barnitz and Lieutenant (junior grade) F.S. Matthews hit a 6,000-ton freighter and sank it. Other aircraft from the *Essex* damaged and sank another six vessels in the harbor.

The Avengers bombed the old Dollar Line Pier, setting it afire, as well as sank a large cargo ship that was tied up to the pier. Later in an attack, Lieutenant (junior grade) Otto R. Bleech's Avenger was hit by anti-aircraft fire that damaged his oil system, as the oil pressure dropped. He had to make a water landing in the northern part of Manila Bay. He and his gunner, T.M Barber, and radioman, W.J. Gormley, scrambled out of the Avenger and got into their life raft as several Japanese sailboats headed their way.

Immediately, Hellcats came in to strafe the enemy boats. A Tony (Kawasaki army fighter) came in toward the yellow raft and Lieutenant (junior grade) Foltz engaged and shot it down. As the Hellcats headed home to the *Essex*, they feared for the three airmen. They were never seen again.

Before McCampbell's strike had returned, Admiral Sherman sent a fighter sweep of twenty-four planes to the Clark Airfield outside Manila. The fighters strafed the area and found several enemy planes on Mabalacat Airfield. Only two of the planes burned, which meant the aircraft had been degassed.

Lieutenant Commander Lambert led a seventy-six plane strike from the three TG carriers off at noon to hit Manila Bay shipping. Lieutenant Roger Noyes led twelve Helldivers in to attack two large merchant ships, the light cruiser *Kiso* and two destroyers. The Helldivers scored hits on *Kiso* and sank her, while also damaging the two destroyers. In the attack run on the *Kiso*, Noyes and his gunner Paul H. Sheehan were killed when anti-aircraft shells hit their engine and wing root, sending them burning and straight in to a sharp dive to the sea.

Nearing home, Lieutenant (junior grade) W.L. Moore with his gunner, T.R. Forrest, had to make a water landing after the rudder had become jammed, making it impossible to land on the carrier. They were soon picked up by a destroyer.

Another fighter sweep from the *Essex* and *Ticonderoga* launched in the afternoon to the Clark Airfield area to look for more enemy fighters. They strafed Bamban Airfield and saw twenty parked planes. Some of these planes turned out to be dummies and others were hidden in revetments off the field.

Since the morning, the Japanese had been sending in planes to hit Admiral Sherman's carriers. The CAP with Lieutenant J.C.C. Symmes shot down a Jake at the other part of the task group. After the *Essex* aircraft had all been recovered, at 1800 radar spotted twenty bogeys heading in. The CAP shot down two Nakajima reconnaissance planes (Myrts), two Frances bombers and one Tojo while the *Hornet* also shot down five more bogeys.

Lieutenant George Carr and his wingman, Jack Taylor, made high-side runs on the Myrt that was carrying a Long Lance torpedo. Carr's gunfire caused a fire to break out, while Taylor's guns exploded the plane into a ball of fire.[25]

Just before dawn at 0400 on the morning of November 14, McCampbell led a ninety-two plane strike from the *Essex*, *Ticonderoga* and *Langley* to Manila Bay. The weather was hazy as the groups attacked any target they found. Since their previous attack mission had been so effective, there were not many targets to bomb. McCampbell encountered a number of Oscars, but he avoided protracted engagements to focus on his primary role as target coordinator.

The ten Helldivers made their dive-bombing attacks, and all made it safely through the flak except one. The Helldiver piloted by Lieutenant (junior grade) Raymond Turner, with his gunner, Aviation Radioman 2nd Class Sam Dorosh, was hit in the dive run and continued straight into a water crash.

At the end of the strike combat, an Oscar came in to engage McCampbell. He turned into the attacker and fired straight into his cockpit, setting the plane on fire. The enemy fighter crashed below. It was the 34th Japanese plane shot down by Commander McCampbell.

The second strike of the day headed off to Manila Bay, but found even slimmer pickings. The enemy ship the dive-bombers had been assigned was actually sitting on the bottom of Manila Bay, with its decks awash. The strike group attacked Cavite buildings and oil tanks that lined the docks. Thankfully, the anti-aircraft fire was light that day. The strike groups returned and landed on their respective carriers. This was the last mission for Carrier Air Group 15 in the Pacific War.[26]

After the all aircraft were recovered, Admiral Sherman's Task Group 38.3 set course eastward for Ulithi. On November 17 at 0630, the *Essex* dropped anchor in Ulithi harbor. The word was on the street. Air Group 15 was finally being relieved by Air Group 4. The air group was excited, as they packed up their gear. On the flight deck of the *Essex* numerous officers and flight crewman were awarded medals.

CDR David Campbell and his Plane Captain AM1 Chester Owens (standing) with the Minsi III showing the 34 Japanese aircraft kills (Official U.S. Navy Photograph).

About 1800 in the evening, the damaged carrier *Bunker Hill* sailed into Ulithi Harbor. On the afternoon of the 18th, some of the men of Air Group 15 were taken by LST to the *Bunker Hill*. Back on November 9, three submarines of the Kikusui Squadron, *I-36*, *I-37* and *I-47*, sailed from Kure Harbor, Japan, into the Inland Sea. Each of these submarines was carrying strange weapons called a Kaiten-a kamikaze version of the Type 95 Long Lance torpedo with a compartment for a human pilot. Their target was Ulithi Harbor. At 0545 on November 19, men aboard the *Essex* and other ships of TG 38.3 heard and felt the oiler *Mississinewa* explode after being hit by a Kaiten at the entrance of Mugai Channel.[27] Wendall Mayes heard the explosion and recalled that at first he felt they had been hit. "The explosion was so big it rocked the *Essex* at anchor like what I thought a torpedo must be like. I ran topside in time to see the fireball, which must have been a thousand feet high."[28]

By the morning of November 20, the final group of men from Air Group 15 boarded the *Bunker Hill*. When the Air Group had departed from Pearl Harbor aboard the *Essex* to begin their combat tour, there were 122 pilots and 99 planes. During the combat tour, Air Group 15 losses were high. Forty-three pilots were killed or missing and twelve were wounded. Of the aircrewmen, twenty-nine were killed or missing and thirteen were wounded. The men of VB-15 had suffered the highest losses with seventeen pilots and fifteen gunners killed or missing in action. Sadly, twenty-five percent of the losses occurred during the last two weeks of the tour. The CAG-15 squadrons had lost 77 planes and 301 damaged.

Around 1400 in the afternoon of the 20th, the *Bunker Hill* departed Ulithi anchorage heading to Pearl Harbor. At 1530 on November 29, 1944, the *Bunker Hill* sailed into Pearl Harbor and docked at Ford Island. The aircraft were taken off the carrier at Ford Island. The officers got liberty that day, but the next day the enlisted men also enjoyed liberty in Honolulu.

The *Bunker Hill* with Air Group 15 steamed out of Pearl Harbor the morning of the first of December. Six days later, the carrier sailed into Puget Sound and docked at the Bremerton Naval Shipyard for a major overhaul. For McCampbell and the men of Air Group 15, the war in the Pacific had ended.[29]

The achievements of Commander David McCampbell and Carrier Air Group Fifteen were astonishing. During his combat tour of duty aboard the *Essex*, McCampbell shot down thirty-four Japanese planes, destroyed twenty-one confirmed planes on the ground and scored another eleven probables. He shot down nine planes in one day on a single sortie. He led all Naval Aviators of World War II in planes shot down to become the Navy's "Ace of Aces."

In addition his Medal of Honor medal he received at the White House on January 10, 1945, by President Franklin D. Roosevelt, David McCampbell was awarded the Navy Cross, the Silver Star Medal with Combat V, the Distinguished Flying Cross with two gold stars, the Air Medal, the Joint Services Commendation Medal, the ribbon for the Presidential Unit Citation awarded Carrier Air Group 15, the American Defense Service Medal with bronze A, the Asiatic-Pacific Campaign Medal with seven engagement stars, the European African-Middle Eastern Campaign Medal with one star, American Campaign Medal, the World War II Victory Medal, the National Defense Service Medal, the Philippine Liberation Medal with two stars and the Navy Expert Rifleman Medal.[30]

As Commander of Air Group 15, McCampbell led a group of aviators that achieved a record that has never been equaled in combat. Air Group 15 shot down 318 enemy aircraft, including 68 planes on a single day, June 19, 1944. They also destroyed 358 Japanese planes on the ground. Either alone or in company with pilots of other air groups, they sank 37

President Roosevelt awarding the Medal of Honor to Commander David McCampbell, USN at the White House on January 10, 1945. Mrs. A.J. McCampbell ties the Medal of Honor around the neck of her son. In the background of the photograph are Fleet Admiral Ernest J. King, and McCampbell's sister, Mrs. Frances Stewart of Washington, D.C. (Official U.S. Navy Photograph # 47649).

Japanese ships and probably sank another ten ships. Along with other air groups, they sank two carriers, a heavy cruiser, the battleship *Musashi*, a light cruiser, as well as damaging three battleships, one carrier, five heavy cruisers, three light cruisers and nineteen destroyers.[31]

Twenty-six of the pilots of Fighter Squadron 15 became aces giving the squadron the name, "Fabled Fifteen."[32] They fulfilled a prediction that came from the captain of the *Essex* after Air Group 15 had joined the carrier. When asked during an interview, Captain Ralph Ofstie displayed a frown and said, "I had to give them hell. Last week I took them up for a little try-out raid on Marcus and Wake islands. By George, they thought they were winning the war then and there! Fifty planes damaged—they went in so low over the AA fire. They were just too damned eager."[33] Smiling he continued, "But they listened to me. They've steadied down now. You know, there's something about the young fellows in this outfit that's a little different. I wouldn't be at all surprised if they turn out to be the best group we've had out here."[34]

The Captain Ofstie prophesy was to become a resounding fact as Air Group 15 took part in twenty-three major engagements in the Pacific War. Everywhere they attacked, they shot down planes in the air and on the ground, neutralized enemy air bases, destroyed building, docks, fuel and ammunition dumps, gun emplacements, supply depots, as well as sinking all manner of enemy ships from PT boats to battleships.[35]

In an article published in 1945 in *Liberty Magazine*, Morris Markey, who was a war correspondent aboard the USS *Essex*, wrote about Air Group 15:

> They went out to the Pacific war, a hundred young men. Seven months later only forty-five of them came home unhurt. But in those immortal seven months of naval history they became the undisputed champions of the Pacific Ocean areas. Indeed they inflicted on the enemy probably more damage and destruction than any other one hundred young men who have fought anywhere in this war. And the price they made the Japanese pay for their own losses is almost fantastic.[36]

Commander McCampbell's squadron commanders played a significant role in helping Air Group 15 to attain such outstanding accomplishments. When McCampbell was promoted to Commander Air Group 15, Commander Charles W. Brewer took over Fighter Squadron 15. He was lost in the first battle of the Philippines over Guam and was replaced by Lieutenant Commander James F. Rigg. He had shot down eleven Japanese planes and five probable on the *Essex* tour. He remained in the Navy and retired as a Captain from the Navy in 1963 having served twenty-seven years. He went into the book binding business and died in 2005 at age 90. Among other awards, he earned the Navy Cross, seven Distinguished Flying Crosses, a Bronze Star and ten Air Medals.[37]

The leader of the Helldivers and Bombing Squadron 15 was Commander James H. Mini. McCampbell said of his death on December 7, 1963, "He died of a heart attack, and he was out in Colorado Springs, where I was on duty. He got up one morning, took his dog out for a walk, and then he climbed the stairs back up to the second floor, and keeled over, and never drew another breath."[38]

The head of Torpedo Squadron 15 was Lieutenant Commander Valdemar G. Lambert. He became the most successful Naval Aviation Cadet (NavCad) in U.S. Navy history. After serving his tour aboard the *Essex*, the Air Group reformed at Los Alamitos, California, during January through June 1945, after which they transferred to Hawaii. After the war, the group was decommissioned. In November 1946, Air Group 153 was redesignated Carrier Air Group 15; Admiral Lambert became Air Group 15 Commander in July 1948, a position he held until the group was decommissioned in December 1949. During the Korean War, Admiral Lambert (then Commander) was assigned to the Staff of the Commander Joint Expeditionary Forces as Aviation Planner for the landing at Inchon. He participated in the initial assault phases of that landing and was on the beach to welcome General McArthur when he came ashore. In addition to the above, Admiral Lambert was Executive Officer of the *Ticonderoga*, (CVA 14) and he commanded the Fleet Oiler *Ashtabula*, (AO 51), the *Saratoga* (CVA 60), and Carrier Division Six. His other commands assignments included the U.S. Naval Base Subic Bay, Philippines, the Naval Technical Training, Millington, Tennessee, and the U.S. Naval Base Long Beach, California. He had four tours of duty in Washington, D.C. He is a graduate of the Naval War College, and served on the staffs of CincPacFleet, and Carrier Divisions Three and Four. He was selected for the rank of Rear Admiral in July 1966. His awards and decorations include the Navy Cross, a Silver Star, three Legions of Merit with Combat V, three Distinguished Flying Crosses, eight Air Medals, the Navy Commendation Ribbon with Combat V, the Presidential Unit Citation with Bronze Star, two Navy Unit Commendation, and other campaign ribbons and service medals. Rear Admiral Lambert retired from active duty on August 1, 1973. Admiral and Mrs. Lambert resided in Monterey, California, from 1973 until his death at his home on August 18, 2008, at age 93.[39]

The officers and men of Carrier Air Group 15 were the most successful Navy air group of World War II, having demonstrated every mission day all the skills and bravery it took to attack and destroy enemy aircraft, ships and ground facilities from a waiting aircraft carrier often hundreds of miles away. During their tour of seven months and more than 20,000 hours of operations, Air Group 15 squadrons destroyed more enemy planes and sank more enemy ships than any other air group in the Pacific war.[40] McCampbell later recalled how proud he was that his air group never lost a bomber or torpedo plane that they escorted due to air-to-air combat, and that the *Essex* was never hit by an enemy bomb or torpedo during their combat tour. These men set the standard for all that an air group could be, delivering the lethal threat represented by the Fast Carrier Task Group during World War II.

20

Post-War Naval Career

"His personal story is unique in all the annals of naval aviation"[1]

On his trip aboard the *Bunker Hill* to Bremerton, McCampbell spent his time flying some ASW patrols off the carrier just to keep up his flying skills. He completed the various combat action reports and got in his share of relaxing and drinking.

After joining his wife, Susan Rankin, in Seattle, the Navy sent McCampbell and Susan to New York where they stayed in the Waldorf-Astoria to attend the National Association of Manufacturers show. There he stayed for three weeks as a guest of Grumman, the manufacturer of his famous Hellcat F6F Minsi III. The Navy assigned him a public relations person to arrange events for him.

Also in New York, McCampbell appeared in several radio shows including the Gulf Oil Show where he and George H. Gay (the only crewmember to survive from the 15 pilots and 15 aircrew members of Torpedo Squadron Eight TBD Devastators that attacked the Japanese fleet during the Battle of Midway in June 1942) were interviewed.

After the show, the Navy sent him to Washington where he learned that he was being presented the Medal of Honor. On January 10, 1945, McCampbell was presented the citation and medal from Franklin D. Roosevelt in the White House Oval Office. He recalled that for the award there he was joined by a submariner, Commander Lawson P. Ramage, USN. He had his wife, mother and father with him. Since he was senior to McCampbell he was called into the presentation first. Next McCampbell was called in to see the President along with his mother and sister. Roosevelt asked him to introduce him to his guests, which he did. He gave the medal to his mother and she pinned the award on her son. Afterward they moved into the anteroom with sister and mother, and got to spend fifteen to twenty minutes with Admiral King, General Marshall and General Hap Arnold individually.[2]

McCampbell also recalled that Roosevelt looked sick, with his eyes sunken with black rings around them, and seemed to have lost weight. "He just didn't look in good health at all."[3] The Navy had arranged all the train travel from California for his mother, father and sister, but his father had fallen down and injured his nose and did not make the trip to Washington.

Then McCampbell was sent on a public relations tour around the country along with his Navy PR officer and another pilot. They traveled to their events in a twin engine Beechcraft SNB. Taking off from Washington, they flew to Glenview, Illinois. The event included the showing of the new movie *The Fighting Lady*, and then McCampbell answered questions about his combat experiences.

The next event was in Ottumwa, Iowa, and then on to California. He went to St. Mary's College at Moraga, California, to make an appearance for the Navy ROTC and guests. From there they flew to San Diego after a refueling stop in Los Angeles. They toured two naval air stations there, North Island and Miramar. They also visited Grumman Aircraft and the Edo Floats Company. Then it was off to the east to Oklahoma for gas, and down to Dallas and Corpus Christi for events at three naval air stations.

The tour then headed off to New Orleans, and on to Florida for events at NAS Pensacola, and at several air stations in the Jacksonville area-NAS Green Cove Springs and NAS Cecil Field-and down to Melbourne and Fort Lauderdale. From there they headed north for events at the University of Georgia in Athens and on to the University of North Carolina at Chapel Hill. Then they flew up to Washington, D.C.

After the tour, McCampbell, who had divorced Susan Rankin, married Sara Jane Heliker on February 18, 1945, in Washington. In March, he reported to his new assignment as Deputy Chief of Staff for the Commander Fleet Air at NAS Quonset Point, Rhode Island. In order that Commodore Gordon Rowe and his staff at Quonset Point could supervise all the air groups, McCampbell was actually stationed at the Oceana Naval Auxiliary Air Station at Virginia Beach, just twelve miles from Norfolk, Virginia.

His job was to monitor the training of naval carrier air groups in the area at Chincoteague, Oceana, Pungo, and another air stations down south at Creeds, Virginia. Working with various group commanders and squadron commanders, McCampbell made sure the training programs were adequate to meet the combat needs of the fleet. Occasionally he would fly up and attend staff meetings and briefings at Quonset Point. He was, in essence, the Virginia representative for the Commander Fleet Air.[4]

While assigned there, McCampbell continued to attend various public appearances because of his Medal of Honor fame. These included visits to local clubs, luncheons, Memorial Day ceremonies and more. He took part in a number of radio shows and a few TV appearances. He participated in the Bob Hope Show in San Francisco, and also did two radio shows at Los Angeles on that same trip.

McCampbell was the Grand Marshall for four parades including Colorado Springs, Pensacola, Washington, and Winchester, Virginia. The Washington parade was with Nimitz and Mitscher. All through the rest of his life, McCampbell did public appearances.[5]

This assignment lasted for eight months until the war ended when McCampbell was assigned to the Commander Air Atlantic Fleet (ComAirLant) staff at Norfolk as the plans and intelligence officer. There he worked on plans to resupply the Mediterranean Six Fleet with nuclear weapons. It took about six months to complete the plans during which he traveled to Fort Campbell Army Base in Kentucky to review the capabilities of the DC-3.

McCampbell and his planning group came up with the procedures that involved ferrying DC-3s loaded with nuclear weapons from Fort Campbell to the Azores, and then to Port Lyautey in French Morocco, Africa. The weapons were stored at Port Lyautey where carrier-based planes, the propeller-driven North American Aviation AJ Savage, would fly in and pick-up the weapons and fly them back to the carriers.[6]

McCampbell held this position until February 3, 1947, when he started at the Armed Forces Staff College in Norfolk. He was in the first class. He applied for the College, which was just a half mile from a house he owned. The college lasted for six months and consisted of lectures, reading and working up a major seminar presentation associated with strategy and tactics. The class was divided up into different areas including personnel, intelligence, planning, operations, logistics and communications. Each section prepared their part of the full seminar and presented it on stage. McCampbell was the supervisor of the Intelligence Division for the seminar work.

McCampbell enjoyed the College and was able to work with Army and Air Force officers, which was a first for him. After completing the courses, McCampbell moved to assume the staff role as Assistant Intelligence Officer based on his student role. He continued to work with the students on developing up-to-date seminars on a variety of subjects like war with China on the Shantung Peninsula.[7]

In February, McCampbell's father, Andrew Jackson McCampbell, came to stay with him in Norfolk for a month. While he was there, Andrew asked him if he could visit the old grounds where his father (David's grandfather) had been imprisoned during the Civil War. So McCampbell drove him up to Richmond and over to the prison camp near Yorktown. Afterwards they headed to Washington and out to Annapolis to show his father around the campus of the Naval Academy.

On their way home to Norfolk outside Annapolis, McCampbell's car was apparently going too fast and hit an icy spot in the road as he rounded a curve. The car went down a hill and flipped over once, coming to rest right side up in a ditch. A salesman from Armour Meat Company came along and assisted McCampbell and his injured father, suffering from a cut on his head, to the hospital back in Annapolis. There they X-rayed his father and did not see anything. The doctor suggested that McCampbell return to Norfolk to attend school and return the following Friday to pick him up.

McCampbell stayed with a friend in Annapolis on Sunday and on Monday, he purchased a new Lincoln to replace his wrecked car, and headed back to Norfolk the next day. On Wednesday, a nurse called from the hospital and said, "If you want to see your father again, you'd better get up here in a hurry. He's lapsed into unconsciousness."[8]

McCampbell signed out a seaplane at Navy FASRon and flew to Annapolis to the hospital. By the time he arrived, his father had died of a diabetic coma. It was February 22, 1947, and Andrew was age 73. He learned that his father had not been taking his injections and that caused his death. McCampbell had his father's body cremated and the ashes sent out to his mother in Los Angeles to be placed in a crypt.[9]

In the summer of 1948, McCampbell was assigned to Buenos Aires, Argentina as the Senior Naval Aviation Advisor to the Argentine Navy. He was also an instructor for the Naval War College in Argentina, where his office was located. For the College he gave advice and instruction, and occasional lectures. He had access to a twin-engine Beechcraft with a pilot, radioman and mechanic. Though the plane was officially assigned to the Naval Attaché, he had full use of the aircraft and crewmembers.[10]

McCampbell's mission was to advice the Argentine Navy on naval matters. The role allowed him great freedom to travel throughout South America. He felt this tour of duty was the most enjoyable he experienced in the Navy. He became professional and personal friends with an Argentine naval aviator, Pio Baroja. He spoke English and set up trips for him. McCampbell was fortunate to have studied Spanish during his college days and had limited ability to speak it on his tour. He took Spanish classes twice a week.

McCampbell's first trip was to the tip of South America to the Argentine naval base and airfield at Ushuaia on the Straits of Magellan. On the 1,800 mile trip down they stopped at a large ranch called Menendes Bette. There they fished and hunted. Other trips were to Rosario, Argentina, Rio de Janeiro, Brazil, Asuncion in Paraguay, and a large lake city at the foot of the Andes called Bariloche. McCampbell learned from a friend that plutonium was being manufactured on an island in the middle of Lake Bariloche, and he reported it to Naval Intelligence. Other more local trips by air for fishing were taken to Salta, JuJuy, and Oran to the north.

McCampbell recalled the living conditions in Argentina where the first few weeks they lived in a hotel as they house-hunted. The old house they selected had four bedrooms since he had his mother-in-law, wife and their two kids. The house, that cost him a rent of $300 per month, had no air-conditioning, or central heating. The mosquitoes came in the rainy part of the year as there were no window screens. McCampbell hired a nurse for the two boys, a female cook who recruited the other help including an upstairs and downstairs maids, a washwoman and another cook. The nurse lived in the house, while the cook and cook's granddaughter lived in a small building behind the house.

He also hired three part-time gardeners, and when one of them died, McCampbell bought a few sheep for $7.50 each to help eating the grass. As it turned out the sheep liked the flowers better than grass, so he gave the sheep to a butcher. Incredible as it seemed, McCampbell's servants excluding the gardeners cost him only $100 per month. He fed all the servants except the washwoman and the gardeners.[11]

While in Argentina, McCampbell received his U.S. Navy commander's salary and flight pay, plus commander's pay from the Argentine Government. His household expenses were low, and he could get breakfast, lunch and dinner at the Naval War College as an instructor for free. Food was cheap, especially beef.[12]

McCampbell ended his tour of duty in Argentina and in February 1951, he became the Executive Officer of the *Franklin D. Roosevelt* fleet carrier. After hearing of his new assignment, he called the commander of the carrier, Captain William V. Davis, Jr. The ship was in the Mediterranean at the time so McCampbell made plans to fly there. He flew to Port Lyautey and was heading toward Nice, France, just past the island of Majorcas in an amphibious PB4Y-A seaplane when it lost an engine. Though he was not officially allowed to land in Spain at that time, he was forced to make an emergency landing at the main airport in Barcelona.

McCampbell called one of the people he had been given by his Argentine friend, Baroja, named Baron MacMahan. MacMahan assisted the Americans to get their money exchanged, get a reservation at the Ritz, as well as taking them out to dinner and even supplying them with female guests. The next day a replacement engine arrived via plane from Port Lyautey, and the plane took McCampbell to Nice. From Nice he got a ride to Cannes where the *Roosevelt* was anchored. McCampbell reported aboard and relieved Commander John L. Crittenden.[13]

The *Roosevelt* was one of the three newest carriers in the fleet and was captained by one of the old and respected aviators. He was born in Savannah in 1902 and graduated from the Naval Academy in 1924. He got his flight training to become a Naval Aviator at Pensacola the next January and served with several squadrons. His naval career was closely associated with naval aviation and he advanced steadily until he took command of the *Roosevelt* in August 1950.[14] McCampbell liked Captain Davis as the skipper, but he was not popular with the crew because he never ventured below decks, staying on the bridge and in his cabin.

During the tour, the *Roosevelt* conducted the routine operations of the Sixth Fleet. McCampbell recalled visiting Valencia, Spain for five days. There were other memorable events during the social periods in port. On the port visits, the usual plan was to anchor out and run boats back and forth to bring the public to an open house on the carrier and guests to a reception.

During the tour in July 1951, Captain Davis was relieved by Captain Fitzhugh Lee who had been a flight instructor for McCampbell. Lee eventually became frustrated by the amount of paperwork as the captain of the *Roosevelt*. McCampbell recalled Lee's actions because he had to read each of the messages and correspondence before the captain did.

Lee started actually counting the number of pieces of paper he had to handle and complained to ComSixthFlt about it.

As the executive officer, McCampbell spent most of his days working on administrative matters. He previewed all captain masts before the captain determined the punishment. If a case were minor, he would throw it out before the captain got involved. The heads of all the ships' departments reported to McCampbell. His staff was a capable team, as were the majority of the other key officers and enlisted personnel.

McCampbell was pressed to keep up his flight time requirements on tour. He had to get in his flying time using a carrier utility plane at the airports nearest the port of call. In March 1952, McCampbell's tour had ended and he was relieved by Commander Edward C. Outlaw on the *Roosevelt*.

Next, McCampbell was assigned to ComAirLant in Norfolk as the Staff Planning Officer where he primarily worked on coordinating resupply of nuclear weapons to the Sixth Fleet. McCampbell was promoted during this tour of duty to the rank of Captain.

He was working with Fort Campbell again where the weapons were stored, as well as with the transport command and the squadron at Norfolk with the AJ aircraft to deliver the weapons to the ships. The nuclear weapons were first manufactured in Washington State and in Tennessee, and transported to Albuquerque, New Mexico. Then they were flown by cargo aircraft to Fort Campbell. From there they took the usual route to the Azores, then to Port Lyautey in French Morocco and then by carrier AJ or the Douglas A3D Skywarrior to the fleet in the Mediterranean.[15]

In the summer of 1953, McCampbell assumed command of the Naval Air Technical Training Center at Jacksonville, Florida. McCampbell's Center reported to the Rear Admiral Wendall G. Switzer, the Chief of Naval Technical Training, with headquarters in Memphis and was responsible for the technical training of 9,000 enlisted personnel. The center trained 1,000 to 1,500 Marines including female Marines (BAMs) and 8,000 Navy enlisted including Navy women (Navy Waves). McCampbell let the senior Marine manage the training of the Marines in his command, while his staff handled the Navy training supervision.

McCampbell was entirely consumed with administrative matters including personnel, discipline and, to some extent, budgeting. His staff covered the same subjects as in Memphis except they trained in missile technology. Half of the instructors were civilians and the rest were GS government employees. The Center included a mired of buildings and facilities including training and residence buildings, a mess hall, a hospital, a swimming

Photograph of Captain David McCampbell, undated (National Museum of Naval Aviation, Emil Buehler Library, Accession Number NNAM.2005.196.009.021).

pool, a PX, and more. McCampbell's staff also included ten barbers, three chaplains, nine dentists, and around twelve doctors.

McCampbell had a residence on the St. Johns River, and was assigned two mess attendants. He had a "nice setup"[16] and enjoyed fishing from the small boat he docked at his residence.[17]

After serving his one-year tour in Jacksonville, McCampbell became the Flight Test Coordinator at the Naval Air Test Center in Patuxent River, Maryland. There he commanded five test divisions-flight test, service test, electronics test, arms test and test pilot school. McCampbell reported to Captain Clifford H. Duerfeldt, the Commander of the Naval Air Test Center.

As Flight Test Coordinator, McCampbell reviewed various test reports from the five divisions. He had little involvement with the test pilot school, except to participate in the selection of people to attend the school. While McCampbell served there, they tested several jet aircraft including the McDonnell's F3H Demon (a jet-powered fighter-bomber that first entered the fleet in the 1950s) and the Grumman F9F-6 swept wing Cougar (a 42-foot long fighter with a wingspan of 36 feet, gross weight of 20,000 pounds and a top speed of 690 miles per hour).

McCampbell learned to fly his first jet, the F9F-6, on this tour. He noted that the chief difference between jets and propeller planes was how quiet the jets were. The landings were difference in jets, having to force the nose down before easing back and flaring.

The testing development methodology started with flight test, and then moved to service tests. Service tests involved suitability trials for arrested landings and catapult shots. Armament tests involved the use of various armaments of planes and missiles, and the electronics test was developing electronic training and severe weather tests including the deep freeze group. A number of famous aviators and future astronauts came though the flight test pilot division while McCampbell was coordinator including John Glenn.[18]

After his tour in Maryland, in June 1956 Captain McCampbell became the Operations Officer for the Sixth Fleet. For most of his tour, he reported to Vice Admiral Charles R. Brown. This change of command ceremony was held while he was anchored in Venice, Italy, on August 4, 1956. McCampbell lived aboard the flag commander's heavy cruiser, which during his tour were the *Salem*, *Des Moines* and *Newport News*.[19] He remembered that his shipboard quarters in his cabin were pretty basic. Aboard the cruiser *Salem* he had a bed that was so soft that it felt more like a hammock. He was able to get another mattress, but it also sunk down too much. He never slept well on that ship.[20]

According to McCampbell, Admiral Brown was a man who demanded to be in control. On his flagship, you could determine what you wanted to eat for breakfast, but for lunch and dinner, the Admiral set the menu. Either you ate what he had the cooks fix or you had nothing to eat. McCampbell later described a day when some guests came aboard and were having fish. He and a senior Marine officer decided to have a lunch of scrambled eggs, and they told the cook to give them eggs. Admiral Brown went ballistic at the cook and called him in to his office to raise hell.[21]

The Sixth Fleet was home ported in "a lovely bay"[22] at Villefranche, France, just ten miles from Nice. They visited nearly every country that bordered the Mediterranean except Israel, Egypt, Tunisia and Algeria. McCampbell noted that he played golf in almost every one of those countries too. He had access to play golf at a Monaco golf club that had no green fees or dues. In Lebanon, he played on a course that was more of a sandlot, where you teed off on rubber mats placed on the sand and drove down the fairway to the sand. He flew down to Morocco to the King's golf course set in an orange grove and played on oil-soaked sand greens. Other golfing locations were Spain, Portugal, Gibraltar, Libya, Italy, Greece, Yugoslavia, and Turkey at Istanbul.

McCampbell was involved along with the other Sixth Fleet staff in organizing, planning and conducting Fleet exercises with American Allies. They held two with the British Bomber Command during which the Sixth Fleet dispersed throughout the Mediterranean to avoid detection. The British bombers had installed new radar that was supposed to be excellent in detecting warships. However, in both exercises the British bombers that flew out of London were unable to locate any of the major Sixth Fleet warships or carriers in the western Mediterranean.[23]

As Operations Officer, McCampbell was primarily responsibility for ensuring that the ships of the Sixth Fleet could carry out their movements successfully. Plans were developed to disperse the fleet around the Med or assemble it as required to meet various threats. Exercises were conducted to test the capability to meet schedules. For example, any ship including a carrier was scheduled to meet a tanker to refuel at an exact date and time and location.

Port visits were strictly controlled by CinCNELM (Commander-in-Chief U.S. Naval Forces in Europe, the East Atlantic, and the Mediterranean) and could not be deviated from. The Sixth Fleet ships received the port call schedules with approximately six-weeks notice or more.[24]

In January 1958, McCampbell was detached for duty as commanding officer of a service force ship. The change in assignment came about when Vice Admiral William V. Davis, Jr., serving as Deputy Chief of Naval Operations (Air), sent a letter to Admiral Brown asking him what he thought about McCampbell becoming a skipper of a service force ship. Admiral Brown felt it was a bad idea because it involved leaving the "brown-shoe"[25] Navy for the "black-shoe"[26] Navy. In those days, aviators wore brown shoes with their khaki or green uniforms, which got them the nickname as brown shoes to distinguish them from the traditional surface ship officers, who are known as black shoes.

Admiral Brown passed the letter along to McCampbell who decided it would be a good move since it was getting difficult to get a deep-draft ship. It was not too long before McCampbell received orders to become the commanding officer the fleet oiler *Severn* (AO–61). The *Severn* was an Ashtabula-class fleet oiler that had been commissioned on July 19, 1944. She displaced 25,440 tons loaded, with a 553-foot length and a 75-foot beam, with a maximum draft of 32 feet. Her maximum speed was 18 knots and she was armed with one 5-inch gun and four 3-inch guns.

McCampbell proceeded to the Todd Shipyard in New York where the oiler was going through an overhaul. When McCampbell reported aboard the *Severn,* he noticed that there was no commission pennant flying and nobody met him at the gangway. He assumed that the captain would be up in the bridge area up above. He ran into the mess attendant and asked where the captain was. He took him to the cabin on the well deck and introduced himself to him. He was a black-shoe Annapolis grad from the class of 1934. To McCampbell's surprise, the ship had not been decommissioned yet even though it did not have its commissioning flag flying. It seemed the captain didn't seem to know that, but he called in the communications officer to get their commission flag up.

McCampbell noticed the lines all over the ship getting their water, electricity and more from the dock. He asked the captain why there was no one posted at the gangway. The response was that he would get that corrected. McCampbell was now convinced that this ship was poorly run. The tour revealed that all the garbage was being piled up on the fantail, to be deposited later out in the ocean. McCampbell later took a picture of what he found and sent it to Admiral Brown. The oiler was supposed to have been in the yard for only three months, but they were heading into the fourth month.[27]

The sea trials experience was another crazy revelation for McCampbell. When the ship was out for sea trials, as soon as they departed the dock, the circuit board failed. There was no electricity in the ship, so they turned around and sailed back for a few days to repair the circuit board. Finally, back at sea some ten miles off the coast off Fire Island Lighthouse, the main steam line sprang a leak.

Since the connections were such that with one steam line down, the second line could not operate. Without steam there was no power to operate the electric generator, so all they could do was drift around. The captain decided to send a whaleboat back to the lighthouse and call for a tug. The coxswain was alerted but he reminded the captain that the lifeboats were all left back at the beach.

Left to drift, the crew attempted to fix the leak as best they could. Finally, after about three hours passed, the steam leak was able to provide enough power to allow them to get underway. They eventually struggled into port. All of these problems indicated that Todd Shipbuilding was doing a terrible job refitting the oiler. The docking pilot aboard took the ship upriver in the dark and came in too fast and did not stop the steam early enough, and the ship hit the end of the dock causing little damage. It had been a trying period for McCampbell.

USS *Severn* (AO-61) underway at sea, after refueling USS *Tarawa* (CVS-40), February 13, 1959 (Official U.S. Navy Photograph # NH 99491).

The ship remained in dock for ten days. During this time McCampbell told the skipper that he would not relieve him as captain until the ship was running well and could pass the sea trials. So, after all was successful with the sea trials, McCampbell and the skipper rode together up to Newport, Rhode Island, without mishap and McCampbell relieved his predecessor.[28]

Almost immediately, the *Severn* was ordered to Guantanamo for more training in gunnery, ship handling and refueling. The ship steamed south for training and ended up with a poor score in gunnery. McCampbell soon discovered that the Chief that set the gunsights on the target from the director was "half blind."[29] The *Severn* did successfully conduct refueling of a destroyer.

With an observer on board to see how you did, the ship was supposed to sail in and anchor within 25 to 35 feet of a certain spot. The process involved taking at least two bearings on two points on the shore, and then determining the point to land. The trick was to accurately determine the time it took to get the word down from the bridge to the first lieutenant who then gave the order to drop anchor, and then add the time it took for the anchor to descend to the bottom which was based on the depth of the water. He overshot the hole to drop the anchor in because the seaman on the forecastle missed the anchor pin to drop the anchor multiple times with his sledgehammer. Although the observer was a former Naval Academy classmate, Captain Lawrence R. Neville, he could not pass the drop because they were too far away from the hole. The *Severn* crew had to repeat the test several times before getting a passing grade.

After training and taking tests for two weeks, the *Severn* sailed back to Newport. On route, they were ordered to the middle of the Atlantic to refuel the *Lake Champlain* (CVS-39), an antisubmarine aircraft carrier, and a few destroyers heading from Norfolk to the Mediterranean. As a first-class boatswain's mate was using a winch to retrieve the span wire on the starboard side of the oiler, he got his sleeve caught between the drum and the wire. The crewman was flipped around four times and was left unconscious. McCampbell called the *Lake Champlain* and asked them if they would send a helicopter over for a badly injured crewman. They flew over and picked him up.

McCampbell's ordeal was not over yet. When the *Severn* was waiting to refuel one of the destroyers, the destroyer collided with the *Severn*. The captain of the destroyer had made two attempts before finally closing on the oiler. His helmsman turned in too close and their anchor put a hole in the port side of the *Severn*. Oil started leaking from the ships' side.[30]

As the *Severn* fueled a destroyer, the winch had been rigged incorrectly by being turned around in the shipyard and when the operator thought he was retrieving the span wire, it was operating in reverse and reeling it out. He reeled it out so far it wound around the port propeller. There was also no way to reel the span wire in because it had reached the bitter end. The problem forced the oiler to turn off its engine.

McCampbell took the motor whaleboat out and using his snorkel, he swam under the ship to confirm the prop was fouled. The *Severn* sent a message to base explaining their problem and indicated he was heading back using the other unfouled propeller to steam back to Newport. They pulled in to the dock next to a repair ship. After getting the port prop unfouled with an underwater blowtorch, orders required that the *Severn* report to the Sixth Fleet to become their fourth oiler tanker.

The *Severn* steamed out of Newport the next day and set a course for the Mediterranean Sea. The ship passed the Straits of Gibraltar and anchored off Algeria. There McCampbell had the crew paint the entire ships' hull. McCampbell reported in to the

Sixth Fleet the next day and was ordered to sail to an oil depot in Pozzuoli, Italy, located near Naples. The *Severn* topped off with fuel and headed to the island of Rhodes, Greece. They spent five days there and then headed to Lebanon, refueling several destroyers on the way.[31]

The 1958 crisis in Lebanon was caused by political and religious tensions in the country that included U.S. military intervention. The intervention lasted around three months until President Camille Chamoun, who had requested the assistance, completed his term as president of Lebanon. When the crisis ended, the United States withdrew shortly after.[32]

During the first month commanding the *Severn,* one of his chief petty officers came to the bridge and told McCampbell that the ship was full of rats. They said the previous night two of the petty officers were bitten by them.[33]

McCampbell called the chief pharmacist's mate and said the crew has reported the ship is full of rats. He said the only way to get rid of them was using strychnine, a poison. Although it was against Navy regulations to use it, McCampbell directed him to put it out and as an incentive, he ordered that anyone who presented a rat tail to the chief pharmacist would receive a carton of cigarettes. After one month over 400 rats had been killed.[34]

The crew of the *Severn* were a mixture of competent and incompetent men. McCampbell had to send two officers off the boat. Their first warrant officer had participated in the Bataan Death March in the Philippines and McCampbell forced him to go to the hospital after the training cruise at Guantanamo. He also replaced his Ensign who had a problem carrying out his duties. During his stay, the ship was investigated three times for pay related issues. In addition to the two officers, McCampbell had to take action against his radiomen who had come to the ship straight from a mental hospital in Philadelphia. When the *Severn* was anchored 80–100 miles off the coast at Athens, Greece, the man dove off the ship and tried to swim across the Mediterranean. It took the whaleboat and five crewmen to get the man back aboard The man had resisted, forcing McCampbell to put him in the brig filled with mattresses until he could reach Athens.

The operations aboard the *Severn* were not too stressful or strenuous for McCampbell and his crew except when the ship had to fuel thirteen ships in a single day. During the daylight hours, McCampbell spent his time on the bridge. For relaxation, the ship would hold bingo games each night either before or after a movie.[35]

As his tour was coming to an end aboard the *Severn,* McCampbell learned from his detailing officer, Hugh Winters, that he was going to command the carrier *Bon Homme Richard.* In preparation for that assignment, McCampbell flew to Olathe, Kansas, to qualify in the latest fighter to be deployed aboard the carrier, the F9F. During the three weeks of training, he qualified in an F6F trainer. Since McCampbell had already flown the jet, it was a breeze for him.

After training, McCampbell flew aboard a Constellation to join the carrier in Manila. After flying from Guam, the Constellation lost an engine and had to return to Guam to get a new engine. From Guam, he flew to Clark Air Force Base, which was 50 miles north of Manila. A helicopter from the carrier flew to Clark and picked up McCampbell and brought him back to the ship.

On February 5, 1959, McCampbell relieved Captain Burdette E. Close as the ninth Commanding Officer of the *Bon Homme Richard* (CVA-31). His delight about being the new skipper was soon diminished on the third night out of Manila heading for Yokosuka, Japan. That night the Commander of Carrier Division Three, Rear Admiral William A. Schoech, riding aboard the *Bon Homme Richard* (BHR), directed McCampbell to refuel with a tanker. McCampbell approached the tanker in rough seas with eight- to ten-foot waves and in wind of 25–30 knots. All seemed well until the carrier overran the tanker. McCampbell reversed the engines a bit and moved back, but the wind caused the carrier to drift into the tanker and had a small collision with it. In order not to have the carrier's propellers hit the tanker, McCampbell moved forward and crossed the tankers' bow by five degrees.

After an investigation, the commander of the Seventh Fleet, Vice Admiral Frederick N. Kivette, indicated in a letter that he planned to issue a reprimand to McCampbell. McCampbell appealed the decision. The investigation found that the tanker was supposed to be steaming at 11 knots, but was only at 9 knots. Also, the tanker's heading was off course by three degrees. When the carrier had pulled alongside, it had the effect of hiding the wind from the tanker and the ship had pulled into the carrier before the rudder had corrected. Since the tanker captain was partially at fault for the collision, the reprimand was canceled.[36]

The carrier reached Yokasuka and spent a week there. Then they started visiting various ports. Heading into the Inland Sea for Osaka at 0600, a small freighter headed toward the carrier from the port side, which placed the *Bon Homme Richard* as the privileged ship, and the freighter thus required to adjust its course.

The freighter continued to hold a collision course to the carrier, so at the last possible moment McCampbell sounded four blasts on the whistle, stopped the engines and turned into the freighter. McCampbell turned into the freighter because the freighter was about to hit the location along the hull where the nuclear weapons were stored. As a result, the carrier barely clipped the stern of the freighter. The only injury of the freighter was the chief engineer who got a cut on his forehead from a broken porthole. The damage on the stern was minor, but the freighter issued a claim for $30,000. After an investigation by Admiral Schoech, he passed it on to Com7thFlt, but no action was ever taken.[37]

After Osaka, the carrier visited Beppu, Japan, where McCampbell had the carrier "dressed up"[38] with flags rigged up from bow to stern. They visited Yokohama north of Yokosuka and spent five days in Hong Kong. After touring in the Far East with Task Force 77, the *Bon Homme Richard* returned to their U.S. homeport at Alameda, California, on June 18, 1959. They spent three months training the new air group off the coast. The carrier made one trip for three days to San Diego to allow McCampbell's division heads to meet the staff at ComAirPac. In July Admiral Kivette was relieved by Rear Admiral Andrew Jackson, Jr.

During McCampbell's tour the carrier brought aboard a new air group, CVG-19, which included squadrons VF-191 flying F11F-1's, VA-192 flying FJ-4B's, VF-193 flying F3H-2's and VA-195 flying AD-6's. In mid-tour VA-192 and VA-195 transitioned to A4D-2 Skyhawks, thus replacing the old Furys and Skyraiders. The carrier operated the first F8U-1P Crusader with VCP-63.

On November 21, 1959, the carrier sailed from Alameda to Hawaii for an operational readiness inspection (ORI). An unfortunate event occurred aboard the carrier as McCampbell later recalled. When they were on course from Alameda to Pearl Harbor there was to be no flying operations that Sunday as directed by Captain Jackson. McCampbell assumed that order did not include respotting the deck. On that rather windy Sunday, while he was lying down taking a nap, a plane was lost overboard during the deck respotting work. It happened when the ship rolled and the plane went over the chocks and fell over the side. Apparently one of the inexperienced plane handlers was in the plane when it went over the side, and he could not swim. Even though they got the helo out to the scene in three

USS *Bon Homme Richard* (CVA-31) being refueled by USS *Kawishiwi* (AO-146) escorted by USS *Hollister* (DD-788) (U.S. Navy and Marine Corps Museum/Naval Aviation Museum, photograph # 1996.488.038.050).

minutes, they could not see him. After some four hours searching for the man, they could not recover his body, They proceeded on to Pearl.[39]

The *Bon Homme Richard* arrived on November 27 at Pearl Harbor. The carrier was scheduled to depart at 0800 on Monday, December 7, 1959, to begin the ORI with Rear Admiral Grover B.H. Hall, the Commander Fleet Air Hawaii, coming aboard as an inspection observer. McCampbell knew there was a ceremony to be held that morning on the Arizona Memorial off Ford Island that was to be attended by Admiral Harry D. Felt, the CinCPac, Senator Barry M. Goldwater of Arizona, Admiral Simmonds, the commander of the Pearl Harbor shipyard, and several other dignitaries.[40]

At 0750, McCampbell came down from the bridge to the flight deck to greet Hall, who was arriving by helicopter. As McCampbell headed back up to the bridge level to take the ship out, the executive officer stood at the handrail and said, "Good morning, Captain. The ship is under way."[41] McCampbell looked down at his watch then responded, "What do you mean, it's under way?"[42] The XO replied, "Well, I don't know, Captain, but it's under way."[43]

With the ship tied up on the starboard side at pier 14, McCampbell dashed to the starboard side to acknowledge that indeed the ship was underway, and heading straight for the Admiral's Quarter K on Ford Island. McCampbell heard the docking pilot yell out all engines stopped, left full rudder. They didn't wipe out the pier, but they did hit four or five piling. The ship was now stopped and out in the stream with enough power to round Ford

Island and pass by the USS *Arizona* while one minute of silence was being observed. Later McCampbell learned that Admiral Felt had inquired to Admiral Simmonds asking if the *Bonne Homme Richard* was supposed to be involved in the celebration. He responded that no, but that the ship was heading out for the ORI. Admiral Felt noted that the carrier served as the perfect backdrop for the one minute of silence.[44]

An investigated took place that revealed a rather incredible series of events during which a test of the communications with the engine order telegraph between engine fire room eight and the bridge was misinterpreted to be the actual orders to get the carrier underway from the pier. The reprimand ultimately went to Lieutenant Williams who was the engineering officer aboard the *Bon Homme Richard* though the actual problem had been initiated by a new interior communications seaman.[45]

The carrier steamed out of Pearl Harbor on December 14 and arrived in Apra Harbor, Guam, on December 23. McCampbell got in some water skiing there before they sailed on December 31. The *Bon Homme Richard* arrived at Buckner Bay, Okinawa, on January 9, and steamed to the next port at Sasebo, Japan, on January 14. The ship anchored at Sasebo on January 16, departing on the 22nd. After spending January 25 back at Buckner Bay, the carrier sailed into Yokosuka Harbor on January 29.[46]

On February 15, 1960, Captain Harold S. Bottomley relieved McCampbell as commanding officer of the *Bon Homme Richard*. McCampbell flew back to the States and took several weeks leave before reporting to his next assignment in Washington at the Joint Chiefs of Staff. During the first three weeks, he studied the various planning documents at the Navy Department. At first, he was supposed to become the aide to the Chief of Plans Division known as J-5, but the incumbent was promoted as a general and departed. McCampbell became the new Chief of Plans with a division staff of twenty-five senior officers from the Navy, Air Force, Army and Marines. Later the Policy area was consolidated and McCampbell's title changed to the Chief of Strategic Plans and Policy.

McCampbell and his staff were responsible for developing plans and policies for the Joint Chiefs of Staff with input from the various military services. There seemed not to be any eight-hour days, as work was often grueling for McCampbell with up to 16-hour days. His office was located in the Pentagon across from the hall from Bobby Kennedy's office, the Attorney General for his brother President Robert Kennedy.[47]

McCampbell's office received their assignments from the Director of the Joint Staff. During his tour at JCS, McCampbell's team became involved in developing contingency plans to invade Cuba during the Cuban Crisis. He was there when the Berlin Wall was being built by the East German regime controlled by the Soviets, when their plans were tested. At first, a platoon of U.S. Army troops marched up to the gate at the Wall and demanded to enter. After a short while, the Americans were allowed to enter. Later they sent in a battalion and a regiment, which also were allowed to enter. His staff also was involved in the Korean situation mainly to establish the proper number of troops to deploy in South Korea. Near the end of his tour, his group did work on the Vietnam War and Laos plans.

Though he was confortable living in an apartment near the Pentagon, which allowed him to walk to work, McCampbell felt the work was not interesting to him. It was strictly a paperwork job, with an endless number of contingency plans coming his way. McCampbell said, "You have a contingency plan for everything-whether you take your umbrella out with you today or not."[48] He was low in the chain of command and only attended one regular session of the JCS. His meetings were with the Joint Staff director.[49]

As his tour was coming to an end, McCampbell was given a choice of his next assignment. He could go to the Air War College at Maxwell Air Force Base in Alabama, or to the Strategic Air Command in Omaha, or head to North American Air Defense Command in Colorado Springs. He chose the North American Air Command because he felt it was good experience, he liked the area and thought it would be a great place to retire.

He arrived in his new job as Assistant Deputy Chief of Staff for Operations, to the Commander in Chief, Continental Air Defense Command in September 1964. He was able to move to head the Programs Division that acted as the "middleman between the Air Force and the Air Defense Command."[50] His group of sixteen officers from the Army, Navy and Air Force were part of a totally staff-oriented function that kept up on new equipment that was coming in to the Air Force associated with air defense squadrons in the U.S. and Canada.

Though he was in programs, the actual direct operational command had a well-equipped "auditorium-like setup for large visual displays."[51] They maintained a round-the-clock surveillance of all air (aircraft and missiles), submarine and ground invasion activities from off the coast of Alaska to the coast of Newfoundland and all the way south to the coast of Florida and to Texas. The DEW line (Distant Early Warning Line) was part of the operational organization, which maintained a chain of 1,200 radar sites managed by the Army. The Cheyenne Mountain headquarters was under construction during McCampbell's tour, so he operated from a facility in Colorado Springs.

His programs group maintained a strong liaison function with the Air Defence Command, the Strategic Air Command (SAC), which had responsibility for maintenance and operations of the offensive bombers and missiles. McCampbell visited their headquarters and five of the missile silo sites.

Aside from his tour in Argentina, he enjoyed this tour the best. He said it was the easiest job he ever had. He held regular hours and no work on weekends. He was able to get out in the Colorado outdoors and hunt elk or do some fly-fishing. His favorite locations were places like Silver City, Colorado. He enjoyed the high altitudes of the mountains, having learned to breathe up there. He recalled that in his aircraft, the usual altitude to put on his oxygen mask was 6,000 feet, but to engage in his mountain sports he was at latitudes of 8,000 and 9,000 feet.

McCampbell left his final tour with the North American Air Defense Command and retired from active duty in the Navy after 31 years of service on July 1, 1964. Though McCampbell had a most remarkable career with extensive and varied command experience, he was passed over for promotion to admiral two times, which forced his departure from the service.

He later recalled that he had not been helped by his tours with the JCS or as the commanding officer of the fleet oiler tanker *Severn*. These two assignments had taken him away from Naval Aviation command. McCampbell later discussed his career: "But it has been a very unusual career, I think. It hasn't been all bad at all. There's been some very good aspects of it, particularly when I was younger. But then as I grew in age and rank, I began to get more privileges and I enjoyed those as much as I could."[52]

McCampbell retired and moved to Palm Beach, Florida. He married Jean Harriet Eckler on July 10, 1965, but the marriage lasted less than a year. McCampbell tried out some other occupations including selling real estate in the Bahamas, and taking on a few consulting engagements. He enjoyed trading in the stock market too.

Because McCampbell was such a celebrated and heroic figure, his primary activity over the years after leaving the Navy was attending events including inaugurations, reunions, and organization engagements. He was a member of twenty-two organizations including the Medal of Honor Society, the American Legion, the Legion of Merit, the Naval Academy and more. He found that he had to limit the number of events it attended. He was an avid reader of books and periodicals on current events and history.[53]

Barrett Tillman, a prolific writer of aviation history books, knew McCampbell after his retirement and spoke of the Ace's celebrated style: "He was a chain smoker who frequently stopped to light one cigarette off another between signing lithographs. He liked to scrawl 'Dashing Dave' for autograph collectors, so he required watching." He also wrote, "Dave enjoyed a joke, including one at his own expense. His demeanor could be disarming, concealing the steel beneath the velvet…. Unlike some warriors, he would tell you that he did not enjoy his war. I remember him commenting about the heat aboard ship, the mediocre food, and general living conditions."[54]

McCampbell had three children. His oldest was Francis McCampbell who was born in 1941 when he was married to Susan Rankin. His oldest son is David Perry McCampbell who was born in February 1945, and graduated from the Naval Academy and served as a commander in the Navy. McCampbell's youngest son is John Calhoun McCampbell who was born in June 1948. Both his sons, David and John, were born when he was married to Sara Jane Heliker.[55]

Though McCampbell felt that the two post-war assignments at the JCS and aboard the fleet oiler command *Severn* had a negative effect on his promotion potential to admiral, he was also aware of the impact of having multiple wives. In 1987 he stated, "I'm not ashamed at all of not being selected for admiral, because along the way I've had considerable marital problems."[56]

McCampbell broke his hip in August 1995 and was moved to the Veterans Affairs Nursing Home Care Unit in Riviera Beach. Captain David McCampbell died on June 30, 1996, at the nursing home at age 86. A few days later an honor guard stood at Palm Beach International Airport's David McCampbell terminal as his body was flown to Washington, D.C. He was buried at Arlington National Cemetery on July 16, 1996 (Plot: Section 60, Lot 3150).[57]

In honor of Captain David McCampbell, on Sunday, July 2, 2000, at the Bath Iron Works at Bath, Maine, the Secretary of State, Madeleine Albright, smashed a bottle of champagne across the bow of the new AEGIS guided-missile destroyer, the USS *McCampbell* (DDG-85), christening it before it slid down the greased ramp into the Kennebec River.[58]

Former Lieutenant Jack Taylor flew in David McCampbell's Carrier Air Group 15 in 1944 as a Hellcat pilot in Fighting Squadron 15. He recalled that the "veteran pilots spoke with sincere admiration" when they openly chatted about him in the squadron ready room aboard the *Essex*. "He was highly respected by those in the squadron and was regarded as a hell of a pilot–a particularly good gunner/marksman." For Taylor, McCampbell was "intense … very aggressive … a throttle-to-the-wall kind of fighter pilot … and one hell of a good air group commander." Taylor praises continues as he described him: "McCampbell impressed me with the businesslike way he ran our air group and his general demeanor and interactions with the pilots…. I'll always remember David McCampbell as a larger-than-life figure–the commander and supreme fighter pilot…. His personal story is unique in all the annals of naval aviation."[59]

Certainly, McCampbell's story was unique, in that he was the leader of the most successful naval air group in combat in World War II and shot down the most enemy aircraft in the Navy. Although he was criticized by his task group commander for aggressively participating in air-to-air combat while serving as Air Group 15 commander, it must be said

Pacific Ocean, July 26, 2005, the guided missile destroyer USS *McCampbell* (DDG 85) prepares to go alongside the Nimitz-class aircraft carrier USS *Ronald Reagan* (CVN 76) to conduct a fueling at sea (FAS) (Official U.S. Navy Photograph).

that he led by example as a truly heroic and unequaled fighter pilot. If he had not been the Air Group Commander, he might have shot down twice the number of Japanese aircraft he did. There has to be something said for a man who gave America both the best fighter pilot in the Navy, and the best carrier air group performance of World War II. That man was David McCampbell. And as a personality, he was just as his Annapolis yearbook described: "Mac will always find life enjoyable because he has an amiable disposition, because he is a gentleman, and because he is an optimist."[60]

Appendix A

Aerial Victories

Reference: Hoyt, Edwin P., *McCampbell's Heroes: The Story of the U.S. Navy's Most Celebrated Carrier Fighters of the Pacific War* (New York: Van Nostrand Reinhold Company, 1983)[1]

Count	Date	Japanese Aircraft Type Shot Down	Allied Code Name	Location
1	11 Jun 1944	Mitsubishi A6M Zero	Zeke	Saipan, Mariana Islands
1	13 Jun 1944	Nakajima Ki-49 Donryu Army Bomber	Helen	Saipan, Mariana Islands
7	19 Jun 1944	5-Yokosuka D4Y Suisei Navy Carrier Dive-bomber	Judy	1st Sortie, Marianas Turkey Shoot, Philippine Sea
		2-Mitsubishi A6M Zero fighter	Zeke	2nd Sortie, Guam, Marianas Islands
1.5	23 Jun 1944	Mitsubishi A6M Zero (Shared one with Ensign C. Plant)	Zeke	Orote Airfield, Guam, Mariana Islands
4	12 Sep 1944	Mitsubishi J2M Raiden Navy fighter	Jack	Ceba Airfield, Philippine Islands
3	13 Sep 1944	1-Yokosuka K5Y Type 93 Navy Bi-plane Trainer,	Willow	Negros Island, Philippine Islands
		1-Nakajima Ki-43 Hayabusa Navy fighter,	Oscar	
		1-Nakajima B5N Navy Torpedo Bomber	Kate	
1	22 Sep 1944	Yokosuka P1Y1 Ginga IJN Land-based Light Bomber	Frances	Manila Bay, Philippine Islands
.5	23 Sep 1944	Mitsubishi F1M2 IJN Reconnaissance Float Biplane (Shared with LTJG Roy Nall)	Pete	Cebu Island, Philippine Islands
2	21 Oct 1944	1-Yokosuka K5Y Type 93 IJN Bi-plane Trainer	Willow	Tablas Island, Philippines Islands
		1-Mitsubishi Ki-46 IJA Air Force Reconnaissance	Dinah	
9	24 Oct 1944	5-Mitsubishi A6M Zero fighter	Zeke	Philippine Sea off Luzon
		2-Nakajima Ki-43 Hayabusa Navy fighter	Oscar	
		2-Mitsubishi A6M3–32	Hamp	

Count	Date	Japanese Aircraft Type Shot Down	Allied Code Name	Location
2	5 Nov 1944	1-Aichi D3A IJN carrier-borne dive-bomber	Val	Subic Bay, Philippine Islands
		1-Mitsubishi A6M Zero	Zeke	Nichols Field, Philippine Islands
1	11 Nov 1944	Nakajima Ki-43 Hayabusa Navy fighter	Oscar	Ormoc Bay, Philippine Islands
1	14 Nov 1944	Nakajima Ki-43 Hayabusa Navy fighter	Oscar	Manila Bay, Philippine Islands
34	Total			

Appendix B

Aces of the Navy Fighting Squadron Fifteen (VF-15), December 1, 1944

This photo of the aces of the U.S. Navy Fighting Squadron Fifteen (VF-15) was taken on December 1, 1944, in the hangar bay of the USS *Essex* (CV-9) after their celebrated six-month combat tour of duty in the Pacific. The original caption states, in part: "Each pilot is credited with five or more enemy planes … their tally reads: 310 enemy planes shot down in combat, with half a million tons of Japanese shipping sunk or damaged…. The squadron's victorious score card is shown in the foreground."

Standing on the right of the scorecard is Commander David McCampbell, the former commanding officer of VF-15 and acting Commander of Carrier Air Group 15. In the background is McCampbell's Grumman F6F-5 Hellcat fighter nicknamed the Minsi III sporting the Japanese flags below the cockpit representing the thirty-four planes he shot down in air combat.

As follows are the names of the VF-15 ace pilots present in the photo:

Front row, left to right:
Lieutenant Junior Grade Roy L. Nall, USNR
Lieutenant John C.C. Symmes, USNR
Lieutenant Commander George C. Duncan, USN
Lieutenant Bert DeWayne Morris, USNR
Lieutenant Commander James F. Rigg, USN, VF-15 Commanding Officer
Lieutenant John R. Strane, USNR
Lieutenant Edward W. Overton, USNR
Lieutenant Junior Grade Richard E. Fowler, Jr., USNR
Lieutenant Junior Grade George R. Carr, USNR
Lieutenant Junior Grade Walter A. Lundin, USNR
Lieutenant Junior Grade Norman R. Berree, USNR
Commander David McCampbell, USN, Air Group 15 Commanding Officer
Lieutenant Junior Grade Roy W. Rushing, USNR
Lieutenant Junior Grade George W. Pigman, Jr., USNR
(One officer to the right of McCampbell is not identified in the original caption.)

Back row, left to right:
Lieutenant Junior Grade Robert P. Pash, USNR
Lieutenant Junior Grade Arthur Singer, Jr., USNR
Lieutenant Junior Grade Wendell Van Twelves, USNR
Ensign Larry R. Self, USNR
Lieutenant Junior Grade Ralph E. Foltz, USNR
Lieutenant Junior Grade James E. Duffy, USNR
Lieutenant Junior Grade Wallace R. Johnson, USNR
Lieutenant Junior Grade Albert C. Slack, USNR
Lieutenant Junior Grade James Dare, USNR.[1]

Appendix C

Medal of Honor Citation of Commander David McCampbell

"For conspicuous gallantry and intrepidity at the risk of his life above and beyond the call of duty as Commander, Air Group Fifteen, during combat against enemy Japanese aerial forces in the First and Second Battles of the Philippine Sea. An inspiring leader, fighting boldly in the face of terrific odds, Commander McCampbell led his fighter planes against a force of 80 Japanese carrier-based aircraft bearing down on our fleet on 19 June 1944. Striking fiercely in valiant defense of our surface force, he personally destroyed seven hostile planes during this single engagement in which the outnumbering attack force was utterly routed and virtually annihilated. During a major fleet engagement with the enemy on 24 October, Commander McCampbell, assisted by but one plane, intercepted and daringly attacked a formation of 60 hostile land-based craft approaching our forces. Fighting desperately but with superb skill against such overwhelming air power, he shot down nine Japanese planes and, completely disorganizing the enemy group, forced the remainder to abandon the attack before a single aircraft could reach the fleet. His great personal valor and indomitable spirit of aggression under extremely perilous combat conditions reflect the highest credit upon Commander McCampbell and the United States Naval Service."[1]

Chapter Notes

Introduction

1. *Quotes from the Past:* http://8tfw.org/pages/quotes.htm.
2. Portz, Captain Matt, USNR (Ret.), *Naval Aviation in WWII, Aviation Training and Expansion, Part 1, Naval Aviation News, July–August 1990,* 2–3.

Chapter 1

1. Cutler, Thomas J., *The Battle of Leyte Gulf: 23 26 October 1944* (Annapolis: Naval Institute Press, 2001), 123.
2. Thomas, Evan, *Sea of Thunder: Four Commanders and the Last Great Naval Campaign 1941-1945* (New York: Simon & Schuster, 2006), 209.
3. Cutler, Thomas J., *The Battle of Leyte Gulf: 23–26 October 1944* (Annapolis: Naval Institute Press, 2001), 122, Thomas, Evan, *Sea of Thunder: Four Commanders and the Last Great Naval Campaign 1941-1945* (New York: Simon & Schuster Paperbacks, 2006), 209, Hoyt, Edwin P., *McCampbell's Heroes: The Story of the U.S. Navy's Most Celebrated Carrier Fighters of the Pacific War* (New York: Van Nostrand Reinhold Company, 1983), xi, Woodward, Comer Vann, *The Battle of Leyte Gulf: The Incredible Story of World War II'S Largest Naval Battle* (New York: Skyhorse Publishing, 2007), 50–51, *Action Report, the Battle of Philippines, October 24-25, 1944, Commanding Officer USS Essex, November 21, 1944,* WWII Archives Foundation, Incorporated, Sims, Edward H., *Greatest Fighter Missions of the Top Navy and Marine Aces of World War II* (New York: Ballantine Books, 1965), 160–161.
4. Cutler, Thomas J., *The Battle of Leyte Gulf: 23–26 October 1944* (Annapolis: Naval Institute Press, 2001), 122.
5. Cutler, Thomas J., *The Battle of Leyte Gulf: 23–26 October 1944* (Annapolis: Naval Institute Press, 2001), 122.
6. Cutler, Thomas J., *The Battle of Leyte Gulf: 23–26 October 1944* (Annapolis: Naval Institute Press, 2001), 122–123.
7. Cutler, Thomas J., *The Battle of Leyte Gulf: 23–26 October 1944* (Annapolis: Naval Institute Press, 2001), 122–123
8. Hoyt, Edwin P., *McCampbell's Heroes: The Story of the U.S. Navy's Most Celebrated Carrier Fighters of the Pacific War* (New York: Van Nostrand Reinhold Company, 1983), xii.
9. Hoyt, Edwin P., *McCampbell's Heroes: The Story of*

the U.S. Navy's Most Celebrated Carrier Fighters of the Pacific War* (New York: Van Nostrand Reinhold Company, 1983), xi–xii, Cutler, Thomas J., *The Battle of Leyte Gulf: 23-26 October 1944* (Annapolis: Naval Institute Press, 2001), 123.
10. Cutler, Thomas J., *The Battle of Leyte Gulf: 23–26 October 1944* (Annapolis: Naval Institute Press, 2001), 123.
11. Cutler, Thomas J., *The Battle of Leyte Gulf: 23–26 October 1944* (Annapolis: Naval Institute Press, 2001), 123.
12. Cutler, Thomas J., *The Battle of Leyte Gulf: 23–26 October 1944* (Annapolis: Naval Institute Press, 2001), 123.
13. Cutler, Thomas J., *The Battle of Leyte Gulf: 23–26 October 1944* (Annapolis: Naval Institute Press, 2001), 124.
14. Cutler, Thomas J., *The Battle of Leyte Gulf: 23–26 October 1944* (Annapolis: Naval Institute Press, 2001), 124.
15. Cutler, Thomas J., *The Battle of Leyte Gulf: 23–26 October 1944* (Annapolis: Naval Institute Press, 2001), 124.
16. Hoyt, Edwin P., *McCampbell's Heroes: The Story of the U.S. Navy's Most Celebrated Carrier Fighters of the Pacific War* (New York: Van Nostrand Reinhold Company, 1983), xi–xii, Cutler, Thomas J., *The Battle of Leyte Gulf: 23-26 October 1944* (Annapolis: Naval Institute Press, 2001), 123–125.
17. Hoyt, Edwin P., *McCampbell's Heroes: The Story of the U.S. Navy's Most Celebrated Carrier Fighters of the Pacific War* (New York: Van Nostrand Reinhold Company, 1983), xii–xiii.
18. Hoyt, Edwin P., *McCampbell's Heroes: The Story of the U.S. Navy's Most Celebrated Carrier Fighters of the Pacific War* (New York: Van Nostrand Reinhold Company, 1983), xiii.
19. Hoyt, Edwin P., *McCampbell's Heroes: The Story of the U.S. Navy's Most Celebrated Carrier Fighters of the Pacific War* (New York: Van Nostrand Reinhold Company, 1983), xiii.
20. Hoyt, Edwin P., *McCampbell's Heroes: The Story of the U.S. Navy's Most Celebrated Carrier Fighters of the Pacific War* (New York: Van Nostrand Reinhold Company, 1983), xiii.
21. *Splash Nine* by Jim "Twitch" Tittle, www.combatsim.com/archive/htm/htm_arc1/ace6.htm.
22. *The Reminiscences of Captain David McCampbell U.S. Navy (Retired)*, Interview by Paul Stillwell (Annapolis, MD.: U.S. Naval Institute, 2010), 203.
23. *The Reminiscences of Captain David McCampbell*

U.S. Navy (Retired), Interview by Paul Stillwell (Annapolis, MD.: U.S. Naval Institute, 2010), 203.

24. *The Reminiscences of Captain David McCampbell U.S. Navy (Retired)*, Interview by Paul Stillwell (Annapolis, MD.: U.S. Naval Institute, 2010), 203.

25. *Splash Nine* by Jim "Twitch" Tittle, www.combatsim.com/archive/htm/htm_arc1/ace6.htm.

26. Hoyt, Edwin P., *McCampbell's Heroes: The Story of the U.S. Navy's Most Celebrated Carrier Fighters of the Pacific War* (New York: Van Nostrand Reinhold Company, 1983), xiv.

27. Hoyt, Edwin P., *McCampbell's Heroes: The Story of the U.S. Navy's Most Celebrated Carrier Fighters of the Pacific War* (New York: Van Nostrand Reinhold Company, 1983), xiii.

28. Hoyt, Edwin P., *McCampbell's Heroes: The Story of the U.S. Navy's Most Celebrated Carrier Fighters of the Pacific War* (New York: Van Nostrand Reinhold Company, 1983), xiv.

29. Hoyt, Edwin P., *McCampbell's Heroes: The Story of the U.S. Navy's Most Celebrated Carrier Fighters of the Pacific War* (New York: Van Nostrand Reinhold Company, 1983), xiv.

30. Cutler, Thomas J., *The Battle of Leyte Gulf: 23–26 October 1944* (Annapolis: Naval Institute Press, 2001), 127.

31. Cutler, Thomas J., *The Battle of Leyte Gulf: 23–26 October 1944* (Annapolis: Naval Institute Press, 2001), 127.

32. *The Reminiscences of Captain David McCampbell U.S. Navy (Retired)*, Interview by Paul Stillwell (Annapolis, MD.: U.S. Naval Institute, 2010), 301.

33. Hoyt, Edwin P., *McCampbell's Heroes: The Story of the U.S. Navy's Most Celebrated Carrier Fighters of the Pacific War* (New York: Van Nostrand Reinhold Company, 1983), xiv–xv, Cutler, Thomas J., *The Battle of Leyte Gulf: 23–26 October 1944* (Annapolis: Naval Institute Press, 2001), 126–127, *The Reminiscences of Captain David McCampbell U.S. Navy (Retired)*, Interview by Paul Stillwell (Annapolis, MD.: U.S. Naval Institute, 2010), 300–301, *Commander David McCampbell—AG-15, Hellcat Ace*, www.ww2wings.com/wings/heroes/davidmccampbell/davidmccampbell.shtml.

Chapter 2

1. *1933 Lucky Bag, U.S. Naval Academy Class of 1933 Yearbook*, 204.

2. *Descendants of John Alexander Perry, Charts of Giles County*, gilestn.genealogyvillage.com/charts/perry.htm.

3. Andrew J McCampbell, *1900 United States Federal Census*, Ancestry.com, William Daniel McCampbell, *1900 United States Federal Census*, Ancestry.com.

4. *The Reminiscences of Captain David McCampbell U.S. Navy (Retired)*, Interview by Paul Stillwell (Annapolis, MD.: U.S. Naval Institute, 2010), 2–3.

5. *Business Bureau of the Beaches, Clewiston News*, Clewiston, Florida, Friday June 20, 1930, 3.

6. Staunton Military Academy Alumni Association, sma-alumni.org.

7. *The Reminiscences of Captain David McCampbell U.S. Navy (Retired)*, Interview by Paul Stillwell (Annapolis, MD.: U.S. Naval Institute, 2010), 4–7, 18.

8. *The Reminiscences of Captain David McCampbell U.S. Navy (Retired)*, Interview by Paul Stillwell (Annapolis, MD.: U.S. Naval Institute, 2010), 12.

9. *Ibid.*, 8–12.

10. *The Reminiscences of Captain David McCampbell U.S. Navy (Retired)*, Interview by Paul Stillwell (Annapolis, MD.: U.S. Naval Institute, 2010), 13.

11. *Ibid.*, 22.

12. *Ibid.*, 20–25.

13. *Ibid.*, 15–17.

14. *1933 Lucky Bag, U.S. Naval Academy Class of 1933 Yearbook*, 480.

15. *The Reminiscences of Captain David McCampbell U.S. Navy (Retired)*, Interview by Paul Stillwell (Annapolis, MD.: U.S. Naval Institute, 2010), 21.

16. *The Reminiscences of Captain David McCampbell U.S. Navy (Retired)*, Interview by Paul Stillwell (Annapolis, MD.: U.S. Naval Institute, 2010), 23, 25–26.

17. *1933 Lucky Bag, U.S. Naval Academy Class of 1933 Yearbook*, 204.

18. *David McCampbell, Military Combat, Enshrined 1996, 1910–1996, National Aviation Hall of Fame*, nationalaviation.org., *David McCampbell*, veterantributes.org, *The Reminiscences of Captain David McCampbell U.S. Navy (Retired)*, Interview by Paul Stillwell (Annapolis, MD.: U.S. Naval Institute, 2010), 26–29.

Chapter 3

1. *The Reminiscences of Captain David McCampbell U.S. Navy (Retired)*, Interview by Paul Stillwell (Annapolis, MD.: U.S. Naval Institute, 2010), 48.

2. *The Reminiscences of Captain David McCampbell U.S. Navy (Retired)*, Interview by Paul Stillwell (Annapolis, MD.: U.S. Naval Institute, 2010), 31.

3. *Ship Information*, Commander Naval Surface Group U.S. Pacific Fleet, public.navy.mil., *The Reminiscences of Captain David McCampbell U.S. Navy (Retired)*, Interview by Paul Stillwell (Annapolis, MD.: U.S. Naval Institute, 2010), 29–30.

4. Generous Jr., William T., *Sweet Pea at War: A History of USS Portland* (Lexington: University Press of Kentucky, 2003), 3–6.

5. Silverstone, Paul, *The Navy of World War II, 1922–1947* (New York City, New York: Routledge, 2007), 32.

6. *The Reminiscences of Captain David McCampbell U.S. Navy (Retired)*, Interview by Paul Stillwell (Annapolis, MD.: U.S. Naval Institute, 2010), 35, Silverstone, Paul, *The Navy of World War II, 1922–1947* (New York City, New York: Routledge, 2007), 32.

7. *Curtiss SOC "Seagull" Scout-Observation Planes*, Department of the Navy, Naval Historical Center, Washington Navy Yard, Washington DC 2037, www.history.navy.mil/photos/ac-usn22/s-types/soc.htm.

8. *Captain David S. McCampbell, U.S. Navy WW-II Top Fighter Ace*, Staunton Military Academy, www.sma-alumni.org/navyace.htm, *The Reminiscences of Captain David McCampbell U.S. Navy (Retired)*, Interview by Paul Stillwell (Annapolis, MD.: U.S. Naval Institute, 2010), 35, 41–42.

9. *The Reminiscences of Captain David McCampbell U.S. Navy (Retired)*, Interview by Paul Stillwell (Annapolis, MD.: U.S. Naval Institute, 2010), 35–37, *Honolulu, Hawaii, Passenger and Crew Lists, 1900–1959*, Susan McCampbell.

10. *The Reminiscences of Captain David McCampbell U.S. Navy (Retired)*, Interview by Paul Stillwell (Annapolis, MD.: U.S. Naval Institute, 2010), 34.

11. *The Reminiscences of Captain David McCampbell U.S. Navy (Retired)*, Interview by Paul Stillwell (Annapolis, MD.: U.S. Naval Institute, 2010), 34.

12. Generous Jr., William T., *Sweet Pea at War: A His-*

tory of USS Portland (Lexington: University Press of Kentucky, 2003), 13–14.

13. *Captain Willis W. Bradley, Jr., USN (Retired) (1884–1954)*, NHHC, www.history.navy.mil/photos/pers-us/uspers-b/w-brdly.htm.

14. *The Reminiscences of Captain David McCampbell U.S. Navy (Retired)*, Interview by Paul Stillwell (Annapolis, MD.: U.S. Naval Institute, 2010), 33–34.

15. Naval Historical Center, *Sicard, Dictionary of American Naval Fighting Ships*, Navy Department, Naval History & Heritage Command, Naval Historical Center, *Waters, Dictionary of American Naval Fighting Ships*, Navy Department, Naval History & Heritage Command.

16. Generous Jr., William T., *Sweet Pea at War: A History of USS Portland* (Lexington: University Press of Kentucky, 2003), 15.

17. Generous Jr., William T., *Sweet Pea at War: A History of USS Portland* (Lexington: University Press of Kentucky, 2003), 19.

18. Naval Historical Center, *Aylwin, Dictionary of American Naval Fighting Ships*, Navy Department, Naval History & Heritage Command, Naval Historical Center, *Tuscaloosa, Dictionary of American Naval Fighting Ships (DANFS)*, Navy Department, Naval History & Heritage Command.

19. *The Reminiscences of Captain David McCampbell U.S. Navy (Retired)*, Interview by Paul Stillwell (Annapolis, MD.: U.S. Naval Institute, 2010), 39–40, Generous Jr., William T., *Sweet Pea at War: A History of USS Portland* (Lexington: University Press of Kentucky, 2003), 13–19.

20. *The Reminiscences of Captain David McCampbell U.S. Navy (Retired)*, Interview by Paul Stillwell (Annapolis, MD.: U.S. Naval Institute, 2010), 43–44, Naval Historical Center, *Tuscaloosa, Dictionary of American Naval Fighting Ships (DANFS)*, Navy Department, Naval History & Heritage Command.

21. Lundstrom, John B., *The First Team: Pacific Naval Air Combat from Pearl Harbor to Midway* (Annapolis, Maryland: Naval Institute Press, 1984), 452–453, *The Reminiscences of Captain David McCampbell U.S. Navy (Retired)*, Interview by Paul Stillwell (Annapolis, MD.: U.S. Naval Institute, 2010), 51.

22. *The Reminiscences of Captain David McCampbell U.S. Navy (Retired)*, Interview by Paul Stillwell (Annapolis, MD.: U.S. Naval Institute, 2010), 47.

23. *The Reminiscences of Captain David McCampbell U.S. Navy (Retired)*, Interview by Paul Stillwell (Annapolis, MD.: U.S. Naval Institute, 2010), 48.

24. *The Reminiscences of Captain David McCampbell U.S. Navy (Retired)*, Interview by Paul Stillwell (Annapolis, MD.: U.S. Naval Institute, 2010), 53.

25. *Ibid.*, 48, 53.

26. *The Reminiscences of Captain David McCampbell U.S. Navy (Retired)*, Interview by Paul Stillwell (Annapolis, MD.: U.S. Naval Institute, 2010), 26.

27. *The Reminiscences of Captain David McCampbell U.S. Navy (Retired)*, Interview by Paul Stillwell (Annapolis, MD.: U.S. Naval Institute, 2010), 50, 52, 54.

Chapter 4

1. *The Reminiscences of Captain David McCampbell U.S. Navy (Retired)*, Interview by Paul Stillwell (Annapolis, MD.: U.S. Naval Institute, 2010), 61.

2. *The Reminiscences of Captain David McCampbell U.S. Navy (Retired)*, Interview by Paul Stillwell (Annapolis, MD.: U.S. Naval Institute, 2010), 54–55.

3. *The Reminiscences of Captain David McCampbell U.S. Navy (Retired)*, Interview by Paul Stillwell (Annapolis, MD.: U.S. Naval Institute, 2010), 55.

4. *Market House Museum: The Naval Career of "Jumpin" Joe Clifton*, markethousemuseum.com.

5. *The Reminiscences of Captain David McCampbell U.S. Navy (Retired)*, Interview by Paul Stillwell (Annapolis, MD.: U.S. Naval Institute, 2010), 55.

6. *The Reminiscences of Captain David McCampbell U.S. Navy (Retired)*, Interview by Paul Stillwell (Annapolis, MD.: U.S. Naval Institute, 2010), 67.

7. *The Reminiscences of Captain David McCampbell U.S. Navy (Retired)*, Interview by Paul Stillwell (Annapolis, MD: U.S. Naval Institute, 2010), 67–68.

8. *The Reminiscences of Captain David McCampbell U.S. Navy (Retired)*, Interview by Paul Stillwell (Annapolis, MD.: U.S. Naval Institute, 2010), 55.

9. *The Reminiscences of Captain David McCampbell U.S. Navy (Retired)*, Interview by Paul Stillwell (Annapolis, MD.: U.S. Naval Institute, 2010), 55.

10. *Ibid.*, 54–56, 58, 60–61.

11. *Ibid.*, 56.

12. *Ranger, Yorktown & Wasp Class Aircraft Carriers (CV 4–8) (Fiscal Years 1930, 1934, 1936 & 1939)*, Online Library of Selected Images, U.S. Navy Fleet Ship Types, Fleet Aircraft Carriers, Naval History and Heritage Command, *USS Ranger (CV-4)*, NavSource Online: Aircraft Carrier Photo Archive, *USS Ranger (CV-4) Aircraft Carrier (1934)*, www.militaryfactory.com/ships/detail.asp?ship_id=USS-Ranger-CV4.

13. Stubblebine, David, *John McCain*, World War II Database, ww2db.com/person_bio.php?person_id=511.

14. Stubblebine, David, *John McCain*, World War II Database, ww2db.com/person_bio.php?person_id=511.

15. Boatner, Mark M. *The Biographical Dictionary of World War II*, Novato, California: Presidio Press, 351, Reynolds, Clark G. *Famous American Admirals*, Naval Institute Press, 2002, 206, *The Great White Fleet*, Department of the Navy, Naval History and Heritage Command, McKinley, Mike, JO2 (Journalist Second Class), *The Cruise of the Great White Fleet*, Stubblebine, David, *John McCain*, World War II Database, ww2db.com/person_bio.php?person_id=511.

16. Scarborough, Capt. William E., USN(Ret.), *the Neutrality Patrol: To Keep Us Out of World War II*, Naval Historical Center, United States Navy.

17. *USS Ranger VI (CV-4)*, *Dictionary of American Naval Fighting Ships (DANFS)*, Navy Department, Naval Historical Center, Naval History & Heritage Command, Scarborough, Capt. William E., USN(Ret.), *the Neutrality Patrol: To Keep Us Out of World War II*, Naval Historical Center, United States Navy.

18. *The Reminiscences of Captain David McCampbell U.S. Navy (Retired)*, Interview by Paul Stillwell (Annapolis, MD.: U.S. Naval Institute, 2010), 61.

19. *The Reminiscences of Captain David McCampbell U.S. Navy (Retired)*, Interview by Paul Stillwell (Annapolis, MD.: U.S. Naval Institute, 2010), 59.

20. *The Reminiscences of Captain David McCampbell U.S. Navy (Retired)*, Interview by Paul Stillwell (Annapolis, MD.: U.S. Naval Institute, 2010), 60–61.

Chapter 5

1. *The Reminiscences of Captain David McCampbell U.S. Navy (Retired)*, Interview by Paul Stillwell (Annapolis, MD.: U.S. Naval Institute, 2010), 90.

2. *The Reminiscences of Captain David McCampbell*

U.S. Navy (Retired), Interview by Paul Stillwell (Annapolis, MD: U.S. Naval Institute, 2010), 69, 73–74.

3. Thomason, Tommy H., *U.S. Navy Aircraft History, Waving Them Aboard—The LSO What Is an LSO?* History, Carrier Landing Consultants, History, carrierlandingconsultants.com/lso.php

4. Thomason, Tommy H., *U.S. Navy Aircraft History, Waving Them Aboard—The LSO What Is an LSO?* History, Carrier Landing Consultants, History, carrierlandingconsultants.com/lso.php.

5. Thomason, Tommy H., *U.S. Navy Aircraft History, Waving Them Aboard—The LSO What Is an LSO?* History, Carrier Landing Consultants, History, carrierlandingconsultants.com/lso.php.

6. Thomason, Tommy H., *U.S. Navy Aircraft History, Waving Them Aboard—The LSO What Is an LSO?* History, Carrier Landing Consultants, History, carrierlandingconsultants.com/lso.php.

7. Morison, Samuel Eliot, *History of United States Naval Operations in World War II/Aleutians, Gilberts and Marshalls, June 1942–April 1944* (Champaign: University of Illinois Press, 1959), xxxvi, Thomason, Tommy H., *U.S. Navy Aircraft History, Waving Them Aboard—The LSO*, thanlont.blogspot.com/2012/11/waving-them-aboard-lso.html.

8. *The Reminiscences of Captain David McCampbell U.S. Navy (Retired)*, Interview by Paul Stillwell (Annapolis, MD.: U.S. Naval Institute, 2010), 70–71.

9. *History of the Silver Eagles*, Naval Aviation Museum Foundation, www.navalaviationmuseum.org/archive/sfl/sflshow.php?id=3, *The Reminiscences of Captain David McCampbell U.S. Navy (Retired)*, Interview by Paul Stillwell (Annapolis, MD.: U.S. Naval Institute, 2010), 73.

10. *The Reminiscences of Captain David McCampbell U.S. Navy (Retired)*, Interview by Paul Stillwell (Annapolis, MD.: U.S. Naval Institute, 2010), 74.

11. *The Reminiscences of Captain David McCampbell U.S. Navy (Retired)*, Interview by Paul Stillwell (Annapolis, MD.: U.S. Naval Institute, 2010), 74.

12. *Dictionary of American Naval Fighting Ships, Wasp*, Naval Historical Center, Department of the Navy, *The Reminiscences of Captain David McCampbell U.S. Navy (Retired)*, Interview by Paul Stillwell (Annapolis, MD.: U.S. Naval Institute, 2010), 94.

13. McKillop, Jack, *United States Navy Aircraft Carriers December 7, 1941*, Bluejacket.Com.

14. *Dictionary of American Naval Fighting Ships, Wasp*, Naval Historical Center, Department of the Navy.

15. Woodman, Richard, *Malta Convoys 1940–1943*, London: John Murray, 320.

16. *The Reminiscences of Captain David McCampbell U.S. Navy (Retired)*, Interview by Paul Stillwell (Annapolis, MD.: U.S. Naval Institute, 2010), 91.

17. *Dictionary of American Naval Fighting Ships, Wasp*, Naval Historical Center, Department of the Navy, Woodman, Richard, *Malta Convoys 1940–1943*, London: John Murray, 320.

18. *The Reminiscences of Captain David McCampbell U.S. Navy (Retired)*, Interview by Paul Stillwell (Annapolis, MD.: U.S. Naval Institute, 2010), 90.

19. *The Reminiscences of Captain David McCampbell U.S. Navy (Retired)*, Interview by Paul Stillwell (Annapolis, MD.: U.S. Naval Institute, 2010), 90.

20. *The Reminiscences of Captain David McCampbell U.S. Navy (Retired)*, Interview by Paul Stillwell (Annapolis, MD.: U.S. Naval Institute, 2010), 91.

21. *The Reminiscences of Captain David McCampbell U.S. Navy (Retired)*, Interview by Paul Stillwell (Annapolis, MD.: U.S. Naval Institute, 2010), 90.

22. *The Reminiscences of Captain David McCampbell U.S. Navy (Retired)*, Interview by Paul Stillwell (Annapolis, MD.: U.S. Naval Institute, 2010), 93.

23. *The Reminiscences of Captain David McCampbell U.S. Navy (Retired)*, Interview by Paul Stillwell (Annapolis, MD.: U.S. Naval Institute, 2010), 95.

24. *Dictionary of American Naval Fighting Ships, Wasp*, Naval Historical Center, Department of the Navy, *The Reminiscences of Captain David McCampbell U.S. Navy (Retired)*, Interview by Paul Stillwell (Annapolis, MD.: U.S. Naval Institute, 2010), 95–96.

25. Tillman, Barrett, and Lawson, Robert L., *U.S. Navy Dive and Torpedo Bombers of World War II* (St. Paul, MN: MBI Publishing Company, 2001), 18, *CV-7 Wasp, U.S. Navy Air Groups—June 1942*, ww2air.altervista.org/ww2/USNair4206.htm.

26. Lieutenant Colonel Frank O. Hough, USMC Major Verle E. Ludwig, USMC, Henry I. Shaw, Jr., *History of U.S. Marine Corps Operations in World War II, Volume I, Part VI, the Turning Point: Guadalcanal, Pearl Harbor to Guadalcanal*, Historical Branch, G-3 Division, Headquarters, U.S. Marine Corps, 242, *Dictionary of American Naval Fighting Ships, Wasp*, Naval Historical Center, Department of the Navy.

27. *The Pacific War Online Encyclopedia, Guadalcanal*, pwencycl.kgbudge.com/G/u/Guadalcanal.htm.

28. *The Reminiscences of Captain David McCampbell U.S. Navy (Retired)*, Interview by Paul Stillwell (Annapolis, MD.: U.S. Naval Institute, 2010), 96–97.

29. *Wasp VIII (CV-7) 1940–1942, Dictionary of American Naval Fighting Ships, Wasp*, Naval Historical Center, Department of the Navy, www.history.navy.mil/research/histories/ship-histories/danfs/w/wasp-viii.html.

30. *Wasp VIII (CV-7) 1940–1942, Dictionary of American Naval Fighting Ships, Wasp*, Naval Historical Center, Department of the Navy, www.history.navy.mil/research/histories/ship-histories/danfs/w/wasp-viii.html.

31. *Wasp VIII (CV-7) 1940–1942, Dictionary of American Naval Fighting Ships, Wasp*, Naval Historical Center, Department of the Navy, www.history.navy.mil/research/histories/ship-histories/danfs/w/wasp-viii.html.

32. *The Pacific War Online Encyclopedia, Vandegrift, Alexander Archer (1887–1973)*, pwencycl.kgbudge.com/V/a/Vandegrift_Alexander_A.htm.

33. *The Pacific War Online Encyclopedia, Guadalcanal, Tulagi*, pwencycl.kgbudge.com/T/u/Tulagi.htm.

34. *The Pacific War Online Encyclopedia, Guadalcanal, Tulagi*, pwencycl.kgbudge.com/T/u/Tulagi.htm

35. *Nakajima A6m2-N Type 2 Float Plane Fighter (Rufe)*, www.pacificwrecks.com/aircraft/a6m2-n/tech.html.

36. *Wasp VIII (CV-7) 1940–1942, Dictionary of American Naval Fighting Ships, Wasp*, Naval Historical Center, Department of the Navy, www.history.navy.mil/research/histories/ship-histories/danfs/w/wasp-viii.html.

37. *Wasp VIII (CV-7) 1940–1942, Dictionary of American Naval Fighting Ships, Wasp*, Naval Historical Center, Department of the Navy, www.history.navy.mil/research/histories/ship-histories/danfs/w/wasp-viii.html.

38. *Dictionary of American Naval Fighting Ships, Wasp*, Naval Historical Center, Department of the Navy, *Nakajima A6m2-N Type 2 Float Plane Fighter (Rufe)*, www.pacificwrecks.com/aircraft/a6m2-n/tech.html.

39. *The Pacific War Online Encyclopedia, Guadalcanal,* pwencycl.kgbudge.com/G/u/Guadalcanal.htm.

40. Coombe, Jack D., *Derailing the Tokyo Express,* Harrisburg, Pennsylvania: Stackpole, 33.

41. *Dictionary of American Naval Fighting Ships, Wasp,* Naval Historical Center, Department of the Navy, Sherman, Captain Forest, *After Action Report Part 1,* davidmclellan0.tripod.com/id20.htm.

42. Boyd, Carl, and Akihiko Yoshida, *The Japanese Submarine Force and World War II* (Annapolis: Naval Institute Press, 1995), 99, Hackett, Bob, & Kingsepp, Sander, *IJN Submarine I-19: Tabular Record of Movement,* www.combinedfleet.com/I-19.htm.

43. Sherman, Captain Forest, *After Action Report Part 1,* davidmclellan0.tripod.com/id20.htm.

44. Sherman, Captain Forest, *After Action Report Part 1,* davidmclellan0.tripod.com/id20.htm.

45. Sherman, Captain Forest, *After Action Report Part 1,* davidmclellan0.tripod.com/id20.htm.

46. Sherman, Captain Forest, *After Action Report Part 1,* davidmclellan0.tripod.com/id20.htm.

47. Sherman, Captain Forest, *After Action Report Part 1,* davidmclellan0.tripod.com/id20.htm.

48. Hackett, Bob, & Sander Kingsepp, *IJN Submarine I-19: Tabular Record of Movement,* www.combinedfleet.com/I-19.htm, Sherman, Captain Forest, *After Action Report Part 1,* davidmclellan0.tripod.com/id20.htm.

49. Bell, Daniel E., *Charlie Cooper Survived the Sinking of the USS Wasp by the Japanese on Sept 15, 1942,* www.pbase.com/image/129458587.

50. Sherman, Captain Forest, *After Action Report Part 1,* davidmclellan0.tripod.com/id20.htm.

51. Sherman, Captain Forest, *After Action Report Part 1,* davidmclellan0.tripod.com/id20.htm, *The Reminiscences of Captain David McCampbell U.S. Navy (Retired),* Interview by Paul Stillwell (Annapolis, MD.: U.S. Naval Institute, 2010), 100.

52. *The Reminiscences of Captain David McCampbell U.S. Navy (Retired),* Interview by Paul Stillwell (Annapolis, MD.: U.S. Naval Institute, 2010), 101.

53. *The Reminiscences of Captain David McCampbell U.S. Navy (Retired),* Interview by Paul Stillwell (Annapolis, MD.: U.S. Naval Institute, 2010), 102.

54. *The Reminiscences of Captain David McCampbell U.S. Navy (Retired),* Interview by Paul Stillwell (Annapolis, MD.: U.S. Naval Institute, 2010), 103.

55. *The Reminiscences of Captain David McCampbell U.S. Navy (Retired),* Interview by Paul Stillwell (Annapolis, MD.: U.S. Naval Institute, 2010), 104.

56. *Ibid.,* 102–104.

57. Sherman, Captain Forest, *After Action Report Part 1,* davidmclellan0.tripod.com/id20.htm, *Dictionary of American Naval Fighting Ships, Wasp,* Naval Historical Center, Department of the Navy.

58. *The Reminiscences of Captain David McCampbell U.S. Navy (Retired),* Interview by Paul Stillwell (Annapolis, MD.: U.S. Naval Institute, 2010), 106.

59. *The Reminiscences of Captain David McCampbell U.S. Navy (Retired),* Interview by Paul Stillwell (Annapolis, MD.: U.S. Naval Institute, 2010), 106.

60. *Ibid.,* 109.

61. *Ibid.,* 105–109.

Chapter 6

1. *The Reminiscences of Captain David McCampbell U.S. Navy (Retired),* Interview by Paul Stillwell (Annapolis, MD.: U.S. Naval Institute, 2010), 65.

2. *The Reminiscences of Captain David McCampbell U.S. Navy (Retired),* Interview by Paul Stillwell (Annapolis, MD.: U.S. Naval Institute, 2010), 109, *Commander, Navy Installations Command (CNIC), Commander, Navy Region Southeast, History,* www.cnic.navy.mil/regions/cnrse/about/history.html, Barnett, William R., *U.S. Naval Air Station, Melbourne Florida, World War II,* Xlibris Corp; 1 edition (February 28, 2001), *NAS Melbourne, Florida,* www.nasmelbourne.freeservers.com, *U.S. Army Corps of Engineers, Southeast and Pacific IMA Region, Site Inspection Report, Naval Air Station Melbourne, Brevard County, Florida,* FUDS Project No. I04FL038601, May 19, 2011, ES-1.

3. *The Reminiscences of Captain David McCampbell U.S. Navy (Retired),* Interview by Paul Stillwell (Annapolis, MD.: U.S. Naval Institute, 2010), 69.

4. *The Reminiscences of Captain David McCampbell U.S. Navy (Retired),* Interview by Paul Stillwell (Annapolis, MD.: U.S. Naval Institute, 2010), 65.

5. *The Reminiscences of Captain David McCampbell U.S. Navy (Retired),* Interview by Paul Stillwell (Annapolis, MD.: U.S. Naval Institute, 2010), 66.

6. *The Reminiscences of Captain David McCampbell U.S. Navy (Retired),* Interview by Paul Stillwell (Annapolis, MD.: U.S. Naval Institute, 2010), 66.

7. *The Reminiscences of Captain David McCampbell U.S. Navy (Retired),* Interview by Paul Stillwell (Annapolis, MD.: U.S. Naval Institute, 2010), 66.

8. *The Reminiscences of Captain David McCampbell U.S. Navy (Retired),* Interview by Paul Stillwell (Annapolis, MD.: U.S. Naval Institute, 2010), 65–66, 69–70, 113.

9. *USS Hornet, WWII Combat, Battle of Santa Cruz Islands (CV-8) & Ship's Log USS Hornet (CV-12),* USS Hornet Museum, The Aircraft Carrier Hornet Foundation, www.uss-hornet.org/history/wwii.

10. Hoyt, Edwin P., *McCampbell's Heroes: The Story of the U.S. Navy's Most Celebrated Carrier Fighters of the Pacific War* (New York: Van Nostrand Reinhold Company, 1983), 1–2.

11. *The Reminiscences of Captain David McCampbell U.S. Navy (Retired),* Interview by Paul Stillwell (Annapolis, MD.: U.S. Naval Institute, 2010), 111, Hoyt, Edwin P., *McCampbell's Heroes: The Story of the U.S. Navy's Most Celebrated Carrier Fighters of the Pacific War* (New York: Van Nostrand Reinhold Company, 1983), 3.

12. *Chapter 7: Naval Air Station Atlantic City, Atlantic City Answers the Call to World War II: How It and the Surrounding Area Contributed to the War Effort,* A Thesis Presented to the Faculty of California State University Dominguez Hills in Partial Fulfillment of the Requirements for the Degree Master of Arts in Humanities: Option In History, by Marston A. Mischlich, Fall 1998.

13. *Atlantic City Naval Air Station, Egg Harbor Township, New Jersey Fact Sheet,* U.S. Army Corps of Engineers. December 2007, www.nan.usace.army.mil/Media/FactSheets/FactSheetArticleView/tabid/11241/Article/9602/fact-sheet-atlantic-city-naval-air-station-egg-harbor-township-nj.aspx.

14. *The Reminiscences of Captain David McCampbell U.S. Navy (Retired),* Interview by Paul Stillwell (Annapolis, MD.: U.S. Naval Institute, 2010), 111–112, Hoyt, Edwin P., *McCampbell's Heroes: The Story of the U.S. Navy's Most Celebrated Carrier Fighters of the Pacific War* (New York: Van Nostrand Reinhold Company, 1983), 2–3.

15. *Matinee Classics, Wayne Morris Biography & Filmography,* www.matineeclassics.com/celebrities/actors/wayne_morris/details, Hopewood, Jon C., *Wayne Mor-*

ris: *Movie Star, War Hero*, www.imdb.com/name/nm0606998/bio, *The Reminiscences of Captain David McCampbell U.S. Navy (Retired)*, Interview by Paul Stillwell (Annapolis, MD.: U.S. Naval Institute, 2010), 114–115.

16. Hoyt, Edwin P., *McCampbell's Heroes: The Story of the U.S. Navy's Most Celebrated Carrier Fighters of the Pacific War* (New York: Van Nostrand Reinhold Company, 1983), 2, 6–7.

17. *The Reminiscences of Captain David McCampbell U.S. Navy (Retired)*, Interview by Paul Stillwell (Annapolis, MD.: U.S. Naval Institute, 2010), 111–112.

18. Andrews, Hal, *F6f Hellcat, Naval Aviation News, September–October 1988*, 1–7, www.history.navy.mil/branches/hist-ac/f6f-5.pdf, Kinzey, Bert. *F6F Hellcat in Detail and Scale (D&S Vol.26)*, Shrewsbury, UK: AirLife Publishing Ltd., 1987, 6, Sullivan, Jim. *F6F Hellcat in Action*, Carrollton, Texas: Squadron/Signal Publications Inc., 1979, 24, 30, 33.

19. *The Reminiscences of Captain David McCampbell U.S. Navy (Retired)*, Interview by Paul Stillwell (Annapolis, MD.: U.S. Naval Institute, 2010), 113.

20. *The Reminiscences of Captain David McCampbell U.S. Navy (Retired)*, Interview by Paul Stillwell (Annapolis, MD.: U.S. Naval Institute, 2010), 117.

21. *The Reminiscences of Captain David McCampbell U.S. Navy (Retired)*, Interview by Paul Stillwell (Annapolis, MD.: U.S. Naval Institute, 2010), 117.

22. Hoyt, Edwin P., *McCampbell's Heroes: The Story of the U.S. Navy's Most Celebrated Carrier Fighters of the Pacific War* (New York: Van Nostrand Reinhold Company, 1983), 3.

23. Hoyt, Edwin P., *McCampbell's Heroes: The Story of the U.S. Navy's Most Celebrated Carrier Fighters of the Pacific War* (New York: Van Nostrand Reinhold Company, 1983), 4.

24. Hoyt, Edwin P., *McCampbell's Heroes: The Story of the U.S. Navy's Most Celebrated Carrier Fighters of the Pacific War* (New York: Van Nostrand Reinhold Company, 1983), 3, *USS Hornet, WWII Combat, Ship's Log USS Hornet (CV-12)*, USS Hornet Museum, The Aircraft Carrier Hornet Foundation, www.usshornet.org/history/wwii.

25. *Curtiss SB2c Helldiver: The Last Dive Bomber, Aviation History Magazine*, Published Online: June 12, 2006.

26. *The Douglas SBD Dauntless & Curtiss SB2c Helldiver*, by Greg Goebel, AirVectors, www.airvectors.net/avsbd.html.

27. Hoyt, Edwin P., *McCampbell's Heroes: The Story of the U.S. Navy's Most Celebrated Carrier Fighters of the Pacific War* (New York: Van Nostrand Reinhold Company, 1983), 3–4, *The Douglas SBD Dauntless & Curtiss SB2c Helldiver*, by Greg Goebel, AirVectors, www.airvectors.net/avsbd.html, *SB2c Helldiver, U.S. Carrier Dive Bomber*, by Kent G. Budge, The Pacific War Online Encyclopedia, pwencycl.kgbudge.com/S/b/SB2C Helldiver.htm, *Curtiss SB2c Helldiver: The Last Dive Bomber, Aviation History Magazine*, Published Online: June 12, 2006.

28. Hoyt, Edwin P., *McCampbell's Heroes: The Story of the U.S. Navy's Most Celebrated Carrier Fighters of the Pacific War* (New York: Van Nostrand Reinhold Company, 1983), 4–5.

29. *Grumman TBF Avenger Carrier-Borne Torpedo Bomber (1942)*, www.MilitaryFactory.com, www.militaryfactory.com/aircraft/detail-page-2.asp?aircraft_id=300.

30. *Grumman TBF Avenger Carrier-Borne Torpedo Bomber (1942)*, www.MilitaryFactory.com, www.militaryfactory.com/aircraft/detail-page-2.asp?aircraft_id=300.

31. *The Reminiscences of Captain David McCampbell U.S. Navy (Retired)*, Interview by Paul Stillwell (Annapolis, MD.: U.S. Naval Institute, 2010), 131–132, *WWII Forums, Theaters of the Second World War, War in the Pacific, Naval Warfare in the Pacific, Carrier Aircraft Navigation: How Did They Do It?*, www.ww2f.com/topic/21346-carrier-aircraft-navigation-how-did-they-do-it.

32. Hoyt, Edwin P., *McCampbell's Heroes: The Story of the U.S. Navy's Most Celebrated Carrier Fighters of the Pacific War* (New York: Van Nostrand Reinhold Company, 1983), 4–7, *The Reminiscences of Captain David McCampbell U.S. Navy (Retired)*, Interview by Paul Stillwell (Annapolis, MD.: U.S. Naval Institute, 2010), 117–119, *Bombing Squadron VB15, Chronology*, by Warren Parrish, Walter Fontaine, and Donna Burney, www.ussessexcv9.org/Bravepages/bombing15.html.

33. *The Reminiscences of Captain David McCampbell U.S. Navy (Retired)*, Interview by Paul Stillwell (Annapolis, MD.: U.S. Naval Institute, 2010), 130.

34. *The Reminiscences of Captain David McCampbell U.S. Navy (Retired)*, Interview by Paul Stillwell (Annapolis, MD.: U.S. Naval Institute, 2010), 131.

35. *The Reminiscences of Captain David McCampbell U.S. Navy (Retired)*, Interview by Paul Stillwell (Annapolis, MD.: U.S. Naval Institute, 2010), 130–131.

36. Hoyt, Edwin P., *McCampbell's Heroes: The Story of the U.S. Navy's Most Celebrated Carrier Fighters of the Pacific War* (New York: Van Nostrand Reinhold Company, 1983), 7–8, 10, 13–14, *The Reminiscences of Captain David McCampbell U.S. Navy (Retired)*, Interview by Paul Stillwell (Annapolis, MD.: U.S. Naval Institute, 2010), 119–122.

37. Cordray, Elmer, *My Diary, WWII Diary 1944 Aboard the USS Essex*, www.ussessexcv9.org/pdfs/Cordray%20Diary.pdf, 4.

38. Hoyt, Edwin P., *McCampbell's Heroes: The Story of the U.S. Navy's Most Celebrated Carrier Fighters of the Pacific War* (New York: Van Nostrand Reinhold Company, 1983), 10, NavSource Online: Aircraft Carrier Photo Archive, *USS HORNET (CV-12)*, contributed by Steve Whitby, Photo NS021236, www.navsource.org/archives/02/12.htm.

39. Graham, A.T., *Pacific War Diary of A.T. Graham, Jr.*, atgrahamjr.blogspot.com/2012_08_01_archive.html.

40. Cleaver, Thomas McKelvey, *Fabled Fifteen: The Pacific War Saga of Carrier Air Group 15*, Pacifica Military History, Kindle Edition, location 1388.

41. Hoyt, Edwin P., *McCampbell's Heroes: The Story of the U.S. Navy's Most Celebrated Carrier Fighters of the Pacific War* (New York: Van Nostrand Reinhold Company, 1983), 10–12.

42. Graham, A.T., *Pacific War Diary of A.T. Graham, Jr.*, atgrahamjr.blogspot.com/2012_08_01_archive.html.

43. *USS Hornet During World War II*, USS Hornet Museum—The Aircraft Carrier Hornet Foundation, www.uss hornet.org/history/wwii, *Abandoned & Little-Known Airfields: Hawaii, Maui Island*, By Paul Freeman, www.airfields-freeman.com/HI/Airfields_HI_Maui.htm, Hoyt, Edwin P., *McCampbell's Heroes: The Story of the U.S. Navy's Most Celebrated Carrier Fighters of the Pacific War* (New York: Van Nostrand Reinhold Company, 1983), 10–12.

44. *The Reminiscences of Captain David McCampbell U.S. Navy (Retired)*, Interview by Paul Stillwell (Annapolis, MD.: U.S. Naval Institute, 2010), 141.

45. *The Reminiscences of Captain David McCampbell*

U.S. Navy (Retired), Interview by Paul Stillwell (Annapolis, MD.: U.S. Naval Institute, 2010), 128.

46. Cordray, Elmer, *My Diary, WWII Diary 1944 Aboard the USS Essex*, www.ussessexcv9.org/pdfs/Cordray%20Diary.pdf, 2.

47. Hoyt, Edwin P., *McCampbell's Heroes: The Story of the U.S. Navy's Most Celebrated Carrier Fighters of the Pacific War* (New York: Van Nostrand Reinhold Company, 1983), 11–12, *Maui No Ka 'Oi Magazine*, Nov.–Dec. 2012, 65, *The Reminiscences of Captain David McCampbell U.S. Navy (Retired)*, Interview by Paul Stillwell (Annapolis, MD.: U.S. Naval Institute, 2010), 126, 128, 140–142, Cordray, Elmer, *My Diary, WWII Diary 1944 Aboard the USS Essex*, www.ussessexcv9.org/pdfs/Cordray%20Diary.pdf, 5, *Revell 1/48 SB2c-3 Helldiver, History*, modelingmadness.com/review/allies/cleaver/us/tmcsb2c3.htm.

Chapter 7

1. *The Reminiscences of Captain David McCampbell U.S. Navy (Retired)*, Interview by Paul Stillwell (Annapolis, MD.: U.S. Naval Institute, 2010), 149.

2. *CV9-USS Essex*, Navy History, historycentral.com/navy/Essex.html, *World War II Service and Diary of John R. McKnight—Ex Rd M 3c USN*, www.wright.edu/~jack.mcknight/diary/diary/44-04.htm, *World War II: USS Essex (CV-9)*, Kennedy Hickman, Military History, militaryhistory.about.com/od/worldwariiwarships/p/World-War-Ii-Uss-Essex-Cv-9.htm.

3. St. John, Philip A., *USS Essex CV/CVA/CVS-9* (Paducah, KY: Turner Publishing Company, 1999), 6.

4. St. John, Philip A., *USS Essex CV/CVA/CVS-9* (Paducah, KY: Turner Publishing Company, 1999), 6–21.

5. St. John, Philip A., *USS Essex CV/CVA/CVS-9* (Paducah, KY: Turner Publishing Company, 1999), 21, Potter, E.B., *Nimitz* (Annapolis: Naval Institute Press, 1979), 278.

6. *Airgroups*, Researcher@Large, www.researcher-atlarge.com, Hoyt, Edwin P., *McCampbell's Heroes: The Story of the U.S. Navy's Most Celebrated Carrier Fighters of the Pacific War* (New York: Van Nostrand Reinhold Company, 1983), 13–14, *World War II Service and Diary of John R. McKnight—Ex Rd M 3c USN*, www.wright.edu/~jack.mcknight/diary/diary/44-04.htm.

7. *Vice Admiral Ralph Andrew Ofstie, U.S. Navy*, Robert Jon Cox, www.bosamar.com/pages/ofstie_bio, *United States Naval Aviation 1910–1995*, by Roy A. Grossnick, Naval Historical Center, Department of the Navy, Washington, D.C., 60, www.history.navy.mil/avh-1910/part03.pdf, Cleaver, Thomas McKelvey, *Fabled Fifteen: The Pacific War Saga of Carrier Air Group 15*, Pacifica Military History, Kindle Edition, location 1449.

8. *The Reminiscences of Captain David McCampbell U.S. Navy (Retired)*, Interview by Paul Stillwell (Annapolis, MD.: U.S. Naval Institute, 2010), 139.

9. *The Reminiscences of Captain David McCampbell U.S. Navy (Retired)*, Interview by Paul Stillwell (Annapolis, MD.: U.S. Naval Institute, 2010), 139, 151.

10. *Ibid.*, 316.

11. Cleaver, Thomas McKelvey, *Fabled Fifteen: The Pacific War Saga of Carrier Air Group 15*, Pacifica Military History, Kindle Edition, location 1449.

12. Cleaver, Thomas McKelvey, *Fabled Fifteen: The Pacific War Saga of Carrier Air Group 15*, Pacifica Military History, Kindle Edition, location 1449.

13. St. John, Philip A., *USS Essex CV/CVA/CVS-9* (Paducah, KY: Turner Publishing Company, 1999), 22.

14. Hoyt, Edwin P., *McCampbell's Heroes: The Story of the U.S. Navy's Most Celebrated Carrier Fighters of the Pacific War* (New York: Van Nostrand Reinhold Company, 1983), 14–17, St. John, Philip A., *USS Essex CV/CVA/CVS-9* (Paducah, KY: Turner Publishing Company, 1999), 22–23, *World War II Service and Diary of John R. McKnight—Ex Rd M 3c USN*, www.wright.edu/~jack.mcknight/diary/diary/44-04.htm, Cleaver, Thomas McKelvey, *Fabled Fifteen: The Pacific War Saga of Carrier Air Group 15*, Pacifica Military History, Kindle Edition, location 1449.

15. Graham, A.T., *Pacific War Diary of A.T. Graham, Jr.*, atgrahamjr.blogspot.com/2012_08_01_archive.html.

16. Graham, A.T., *Pacific War Diary of A.T. Graham, Jr.*, atgrahamjr.blogspot.com/2012_08_01_archive.html.

17. *The Reminiscences of Captain David McCampbell U.S. Navy (Retired)*, Interview by Paul Stillwell (Annapolis, MD.: U.S. Naval Institute, 2010), 162.

18. *The Reminiscences of Captain David McCampbell U.S. Navy (Retired)*, Interview by Paul Stillwell (Annapolis, MD.: U.S. Naval Institute, 2010), 158–160, 161.

19. Hoyt, Edwin P., *McCampbell's Heroes: The Story of the U.S. Navy's Most Celebrated Carrier Fighters of the Pacific War* (New York: Van Nostrand Reinhold Company, 1983), 17–20, *Action Report: Operations Against Marcus and Wake Islands, 15–25 May 1944*, Commanding Officer USS Essex, March 30, 1944, WWII Archives Foundation, Incorporated.

20. *The Reminiscences of Captain David McCampbell U.S. Navy (Retired)*, Interview by Paul Stillwell (Annapolis, MD.: U.S. Naval Institute, 2010), 149.

21. Hoyt, Edwin P., *McCampbell's Heroes: The Story of the U.S. Navy's Most Celebrated Carrier Fighters of the Pacific War* (New York: Van Nostrand Reinhold Company, 1983), 17–20, *Action Report: Operations Against Marcus and Wake Islands, 15–25 May 1944*, Commanding Officer USS Essex, March 30, 1944, WWII Archives Foundation, Incorporated.

22. *Action Report: Operations Against Marcus and Wake Islands, 15–25 May 1944*, Commanding Officer USS Essex, March 30, 1944, WWII Archives Foundation, Incorporated.

23. Hoyt, Edwin P., *McCampbell's Heroes: The Story of the U.S. Navy's Most Celebrated Carrier Fighters of the Pacific War* (New York: Van Nostrand Reinhold Company, 1983), 20–21, *Action Report: Operations Against Marcus and Wake Islands, 15–25 May 1944*, Commanding Officer USS Essex, March 30, 1944, WWII Archives Foundation, Incorporated, St. John, Philip A., *USS Essex CV/CVA/CVS-9* (Paducah, KY: Turner Publishing Company, 1999), 22.

24. Cleaver, Thomas McKelvey, *Fabled Fifteen: The Pacific War Saga of Carrier Air Group 15*, Pacifica Military History, Kindle Edition, location 1614.

25. *Action Report: Operations Against Marcus and Wake Islands, 15–25 May 1944*, Commanding Officer USS Essex, March 30, 1944, WWII Archives Foundation, Incorporated.

26. *Action Report: Operations Against Marcus and Wake Islands, 15–25 May 1944*, Commanding Officer USS Essex, March 30, 1944, WWII Archives Foundation, Incorporated.

Chapter 8

1. Tillman, Barrett, *Clash of the Carriers: The True Story of the Marianas Turkey Shoot of World War II* (New York: NAL Caliber, 2006), 16.

2. Morison, Samuel Eliot, *History of United States Naval Operations in World War II: New Guinea and the Marianas, March 1944–August 1944* (Champaign, IL: University of Illinois Press, 1981), 5.

3. Morison, Samuel Eliot, *History of United States Naval Operations in World War II: New Guinea and the Marianas, March 1944–August 1944* (Champaign, IL: University of Illinois Press, 1981), 4.

4. Henry I. Shaw, Jr., Bernard C. Nalty, Edwin T. Turnbladh, *Part IV Saipan: The Decisive Battle, Chapter 1, Background to Forager, Central Pacific Drive, History of U.S, Marine Corps Operations in World War II*, Historical Branch, G-3 Headquarters, U.S. Marine Corps, 232, ibiblio.org/hyperwar/USMC/III/USMC-III-IV-1.html.

5. Morison, Samuel Eliot, *History of United States Naval Operations in World War II: New Guinea and the Marianas, March 1944–August 1944* (Champaign, IL: University of Illinois Press, 1981), 9.

6. Tillman, Barrett, *Clash of the Carriers: The True Story of the Marianas Turkey Shoot of World War II* (New York: NAL Caliber, 2006), 16.

7. Tillman, Barrett, *Clash of the Carriers: The True Story of the Marianas Turkey Shoot of World War II* (New York: NAL Caliber, 2006), 15.

8. Tillman, Barrett, *Clash of the Carriers: The True Story of the Marianas Turkey Shoot of World War II* (New York: NAL Caliber, 2006), 15–16.

9. *Operation Vengeance: The Mission to Kill Admiral Yamamoto*, by Dwight Jon Zimmerman, Defense Media Network, May 8, 2013, www.defensemedianetwork.com/stories/operation-vengeance-the-mission-to-kill-admiral-yamamoto.

10. *Operation Vengeance: The Mission to Kill Admiral Yamamoto*, by Dwight Jon Zimmerman, Defense Media Network, May 8, 2013, www.defensemedianetwork.com/stories/operation-vengeance-the-mission-to-kill-admiral-yamamoto.

11. Morison, Samuel Eliot, *History of United States Naval Operations in World War II: New Guinea and the Marianas, March 1944–August 1944* (Champaign, IL: University of Illinois Press, 1981), 12.

12. Morison, Samuel Eliot, *History of United States Naval Operations in World War II: New Guinea and the Marianas, March 1944–August 1944* (Champaign, IL: University of Illinois Press, 1981), 13.

13. Morison, Samuel Eliot, *New Guinea and the Marianas: March 1944–August 1944, Volume Eight* (Annapolis: U.S. Naval Institute Press, 1953), 216.

14. Prange, Gordon William, with Donald M. Goldstein, Katherine V. Dillon, *God's Samurai: Lead Pilot at Pearl Harbor* (Dulles, VA: Brassey's Inc., 2004), 122–124, *Interrogations of Japanese Officials, Vice Admiral OZAWA, Jisaburo, IJN, the Battle of the Philippine Sea, 19–20 June 1944*, Interrogation NAV No. 3 USSBS No. 32, October 16, 1945, 7–8, Henry I. Shaw, Jr., Bernard C. Nalty, Edwin T. Turnbladh, *Part IV Saipan: The Decisive Battle, Chapter 1, Background to Forager, Central Pacific Drive, History of U.S, Marine Corps Operations in World War II*, Historical Branch, G-3 Headquarters, U.S. Marine Corps, 256, Morison, Samuel Eliot, *New Guinea and the Marianas: March 1944–August 1944, Volume Eight* (Annapolis: U.S. Naval Institute Press, 1953), 216.

15. Henry I. Shaw, Jr., Bernard C. Nalty, Edwin T. Turnbladh, *Part IV Saipan: The Decisive Battle, Chapter 1, Background to Forager, Central Pacific Drive, History of U.S, Marine Corps Operations in World War II*, Historical Branch, G-3 Headquarters, U.S. Marine Corps, 256–257, ibiblio.org/hyperwar/USMC/III/USMC-III-IV-1.html.

16. Henry I. Shaw, Jr., Bernard C. Nalty, Edwin T. Turnbladh, *Part IV Saipan: The Decisive Battle, Chapter 1, Background to Forager, Central Pacific Drive, History of U.S, Marine Corps Operations in World War II*, Historical Branch, G-3 Headquarters, U.S. Marine Corps, 258, ibiblio.org/hyperwar/USMC/III/USMC-III-IV-1.html.

17. Morison, Samuel Eliot, *New Guinea and the Marianas: March 1944–August 1944, Volume Eight* (Annapolis: U.S. Naval Institute Press, 1953), 161.

18. Goldberg, Harold J., *D-Day in the Pacific: The Battle of Saipan* (Bloomington, IN: Indiana University Press, 2007), 51–53, Hoyt, Edwin P., *McCampbell's Heroes: The Story of the U.S. Navy's Most Celebrated Carrier Fighters of the Pacific War* (New York: Van Nostrand Reinhold Company, 1983), 21–22, *World War II Service and Diary of John R. McKnight—Ex Rd M 3c USN*, www.wright.edu/~jack.mcknight/diary/diary/44–04.htm, Potter, E.B., *Nimitz* (Annapolis: Naval Institute Press, 1979), 296, Tillman, Barrett, *Clash of the Carriers: The True Story of the Marianas Turkey Shoot of World War II* (New York: NAL Caliber, 2006), 50–51.

19. *Action Report: Forager, June 6–July 6, 1944, Commanding Officer USS Essex, July 6, 1944*, WWII Archives Foundation, Incorporated.

20. *Action Report: Forager, June 6–July 6, 1944, Commanding Officer USS Essex, July 6, 1944*, WWII Archives Foundation, Incorporated.

21. *The Reminiscences of Captain David McCampbell U.S. Navy (Retired)*, Interview by Paul Stillwell (Annapolis, MD.: U.S. Naval Institute, 2010), 164.

22. *The Reminiscences of Captain David McCampbell U.S. Navy (Retired)*, Interview by Paul Stillwell (Annapolis, MD.: U.S. Naval Institute, 2010), 138.

23. *The Reminiscences of Captain David McCampbell U.S. Navy (Retired)*, Interview by Paul Stillwell (Annapolis, MD.: U.S. Naval Institute, 2010), 164–165, 168–170.

24. *The Reminiscences of Captain David McCampbell U.S. Navy (Retired)*, Interview by Paul Stillwell (Annapolis, MD.: U.S. Naval Institute, 2010), 170.

25. Hoyt, Edwin P., *McCampbell's Heroes: The Story of the U.S. Navy's Most Celebrated Carrier Fighters of the Pacific War* (New York: Van Nostrand Reinhold Company, 1983), 27.

26. Hoyt, Edwin P., *McCampbell's Heroes: The Story of the U.S. Navy's Most Celebrated Carrier Fighters of the Pacific War* (New York: Van Nostrand Reinhold Company, 1983), 26–29, *Action Report: Forager, June 6–July 6, 1944, Commanding Officer USS Essex, July 6, 1944*, WWII Archives Foundation, Incorporated, Tillman, Barrett, *Clash of the Carriers: The True Story of the Marianas Turkey Shoot of World War II* (New York: NAL Caliber, 2006), 54.

27. Cleaver, Thomas McKelvey, *Fabled Fifteen: The Pacific War Saga of Carrier Air Group 15*, Pacifica Military History, Kindle Edition, locations 1785–1786.

28. Hoyt, Edwin P., *McCampbell's Heroes: The Story of the U.S. Navy's Most Celebrated Carrier Fighters of the Pacific War* (New York: Van Nostrand Reinhold Company, 1983), 26–29, *Action Report: Forager, June 6–July 6, 1944, Commanding Officer USS Essex, July 6, 1944*, WWII Archives Foundation, Incorporated, Tillman, Barrett, *Clash of the Carriers: The True Story of the Marianas Turkey Shoot of World War II* (New York: NAL Caliber, 2006), 54.

29. *Action Report: Forager, June 6–July 6, 1944, Commanding Officer USS Essex, July 6, 1944*, WWII Archives Foundation, Incorporated, Hoyt, Edwin P., *McCamp-*

bell's Heroes: The Story of the U.S. Navy's Most Celebrated Carrier Fighters of the Pacific War (New York: Van Nostrand Reinhold Company, 1983), 26–29, Rottman, Gordon L., *World War 2 Pacific Island Guide: A Geo-Military Study* (Westport, CT: Greenwood Press, 2002), 394.

30. Hoyt, Edwin P., *McCampbell's Heroes: The Story of the U.S. Navy's Most Celebrated Carrier Fighters of the Pacific War* (New York: Van Nostrand Reinhold Company, 1983), 33–35, *Action Report: Forager, June 6–July 6, 1944, Commanding Officer USS Essex, July 6, 1944*, WWII Archives Foundation, Incorporated.

31. Hoyt, Edwin P., *McCampbell's Heroes: The Story of the U.S. Navy's Most Celebrated Carrier Fighters of the Pacific War* (New York: Van Nostrand Reinhold Company, 1983), 34–36, *Action Report: Forager, June 6–July 6, 1944, Commanding Officer USS Essex, July 6, 1944*, WWII Archives Foundation, Incorporated.

32. Hoyt, Edwin P., *McCampbell's Heroes: The Story of the U.S. Navy's Most Celebrated Carrier Fighters of the Pacific War* (New York: Van Nostrand Reinhold Company, 1983), 37.

33. *Action Report: Forager, June 6–July 6, 1944, Commanding Officer USS Essex, July 6, 1944*, WWII Archives Foundation, Incorporated.

34. *Action Report: Forager, June 6–July 6, 1944, Commanding Officer USS Essex, July 6, 1944*, WWII Archives Foundation, Incorporated.

35. *Action Report: Forager, June 6–July 6, 1944, Commanding Officer USS Essex, July 6, 1944*, WWII Archives Foundation, Incorporated.

36. *Action Report: Forager, June 6–July 6, 1944, Commanding Officer USS Essex, July 6, 1944*, WWII Archives Foundation, Incorporated.

37. Hoyt, Edwin P., *McCampbell's Heroes: The Story of the U.S. Navy's Most Celebrated Carrier Fighters of the Pacific War* (New York: Van Nostrand Reinhold Company, 1983), 36–39, *Action Report: Forager, June 6–July 6, 1944, Commanding Officer USS Essex, July 6, 1944*, WWII Archives Foundation, Incorporated, Tillman, Barrett, *Clash of the Carriers: The True Story of the Marianas Turkey Shoot of World War II* (New York: NAL Caliber, 2006), 24.

38. Morison, Samuel Eliot, *New Guinea and the Marianas: March 1944–August 1944, Volume Eight* (Annapolis: U.S. Naval Institute Press, 1953), 221.

Chapter 9

1. Tillman, Barrett, *Clash of the Carriers: The True Story of the Marianas Turkey Shoot of World War II* (New York: NAL Caliber, 2006), 75.

2. Tillman, Barrett, *Clash of the Carriers: The True Story of the Marianas Turkey Shoot of World War II* (New York: NAL Caliber, 2006), 75.

3. Tillman, Barrett, *Clash of the Carriers: The True Story of the Marianas Turkey Shoot of World War II* (New York: NAL Caliber, 2006), 75.

4. Hoyt, Edwin P., *McCampbell's Heroes: The Story of the U.S. Navy's Most Celebrated Carrier Fighters of the Pacific War* (New York: Van Nostrand Reinhold Company, 1983), 41.

5. Hoyt, Edwin P., *McCampbell's Heroes: The Story of the U.S. Navy's Most Celebrated Carrier Fighters of the Pacific War* (New York: Van Nostrand Reinhold Company, 1983), 40, *Action Report: Forager, June 6–July 6, 1944, Commanding Officer USS Essex, July 6, 1944*, WWII Archives Foundation, Incorporated, Tillman, Barrett, *Clash of the Carriers: The True Story of the Mar-*

ianas Turkey Shoot of World War II (New York: NAL Caliber, 2006), 75.

6. *Action Report: Forager, June 6–July 6, 1944, Commanding Officer USS Essex, July 6, 1944*, WWII Archives Foundation, Incorporated.

7. Hoyt, Edwin P., *McCampbell's Heroes: The Story of the U.S. Navy's Most Celebrated Carrier Fighters of the Pacific War* (New York: Van Nostrand Reinhold Company, 1983), 40.

8. Hoyt, Edwin P., *McCampbell's Heroes: The Story of the U.S. Navy's Most Celebrated Carrier Fighters of the Pacific War* (New York: Van Nostrand Reinhold Company, 1983), 40–41.

9. Hoyt, Edwin P., *McCampbell's Heroes: The Story of the U.S. Navy's Most Celebrated Carrier Fighters of the Pacific War* (New York: Van Nostrand Reinhold Company, 1983), 41.

10. Tillman, Barrett, *Clash of the Carriers: The True Story of the Marianas Turkey Shoot of World War II* (New York: NAL Caliber, 2006), 80, *McCampbell's Heroes: The Story of the U.S. Navy's Most Celebrated Carrier Fighters of the Pacific War* (New York: Van Nostrand Reinhold Company, 1983), 41.

11. *Action Report: Forager, June 6–July 6, 1944, Commanding Officer USS Essex, July 6, 1944*, WWII Archives Foundation, Incorporated.

12. Hoyt, Edwin P., *McCampbell's Heroes: The Story of the U.S. Navy's Most Celebrated Carrier Fighters of the Pacific War* (New York: Van Nostrand Reinhold Company, 1983), 42.

13. Graham, A.T., *Pacific War Diary of A.T. Graham, Jr.*, atgrahamjr.blogspot.com/2012_08_01_archive.html.

14. Graham, A.T., *Pacific War Diary of A.T. Graham, Jr.*, atgrahamjr.blogspot.com/2012_08_01_archive.html.

15. Graham, A.T., *Pacific War Diary of A.T. Graham, Jr.*, atgrahamjr.blogspot.com/2012_08_01_archive.html.

16. Graham, A.T., *Pacific War Diary of A.T. Graham, Jr.*, atgrahamjr.blogspot.com/2012_08_01_archive.html.

17. *Action Report: Forager, June 6–July 6, 1944, Commanding Officer USS Essex, July 6, 1944*, WWII Archives Foundation, Incorporated.

18. Hoyt, Edwin P., *McCampbell's Heroes: The Story of the U.S. Navy's Most Celebrated Carrier Fighters of the Pacific War* (New York: Van Nostrand Reinhold Company, 1983), 41–43, Cleaver, Thomas McKelvey, *Fabled Fifteen: The Pacific War Saga of Carrier Air Group 15*, Pacifica Military History, Kindle Edition, locations 1890–1902, Graham, A.T., *Pacific War Diary of A.T. Graham, Jr.*, atgrahamjr.blogspot.com/2012_08_01_archive.html, *Action Report: Forager, June 6–July 6, 1944, Commanding Officer USS Essex, July 6, 1944*, WWII Archives Foundation, Incorporated.

19. Goldberg, Harold J., *D-Day in the Pacific: The Battle of Saipan* (Bloomington, IN: Indiana University Press, 2007), 59.

20. Goldberg, Harold J., *D-Day in the Pacific: The Battle of Saipan* (Bloomington, IN: Indiana University Press, 2007), 59.

21. Morison, Samuel Eliot, *New Guinea and the Marianas: March 1944–August 1944, Volume Eight*, (Annapolis: U.S. Naval Institute Press, 1953), 198.

22. Goldberg, Harold J., *D-Day in the Pacific: The Battle of Saipan* (Bloomington, IN: Indiana University Press, 2007), 54, Morison, Samuel Eliot, *New Guinea and the Marianas: March 1944–August 1944, Volume Eight* (Annapolis: U.S. Naval Institute Press, 1953), 198, Tillman, Barrett, *Clash of the Carriers: The True Story of the Marianas Turkey Shoot of World War II* (New York: NAL Caliber, 2006), 76–77.

23. Tillman, Barrett, *Clash of the Carriers: The True Story of the Marianas Turkey Shoot of World War II* (New York: NAL Caliber, 2006), 81–82.

24. Morison, Samuel Eliot, *New Guinea and the Marianas: March 1944–August 1944, Volume Eight* (Annapolis: U.S. Naval Institute Press, 1953), 221.

25. Tillman, Barrett, *Clash of the Carriers: The True Story of the Marianas Turkey Shoot of World War II* (New York: NAL Caliber, 2006), 84.

26. Tillman, Barrett, *Clash of the Carriers: The True Story of the Marianas Turkey Shoot of World War II* (New York: NAL Caliber, 2006), 83–84.

27. Morison, Samuel Eliot, *New Guinea and the Marianas: March 1944–August 1944, Volume Eight* (Annapolis: U.S. Naval Institute Press, 1953), 241.

28. *Action Report: Forager, June 6–July 6, 1944, Commanding Officer USS Essex, July 6, 1944*, WWII Archives Foundation, Incorporated.

29. Tillman, Barrett, *Clash of the Carriers: The True Story of the Marianas Turkey Shoot of World War II* (New York: NAL Caliber, 2006), 84–85.

30. Morison, Samuel Eliot, *New Guinea and the Marianas: March 1944–August 1944, Volume Eight* (Annapolis: U.S. Naval Institute Press, 1953), 243.

31. Morison, Samuel Eliot, *New Guinea and the Marianas: March 1944–August 1944, Volume Eight* (Annapolis: U.S. Naval Institute Press, 1953), 231–232, 242–243.

32. Morison, Samuel Eliot, *New Guinea and the Marianas: March 1944–August 1944, Volume Eight* (Annapolis: U.S. Naval Institute Press, 1953), 243.

33. Morison, Samuel Eliot, *New Guinea and the Marianas: March 1944–August 1944, Volume Eight* (Annapolis: U.S. Naval Institute Press, 1953), 243.

34. *Action Report: Forager, June 6–July 6, 1944, Commanding Officer USS Essex, July 6, 1944*, WWII Archives Foundation, Incorporated.

35. Correll, John T., *The Matterhorn Missions, Air Force Magazine* (March 2009), 63, *Action Report: Forager, June 6–July 6, 1944, Commanding Officer USS Essex, July 6, 1944*, WWII Archives Foundation, Incorporated, *McCampbell's Heroes: The Story of the U.S. Navy's Most Celebrated Carrier Fighters of the Pacific War* (New York: Van Nostrand Reinhold Company, 1983), 47–48, Cordray, Elmer, *My Diary, WWII Diary 1944 Aboard the USS Essex*, www.ussessexcv9.org/pdfs/Cordray%20Diary.pdf, 7, Graham, A.T., *Pacific War Diary of A.T. Graham, Jr.*, atgrahamjr.blogspot.com/2012_08_01_archive.html.

36. Morison, Samuel Eliot, *New Guinea and the Marianas: March 1944–August 1944, Volume Eight* (Annapolis: U.S. Naval Institute Press, 1953), 231–232, 243.

37. Tillman, Barrett, *Clash of the Carriers: The True Story of the Marianas Turkey Shoot of World War II* (New York: NAL Caliber, 2006), 93–94.

38. Tillman, Barrett, *Clash of the Carriers: The True Story of the Marianas Turkey Shoot of World War II* (New York: NAL Caliber, 2006), 95.

39. Tillman, Barrett, *Clash of the Carriers: The True Story of the Marianas Turkey Shoot of World War II* (New York: NAL Caliber, 2006), 95.

40. Tillman, Barrett, *Clash of the Carriers: The True Story of the Marianas Turkey Shoot of World War II* (New York: NAL Caliber, 2006), 95.

41. *Action Report: Forager, June 6–July 6, 1944, Commanding Officer USS Essex, July 6, 1944*, WWII Archives Foundation, Incorporated, Tillman, Barrett, *Clash of the Carriers: The True Story of the Marianas Turkey Shoot of World War II* (New York: NAL Caliber, 2006), 93–95.

Chapter 10

1. Cleaver, Thomas McKelvey, *Fabled Fifteen: The Pacific War Saga of Carrier Air Group 15*, Pacifica Military History, Kindle Edition, locations 2200.

2. Tillman, Barrett, *Clash of the Carriers: The True Story of the Marianas Turkey Shoot of World War II* (New York: NAL Caliber, 2006), 102, 106.

3. Morison, Samuel Eliot, *New Guinea and the Marianas: March 1944–August 1944, Volume Eight* (Annapolis: U.S. Naval Institute Press, 1953), 263–264, Reyonds, Clark G., *The Fast Carriers: The Forging of an Air Navy* (Annapolis: Naval Institute Press, 1968), 160, Muir, Dan, *Order of Battle: The Battle of the Philippine Sea, 19–20 June 1944*, http://www.navweaps.com/index_oob/OOB_WWII_Pacific/OOB_WWII_Phillipine_Sea.htm.

4. Morison, Samuel Eliot, *New Guinea and the Marianas: March 1944–August 1944, Volume Eight* (Annapolis: U.S. Naval Institute Press, 1953), 249.

5. Morison, Samuel Eliot, *New Guinea and the Marianas: March 1944–August 1944, Volume Eight* (Annapolis: U.S. Naval Institute Press, 1953), 249–250.

6. Tillman, Barrett, *Clash of the Carriers: The True Story of the Marianas Turkey Shoot of World War II* (New York: NAL Caliber, 2006), 127.

7. Tillman, Barrett, *Clash of the Carriers: The True Story of the Marianas Turkey Shoot of World War II* (New York: NAL Caliber, 2006), 124–127.

8. Backer, Steve, *Essex Class Aircraft Carriers of the Second World War* (Barnsley, South Yorkshire, UK: Seaforth Publishing, 2009), 55–56.

9. Simpson, Joanne Cavanaugh, *The Funny Little Fuze with Devastating Aim, John Hopkins Magazine*, April 2000.

10. Simpson, Joanne Cavanaugh, *The Funny Little Fuze with Devastating Aim, John Hopkins Magazine*, April 2000, Tillman, Barrett, *Clash of the Carriers: The True Story of the Marianas Turkey Shoot of World War II* (New York: NAL Caliber, 2006), 124.

11. Tillman, Barrett, *Clash of the Carriers: The True Story of the Marianas Turkey Shoot of World War II* (New York: NAL Caliber, 2006), 126.

12. Morison, Samuel Eliot, *New Guinea and the Marianas: March 1944–August 1944, Volume Eight* (Annapolis: U.S. Naval Institute Press, 1953), 261–262, Tillman, Barrett, *Clash of the Carriers: The True Story of the Marianas Turkey Shoot of World War II* (New York: NAL Caliber, 2006), 126.

13. Morison, Samuel Eliot, *New Guinea and the Marianas: March 1944–August 1944, Volume Eight* (Annapolis: U.S. Naval Institute Press, 1953), 250.

14. Morison, Samuel Eliot, *New Guinea and the Marianas: March 1944–August 1944, Volume Eight* (Annapolis: U.S. Naval Institute Press, 1953), 251.

15. Morison, Samuel Eliot, *New Guinea and the Marianas: March 1944–August 1944, Volume Eight* (Annapolis: U.S. Naval Institute Press, 1953), 250–252, Blair, Clay, *Silent Victory: The U.S. Submarine War Against Japan* (Annapolis: Naval Institute Press, 2001), 654.

16. Morison, Samuel Eliot, *New Guinea and the Marianas: March 1944–August 1944, Volume Eight* (Annapolis: U.S. Naval Institute Press, 1953), 252.

17. Tillman, Barrett, *Clash of the Carriers: The True Story of the Marianas Turkey Shoot of World War II* (New York: NAL Caliber, 2006), 107.

18. Hoyt, Edwin P., *McCampbell's Heroes: The Story of the U.S. Navy's Most Celebrated Carrier Fighters of the Pacific War* (New York: Van Nostrand Reinhold Company, 1983), 57.

19. Hoyt, Edwin P., *McCampbell's Heroes: The Story of the U.S. Navy's Most Celebrated Carrier Fighters of the Pacific War* (New York: Van Nostrand Reinhold Company, 1983), 57.

20. Hoyt, Edwin P., *McCampbell's Heroes: The Story of the U.S. Navy's Most Celebrated Carrier Fighters of the Pacific War* (New York: Van Nostrand Reinhold Company, 1983), 58.

21. Morison, Samuel Eliot, *New Guinea and the Marianas: March 1944–August 1944, Volume Eight*, (Annapolis: U.S. Naval Institute Press, 1953), 267.

22. Morison, Samuel Eliot, *New Guinea and the Marianas: March 1944–August 1944, Volume Eight* (Annapolis: U.S. Naval Institute Press, 1953), 267.

23. *Action Report: Forager, June 6–July 6, 1944, Commanding Officer USS Essex*, July 6, 1944, WWII Archives Foundation, Incorporated, Tillman, Barrett, *Clash of the Carriers: The True Story of the Marianas Turkey Shoot of World War II* (New York: NAL Caliber, 2006), 146–147, Morison, Samuel Eliot, *New Guinea and the Marianas: March 1944–August 1944, Volume Eight* (Annapolis: U.S. Naval Institute Press, 1953), 266–267, Hoyt, Edwin P., *McCampbell's Heroes: The Story of the U.S. Navy's Most Celebrated Carrier Fighters of the Pacific War* (New York: Van Nostrand Reinhold Company, 1983), 58–59.

24. Morison, Samuel Eliot, *New Guinea and the Marianas: March 1944–August 1944, Volume Eight*, (Annapolis: U.S. Naval Institute Press, 1953), 268–269.

25. Lippman, David H., *The Turkey Shoot*, Published November 3, 2013, by Peter Laurentis, Locations 372.

26. Lippman, David H., *The Turkey Shoot*, Published November 3, 2013, by Peter Laurentis, Locations 405.

27. Tillman, Barrett, *Clash of the Carriers: The True Story of the Marianas Turkey Shoot of World War II* (New York: NAL Caliber, 2006), 155.

28. Lippman, David H., *The Turkey Shoot*, Published November 3, 2013, by Peter Laurentis, Locations 423.

29. Morison, Samuel Eliot, *New Guinea and the Marianas: March 1944–August 1944, Volume Eight* (Annapolis: U.S. Naval Institute Press, 1953), 280.

30. Morison, Samuel Eliot, *New Guinea and the Marianas: March 1944–August 1944, Volume Eight* (Annapolis: U.S. Naval Institute Press, 1953), 280.

31. Lippman, David H., *The Turkey Shoot*, Published November 3, 2013, by Peter Laurentis, Locations 430.

32. Tillman, Barrett, *Clash of the Carriers: The True Story of the Marianas Turkey Shoot of World War II* (New York: NAL Caliber, 2006), 158.

33. Tillman, Barrett, *Clash of the Carriers: The True Story of the Marianas Turkey Shoot of World War II* (New York: NAL Caliber, 2006), 158.

34. Morison, Samuel Eliot, *New Guinea and the Marianas: March 1944–August 1944, Volume Eight* (Annapolis: U.S. Naval Institute Press, 1953), 281.

35. Tillman, Barrett, *Clash of the Carriers: The True Story of the Marianas Turkey Shoot of World War II* (New York: NAL Caliber, 2006), 160.

36. Tillman, Barrett, *Clash of the Carriers: The True Story of the Marianas Turkey Shoot of World War II* (New York: NAL Caliber, 2006), 155–160, Morison, Samuel Eliot, *New Guinea and the Marianas: March 1944–August 1944, Volume Eight* (Annapolis: U.S. Naval Institute Press, 1953), 278–281.

37. Tillman, Barrett, *Clash of the Carriers: The True Story of the Marianas Turkey Shoot of World War II* (New York: NAL Caliber, 2006),154.

38. Tillman, Barrett, *Clash of the Carriers: The True Story of the Marianas Turkey Shoot of World War II* (New York: NAL Caliber, 2006), 153–154.

39. *The Reminiscences of Captain David McCampbell U.S. Navy (Retired)*, Interview by Paul Stillwell (Annapolis, MD.: U.S. Naval Institute, 2010), 179–180.

40. Hoyt, Edwin P., *McCampbell's Heroes: The Story of the U.S. Navy's Most Celebrated Carrier Fighters of the Pacific War* (New York: Van Nostrand Reinhold Company, 1983), 66.

41. Hoyt, Edwin P., *McCampbell's Heroes: The Story of the U.S. Navy's Most Celebrated Carrier Fighters of the Pacific War* (New York: Van Nostrand Reinhold Company, 1983), 66.

42. Hoyt, Edwin P., *McCampbell's Heroes: The Story of the U.S. Navy's Most Celebrated Carrier Fighters of the Pacific War* (New York· Van Nostrand Reinhold Company, 1983), 66.

43. Hoyt, Edwin P., *McCampbell's Heroes: The Story of the U.S. Navy's Most Celebrated Carrier Fighters of the Pacific War* (New York: Van Nostrand Reinhold Company, 1983), 68.

44. Hoyt, Edwin P., *McCampbell's Heroes: The Story of the U.S. Navy's Most Celebrated Carrier Fighters of the Pacific War* (New York: Van Nostrand Reinhold Company, 1983), 67–68.

45. Hoyt, Edwin P., *McCampbell's Heroes: The Story of the U.S. Navy's Most Celebrated Carrier Fighters of the Pacific War* (New York: Van Nostrand Reinhold Company, 1983), 69.

46. Cleaver, Thomas McKelvey, *Fabled Fifteen: The Pacific War Saga of Carrier Air Group 15*, Pacifica Military History, Kindle Edition, locations 2163.

47. Cleaver, Thomas McKelvey, *Fabled Fifteen: The Pacific War Saga of Carrier Air Group 15*, Pacifica Military History, Kindle Edition, locations 2166.

48. Cleaver, Thomas McKelvey, *Fabled Fifteen: The Pacific War Saga of Carrier Air Group 15*, Pacifica Military History, Kindle Edition, locations 2172.

49. Cleaver, Thomas McKelvey, *Fabled Fifteen: The Pacific War Saga of Carrier Air Group 15*, Pacifica Military History, Kindle Edition, locations 2176.

50. Cleaver, Thomas McKelvey, *Fabled Fifteen: The Pacific War Saga of Carrier Air Group 15*, Pacifica Military History, Kindle Edition, locations 2178.

51. Cleaver, Thomas McKelvey, *Fabled Fifteen: The Pacific War Saga of Carrier Air Group 15*, Pacifica Military History, Kindle Edition, locations 2182.

52. Cleaver, Thomas McKelvey, *Fabled Fifteen: The Pacific War Saga of Carrier Air Group 15*, Pacifica Military History, Kindle Edition, locations 2188.

53. Cleaver, Thomas McKelvey, *Fabled Fifteen: The Pacific War Saga of Carrier Air Group 15*, Pacifica Military History, Kindle Edition, locations 2195.

54. Cleaver, Thomas McKelvey, *Fabled Fifteen: The Pacific War Saga of Carrier Air Group 15*, Pacifica Military History, Kindle Edition, locations 2200.

55. Hoyt, Edwin P., *McCampbell's Heroes: The Story of the U.S. Navy's Most Celebrated Carrier Fighters of the Pacific War* (New York: Van Nostrand Reinhold Company, 1983), 72.

56. Cleaver, Thomas McKelvey, *Fabled Fifteen: The Pacific War Saga of Carrier Air Group 15*, Pacifica Military History, Kindle Edition, locations 2205.

57. Hoyt, Edwin P., *McCampbell's Heroes: The Story of the U.S. Navy's Most Celebrated Carrier Fighters of the Pacific War* (New York: Van Nostrand Reinhold Company, 1983), 73.

58. Hoyt, Edwin P., *McCampbell's Heroes: The Story

of the U.S. Navy's Most Celebrated Carrier Fighters of the Pacific War (New York: Van Nostrand Reinhold Company, 1983), 72–74, *Action Report: Forager, June 6–July 6, 1944, Commanding Officer USS Essex, July 6, 1944,* WWII Archives Foundation, Incorporated.

59. Cleaver, Thomas McKelvey, *Fabled Fifteen: The Pacific War Saga of Carrier Air Group 15,* Pacifica Military History, Kindle Edition, locations 2260.

60. Tillman, Barrett, *Clash of the Carriers: The True Story of the Marianas Turkey Shoot of World War II* (New York: NAL Caliber, 2006), 196.

61. Tillman, Barrett, *Clash of the Carriers: The True Story of the Marianas Turkey Shoot of World War II* (New York: NAL Caliber, 2006), 196.

62. Hoyt, Edwin P., *McCampbell's Heroes: The Story of the U.S. Navy's Most Celebrated Carrier Fighters of the Pacific War* (New York: Van Nostrand Reinhold Company, 1983), 74.

Chapter 11

1. Morison, Samuel Eliot, *New Guinea and the Marianas: March 1944–August 1944, Volume Eight,* (Annapolis: U.S. Naval Institute Press, 1953), 291.

2. Morison, Samuel Eliot, *New Guinea and the Marianas: March 1944–August 1944, Volume Eight* (Annapolis: U.S. Naval Institute Press, 1953), 284.

3. Morison, Samuel Eliot, *New Guinea and the Marianas: March 1944–August 1944, Volume Eight* (Annapolis: U.S. Naval Institute Press, 1953), 282–286, Barrett, *Clash of the Carriers: The True Story of the Marianas Turkey Shoot of World War II* (New York: NAL Caliber, 2006), 201.

4. Hoyt, Edwin P., *McCampbell's Heroes: The Story of the U.S. Navy's Most Celebrated Carrier Fighters of the Pacific War* (New York: Van Nostrand Reinhold Company, 1983), 79.

5. Hoyt, Edwin P., *McCampbell's Heroes: The Story of the U.S. Navy's Most Celebrated Carrier Fighters of the Pacific War* (New York: Van Nostrand Reinhold Company, 1983), 80.

6. Hoyt, Edwin P., *McCampbell's Heroes: The Story of the U.S. Navy's Most Celebrated Carrier Fighters of the Pacific War* (New York: Van Nostrand Reinhold Company, 1983), 81.

7. Hoyt, Edwin P., *McCampbell's Heroes: The Story of the U.S. Navy's Most Celebrated Carrier Fighters of the Pacific War* (New York: Van Nostrand Reinhold Company, 1983), 82.

8. Hoyt, Edwin P., *McCampbell's Heroes: The Story of the U.S. Navy's Most Celebrated Carrier Fighters of the Pacific War* (New York: Van Nostrand Reinhold Company, 1983), 81–82, *Action Report: Forager, June 6–July 6, 1944, Commanding Officer USS Essex, July 6, 1944,* WWII Archives Foundation, Incorporated.

9. Morison, Samuel Eliot, *New Guinea and the Marianas: March 1944–August 1944, Volume Eight* (Annapolis: U.S. Naval Institute Press, 1953), 288–291, Tillman, Barrett, *Clash of the Carriers: The True Story of the Marianas Turkey Shoot of World War II* (New York: NAL Caliber, 2006), 203–209.

10. Tillman, Barrett, *Clash of the Carriers: The True Story of the Marianas Turkey Shoot of World War II* (New York: NAL Caliber, 2006), 206.

11. Tillman, Barrett, *Clash of the Carriers: The True Story of the Marianas Turkey Shoot of World War II* (New York: NAL Caliber, 2006), 207.

12. Tillman, Barrett, *Clash of the Carriers: The True Story of the Marianas Turkey Shoot of World War II* (New York: NAL Caliber, 2006), 207.

13. Tillman, Barrett, *Clash of the Carriers: The True Story of the Marianas Turkey Shoot of World War II* (New York: NAL Caliber, 2006), 208.

14. Morison, Samuel Eliot, *New Guinea and the Marianas: March 1944–August 1944, Volume Eight* (Annapolis: U.S. Naval Institute Press, 1953), 288–291, Tillman, Barrett, *Clash of the Carriers: The True Story of the Marianas Turkey Shoot of World War II* (New York: NAL Caliber, 2006), 203–209.

15. Tillman, Barrett, *Clash of the Carriers: The True Story of the Marianas Turkey Shoot of World War II* (New York: NAL Caliber, 2006), 209.

16. Tillman, Barrett, *Clash of the Carriers: The True Story of the Marianas Turkey Shoot of World War II* (New York: NAL Caliber, 2006), 209.

17. Morison, Samuel Eliot, *New Guinea and the Marianas: March 1944–August 1944, Volume Eight,* (Annapolis: U.S. Naval Institute Press, 1953), 291.

18. Morison, Samuel Eliot, *New Guinea and the Marianas: March 1944–August 1944, Volume Eight,* (Annapolis: U.S. Naval Institute Press, 1953), 300.

19. Tillman, Barrett, *Clash of the Carriers: The True Story of the Marianas Turkey Shoot of World War II* (New York: NAL Caliber, 2006), 233.

20. Tillman, Barrett, *Clash of the Carriers: The True Story of the Marianas Turkey Shoot of World War II* (New York: NAL Caliber, 2006), 234.

21. Tillman, Barrett, *Clash of the Carriers: The True Story of the Marianas Turkey Shoot of World War II* (New York: NAL Caliber, 2006), 234.

22. Morison, Samuel Eliot, *New Guinea and the Marianas: March 1944–August 1944, Volume Eight* (Annapolis: U.S. Naval Institute Press, 1953), 290–301, Tillman, Barrett, *Clash of the Carriers: The True Story of the Marianas Turkey Shoot of World War II* (New York: NAL Caliber, 2006), 208–240.

23. Morison, Samuel Eliot, *New Guinea and the Marianas: March 1944–August 1944, Volume Eight,* (Annapolis: U.S. Naval Institute Press, 1953), 301–302, Tillman, Barrett, *Clash of the Carriers: The True Story of the Marianas Turkey Shoot of World War II* (New York: NAL Caliber, 2006), 241–242.

24. Taylor, Theodore, *The Magnificent Mitscher* (Annapolis: U.S. Naval Institute Press, 1954), 234.

25. Taylor, Theodore, *The Magnificent Mitscher* (Annapolis: U.S. Naval Institute Press, 1954), 234.

26. Taylor, Theodore, *The Magnificent Mitscher* (Annapolis: U.S. Naval Institute Press, 1954), 234.

27. Taylor, Theodore, *The Magnificent Mitscher* (Annapolis: U.S. Naval Institute Press, 1954), 234.

28. Taylor, Theodore, *The Magnificent Mitscher* (Annapolis: U.S. Naval Institute Press, 1954), 234–235.

29. Morison, Samuel Eliot, *New Guinea and the Marianas: March 1944–August 1944, Volume Eight* (Annapolis: U.S. Naval Institute Press, 1953), 304–309.

30. Taylor, Theodore, *The Magnificent Mitscher* (Annapolis: U.S. Naval Institute Press, 1954), 237.

Chapter 12

1. Morison, Samuel Eliot, *New Guinea and the Marianas: March 1944–August 1944, Volume Eight* (Annapolis: U.S. Naval Institute Press, 1953), 340.

2. Hoyt, Edwin P., *McCampbell's Heroes: The Story of the U.S. Navy's Most Celebrated Carrier Fighters of the Pacific War* (New York: Van Nostrand Reinhold Com-

pany, 1983), 86–87, *Action Report: Forager, June 6–July 6, 1944, Commanding Officer USS Essex, July 6, 1944*, WWII Archives Foundation, Incorporated.

3. Cleaver, Thomas McKelvey, *Fabled Fifteen: The Pacific War Saga of Carrier Air Group 15*, Pacifica Military History, locations 2302.

4. Cleaver, Thomas McKelvey, *Fabled Fifteen: The Pacific War Saga of Carrier Air Group 15*, Pacifica Military History, locations 2303.

5. Cleaver, Thomas McKelvey, *Fabled Fifteen: The Pacific War Saga of Carrier Air Group 15*, Pacifica Military History, Kindle Edition, location 2349.

6. Cleaver, Thomas McKelvey, *Fabled Fifteen: The Pacific War Saga of Carrier Air Group 15*, Pacifica Military History, Kindle Edition, locations 2322.

7. Cleaver, Thomas McKelvey, *Fabled Fifteen: The Pacific War Saga of Carrier Air Group 15*, Pacifica Military History, locations 2356.

8. Cleaver, Thomas McKelvey, *Fabled Fifteen: The Pacific War Saga of Carrier Air Group 15*, Pacifica Military History, locations 2357.

9. Hoyt, Edwin P., *McCampbell's Heroes: The Story of the U.S. Navy's Most Celebrated Carrier Fighters of the Pacific War* (New York: Van Nostrand Reinhold Company, 1983), 89–90.

10. Hoyt, Edwin P., *McCampbell's Heroes: The Story of the U.S. Navy's Most Celebrated Carrier Fighters of the Pacific War* (New York: Van Nostrand Reinhold Company, 1983), 88–92.

11. Cleaver, Thomas McKelvey, *Fabled Fifteen: The Pacific War Saga of Carrier Air Group 15*, Pacifica Military History, Kindle Edition, locations 2376.

12. Cleaver, Thomas McKelvey, *Fabled Fifteen: The Pacific War Saga of Carrier Air Group 15*, Pacifica Military History, locations 2383.

13. *Action Report: Forager, June 6–July 6, 1944, Commanding Officer USS Essex, July 6, 1944*, WWII Archives Foundation, Incorporated, Hoyt, Edwin P., *McCampbell's Heroes: The Story of the U.S. Navy's Most Celebrated Carrier Fighters of the Pacific War* (New York: Van Nostrand Reinhold Company, 1983), 92–93, Cleaver, Thomas McKelvey, *Fabled Fifteen: The Pacific War Saga of Carrier Air Group 15*, Pacifica Military History, locations 2386–2394.

14. *Action Report: Forager, June 6–July 6, 1944, Commanding Officer USS Essex, July 6, 1944*, WWII Archives Foundation, Incorporated.

15. *Action Report: Forager, June 6–July 6, 1944, Commanding Officer USS Essex, July 6, 1944*, WWII Archives Foundation, Incorporated, Hoyt, Edwin P., *McCampbell's Heroes: The Story of the U.S. Navy's Most Celebrated Carrier Fighters of the Pacific War* (New York: Van Nostrand Reinhold Company, 1983), 93–95, Cleaver, Thomas McKelvey, *Fabled Fifteen: The Pacific War Saga of Carrier Air Group 15*, Pacifica Military History, locations 2402–2409.

16. Tillman, Barrett, *Clash of the Carriers: The True Story of the Marianas Turkey Shoot of World War II* (New York: NAL Caliber, 2006), 277.

17. *Action Report: Forager, June 6–July 6, 1944, Commanding Officer USS Essex, July 6, 1944*, WWII Archives Foundation, Incorporated, Hoyt, Edwin P., *McCampbell's Heroes: The Story of the U.S. Navy's Most Celebrated Carrier Fighters of the Pacific War* (New York: Van Nostrand Reinhold Company, 1983), 95.

18. *Action Report: Forager, June 6–July 6, 1944, Commanding Officer USS Essex, July 6, 1944*, WWII Archives Foundation, Incorporated, Hoyt, Edwin P., *McCampbell's Heroes: The Story of the U.S. Navy's Most Celebrated Carrier Fighters of the Pacific War* (New York: Van Nostrand Reinhold Company, 1983), 95.

19. Cleaver, Thomas McKelvey, *Fabled Fifteen: The Pacific War Saga of Carrier Air Group 15*, Pacifica Military History, location 2402.

20. *Action Report: Forager, June 6–July 6, 1944, Commanding Officer USS Essex, July 6, 1944*, WWII Archives Foundation, Incorporated.

21. *Action Report: Forager, June 6–July 6, 1944, Commanding Officer USS Essex, July 6, 1944*, WWII Archives Foundation, Incorporated, Tillman, Barrett, *Clash of the Carriers: The True Story of the Marianas Turkey Shoot of World War II* (New York: NAL Caliber, 2006), 283.

22. Cleaver, Thomas McKelvey, *Fabled Fifteen: The Pacific War Saga of Carrier Air Group 15*, Pacifica Military History, location 2451.

23. Cleaver, Thomas McKelvey, *Fabled Fifteen: The Pacific War Saga of Carrier Air Group 15*, Pacifica Military History, location 2451.

24. Cleaver, Thomas McKelvey, *Fabled Fifteen: The Pacific War Saga of Carrier Air Group 15*, Pacifica Military History, location 2460.

25. Cleaver, Thomas McKelvey, *Fabled Fifteen: The Pacific War Saga of Carrier Air Group 15*, Pacifica Military History, location 2472.

26. Cleaver, Thomas McKelvey, *Fabled Fifteen: The Pacific War Saga of Carrier Air Group 15*, Pacifica Military History, location 2472.

27. *Action Report: Forager, July 6–August 13, 1944, Commanding Officer USS Essex, August 14, 1944*, WWII Archives Foundation, Incorporated.

28. Cordray, Elmer, *My Diary, WWII Diary 1944 Aboard the USS Essex*, www.ussessexcv9.org/pdfs/Cordray%20Diary.pdf, 9.

29. Cordray, Elmer, *My Diary, WWII Diary 1944 Aboard the USS Essex*, www.ussessexcv9.org/pdfs/Cordray%20Diary.pdf, 9.

30. *The Reminiscences of Captain David McCampbell U.S. Navy (Retired)*, Interview by Paul Stillwell (Annapolis, MD.: U.S. Naval Institute, 2010), 191.

31. *Action Report: Forager, June 6–July 6, 1944, Commanding Officer USS Essex, July 6, 1944*, WWII Archives Foundation, Incorporated.

32. Morison, Samuel Eliot, *New Guinea and the Marianas: March 1944–August 1944, Volume Eight* (Annapolis: U.S. Naval Institute Press, 1953), 340.

33. Morison, Samuel Eliot, *New Guinea and the Marianas: March 1944–August 1944, Volume Eight* (Annapolis: U.S. Naval Institute Press, 1953), 340.

34. Morison, Samuel Eliot, *New Guinea and the Marianas: March 1944–August 1944, Volume Eight* (Annapolis: U.S. Naval Institute Press, 1953), 339.

35. Morison, Samuel Eliot, *New Guinea and the Marianas: March 1944–August 1944, Volume Eight* (Annapolis: U.S. Naval Institute Press, 1953), 339–340.

Chapter 13

1. Admiral Raymond A. Spruance letter to CMC, dated 27 Nov. 50.

2. *Action Report: Forager, July 6–August 13, 1944, Commanding Officer USS Essex, August 14, 1944*, WWII Archives Foundation, Incorporated.

3. *Action Report: Forager, July 6–August 13, 1944, Commanding Officer USS Essex, August 14, 1944*, WWII Archives Foundation, Incorporated.

4. *Action Report: Forager, July 6–August 13, 1944, Commanding Officer USS Essex, August 14, 1944*, WWII Archives Foundation, Incorporated.

5. Cleaver, Thomas McKelvey, *Fabled Fifteen: The

Pacific War Saga of Carrier Air Group 15, Pacifica Military History, location 2502.

6. Morison, Samuel Eliot, *New Guinea and the Marianas: March 1944–August 1944, Volume Eight* (Annapolis: U.S. Naval Institute Press, 1953), 382–386, 289–390, 401.

7. *Action Report: Forager, July 6–August 13, 1944, Commanding Officer USS Essex, August 14, 1944*, WWII Archives Foundation, Incorporated.

8. *Napalm*, www.globalsecurity.org/military/systems/munitions/napalm.htm.

9. *Napalm*, www.globalsecurity.org/military/systems/munitions/napalm.htm.

10. Hoyt, Edwin P., *McCampbell's Heroes: The Story of the U.S. Navy's Most Celebrated Carrier Fighters of the Pacific War* (New York: Van Nostrand Reinhold Company, 1983), 98–99, *Action Report: Forager, July 6–August 13, 1944, Commanding Officer USS Essex, August 14, 1944*, WWII Archives Foundation, Incorporated, Cleaver, Thomas McKelvey, *Fabled Fifteen: The Pacific War Saga of Carrier Air Group 15*, Pacifica Military History, locations 2509, 2527, Prefer, Nathan N., *Battle for Tinian, The: Vital Stepping Stone in America's War Against Japan* (Havertown, PA: Casemate Publishers, 2012), 59.

11. Morison, Samuel Eliot, *New Guinea and the Marianas: March 1944–August 1944, Volume Eight* (Annapolis: U.S. Naval Institute Press, 1953), 351–353.

12. Shaw, Henry I. Jr., Nalty, Bernard C., Turnbladh, Edwin T., *History of U.S. Marine Corps Operations in World War II, Volume III: Central Pacific Drive*, Historical Branch, G-3 Division, Headquarters, U.S. Marine Corps, 1966, 376–377, Hoyt, Edwin P., *McCampbell's Heroes: The Story of the U.S. Navy's Most Celebrated Carrier Fighters of the Pacific War* (New York: Van Nostrand Reinhold Company, 1983), 99, *Action Report: Forager, July 6–August 13, 1944, Commanding Officer USS Essex, August 14, 1944*, WWII Archives Foundation, Incorporated.

13. Hoyt, Edwin P., *McCampbell's Heroes: The Story of the U.S. Navy's Most Celebrated Carrier Fighters of the Pacific War* (New York: Van Nostrand Reinhold Company, 1983), 99, *Action Report: Forager, July 6–August 13, 1944, Commanding Officer USS Essex, August 14, 1944*, WWII Archives Foundation, Incorporated.

14. *Action Report: Forager, July 6–August 13, 1944, Commanding Officer USS Essex, August 14, 1944*, WWII Archives Foundation, Incorporated.

15. Hoyt, Edwin P., *McCampbell's Heroes: The Story of the U.S. Navy's Most Celebrated Carrier Fighters of the Pacific War* (New York: Van Nostrand Reinhold Company, 1983), 99–101, *Action Report: Forager, July 6–August 13, 1944, Commanding Officer USS Essex, August 14, 1944*, WWII Archives Foundation, Incorporated.

16. *Action Report: Forager, July 6–August 13, 1944, Commanding Officer USS Essex, August 14, 1944*, WWII Archives Foundation, Incorporated.

17. Hoyt, Edwin P., *McCampbell's Heroes: The Story of the U.S. Navy's Most Celebrated Carrier Fighters of the Pacific War* (New York: Van Nostrand Reinhold Company, 1983), 101–102, *Action Report: Forager, July 6–August 13, 1944, Commanding Officer USS Essex, August 14, 1944*, WWII Archives Foundation, Incorporated.

18. Morison, Samuel Eliot, *New Guinea and the Marianas: March 1944–August 1944, Volume Eight*, (Annapolis: U.S. Naval Institute Press, 1953), 370.

19. Admiral Raymond A. Spruance letter to CMC, dated 27 Nov. 50.

20. Morison, Samuel Eliot, *New Guinea and the Marianas: March 1944–August 1944, Volume Eight* (Annapolis: U.S. Naval Institute Press, 1953), 369, Rottman, Gordon, *Saipan & Tinian 1944: Piercing the Japanese Empire* (Botley, Oxford: Osprey Publishing, April 27, 2004), 34, 88–89, Willis, David, *Boeing B-29 and B-50 Superfortress, International Air Power Review, Volume 22, 2007*, 136–169, Westport, Connecticut: AIRtime Publishing, *Manhattan Project History: Putting the "Weapon" to Military Use, 509th Composite Group, the Hiroshima Mission—Timeline*, www.mphpa.org/classic/HISTORY/H-07L1.htm, Prefer, Nathan N., *Battle for Tinian, The: Vital Stepping Stone in America's War Against Japan* (Havertown, PA: Casemate Publishers, 2012), 11.

21. Morison, Samuel Eliot, *New Guinea and the Marianas: March 1944–August 1944, Volume Eight* (Annapolis: U.S. Naval Institute Press, 1953), 400–402.

Chapter 14

1. Hoyt, Edwin P., *McCampbell's Heroes: The Story of the U.S. Navy's Most Celebrated Carrier Fighters of the Pacific War* (New York: Van Nostrand Reinhold Company, 1983), 110.

2. Hearn, Chester G., *Carriers in Combat: The Air War at Sea* (Westport, CT.: Praeger Publishing, 2005), 183, St. John, Philip A., *USS Essex (CV/CVA/CVS-9)*, Paducah, KT.: Turner Publishing, 1999), 27.

3. *Admiral Frederick C. Sherman*, Navy Biographies Branch, OI-450, 6 August 1957, Modern Biographies files, Navy Department Library, Naval History & Heritage Command, *Sherman, Frederick Carl (1888–1957)*, The Pacific War Online Dictionary, pwencycl.kgbudge.com/S/h/Sherman_Frederick_C.htm.

4. Carter, Rear Admiral Worrall Reed, *Beans, Bullets and Black Oil, Chapter XVI, Stalemate II: The Western Carolines Operation*, 171–172, www.ibiblio.org/hyperwar/USN/BBBO/BBBO-16.html.

5. Carter, Rear Admiral Worrall Reed, *Beans, Bullets and Black Oil, Chapter XVI, Stalemate II: The Western Carolines Operation*, 171–172, www.ibiblio.org/hyperwar/USN/BBBO/BBBO-16.html.

6. Carter, Rear Admiral Worrall Reed, *Beans, Bullets and Black Oil, Chapter XVI, Stalemate II: The Western Carolines Operation*, 171–172, www.ibiblio.org/hyperwar/USN/BBBO/BBBO-16.html.

7. Cleaver, Thomas McKelvey, *Fabled Fifteen: The Pacific War Saga of Carrier Air Group 15*, Pacifica Military History, locations 2563.

8. Cleaver, Thomas McKelvey, *Fabled Fifteen: The Pacific War Saga of Carrier Air Group 15*, Pacifica Military History, locations 2568.

9. Cleaver, Thomas McKelvey, *Fabled Fifteen: The Pacific War Saga of Carrier Air Group 15*, Pacifica Military History, locations 2570.

10. *First Action Report: Stalemate II: Palau, August 29–September 8, 1944, Commanding Officer USS Essex, October 1, 1944*, WWII Archives Foundation, Incorporated, Hoyt, Edwin P., *McCampbell's Heroes: The Story of the U.S. Navy's Most Celebrated Carrier Fighters of the Pacific War* (New York: Van Nostrand Reinhold Company, 1983), 106.

11. Hoyt, Edwin P., *McCampbell's Heroes: The Story of the U.S. Navy's Most Celebrated Carrier Fighters of the Pacific War* (New York: Van Nostrand Reinhold Company, 1983), 108.

12. Hoyt, Edwin P., *McCampbell's Heroes: The Story of the U.S. Navy's Most Celebrated Carrier Fighters of the Pacific War* (New York: Van Nostrand Reinhold Company, 1983), 106–108, *First Action Report: Stalemate II:*

Palau, August 29–September 8, 1944, Commanding Officer USS Essex, October 1, 1944, WWII Archives Foundation, Incorporated.

13. *The Reminiscences of Captain David McCampbell U.S. Navy (Retired)*, Interview by Paul Stillwell (Annapolis, MD.: U.S. Naval Institute, 2010), 194.

14. Cleaver, Thomas McKelvey, *Fabled Fifteen: The Pacific War Saga of Carrier Air Group 15*, Pacifica Military History, locations 2677.

15. Cleaver, Thomas McKelvey, *Fabled Fifteen: The Pacific War Saga of Carrier Air Group 15*, Pacifica Military History, locations 2680.

16. Cleaver, Thomas McKelvey, *Fabled Fifteen: The Pacific War Saga of Carrier Air Group 15*, Pacifica Military History, locations 2705.

17. Cleaver, Thomas McKelvey, *Fabled Fifteen: The Pacific War Saga of Carrier Air Group 15*, Pacifica Military History, locations 2665, 2674, 2676–2684, 2713–2719, *Second Action Report: Stalemate II: Southern Philippines, September 9–10, 1944, Commanding Officer USS Essex, October 1, 1944*, WWII Archives Foundation, Incorporated.

18. Hoyt, Edwin P., *McCampbell's Heroes: The Story of the U.S. Navy's Most Celebrated Carrier Fighters of the Pacific War* (New York: Van Nostrand Reinhold Company, 1983), 110.

19. *Second Action Report: Stalemate II: Southern Philippines, September 9–10, 1944, Commanding Officer USS Essex, October 1, 1944*, WWII Archives Foundation, Incorporated.

20. *The Reminiscences of Captain David McCampbell U.S. Navy (Retired)*, Interview by Paul Stillwell (Annapolis, MD.: U.S. Naval Institute, 2010), 155–156.

21. Cleaver, Thomas McKelvey, *Fabled Fifteen: The Pacific War Saga of Carrier Air Group 15*, Pacifica Military History, Kindle Edition, locations 2710.

22. Hoyt, Edwin P., *McCampbell's Heroes: The Story of the U.S. Navy's Most Celebrated Carrier Fighters of the Pacific War* (New York: Van Nostrand Reinhold Company, 1983), 111–112, *Second Action Report: Stalemate II: Southern Philippines, September 9–10, 1944, Commanding Officer USS Essex, October 1, 1944*, WWII Archives Foundation, Incorporated.

23. *Second Action Report: Stalemate II: Southern Philippines, September 9–10, 1944, Commanding Officer USS Essex, October 1, 1944*, WWII Archives Foundation, Incorporated.

24. Hoyt, Edwin P., *McCampbell's Heroes: The Story of the U.S. Navy's Most Celebrated Carrier Fighters of the Pacific War* (New York: Van Nostrand Reinhold Company, 1983), 111–112, *Second Action Report: Stalemate II: Southern Philippines, September 9–10, 1944, Commanding Officer USS Essex, October 1, 1944*, WWII Archives Foundation, Incorporated.

Chapter 15

1. Hoyt, Edwin P., *McCampbell's Heroes: The Story of the U.S. Navy's Most Celebrated Carrier Fighters of the Pacific War* (New York: Van Nostrand Reinhold Company, 1983), 114.

2. *Third Action Report: Stalemate II: First Visayas, September 12–14, 1944, Commanding Officer USS Essex, October 1, 1944*, WWII Archives Foundation, Incorporated, Hoyt, Edwin P., *McCampbell's Heroes: The Story of the U.S. Navy's Most Celebrated Carrier Fighters of the Pacific War* (New York: Van Nostrand Reinhold Company, 1983), 113–114.

3. Hoyt, Edwin P., *McCampbell's Heroes: The Story of the U.S. Navy's Most Celebrated Carrier Fighters of the Pacific War* (New York: Van Nostrand Reinhold Company, 1983), 114.

4. Hoyt, Edwin P., *McCampbell's Heroes: The Story of the U.S. Navy's Most Celebrated Carrier Fighters of the Pacific War* (New York: Van Nostrand Reinhold Company, 1983), 114.

5. *Third Action Report: Stalemate II: First Visayas, September 12–14, 1944, Commanding Officer USS Essex, October 1, 1944*, WWII Archives Foundation, Incorporated, Hoyt, Edwin P., *McCampbell's Heroes: The Story of the U.S. Navy's Most Celebrated Carrier Fighters of the Pacific War* (New York: Van Nostrand Reinhold Company, 1983), 114–116.

6. Cleaver, Thomas McKelvey, *Fabled Fifteen: The Pacific War Saga of Carrier Air Group 15*, Pacifica Military History, locations 2748.

7. *Third Action Report: Stalemate II: First Visayas, September 12–14, 1944, Commanding Officer USS Essex, October 1, 1944*, WWII Archives Foundation, Incorporated, Hoyt, Edwin P., *McCampbell's Heroes: The Story of the U.S. Navy's Most Celebrated Carrier Fighters of the Pacific War* (New York: Van Nostrand Reinhold Company, 1983), 113–117.

8. *Third Action Report: Stalemate II: First Visayas, September 12–14, 1944, Commanding Officer USS Essex, October 1, 1944*, WWII Archives Foundation, Incorporated, Hoyt, Edwin P., *McCampbell's Heroes: The Story of the U.S. Navy's Most Celebrated Carrier Fighters of the Pacific War* (New York: Van Nostrand Reinhold Company, 1983), 118–120.

9. Hoyt, Edwin P., *McCampbell's Heroes: The Story of the U.S. Navy's Most Celebrated Carrier Fighters of the Pacific War* (New York: Van Nostrand Reinhold Company, 1983), 119–120.

10. Hoyt, Edwin P., *McCampbell's Heroes: The Story of the U.S. Navy's Most Celebrated Carrier Fighters of the Pacific War* (New York: Van Nostrand Reinhold Company, 1983), 120.

11. Hoyt, Edwin P., *McCampbell's Heroes: The Story of the U.S. Navy's Most Celebrated Carrier Fighters of the Pacific War* (New York: Van Nostrand Reinhold Company, 1983), 120–121.

12. Hoyt, Edwin P., *McCampbell's Heroes: The Story of the U.S. Navy's Most Celebrated Carrier Fighters of the Pacific War* (New York: Van Nostrand Reinhold Company, 1983), 122.

13. Hoyt, Edwin P., *McCampbell's Heroes: The Story of the U.S. Navy's Most Celebrated Carrier Fighters of the Pacific War* (New York: Van Nostrand Reinhold Company, 1983), 122–123.

14. Cleaver, Thomas McKelvey, *Fabled Fifteen: The Pacific War Saga of Carrier Air Group 15*, Pacifica Military History, locations 2805.

15. Cleaver, Thomas McKelvey, *Fabled Fifteen: The Pacific War Saga of Carrier Air Group 15*, Pacifica Military History, locations 2813.

16. Hoyt, Edwin P., *McCampbell's Heroes: The Story of the U.S. Navy's Most Celebrated Carrier Fighters of the Pacific War* (New York: Van Nostrand Reinhold Company, 1983), 123–124, *Third Action Report: Stalemate II: First Visayas, September 12–14, 1944, Commanding Officer USS Essex, October 1, 1944*, WWII Archives Foundation, Incorporated, Cleaver, Thomas McKelvey, *Fabled Fifteen: The Pacific War Saga of Carrier Air Group 15*, Pacifica Military History, locations 2748–2813.

17. Hoyt, Edwin P., *McCampbell's Heroes: The Story of the U.S. Navy's Most Celebrated Carrier Fighters of the*

Pacific War (New York: Van Nostrand Reinhold Company, 1983), 127–129, 131, *Third Action Report: Stalemate II: First Visayas, September 12–14, 1944, Commanding Officer USS Essex, October 1, 1944*, WWII Archives Foundation, Incorporated.

18. FAdm William F. Halsey and LCdr Julian Bryan, III, *Admiral Halsey's Story* (New York: McGraw-Hill Book Company, Inc., 1947), p. 199.

19. Antill, Peter, *Peleliu, Battle for (Operation Stalemate II), the Pacific War's Forgotten Battle, September–November 1944, The Decision, Chapter 2, Peleliu, September 1944: Amphibious Combat Against a Clever, Defensive-Minded Enemy*, erenow.com/ww/grunts-inside-american-infantry-combat-experience/3.php.

20. Antill, Peter, *Peleliu, Battle for (Operation Stalemate II), the Pacific War's Forgotten Battle, September–November 1944, The Decision, Chapter 2, Peleliu, September 1944: Amphibious Combat Against a Clever, Defensive-Minded Enemy*, erenow.com/ww/grunts-inside-american-infantry-combat-experience/3.php.

21. O'Neill, Robert, *The Road to Victory: From Pearl Harbor to Okinawa, Peleliu, Battle for (Operation Stalemate II)—The Pacific War's Forgotten Battle, September–November 1944*, www.historyofwar.org/articles/battles_peleliu.html, McManus, John C., *Grunts: Inside the American Infantry Combat Experience, World War II Through Iraq* (New York: New American Library-Div. of Penguin Group, 2010), Chapter 2., Polmar, Norman, *Aircraft Carriers: A History of Carrier Aviation and Its Influence on World Events, Volume I, 1909–1945* (Dulles, Virginia: Potomac Books, 2006), Manchester, William, *American Caesar: Douglas MacArthur 1880–1964* (New York: Back Bay Books/Little, Brown and Company, 1978).

22. Hoyt, Edwin P., *McCampbell's Heroes: The Story of the U.S. Navy's Most Celebrated Carrier Fighters of the Pacific War* (New York: Van Nostrand Reinhold Company, 1983), 127–129, 131, *Third Action Report: Stalemate II: First Visayas, September 12–14, 1944, Commanding Officer USS Essex, October 1, 1944*, WWII Archives Foundation, Incorporated.

23. Cleaver, Thomas McKelvey, *Fabled Fifteen: The Pacific War Saga of Carrier Air Group 15*, Pacifica Military History, locations 2841.

24. Cleaver, Thomas McKelvey, *Fabled Fifteen: The Pacific War Saga of Carrier Air Group 15*, Pacifica Military History, locations 2845.

25. Hoyt, Edwin P., *McCampbell's Heroes: The Story of the U.S. Navy's Most Celebrated Carrier Fighters of the Pacific War* (New York: Van Nostrand Reinhold Company, 1983), 133.

26. Hoyt, Edwin P., *McCampbell's Heroes: The Story of the U.S. Navy's Most Celebrated Carrier Fighters of the Pacific War* (New York: Van Nostrand Reinhold Company, 1983), 132–134.

27. Hoyt, Edwin P., *McCampbell's Heroes: The Story of the U.S. Navy's Most Celebrated Carrier Fighters of the Pacific War* (New York: Van Nostrand Reinhold Company, 1983), 134.

28. Hoyt, Edwin P., *McCampbell's Heroes: The Story of the U.S. Navy's Most Celebrated Carrier Fighters of the Pacific War* (New York: Van Nostrand Reinhold Company, 1983), 131–137, *Third Action Report: Stalemate II: First Visayas, September 12–14, 1944, Commanding Officer USS Essex, October 1, 1944*, WWII Archives Foundation, Incorporated, Cleaver, Thomas McKelvey, *Fabled Fifteen: The Pacific War Saga of Carrier Air Group 15*, Pacifica Military History, locations 2851–2858, 2872.

29. Cleaver, Thomas McKelvey, *Fabled Fifteen: The Pacific War Saga of Carrier Air Group 15*, Pacifica Military History, location 2894.

30. Hoyt, Edwin P., *McCampbell's Heroes: The Story of the U.S. Navy's Most Celebrated Carrier Fighters of the Pacific War* (New York: Van Nostrand Reinhold Company, 1983), 141.

31. Hoyt, Edwin P., *McCampbell's Heroes: The Story of the U.S. Navy's Most Celebrated Carrier Fighters of the Pacific War* (New York: Van Nostrand Reinhold Company, 1983), 138–141, *Fourth Action Report: Stalemate II: Manila Strikes, 21–22 September, Commanding Officer USS Essex, October 1, 1944*, WWII Archives Foundation, Incorporated, Cleaver, Thomas McKelvey, *Fabled Fifteen: The Pacific War Saga of Carrier Air Group 15*, Pacifica Military History, locations 2906–2909, 2922.

32. *Fifth Action Report: Stalemate II: Second Visayas, 24 September 1944, Commanding Officer USS Essex, October 1, 1944*, WWII Archives Foundation, Incorporated.

33. *Fifth Action Report: Stalemate II: Second Visayas, 24 September 1944, Commanding Officer USS Essex, October 1, 1944*, WWII Archives Foundation, Incorporated.

34. *Fifth Action Report: Stalemate II: Second Visayas, 24 September 1944, Commanding Officer USS Essex, October 1, 1944*, WWII Archives Foundation, Incorporated.

35. Hoyt, Edwin P., *McCampbell's Heroes: The Story of the U.S. Navy's Most Celebrated Carrier Fighters of the Pacific War* (New York: Van Nostrand Reinhold Company, 1983), 141–143, *Fifth Action Report: Stalemate II: Second Visayas, 24 September 1944, Commanding Officer USS Essex, October 1, 1944*, WWII Archives Foundation, Incorporated.

36. *First Action Report: Stalemate II: Palau, August 29–September 8, 1944, Commanding Officer USS Essex, October 1, 1944*, WWII Archives Foundation, Incorporated, Reynolds, Clark G., *The Fast Carriers: The Forging of an Air Navy* (Annapolis: Naval Institute Press, 1968), 250–251, Cordray, Elmer, *My Diary, WWII Diary 1944 Aboard the USS Essex, USS Essex WWII Air Groups Their Squadrons and Their Aircraft*, www.ussessexcv9.org/pdfs/Cordray%20Diary.pdf, 13.

Chapter 16

1. Hoyt, Edwin P., *McCampbell's Heroes: The Story of the U.S. Navy's Most Celebrated Carrier Fighters of the Pacific War* (New York: Van Nostrand Reinhold Company, 1983), 147.

2. Cleaver, Thomas McKelvey, *Fabled Fifteen: The Pacific War Saga of Carrier Air Group 15*, Pacifica Military History, locations 2933.

3. Cleaver, Thomas McKelvey, *Fabled Fifteen: The Pacific War Saga of Carrier Air Group 15*, Pacifica Military History, locations 2953.

4. Cordray, Elmer, *My Diary, WWII Diary 1944 Aboard the USS Essex, USS Essex WWII Air Groups Their Squadrons and Their Aircraft*, www.ussessexcv9.org/pdfs/Cordray%20Diary.pdf, 13, *World War II Service and Diary of John R. McKnight—Ex Rd M 3c USN*, www.wright.edu/~jack.mcknight/diary/diary/44-04.htm, Reynolds, Clark G., *The Fast Carriers: The Forging of an Air Navy* (Annapolis: Naval Institute Press, 1968), 251, 259, Cleaver, Thomas McKelvey, *Fabled Fifteen: The Pacific War Saga of Carrier Air Group 15*, Pacifica Military History, locations 2933–2948.

5. Morison, Samuel Eliot, *Leyte: June 1944–January 1945, History of the United States Naval Operations in World War II, Volume 12* (Annapolis, MD: Naval Institute Press, 1958), 87.

6. Morison, Samuel Eliot, *Leyte: June 1944–January 1945, History of the United States Naval Operations in World War II, Volume 12* (Annapolis, MD: Naval Institute Press, 1958), 86–90.

7. Hoyt, Edwin P., *McCampbell's Heroes: The Story of the U.S. Navy's Most Celebrated Carrier Fighters of the Pacific War* (New York: Van Nostrand Reinhold Company, 1983), 147.

8. Hoyt, Edwin P., *McCampbell's Heroes: The Story of the U.S. Navy's Most Celebrated Carrier Fighters of the Pacific War* (New York: Van Nostrand Reinhold Company, 1983), 147.

9. Hoyt, Edwin P., *McCampbell's Heroes: The Story of the U.S. Navy's Most Celebrated Carrier Fighters of the Pacific War* (New York: Van Nostrand Reinhold Company, 1983), 148.

10. Hoyt, Edwin P., *McCampbell's Heroes: The Story of the U.S. Navy's Most Celebrated Carrier Fighters of the Pacific War* (New York: Van Nostrand Reinhold Company, 1983), 144–149, *Action Report Nanei Shoto, October 10, 1944, Commanding Officer USS Essex, November 21, 1944*, WWII Archives Foundation, Incorporated.

Chapter 17

1. Morison, Samuel Eliot, *Leyte: June 1944–January 1945, History of the United States Naval Operations in World War II, Volume 12* (Annapolis, MD: Naval Institute Press, 1958), 93.

2. Morison, Samuel Eliot, *Leyte: June 1944–January 1945, History of the United States Naval Operations in World War II, Volume 12* (Annapolis, MD: Naval Institute Press, 1958), 91.

3. *Vego, Milan N., the Battle for Leyte, 1944: Allied and Japanese Plans, Preparations, and Execution* (Annapolis, MD: Naval Institute Press, 2006), Chapter 6, Morison, Samuel Eliot, *Leyte: June 1944–January 1945, History of the United States Naval Operations in World War II, Volume 12*, (Annapolis, MD: Naval Institute Press, 1958), 91.

4. Morison, Samuel Eliot, *Leyte: June 1944–January 1945, History of the United States Naval Operations in World War II, Volume 12* (Annapolis, MD: Naval Institute Press, 1958), 92, *Action Report, USS Cowpens, During Period 2–15 October, 1944 and 21–28 October 1944*, Commanding Officer USS Cowpens, October 28 1944.

5. Morison, Samuel Eliot, *Leyte: June 1944–January 1945, History of the United States Naval Operations in World War II, Volume 12* (Annapolis, MD: Naval Institute Press, 1958), 92.

6. *Action Report, the Battle of Formosa, October 12–14, 1944, Commanding Officer USS Essex, November 21, 1944*, WWII Archives Foundation, Incorporated.

7. *Action Report, the Battle of Formosa, October 12–14, 1944, Commanding Officer USS Essex, November 21, 1944*, WWII Archives Foundation, Incorporated.

8. Cleaver, Thomas McKelvey, *Fabled Fifteen: The Pacific War Saga of Carrier Air Group 15*, Pacifica Military History, locations 3010.

9. Cleaver, Thomas McKelvey, *Fabled Fifteen: The Pacific War Saga of Carrier Air Group 15*, Pacifica Military History, locations 3013.

10. Cleaver, Thomas McKelvey, *Fabled Fifteen: The Pacific War Saga of Carrier Air Group 15*, Pacifica Military History, locations 3021.

11. *Action Report, the Battle of Formosa, October 12–14, 1944, Commanding Officer USS Essex, November 21,*

1944, WWII Archives Foundation, Incorporated, Morison, Samuel Eliot, *Leyte: June 1944–January 1945, History of the United States Naval Operations in World War II, Volume 12*, (Annapolis, MD: Naval Institute Press, 1958), 92–93.

12. Hoyt, Edwin P., *McCampbell's Heroes: The Story of the U.S. Navy's Most Celebrated Carrier Fighters of the Pacific War* (New York: Van Nostrand Reinhold Company, 1983), 150.

13. Hoyt, Edwin P., *McCampbell's Heroes: The Story of the U.S. Navy's Most Celebrated Carrier Fighters of the Pacific War* (New York: Van Nostrand Reinhold Company, 1983), 150.

14. Hoyt, Edwin P., *McCampbell's Heroes: The Story of the U.S. Navy's Most Celebrated Carrier Fighters of the Pacific War* (New York: Van Nostrand Reinhold Company, 1983), 152.

15. Hoyt, Edwin P., *McCampbell's Heroes: The Story of the U.S. Navy's Most Celebrated Carrier Fighters of the Pacific War* (New York: Van Nostrand Reinhold Company, 1983), 150–153.

16. Cleaver, Thomas McKelvey, *Fabled Fifteen: The Pacific War Saga of Carrier Air Group 15*, Pacifica Military History, locations 3070.

17. Hoyt, Edwin P., *McCampbell's Heroes: The Story of the U.S. Navy's Most Celebrated Carrier Fighters of the Pacific War* (New York: Van Nostrand Reinhold Company, 1983), 154–155.

18. Cleaver, Thomas McKelvey, *Fabled Fifteen: The Pacific War Saga of Carrier Air Group 15*, Pacifica Military History, locations 3103.

19. Hoyt, Edwin P., *McCampbell's Heroes: The Story of the U.S. Navy's Most Celebrated Carrier Fighters of the Pacific War* (New York: Van Nostrand Reinhold Company, 1983), 155–158.

20. *The Reminiscences of Captain David McCampbell U.S. Navy (Retired)*, Interview by Paul Stillwell (Annapolis, MD.: U.S. Naval Institute, 2010), 196–197.

21. *The Reminiscences of Captain David McCampbell U.S. Navy (Retired)*, Interview by Paul Stillwell (Annapolis, MD.: U.S. Naval Institute, 2010), 196–197.

22. Morison, Samuel Eliot, *Leyte: June 1944–January 1945, History of the United States Naval Operations in World War II, Volume 12* (Annapolis, MD: Naval Institute Press, 1958), 93.

23. Morison, Samuel Eliot, *Leyte: June 1944–January 1945, History of the United States Naval Operations in World War II, Volume 12* (Annapolis, MD: Naval Institute Press, 1958), 93.

24. Hoyt, Edwin P., *McCampbell's Heroes: The Story of the U.S. Navy's Most Celebrated Carrier Fighters of the Pacific War* (New York: Van Nostrand Reinhold Company, 1983), 158.

25. Hoyt, Edwin P., *McCampbell's Heroes: The Story of the U.S. Navy's Most Celebrated Carrier Fighters of the Pacific War* (New York: Van Nostrand Reinhold Company, 1983), 158.

26. Hoyt, Edwin P., *McCampbell's Heroes: The Story of the U.S. Navy's Most Celebrated Carrier Fighters of the Pacific War* (New York: Van Nostrand Reinhold Company, 1983), 158–159, Morison, Samuel Eliot, *Leyte: June 1944–January 1945, History of the United States Naval Operations in World War II, Volume 12* (Annapolis, MD: Naval Institute Press, 1958), 93.

27. Hoyt, Edwin P., *McCampbell's Heroes: The Story of the U.S. Navy's Most Celebrated Carrier Fighters of the Pacific War* (New York: Van Nostrand Reinhold Company, 1983), 160.

28. *Action Report, the Battle of Formosa, October 12–*

14, 1944, Commanding Officer USS Essex, November 21, 1944, WWII Archives Foundation, Incorporated.

29. Hoyt, Edwin P., *McCampbell's Heroes: The Story of the U.S. Navy's Most Celebrated Carrier Fighters of the Pacific War* (New York: Van Nostrand Reinhold Company, 1983), 159–161, Morison, Samuel Eliot, *Leyte: June 1944–January 1945, History of the United States Naval Operations in World War II, Volume 12* (Annapolis, MD: Naval Institute Press, 1958), 93, *Action Report, the Battle of Formosa, October 12–14, 1944, Commanding Officer USS Essex, November 21, 1944*, WWII Archives Foundation, Incorporated, Cleaver, Thomas McKelvey, *Fabled Fifteen: The Pacific War Saga of Carrier Air Group 15*, Pacifica Military History, Kindle Edition, locations 3170–3176.

30. *Action Report, the Battle of Formosa, October 12–14, 1944, Commanding Officer USS Essex, November 21, 1944*, WWII Archives Foundation, Incorporated.

31. Morison, Samuel Eliot, *Leyte: June 1944–January 1945, History of the United States Naval Operations in World War II, Volume 12* (Annapolis, MD: Naval Institute Press, 1958), 96.

32. *U.S.S. Houston (CL81) Torpedo Damage Off Formosa 14 and 16 October, 1944, War Damage Report No. 53*, March 15, 1947, Bureau of Ships, Navy Department, Naval History & Heritage Command, pg.1.

33. *USS Canberra (CA70) Torpedo Damage, Formosa, October 13, 1944, Bureau of Ships, Navy Department, August 1, 1946, War Damage Report No. 54*, USS Canberra Danfs History, Naval History and Heritage Command, Morison, Samuel Eliot, *Leyte: June 1944–January 1945, History of the United States Naval Operations in World War II, Volume 12* (Annapolis, MD: Naval Institute Press, 1958), 93–100, *Action Report, the Battle of Formosa, October 12–14, 1944, Commanding Officer USS Essex, November 21, 1944*, WWII Archives Foundation, Incorporated, Hoyt, Edwin P., *McCampbell's Heroes: The Story of the U.S. Navy's Most Celebrated Carrier Fighters of the Pacific War* (New York: Van Nostrand Reinhold Company, 1983), 161–167, *U.S.S. Houston (CL81) Torpedo Damage Off Formosa 14 and 16 October, 1944, War Damage Report No. 53*, March 15, 1947, Bureau of Ships, Navy Department, Naval History & Heritage Command.

34. Morison, Samuel Eliot, *Leyte: June 1944–January 1945, History of the United States Naval Operations in World War II, Volume 12* (Annapolis, MD: Naval Institute Press, 1958), 104.

35. Morison, Samuel Eliot, *Leyte: June 1944–January 1945, History of the United States Naval Operations in World War II, Volume 12* (Annapolis, MD: Naval Institute Press, 1958), 104.

36. Morison, Samuel Eliot, *Leyte: June 1944–January 1945, History of the United States Naval Operations in World War II, Volume 12* (Annapolis, MD: Naval Institute Press, 1958), 103.

37. Morison, Samuel Eliot, *Leyte: June 1944–January 1945, History of the United States Naval Operations in World War II, Volume 12* (Annapolis, MD: Naval Institute Press, 1958), 106.

38. Morison, Samuel Eliot, *Leyte: June 1944–January 1945, History of the United States Naval Operations in World War II, Volume 12* (Annapolis, MD: Naval Institute Press, 1958), 104.

39. Hoyt, Edwin P., *McCampbell's Heroes: The Story of the U.S. Navy's Most Celebrated Carrier Fighters of the Pacific War* (New York: Van Nostrand Reinhold Company, 1983), 166–168, Morison, Samuel Eliot, *Leyte: June 1944–January 1945, History of the United States Naval Operations in World War II, Volume 12* (Annapolis, MD: Naval Institute Press, 1958), 101–106.

40. Morison, Samuel Eliot, *Leyte: June 1944–January 1945, History of the United States Naval Operations in World War II, Volume 12* (Annapolis, MD: Naval Institute Press, 1958), 108.

41. Morison, Samuel Eliot, *Leyte: June 1944–January 1945, History of the United States Naval Operations in World War II, Volume 12* (Annapolis, MD: Naval Institute Press, 1958), 109.

42. Morison, Samuel Eliot, *Leyte: June 1944–January 1945, History of the United States Naval Operations in World War II, Volume 12* (Annapolis, MD: Naval Institute Press, 1958), 109.

Chapter 18

1. Cleaver, Thomas McKelvey, *Fabled Fifteen: The Pacific War Saga of Carrier Air Group 15*, Pacifica Military History, locations 3461.

2. Cutler, Thomas J., *The Battle of Leyte Gulf: 23–26 October 1944* (Annapolis: Naval Institute Press, 2001), xiii.

3. Woodward, Comer Vann, *The Battle of Leyte Gulf: The Incredible Story of World War II'S Largest Naval Battle* (New York: Skyhorse Publishing, 2007), 1.

4. Woodward, Comer Vann, *The Battle of Leyte Gulf: The Incredible Story of World War II'S Largest Naval Battle* (New York: Skyhorse Publishing, 2007), 1, Cutler, Thomas J., *The Battle of Leyte Gulf: 23–26 October 1944* (Annapolis: Naval Institute Press, 2001), xiii.

5. Morison, Samuel Eliot, *Leyte: June 1944–January 1945, History of the United States Naval Operations in World War II, Volume 12* (Annapolis, MD: Naval Institute Press, 1958), 116.

6. *Cincpac Monthly Analysis for October 1944*, Morison, Samuel Eliot, *Leyte: June 1944–January 1945, History of the United States Naval Operations in World War II, Volume 12* (Annapolis, MD: Naval Institute Press, 1958), 55–56, 113, 116.

7. Morison, Samuel Eliot, *Leyte: June 1944–January 1945, History of the United States Naval Operations in World War II, Volume 12* (Annapolis, MD: Naval Institute Press, 1958), 106, 116, 118–119.

8. Cutler, Thomas J., *The Battle of Leyte Gulf: 23–26 October 1944* (Annapolis: Naval Institute Press, 2001), 66.

9. Cutler, Thomas J., *The Battle of Leyte Gulf: 23–26 October 1944* (Annapolis: Naval Institute Press, 2001), 66.

10. Cutler, Thomas J., *The Battle of Leyte Gulf: 23–26 October 1944* (Annapolis: Naval Institute Press, 2001), 66.

11. Cutler, Thomas J., *The Battle of Leyte Gulf: 23–26 October 1944* (Annapolis: Naval Institute Press, 2001), 69.

12. *Japanese Operations in the Southwest Pacific Area, MacArthur Historical Report II*, page 337, Cutler, Thomas J., *The Battle of Leyte Gulf: 23–26 October 1944* (Annapolis: Naval Institute Press, 2001), 66–67.

13. Tucker, Spencer C., *Leyte Gulf, Battle of (23–26 October 1944)*, *ABC-CLIO'S Encyclopedia of World War II: A Political, Social, and Military History*, www.historyandtheheadlines.abc-clio.com, Cleaver, Thomas McKelvey, *Fabled Fifteen: The Pacific War Saga of Carrier Air Group 15*, Pacifica Military History, locations 3383–3394, 3401–3405, Morison, Samuel Eliot, *Leyte: June 1944–January 1945, History of the United States Naval Operations in World War II, Volume 12* (Annapolis, MD: Naval Institute Press, 1958), 191.

14. Morison, Samuel Eliot, *Leyte: June 1944–January 1945, History of the United States Naval Operations in World War II, Volume 12* (Annapolis, MD: Naval Institute Press, 1958), 136–137.

15. Morison, Samuel Eliot, *Leyte: June 1944–January 1945, History of the United States Naval Operations in World War II, Volume 12* (Annapolis, MD: Naval Institute Press, 1958), 127, 131–133, 136–137, Woodward, Comer Vann, *The Battle of Leyte Gulf: The Incredible Story of World War II'S Largest Naval Battle* (New York: Skyhorse Publishing, 2007), 29–31.

16. Hoyt, Edwin P., *McCampbell's Heroes: The Story of the U.S. Navy's Most Celebrated Carrier Fighters of the Pacific War* (New York: Van Nostrand Reinhold Company, 1983), 170.

17. Hoyt, Edwin P., *McCampbell's Heroes: The Story of the U.S. Navy's Most Celebrated Carrier Fighters of the Pacific War* (New York: Van Nostrand Reinhold Company, 1983), 171.

18. Hoyt, Edwin P., *McCampbell's Heroes: The Story of the U.S. Navy's Most Celebrated Carrier Fighters of the Pacific War* (New York: Van Nostrand Reinhold Company, 1983), 171.

19. Hoyt, Edwin P., *McCampbell's Heroes: The Story of the U.S. Navy's Most Celebrated Carrier Fighters of the Pacific War* (New York: Van Nostrand Reinhold Company, 1983), 171.

20. Hoyt, Edwin P., *McCampbell's Heroes: The Story of the U.S. Navy's Most Celebrated Carrier Fighters of the Pacific War* (New York: Van Nostrand Reinhold Company, 1983), 170–173.

21. Cutler, Thomas J., *The Battle of Leyte Gulf: 23–26 October 1944* (Annapolis: Naval Institute Press, 2001), 115.

22. Cutler, Thomas J., *The Battle of Leyte Gulf: 23–26 October 1944* (Annapolis: Naval Institute Press, 2001), 115.

23. Cutler, Thomas J., *The Battle of Leyte Gulf: 23–26 October 1944* (Annapolis: Naval Institute Press, 2001), 114–115, Woodward, Comer Vann, *The Battle of Leyte Gulf: The Incredible Story of World War II'S Largest Naval Battle* (New York: Skyhorse Publishing, 2007), 43.

24. Morison, Samuel Eliot, *Leyte: June 1944–January 1945, History of the United States Naval Operations in World War II, Volume 12* (Annapolis, MD: Naval Institute Press, 1958), 170.

25. Morison, Samuel Eliot, *Leyte: June 1944–January 1945, History of the United States Naval Operations in World War II, Volume 12* (Annapolis, MD: Naval Institute Press, 1958), 169–173.

26. Cutler, Thomas J., *The Battle of Leyte Gulf: 23–26 October 1944* (Annapolis: Naval Institute Press, 2001), 114–115.

27. *Action Report, the Battle of Philippines, October 24–25, 1944, Commanding Officer USS Essex, November 21, 1944,* WWII Archives Foundation, Incorporated, Hoyt, Edwin P., *McCampbell's Heroes: The Story of the U.S. Navy's Most Celebrated Carrier Fighters of the Pacific War* (New York: Van Nostrand Reinhold Company, 1983), ix–xi.

28. Cutler, Thomas J., *The Battle of Leyte Gulf: 23–26 October 1944* (Annapolis: Naval Institute Press, 2001), 118.

29. Cutler, Thomas J., *The Battle of Leyte Gulf: 23–26 October 1944* (Annapolis: Naval Institute Press, 2001), 119.

30. Cutler, Thomas J., *The Battle of Leyte Gulf: 23–26 October 1944* (Annapolis: Naval Institute Press, 2001), 119.

31. Woodward, Comer Vann, *The Battle of Leyte Gulf: The Incredible Story of World War II'S Largest Naval Battle* (New York: Skyhorse Publishing, 2007), 47, Morison, Samuel Eliot, *Leyte: June 1944–January 1945, History of the United States Naval Operations in World War II, Volume 12,* (Annapolis, MD: Naval Institute Press, 1958), 174–175, Thomas, Evan, *Sea of Thunder: Four Commanders and the Last Great Naval Campaign 1941–1945* (New York: Simon & Schuster Paperbacks, 2006), 209.

32. *Glossary of U.S. Naval Abbreviations,* Department of the Navy, Naval Historical Center, Washington Navy Yard, Washington, D.C.

33. Cutler, Thomas J., *The Battle of Leyte Gulf: 23–26 October 1944* (Annapolis: Naval Institute Press, 2001), 121.

34. Hoyt, Edwin P., *McCampbell's Heroes: The Story of the U.S. Navy's Most Celebrated Carrier Fighters of the Pacific War* (New York: Van Nostrand Reinhold Company, 1983), 175, 179.

35. Cutler, Thomas J., *The Battle of Leyte Gulf: 23–26 October 1944* (Annapolis: Naval Institute Press, 2001), 129.

36. Cutler, Thomas J., *The Battle of Leyte Gulf: 23–26 October 1944* (Annapolis: Naval Institute Press, 2001), 129.

37. Buracker, William H., *Saga of the Carrier Princeton, The National Graphic Magazine,* Aug. 1945.

38. Buracker, William H., *Saga of the Carrier Princeton, The National Graphic Magazine,* Aug. 1945, Cutler, Thomas J., *The Battle of Leyte Gulf: 23–26 October 1944* (Annapolis: Naval Institute Press, 2001), 128–131.

39. Hoyt, Edwin P., *McCampbell's Heroes: The Story of the U.S. Navy's Most Celebrated Carrier Fighters of the Pacific War* (New York: Van Nostrand Reinhold Company, 1983), 175–181.

40. Cleaver, Thomas McKelvey, *Fabled Fifteen: The Pacific War Saga of Carrier Air Group 15,* Pacifica Military History, locations 3461–3471.

41. Cleaver, Thomas McKelvey, *Fabled Fifteen: The Pacific War Saga of Carrier Air Group 15,* Pacifica Military History, locations 3474.

42. Cleaver, Thomas McKelvey, *Fabled Fifteen: The Pacific War Saga of Carrier Air Group 15,* Pacifica Military History, locations 3474–3499.

43. Cleaver, Thomas McKelvey, *Fabled Fifteen: The Pacific War Saga of Carrier Air Group 15,* Pacifica Military History, Kindle Edition, locations 3508.

44. Cleaver, Thomas McKelvey, *Fabled Fifteen: The Pacific War Saga of Carrier Air Group 15,* Pacifica Military History, Kindle Edition, locations 3513.

45. Cleaver, Thomas McKelvey, *Fabled Fifteen: The Pacific War Saga of Carrier Air Group 15,* Pacifica Military History, Kindle Edition, locations 3525.

46. Cleaver, Thomas McKelvey, *Fabled Fifteen: The Pacific War Saga of Carrier Air Group 15,* Pacifica Military History, locations 3526–3527, 3537–3538, 3550–3556, Hoyt, Edwin P., *McCampbell's Heroes: The Story of the U.S. Navy's Most Celebrated Carrier Fighters of the Pacific War* (New York: Van Nostrand Reinhold Company, 1983), 181.

47. Cleaver, Thomas McKelvey, *Fabled Fifteen: The Pacific War Saga of Carrier Air Group 15,* Pacifica Military History, locations 3556–3565, 3660–3662.

48. Cutler, Thomas J., *The Battle of Leyte Gulf: 23–26 October 1944* (Annapolis: Naval Institute Press, 2001), 150–151.

49. Cutler, Thomas J., *The Battle of Leyte Gulf: 23–26 October 1944* (Annapolis: Naval Institute Press, 2001), 149–153.

50. Morison, Samuel Eliot, *Leyte: June 1944–January 1945, History of the United States Naval Operations in World War II, Volume 12* (Annapolis, MD: Naval Institute Press, 1958), 190, Cutler, Thomas J., *The Battle of Leyte Gulf: 23–26 October 1944* (Annapolis: Naval Institute Press, 2001), 139–140.

51. Morison, Samuel Eliot, *Leyte: June 1944–January 1945, History of the United States Naval Operations in World War II, Volume 12* (Annapolis, MD: Naval Institute Press, 1958), 142.

52. Cutler, Thomas J., *The Battle of Leyte Gulf: 23–26 October 1944* (Annapolis: Naval Institute Press, 2001), 156.

53. Cutler, Thomas J., *The Battle of Leyte Gulf: 23–26 October 1944* (Annapolis: Naval Institute Press, 2001), 156.

54. Morison, Samuel Eliot, *Leyte: June 1944–January 1945, History of the United States Naval Operations in World War II, Volume 12* (Annapolis, MD: Naval Institute Press, 1958), 192, Cutler, Thomas J., *The Battle of Leyte Gulf: 23–26 October 1944* (Annapolis: Naval Institute Press, 2001), 162.

55. Reynolds, Clark G., *The Fast Carriers: The Forging of an Air Navy* (Annapolis: Naval Institute Press, 1968), 267.

56. Morison, Samuel Eliot, *Leyte: June 1944–January 1945, History of the United States Naval Operations in World War II, Volume 12* (Annapolis, MD: Naval Institute Press, 1958), 290.

57. Cutler, Thomas J., *The Battle of Leyte Gulf: 23–26 October 1944* (Annapolis: Naval Institute Press, 2001), 170.

58. Morison, Samuel Eliot, *Leyte: June 1944–January 1945, History of the United States Naval Operations in World War II, Volume 12* (Annapolis, MD: Naval Institute Press, 1958), 189.

59. Cutler, Thomas J., *The Battle of Leyte Gulf: 23–26 October 1944* (Annapolis: Naval Institute Press, 2001), 171.

60. Cutler, Thomas J., *The Battle of Leyte Gulf: 23–26 October 1944* (Annapolis: Naval Institute Press, 2001), 160, Reynolds, Clark G., *The Fast Carriers: The Forging of an Air Navy* (Annapolis: Naval Institute Press, 1968), 269.

61. Reynolds, Clark G., *The Fast Carriers: The Forging of an Air Navy* (Annapolis: Naval Institute Press, 1968), 268.

62. *Ibid.*, 268.

63. Morison, Samuel Eliot, *Leyte: June 1944–January 1945, History of the United States Naval Operations in World War II, Volume 12* (Annapolis, MD: Naval Institute Press, 1958), 194.

64. Morison, Samuel Eliot, *Leyte: June 1944–January 1945, History of the United States Naval Operations in World War II, Volume 12* (Annapolis, MD: Naval Institute Press, 1958), 193–194.

65. Cleaver, Thomas McKelvey, *Fabled Fifteen: The Pacific War Saga of Carrier Air Group 15*, Pacifica Military History, locations 3697.

66. Hoyt, Edwin P., *McCampbell's Heroes: The Story of the U.S. Navy's Most Celebrated Carrier Fighters of the Pacific War* (New York: Van Nostrand Reinhold Company, 1983), 185.

67. Reynolds, Clark G., *The Fast Carriers: The Forging of an Air Navy* (Annapolis: Naval Institute Press, 1968), 273, Hoyt, Edwin P., *McCampbell's Heroes: The Story of the U.S. Navy's Most Celebrated Carrier Fighters of the Pacific War* (New York: Van Nostrand Reinhold Company, 1983), 184–185, *Action Report, the Battle of Philippines, October 24–25, 1944, Commanding Officer USS Essex, November 21, 1944*, WWII Archives Foundation, Incorporated.

68. Cleaver, Thomas McKelvey, *Fabled Fifteen: The Pacific War Saga of Carrier Air Group 15*, Pacifica Military History, locations 3734.

69. Cleaver, Thomas McKelvey, *Fabled Fifteen: The Pacific War Saga of Carrier Air Group 15*, Pacifica Military History, locations 3746–3753, Hoyt, Edwin P., *McCampbell's Heroes: The Story of the U.S. Navy's Most Celebrated Carrier Fighters of the Pacific War* (New York: Van Nostrand Reinhold Company, 1983), 185–187.

70. Morison, Samuel Eliot, *Leyte: June 1944–January 1945, History of the United States Naval Operations in World War II, Volume 12* (Annapolis, MD: Naval Institute Press, 1958), 325.

71. Morison, Samuel Eliot, *Leyte: June 1944–January 1945, History of the United States Naval Operations in World War II, Volume 12* (Annapolis, MD: Naval Institute Press, 1958), 325.

72. Morison, Samuel Eliot, *Leyte: June 1944–January 1945, History of the United States Naval Operations in World War II, Volume 12* (Annapolis, MD: Naval Institute Press, 1958), 325–327.

73. Hoyt, Edwin P., *McCampbell's Heroes: The Story of the U.S. Navy's Most Celebrated Carrier Fighters of the Pacific War* (New York: Van Nostrand Reinhold Company, 1983), 188.

74. Hoyt, Edwin P., *McCampbell's Heroes: The Story of the U.S. Navy's Most Celebrated Carrier Fighters of the Pacific War* (New York: Van Nostrand Reinhold Company, 1983), 187–188, Morison, Samuel Eliot, *Leyte: June 1944–January 1945, History of the United States Naval Operations in World War II, Volume 12* (Annapolis, MD: Naval Institute Press, 1958), 326–328, Woodward, Comer Vann, *The Battle of Leyte Gulf: The Incredible Story of World War II'S Largest Naval Battle* (New York: Skyhorse Publishing, 2007), 143–146.

75. Morison, Samuel Eliot, *Leyte: June 1944–January 1945, History of the United States Naval Operations in World War II, Volume 12* (Annapolis, MD: Naval Institute Press, 1958), 198–240.

76. Reynolds, Clark G., *The Fast Carriers: The Forging of an Air Navy* (Annapolis: Naval Institute Press, 1968), 272.

77. Reynolds, Clark G., *The Fast Carriers: The Forging of an Air Navy* (Annapolis: Naval Institute Press, 1968), 272.

78. Reynolds, Clark G., *The Fast Carriers: The Forging of an Air Navy* (Annapolis: Naval Institute Press, 1968), 274.

79. Reynolds, Clark G., *The Fast Carriers: The Forging of an Air Navy* (Annapolis: Naval Institute Press, 1968), 275.

80. Reynolds, Clark G., *The Fast Carriers: The Forging of an Air Navy* (Annapolis: Naval Institute Press, 1968), 272–275.

81. Morison, Samuel Eliot, *Leyte: June 1944–January 1945, History of the United States Naval Operations in World War II, Volume 12* (Annapolis, MD: Naval Institute Press, 1958), 242–259,

82. Woodward, Comer Vann, *The Battle of Leyte Gulf: The Incredible Story of World War II'S Largest Naval Battle* (New York: Skyhorse Publishing, 2007), 156.

83. Woodward, Comer Vann, *The Battle of Leyte Gulf: The Incredible Story of World War II'S Largest Naval Battle* (New York: Skyhorse Publishing, 2007), 171.

84. Morison, Samuel Eliot, *Leyte: June 1944–January 1945, History of the United States Naval Operations in World War II, Volume 12* (Annapolis, MD: Naval Institute Press, 1958), 255–271, Woodward, Comer Vann, *The Battle of Leyte Gulf: The Incredible Story of World War II'S Largest Naval Battle* (New York: Skyhorse Publishing, 2007), 163–171.

85. Morison, Samuel Eliot, *Leyte: June 1944–January 1945, History of the United States Naval Operations in World War II, Volume 12* (Annapolis, MD: Naval Institute Press, 1958), 285–287.

86. Morison, Samuel Eliot, *Leyte: June 1944–January 1945, History of the United States Naval Operations in World War II, Volume 12* (Annapolis, MD: Naval Institute Press, 1958), 297.

87. *Ibid.*, 299.

88. *Ibid.*, 299.

89. *Ibid.*, 300.

90. Woodward, Comer Vann, *The Battle of Leyte Gulf: The Incredible Story of World War II'S Largest Naval Battle* (New York: Skyhorse Publishing, 2007), 198–201, Reynolds, Clark G., *The Fast Carriers: The Forging of an Air Navy* (Annapolis: Naval Institute Press, 1968), 275–276.

91. Morison, Samuel Eliot, *Leyte: June 1944–January 1945, History of the United States Naval Operations in World War II, Volume 12* (Annapolis, MD: Naval Institute Press, 1958), 329, Woodward, Comer Vann, *The Battle of Leyte Gulf: The Incredible Story of World War II'S Largest Naval Battle* (New York: Skyhorse Publishing, 2007), 198–201, Reynolds, Clark G., *The Fast Carriers: The Forging of an Air Navy* (Annapolis: Naval Institute Press, 1968), 207–208, *CTF 34 Action Report (Vice Admiral Lee)*, December 14, 1944.

92. Morison, Samuel Eliot, *Leyte: June 1944–January 1945, History of the United States Naval Operations in World War II, Volume 12* (Annapolis, MD: Naval Institute Press, 1958), 315–316.

Chapter 19

1. *AirGroup 15 of the United States Ship ESSEX*, by Morris Markey, *Liberty Magazine*, May 26, 1945.

2. Hoyt, Edwin P., *McCampbell's Heroes: The Story of the U.S. Navy's Most Celebrated Carrier Fighters of the Pacific War* (New York: Van Nostrand Reinhold Company, 1983), 193.

3. Hoyt, Edwin P., *McCampbell's Heroes: The Story of the U.S. Navy's Most Celebrated Carrier Fighters of the Pacific War* (New York: Van Nostrand Reinhold Company, 1983), 193.

4. Hoyt, Edwin P., *McCampbell's Heroes: The Story of the U.S. Navy's Most Celebrated Carrier Fighters of the Pacific War* (New York: Van Nostrand Reinhold Company, 1983), 192–194.

5. Morison, Samuel Eliot, *Leyte: June 1944–January 1945, History of the United States Naval Operations in World War II, Volume 12* (Annapolis, MD: Naval Institute Press, 1958), 340–341.

6. Cordray, Elmer, *My Diary, WWII Diary 1944 Aboard the USS Essex, USS Essex WWII Air Groups Their Squadrons and Their Aircraft*, www.ussessexcv9. org/pdfs/Cordray%20Diary.pdf, 15.

7. Hoyt, Edwin P., *McCampbell's Heroes: The Story of the U.S. Navy's Most Celebrated Carrier Fighters of the Pacific War* (New York: Van Nostrand Reinhold Company, 1983), 195.

8. Morison, Samuel Eliot, *Leyte: June 1944–January 1945, History of the United States Naval Operations in World War II, Volume 12* (Annapolis, MD: Naval Institute Press, 1958), 341.

9. Morison, Samuel Eliot, *Leyte: June 1944–January 1945, History of the United States Naval Operations in World War II, Volume 12* (Annapolis, MD: Naval Institute Press, 1958), 346.

10. Morison, Samuel Eliot, *Leyte: June 1944–January 1945, History of the United States Naval Operations in World War II, Volume 12* (Annapolis, MD: Naval Institute Press, 1958), 346–349, Hoyt, Edwin P., *McCampbell's Heroes: The Story of the U.S. Navy's Most Celebrated Carrier Fighters of the Pacific War* (New York: Van Nostrand Reinhold Company, 1983), 195–196, Cordray, Elmer, *My Diary, WWII Diary 1944 Aboard the USS Essex, USS Essex WWII Air Groups Their Squadrons and Their Aircraft*, www.ussessexcv9.org/pdfs/Cordray%20Diary.pdf, 16.

11. Hoyt, Edwin P., *McCampbell's Heroes: The Story of the U.S. Navy's Most Celebrated Carrier Fighters of the Pacific War* (New York: Van Nostrand Reinhold Company, 1983), 197.

12. Hoyt, Edwin P., *McCampbell's Heroes: The Story of the U.S. Navy's Most Celebrated Carrier Fighters of the Pacific War* (New York: Van Nostrand Reinhold Company, 1983), 198.

13. Hoyt, Edwin P., *McCampbell's Heroes: The Story of the U.S. Navy's Most Celebrated Carrier Fighters of the Pacific War* (New York: Van Nostrand Reinhold Company, 1983), 199.

14. Cleaver, Thomas McKelvey, *Fabled Fifteen: The Pacific War Saga of Carrier Air Group 15*, Pacifica Military, locations 4043–4061, Hoyt, Edwin P., *McCampbell's Heroes: The Story of the U.S. Navy's Most Celebrated Carrier Fighters of the Pacific War* (New York: Van Nostrand Reinhold Company, 1983), 196–200.

15. Hoyt, Edwin P., *McCampbell's Heroes: The Story of the U.S. Navy's Most Celebrated Carrier Fighters of the Pacific War* (New York: Van Nostrand Reinhold Company, 1983), 200–201.

16. Morison, Samuel Eliot, *Leyte: June 1944–January 1945, History of the United States Naval Operations in World War II, Volume 12* (Annapolis, MD: Naval Institute Press, 1958), 349, Hoyt, Edwin P., *McCampbell's Heroes: The Story of the U.S. Navy's Most Celebrated Carrier Fighters of the Pacific War* (New York: Van Nostrand Reinhold Company, 1983), 201–203.

17. Hoyt, Edwin P., *McCampbell's Heroes: The Story of the U.S. Navy's Most Celebrated Carrier Fighters of the Pacific War* (New York: Van Nostrand Reinhold Company, 1983), 203.

18. Cleaver, Thomas McKelvey, Fabled Fifteen: The Pacific War Saga of Carrier Air Group 15, Pacifica Military History, locations 4103–4105, *World War II Service and Diary of John R. McKnight-Ex Rd M 3c USN*, www.wright.edu/~jack.mcknight/diary/diary/44–04.htm.

19. Graham, A.T., *Pacific War Diary of A.T. Graham, Jr.*, atgrahamjr.blogspot.com/2012_08_01_archive.html.

20. Hoyt, Edwin P., *McCampbell's Heroes: The Story of the U.S. Navy's Most Celebrated Carrier Fighters of the Pacific War* (New York: Van Nostrand Reinhold Company, 1983), 204.

21. Cleaver, Thomas McKelvey, Fabled Fifteen: The Pacific War Saga of Carrier Air Group 15, Pacifica Military History, locations 4112–4113, 4144–4161, Hoyt, Edwin P., *McCampbell's Heroes: The Story of the U.S. Navy's Most Celebrated Carrier Fighters of the Pacific War* (New York: Van Nostrand Reinhold Company, 1983), 203–209.

22. Hoyt, Edwin P., *McCampbell's Heroes: The Story of the U.S. Navy's Most Celebrated Carrier Fighters of the Pacific War* (New York: Van Nostrand Reinhold Company, 1983), 211.

23. Hoyt, Edwin P., *McCampbell's Heroes: The Story of the U.S. Navy's Most Celebrated Carrier Fighters of the Pacific War* (New York: Van Nostrand Reinhold Company, 1983), 211.

24. Cleaver, Thomas McKelvey, Fabled Fifteen: The Pacific War Saga of Carrier Air Group 15, Pacifica Military History, locations 4162–4175, 4176–4178, Hoyt, Edwin P., *McCampbell's Heroes: The Story of the U.S. Navy's Most Celebrated Carrier Fighters of the Pacific War* (New York: Van Nostrand Reinhold Company, 1983), 209–211, Morison, Samuel Eliot, *Leyte: June 1944–January 1945, History of the United States Naval Operations in World War II, Volume 12* (Annapolis, MD: Naval Institute Press, 1958), 353.

25. Hoyt, Edwin P., *McCampbell's Heroes: The Story of the U.S. Navy's Most Celebrated Carrier Fighters of the Pacific War* (New York: Van Nostrand Reinhold Company, 1983), 213–215, Cleaver, Thomas McKelvey, *Fabled Fifteen: The Pacific War Saga of Carrier Air Group 15*, Pacifica Military History, locations 4213–4238, Cordray, Elmer, *My Diary, WWII Diary 1944 Aboard the USS Essex, USS Essex WWII Air Squadrons and Their Aircraft*, www.ussessexcv9.org/pdfs/Cordray%20Diary.pdf, 16.

26. Hoyt, Edwin P., *McCampbell's Heroes: The Story of the U.S. Navy's Most Celebrated Carrier Fighters of the Pacific War* (New York: Van Nostrand Reinhold Company, 1983), 215–216.

27. Cleaver, Thomas McKelvey, *Fabled Fifteen: The Pacific War Saga of Carrier Air Group 15*, Pacifica Military History, locations 4276–4282, Cordray, Elmer, *My Diary, WWII Diary 1944 Aboard the USS Essex, USS Essex WWII Air Groups Their Squadrons and Their Aircraft*, www.ussessexcv9.org/pdfs/Cordray%20Diary.pdf, 17.

28. Cleaver, Thomas McKelvey, *Fabled Fifteen: The Pacific War Saga of Carrier Air Group 15*, Pacifica Military History, locations 4250.

29. Cleaver, Thomas McKelvey, *Fabled Fifteen: The Pacific War Saga of Carrier Air Group 15*, Pacifica Military History, locations 4255–4271, Cordray, Elmer, *My Diary, WWII Diary 1944 Aboard the USS Essex, USS Essex WWII Air Groups Their Squadrons and Their Aircraft*, www.ussessexcv9.org/pdfs/Cordray%20Diary.pdf, 17, *AirGroup 15 of the United States Ship Essex*, by Morris Markey, *Liberty Magazine*, May 26, 1945, *Airgroups*, Researcher@Large, www.researcheratlarge.com, www.researcheratlarge.com, Hoyt, Edwin P., *McCampbell's Heroes: The Story of the U.S. Navy's Most Celebrated Carrier Fighters of the Pacific War* (New York: Van Nostrand Reinhold Company, 1983), 13–14.

30. *The Reminiscences of Captain David McCampbell U.S. Navy (Retired)*, Interview by Paul Stillwell (Annapolis, MD.: U.S. Naval Institute, 2010), 4.

31. *The Reminiscences of Captain David McCampbell U.S. Navy (Retired)*, Interview by Paul Stillwell (Annapolis, MD.: U.S. Naval Institute, 2010), 134, Cleaver, Thomas McKelvey, *Fabled Fifteen: The Pacific War Saga of Carrier Air Group 15*, Pacifica Military History, locations 4339–4345.

32. *The Reminiscences of Captain David McCampbell U.S. Navy (Retired)*, Interview by Paul Stillwell (Annapolis, MD.: U.S. Naval Institute, 2010), 4.

33. *AirGroup 15 of the United States Ship ESSEX*, by Morris Markey, *Liberty Magazine*, May 26, 1945.

34. *AirGroup 15 of the United States Ship ESSEX*, by Morris Markey, *Liberty Magazine*, May 26, 1945.

35. *AirGroup 15 of the United States Ship ESSEX*, by Morris Markey, *Liberty Magazine*, May 26, 1945.

36. Cleaver, Thomas McKelvey, *Relentless in Battle*, Aviation History Magazine, June 2, 2014, www.historynet.com/relentless-in-battle.htm.

37. Layton, Andrew, *Wolverines in the Sky* (Xulon Press, 2007), 39.

38. *The Reminiscences of Captain David McCampbell U.S. Navy (Retired)*, Interview by Paul Stillwell (Annapolis, MD.: U.S. Naval Institute, 2010), 2–133.

39. *Valdemar Greene Lambert, the Monterey Herald* on Aug. 29, 2008, www.legacy.com/obituaries/monterey herald/obituary.aspx?

40. *David McCampbell, Military Combat, Enshrined 1996, 1910–1996, National Aviation Hall of Fame*, nationalaviation.org, *The Reminiscences of Captain David McCampbell U.S. Navy (Retired)*, Interview by Paul Stillwell (Annapolis, MD.: U.S. Naval Institute, 2010), 227.

Chapter 20

1. *Quote from Jack C. Taylor, Former Lieutenant, USNR, The Reminiscences of Captain David McCampbell U.S. Navy (Retired)*, Interview by Paul Stillwell (Annapolis, MD.: U.S. Naval Institute, 2010), Forward.

2. *The Reminiscences of Captain David McCampbell U.S. Navy (Retired)*, Interview by Paul Stillwell (Annapolis, MD.: U.S. Naval Institute, 2010), 221–225.

3. *The Reminiscences of Captain David McCampbell U.S. Navy (Retired)*, Interview by Paul Stillwell (Annapolis, MD.: U.S. Naval Institute, 2010), 225.

4. *Ibid.*, 222–232.

5. *Ibid.*, 233.

6. *Ibid.*, 229–231.

7. *Ibid.*, 244–250.

8. *The Reminiscences of Captain David McCampbell U.S. Navy (Retired)*, Interview by Paul Stillwell (Annapolis, MD.: U.S. Naval Institute, 2010), 269.

9. *Ibid.*, 268–269.

10. *Ibid.*, 253.

11. *The Reminiscences of Captain David McCampbell U.S. Navy (Retired)*, Interview by Paul Stillwell (Annapolis, MD.: U.S. Naval Institute, 2010), 262.

12. *Ibid.*, 261–263.

13. *Ibid.*, 276–277.

14. *Vice Admiral (Retired) William V. ""Bill"" Davis, Jr.*, United State Navy Biography, U.S. Navy Website.

15. *The Reminiscences of Captain David McCampbell U.S. Navy (Retired)*, Interview by Paul Stillwell (Annapolis, MD.: U.S. Naval Institute, 2010), 280–286.

16. *The Reminiscences of Captain David McCampbell U.S. Navy (Retired)*, Interview by Paul Stillwell (Annapolis, MD.: U.S. Naval Institute, 2010), 284.

17. *Ibid.*, pp.286–294.

18. *Ibid.*, 294–297.

19. *The Reminiscences of Captain David McCampbell U.S. Navy (Retired)*, Interview by Paul Stillwell (Annapolis, MD.: U.S. Naval Institute, 2010), 300.

20. *The Reminiscences of Captain David McCampbell U.S. Navy (Retired)*, Interview by Paul Stillwell (Annapolis, MD.: U.S. Naval Institute, 2010), 302.

21. *Ibid.*, 301.

22. *The Reminiscences of Captain David McCampbell U.S. Navy (Retired)*, Interview by Paul Stillwell (Annapolis, MD.: U.S. Naval Institute, 2010), 320.

23. *Ibid.*, 320–325.

24. *Ibid.*, 303–304.
25. *The Reminiscences of Captain David McCampbell U.S. Navy (Retired)*, Interview by Paul Stillwell (Annapolis, MD.: U.S. Naval Institute, 2010), 326.
26. *The Reminiscences of Captain David McCampbell U.S. Navy (Retired)*, Interview by Paul Stillwell (Annapolis, MD.: U.S. Naval Institute, 2010), 326.
27. *Ibid.*, 327.
28. *Ibid.*, 327–329.
29. *Ibid.*, 329.
30. *Ibid.*, 329–330, 338.
31. *Ibid.*, 331–333.
32. "B&J": *Jacob Bercovitch and Richard Jackson, International Conflict: A Chronological Encyclopedia of Conflicts and Their Management 1945–1995* (1997).
33. *The Reminiscences of Captain David McCampbell U.S. Navy (Retired)*, Interview by Paul Stillwell (Annapolis, MD.: U.S. Naval Institute, 2010), 335.
34. *The Reminiscences of Captain David McCampbell U.S. Navy (Retired)*, Interview by Paul Stillwell (Annapolis, MD.: U.S. Naval Institute, 2010), 335.
35. *The Reminiscences of Captain David McCampbell U.S. Navy (Retired)*, Interview by Paul Stillwell (Annapolis, MD.: U.S. Naval Institute, 2010), 334–335.
36. *Ibid.*, 337–340.
37. *Ibid.*, 340–342.
38. *The Reminiscences of Captain David McCampbell U.S. Navy (Retired)*, Interview by Paul Stillwell (Annapolis, MD.: U.S. Naval Institute, 2010), 342.
39. *Ibid.*, 348.
40. *USS Bon Homme Richard, Aircraft Carrier Thirty One, Ships History,* www.ussbhr.org.
41. *The Reminiscences of Captain David McCampbell U.S. Navy (Retired)*, Interview by Paul Stillwell (Annapolis, MD.: U.S. Naval Institute, 2010), 344.
42. *The Reminiscences of Captain David McCampbell U.S. Navy (Retired)*, Interview by Paul Stillwell (Annapolis, MD.: U.S. Naval Institute, 2010), 344.
43. *The Reminiscences of Captain David McCampbell U.S. Navy (Retired)*, Interview by Paul Stillwell (Annapolis, MD.: U.S. Naval Institute, 2010), 344.
44. *The Reminiscences of Captain David McCampbell U.S. Navy (Retired)*, Interview by Paul Stillwell (Annapolis, MD.: U.S. Naval Institute, 2010), 344–345.
45. *The Reminiscences of Captain David McCampbell U.S. Navy (Retired)*, Interview by Paul Stillwell (Annapolis, MD.: U.S. Naval Institute, 2010), 346.
46. *1960 Cruise Book of USS Bon Homme Richard CVA-31, the Archive,* Navy Department Library, Washington, D.C., 3, 11.

47. *The Reminiscences of Captain David McCampbell U.S. Navy (Retired)*, Interview by Paul Stillwell (Annapolis, MD.: U.S. Naval Institute, 2010), 352–354.
48. *Ibid.*, 356.
49. *Ibid.*, 354–356.
50. *Ibid.*, 361.
51. *Ibid.*, 359.
52. *Ibid.*, 368.
53. *Ibid.*, 363–365.
54. Cleaver, Thomas McKelvey, *Fabled Fifteen: The Pacific War Saga of Carrier Air Group 15,* Pacifica Military History, location: Preface.
55. *The Reminiscences of Captain David McCampbell U.S. Navy (Retired)*, Interview by Paul Stillwell (Annapolis, MD.: U.S. Naval Institute, 2010), 366–368.
56. *Ibid.* 368.
57. *McCampbell: No Swagger, Just Heroism, the Palm Beach Post,* July 4, 1996, 18A, www.emedals.com.
58. *Destroyer Named After the Navy's 'Ace of Aces,'* by Eliot Kleinberg, *Palm Beach Post, July 3, 2000,* 1B.
59. *Quote from Jack C. Taylor, Former Lieutenant, USNR, The Reminiscences of Captain David McCampbell U.S. Navy (Retired)*, Interview by Paul Stillwell (Annapolis, MD.: U.S. Naval Institute, 2010), Forward.
60. *1933 Lucky Bag, U.S. Naval Academy Class of 1933 Yearbook,* 204.

Appendix A

1. Hoyt, Edwin P., *McCampbell's Heroes: The Story of the U.S. Navy's Most Celebrated Carrier Fighters of the Pacific War* (New York: Van Nostrand Reinhold Company, 1983).

Appendix B

1. *Collection of Rear Admiral Samuel E. Morison, USN (Retired). Photo # NH 106328,* Official U.S. Navy Photograph, Naval History and Heritage Command collection.

Appendix C

1. *Medal of Honor Citation of Commander David McCampbell, USN,* Printed in the official publication *Medal of Honor, 1861–1949, The Navy,* 22.

Bibliography

Abandoned & Little-Known Airfields: Hawaii, Maui Island, By Paul Freeman, www.airfields-freeman.com/HI/Airfields_HI_Maui.htm.

Action Report, the Battle of Formosa, October 12–14, 1944, Commanding Officer USS Essex, November 21, 1944, WWII Archives Foundation, Incorporated.

Action Report, the Battle of Philippines, October 24–25, 1944, Commanding Officer USS Essex, November 21, 1944, WWII Archives Foundation, Incorporated.

Action Report, USS Cowpens, During Period 2–15 October 1944 and 21–28 October 1944, Commanding Officer USS Cowpens, October 28, 1944.

Action Report: Forager, July 6–August 13, 1944, Commanding Officer USS Essex, August 14, 1944, WWII Archives Foundation, Incorporated.

Action Report: Forager, June 6–July 6, 1944, Commanding Officer USS Essex, July 6, 1944, WWII Archives Foundation, Incorporated.

Action Report Nanei Shoto, October 10, 1944, Commanding Officer USS Essex, November 21, 1944, WWII Archives Foundation, Incorporated.

Action Report: Operations Against Marcus and Wake Islands, 15–25 May 1944, Commanding Officer USS Essex, March 30, 1944, WWII Archives Foundation, Incorporated.

Admiral Frederick C. Sherman, Navy Biographies Branch, OI-450, 6 August 1957, Modern Biographies files, Navy Department Library, Naval History & Heritage Command.

AirGroup 15 of the United States Ship Essex, by Morris Markey, *Liberty Magazine,* May 26, 1945.

Airgroups, Researcher@Large, www.researcheratlarge.com.

Andrews, Hal, *F6f Hellcat, Naval Aviation News,* September–October 1988, www.history.navy.mil/branches/hist-ac/f6f-5.pdf.

Antill, Peter, *Peleliu, Battle for (Operation Stalemate II)—The Pacific War's Forgotten Battle, September–November 1944* (2003), www.historyofwar.org/articles/battles_peleliu.

Atlantic City Naval Air Station, Egg Harbor Township, New Jersey Fact Sheet, U.S. Army Corps of Engineers, December 2007, www.nan.usace.army.mil/Media/FactSheets/FactSheetArticleView/tabid/11241/Article/9602/fact-sheet-atlantic-city-naval-air-station-egg-harbor-township-nj.aspx.

Aylwin, Dictionary of American Naval Fighting Ships, Navy Department, Naval History & Heritage Command, Naval Historical Center.

"B&J": Jacob Bercovitch and Richard Jackson, International Conflict: A Chronological Encyclopedia of Conflicts and Their Management 1945–1995 (1997).

Backer, Steve, *Essex Class Aircraft Carriers of the Second World War.* Barnsley, South Yorkshire, UK: Seaforth Publishing, 2009.

Barnett, William R., *US Naval Air Station, Melbourne Florida, World War II,* Xlibris Corp; 1st edition (February 28, 2001).

Bell, Daniel E., *Charlie Cooper Survived the Sinking of the USS Wasp by the Japanese on Sept 15, 1942,* www.pbase.com/image/129458587.

Blair, Clay, *Silent Victory: The U.S. Submarine War Against Japan.* Annapolis, MD: Naval Institute Press, 2001.

Boatner, Mark M. *The Biographical Dictionary of World War II,* Novato, California: Presidio Press.

The Bomber Pilots and Crews, USS Essex Association, www.ussessexcv9.org.

Bombing Squadron VB15, Chronology, by Warren Parrish, Walter Fontaine, and Donna Burney, www.ussessexcv9.org/Bravepages/bombing15.html.

USS Bon Homme Richard, Aircraft Carrier Thirty One, Ships History, www.ussbhr.org.

Boyd, Carl, and Akihiko Yoshida, *The Japanese Submarine Force and World War II.* Annapolis, MD: Naval Institute Press, 1995.

Budge, Kent G., *SB2c Helldiver, U.S. Carrier Dive Bomber,* The Pacific War Online Encyclopedia, pwencycl.kgbudge.com/S/b/SB2C_Helldiver.htm.

Buracker, William H., *Saga of the Carrier Princeton, the National Graphic Magazine,* Aug. 1945.

Business Bureau of the Beaches, Clewiston News, Clewiston, Florida, Friday, June 20, 1930.

USS Canberra (CA70) Torpedo Damage, Formosa, October 13, 1944, Bureau of Ships, Navy Department, August 1, 1946, War Damage Report No. 54, USS Canberra Danfs History, Naval History and Heritage Command.

Captain David McCampbell, USN (1910–1996), U.S. Naval History and Heritage Command, www.history.navy.mil/our-collections/photography/us-people/m/mccampbell-david.html.

Captain David S. McCampbell, U.S. Navy WW-II Top Fighter Ace, Staunton Military Academy, www.sma-alumni.org/navyace.htm.

Captain Willis W. Bradley, Jr., USN (Retired) (1884–1954), NHHC, www.history.navy.mil/photos/pers-us/uspers-b/w-brdly.htm.

Carter, Rear Admiral Worrall Reed, *Beans, Bullets and Black Oil, Chapter XVI, Stalemate II: The Western Carolines Operation,* www.ibiblio.org/hyperwar/USN/BBBO/BBBO-16.html.

Chen, C. Peter, *Palau Islands and Ulithi Islands Campaigns, 15 Sep 1944–1 Dec 1944*, ww2db.com/battle_spec.php?battle_id=77.

Cincpac Monthly Analysis for October 1944.

Cleaver, Thomas McKelvey, *Fabled Fifteen: The Pacific War Saga of Carrier Air Group 15*, Pacifica Military History.

Cleaver, Thomas McKelvey, *Relentless in Battle, Aviation History Magazine, June 2, 2014*, www.historynet.com/relentless-in-battle.htm.

Cleaver, Thomas McKelvey, *VF-15—Satan's Playmates, F6f-3 Hellcat, History*, HobbyBoss 1/48, January 2012, modelingmadness.com/review/allies/cleaver/us/tmcf6f.htm.

Collection of Rear Admiral Samuel E. Morison, USN (Retired). Photo # NH 106328, Official U.S. Navy Photograph, Naval History and Heritage Command collection.

Commander, Navy Installations Command (CNIC), Commander, Navy Region Southeast, History, www.cnic.navy.mil/regions/cnrse/about/history.html.

Commander David McCampbell—AG-15, Hellcat Ace, www.ww2wings.com/wings/heroes/davidmccampbell/davidmccampbell.shtml.

Cordray, Elmer, *My Diary, WWII Diary 1944 Aboard the USS Essex*, www.ussessexcv9.org/pdfs/Cordray%20Diary.pdf.

Correll, John T., *The Matterhorn Missions, Air Force Magazine* (March 2009).

Cox, Robert Jon, *Vice Admiral Ralph Andrew Ofstie, U.S. Navy*, www.bosamar.com/pages/ofstie_bio.

CTF 34 Action Report (Vice Admiral Lee), December 14, 1944.

Curtiss SOC "Seagull" Scout-Observation Planes, Department of the Navy, Naval Historical Center, Washington Navy Yard, Washington, D.C., www.history.navy.mil/photos/ac-usn22/s-types/soc.htm.

"Curtiss SB2c Helldiver: The Last Dive Bomber," *Aviation History Magazine*, Published Online: June 12, 2006.

Cutler, Thomas J., *The Battle of Leyte Gulf: 23–26 October 1944*. Annapolis, MD: Naval Institute Press, 2001.

CV9 USS Essex, Navy History, historycentral.com/navy/Essex.html.

CV-7 Wasp, US Navy Air Groups—June 1942, ww2air.altervista.org/ww2/USNair4206.htm.

David McCampbell, Military Combat, Enshrined 1996, 1910–1996, National Aviation Hall of Fame, nationalaviation.org.

David McCampbell, veterantributes.org.

The Decision, Chapter 2, Peleliu, September 1944: Amphibious Combat Against a Clever, Defensive-Minded Enemy, erenow.com/ww/grunts-inside-american-infantry-combat-experience/3.php.

Descendants of John Alexander Perry, Charts of Giles County, gilestn.genealogyvillage.com/charts/perry.htm.

The Douglas SBD Dauntless & Curtiss SB2c Helldiver, by Greg Goebel, AirVectors, www.airvectors.net/avsbd.html.

Fifth Action Report: Stalemate II: Second Visayas, 24 September 1944, Commanding Officer USS Essex, October 1, 1944, WWII Archives Foundation, Incorporated.

First Action Report: Stalemate II: Palau, August 29–September 8, 1944, Commanding Officer USS Essex, October 1, 1944, WWII Archives Foundation, Incorporated.

Fourth Action Report: Stalemate II: Manila Strikes, 21–22 September, Commanding Officer USS Essex, October 1, 1944, WWII Archives Foundation, Incorporated.

Generous, William T., Jr., *Sweet Pea at War: A History of USS Portland*. Lexington: University Press of Kentucky, 2003.

Glossary of U.S. Naval Abbreviations, Department of the Navy, Naval Historical Center, Washington Navy Yard, Washington, D.C.

Goldberg, Harold J., *D-Day in the Pacific: The Battle of Saipan*. Bloomington: Indiana University Press, 2007.

Graham, A.T., *Pacific War Diary of A.T. Graham, Jr.*, atgrahamjr.blogspot.com/2012_08_01_archive.html.

The Great White Fleet, Department of the Navy, Naval History and Heritage Command.

Grossnick, Roy A., *United States Naval Aviation 1910–1995*, Naval Historical Center, Department of the Navy, Washington, D C., 60, www.history.navy.mil/avh-1910/part03.pdf.

Grumman TBF Avenger Carrier-Borne Torpedo Bomber (1942), www.militaryfactory.com/aircraft/detail-page-2.asp?aircraft_id=300.

Hackett, Bob, and Sander Kingsepp, *IJN Submarine I-19: Tabular Record of Movement*, www.combinedfleet.com/I-19.htm.

Hearn, Chester G., *Carriers in Combat: The Air War at Sea*. Westport, CT: Praeger, 2005.

Hickman, Kennedy, *World War II: USS Essex (CV-9)*, Military History, militaryhistory.about.com/od/world wariiwarships/p/World-War-II-Uss-Essex-Cv-9.htm.

History of the Silver Eagles, Naval Aviation Museum Foundation, www.navalaviationmuseum.org/archive/sfl/sflshow.php?id=3.

Honolulu, Hawaii, Passenger and Crew Lists, 1900–1959, Susan McCampbell.

Hopewood, Jon C., *Wayne Morris: Movie Star, War Hero*, www.imdb.com/name/nm0606998/bio.

USS Hornet, WWII Combat, Battle of Santa Cruz Islands (CV-8) & Ship's Log USS Hornet (CV-12), USS Hornet Museum, The Aircraft Carrier Hornet Foundation, www.uss-hornet.org/history/wwii.

USS Hornet, WWII Combat, Ship's Log USS Hornet (CV-12), USS Hornet Museum, The Aircraft Carrier Hornet Foundation, www.usshornet.org/history/wwii.

USS Hornet During World War II, USS Hornet Museum—The Aircraft Carrier Hornet Foundation, www.uss hornet.org/history/wwii.

Hough, USMC, Lieutenant Colonel Frank O., Major Verle E. Ludwig, USMC, Henry I. Shaw, Jr., *History of U. S. Marine Corps Operations in World War II, Volume I, Part VI, the Turning Point: Guadalcanal, Pearl Harbor to Guadalcanal*, Historical Branch, G-3 Division, Headquarters, U.S. Marine Corps.

U.S.S. Houston (CL81) Torpedo Damage Off Formosa 14 and 16 October, 1944, War Damage Report No. 53, March 15, 1947, Bureau of Ships, Navy Department, Naval History & Heritage Command.

Hoyt, Edwin P., *McCampbell's Heroes: The Story of the U.S. Navy's Most Celebrated Carrier Fighters of the Pacific War*. New York: Van Nostrand Reinhold Company, 1983.

Interrogations of Japanese Officials, Vice Admiral OZAWA, Jisaburo, IJN, the Battle of the Philippine Sea, 19–20 June 1944, Interrogation NAV No. 3 USSBS No. 32, October 16, 1945.

Japanese Operations in the Southwest Pacific Area, MacArthur Historical Report II.

Kinzey, Bert. *F6F Hellcat in Detail and Scale (D&S Vol.26)*. Shrewsbury, UK: AirLife Publishing Ltd., 1987.

Kleinberg, Eliot, "Destroyer Named After the Navy's 'Ace of Aces,'" *Palm Beach Post,* July 3, 2000.

Layton, Andrew, *Wolverines in the Sky.* Xulon Press, 2007.

Lippman, David H., *The Turkey Shoot.* Peter Laurentis, 2013.

Lundstrom, John B., *The First Team: Pacific Naval Air Combat from Pearl Harbor to Midway.* Annapolis, MD: Naval Institute Press, 1984.

Manchester, William, *American Caesar: Douglas MacArthur 1880-1964.* New York: Back Bay Books/ Little, Brown and Company, 1978.

Manhattan Project History: Putting the "Weapon" to Military Use, 509th Composite Group, the Hiroshima Mission—Timeline, www.mphpa.org/classic/HISTORY/ H-07L1.htm.

Market House Museum: The Naval Career of "Jumpin" Joe Clifton, markethousemuseum.com.

Matinee Classics, Wayne Morris Biography & Filmography, www.matineeclassics.com/celebrities/actors/ wayne_morris/details.

Maui No Ka 'Oi Magazine, Nov.-Dec. 2012.

McCampbell, Andrew J., *1900 United States Federal Census,* Ancestry.com,

McCampbell, William Daniel, *1900 United States Federal Census,* Ancestry.com.

"McCampbell: No Swagger, Just Heroism," *Palm Beach Post,* July 4, 1996, 18A, www.emedals.com.

McKillop, Jack, *United States Navy Aircraft Carriers December 7, 1941,* Bluejacket.com.

McKinley, Mike, JO2 (Journalist Second Class), *The Cruise of the Great White Fleet.*

McManus, John C., *Grunts: Inside the American Infantry Combat Experience, World War II Through Iraq.* New York: New American Library, 2010.

Medal of Honor Citation of Commander David McCampbell, USN, Printed in the official publication *Medal of Honor, 1861-1949, the Navy.*

Mischlich, Marston A., *Chapter 7: Naval Air Station Atlantic City, Atlantic City Answers the Call to World War II: How It and the Surrounding Area Contributed to the War Effort,* M.A. thesis, California State University Dominguez Hills, 1998.

Morison, Samuel Eliot, *History of United States Naval Operations in World War II: Aleutians, Gilberts and Marshalls, June 1942-April 1944.* Champaign: University of Illinois Press, 1959.

Morison, Samuel Eliot, *History of United States Naval Operations in World War II: New Guinea and the Marianas, March 1944-August 1944.* Champaign: University of Illinois Press, 1981.

Morison, Samuel Eliot, *Leyte: June 1944-January 1945, History of the United States Naval Operations in World War II, Volume 12.* Annapolis, MD: Naval Institute Press, 1958.

Morison, Samuel Eliot, *New Guinea and the Marianas: March 1944-August 1944, Volume Eight.* Annapolis, MD: U.S. Naval Institute Press, 1953.

Muir, Dan, *Order of Battle: The Battle of the Philippine Sea,* 19-20 June 1944, www.navweaps.com/index_ oob/OOB_WWII_Pacific/OOB_WWII_Phillipine_ Sea.htm.

Nakajima A6m2-N Type 2 Float Plane Fighter (Rufe), www.pacificwrecks.com/aircraft/a6m2-n/tech.html.

Napalm, www.globalsecurity.org/military/systems/ munitions/napalm.htm.

NAS Melbourne, Florida, www.nasmelbourne.freeservers. com.

NavSource Online: Aircraft Carrier Photo Archive, *USS Hornet (CV-12),* contributed by Steve Whitby, www. navsource.org/archives/02/12.htm.

1960 Cruise Book of USS Bon Homme Richard CVA-31, the Archive, Navy Department Library, Washington, D.C.

1933 Lucky Bag, US Naval Academy Class of 1933 Yearbook.

O'Neill, Robert, *The Road to Victory: From Pearl Harbor to Okinawa.* Botley, Oxford: Osprey Publishing, 2011.

The Pacific War Online Encyclopedia, Guadalcanal, pwencycl.kgbudge.com/G/u/Guadalcanal.htm.

The Pacific War Online Encyclopedia, Guadalcanal, Tulagi, pwencycl.kgbudge.com.

Peleliu, Battle for (Operation Stalemate II)—The Pacific War's Forgotten Battle, September–November 1944, www.historyofwar.org/articles/battles_peleliu.html.

Polmar, Norman, *Aircraft Carriers: A History of Carrier Aviation and Its Influence on World Events, Volume I, 1909-1945.* Dulles, VA: Potomac Books, 2006.

Portz, USNR (Ret.), Captain Matt, *Naval Aviation in WWII, Aviation Training and Expansion, Part 1, Naval Aviation News,* July-August 1990.

Potter, E.B., *Nimitz.* Annapolis, MD: Naval Institute Press, 1979.

Prange, Gordon William, with Donald M. Goldstein and Katherine V. Dillon, *God's Samurai: Lead Pilot at Pearl Harbor.* Dulles, VA: Brassey's, 2004.

Prefer, Nathan N., *The Battle for Tinian: Vital Stepping Stone in America's War Against Japan.* Havertown, PA: Casemate Publishers, 2012.

USS Ranger (CV-4), NavSource Online: Aircraft Carrier Photo Archive, *USS Ranger (CV-4) Aircraft Carrier (1934),* www.militaryfactory.com/ships/detail.asp? ship_id=USS-Ranger-CV4.

USS Ranger VI (CV-4), Dictionary of American Naval Fighting Ships (DANFS), Navy Department, Naval Historical Center, Naval History & Heritage Command.

Ranger, Yorktown & Wasp Class Aircraft Carriers (CV 4-8) (Fiscal Years 1930, 1934, 1936 & 1939), Online Library of Selected Images, U.S. Navy Fleet Ship Types, Fleet Aircraft Carriers, Naval History and Heritage Command.

The Reminiscences of Captain David McCampbell U.S. Navy (Retired), Interview by Paul Stillwell. Annapolis, MD: U.S. Naval Institute, 2010.

Revell 1/48 SB2c-3 Helldiver, History, modelingmadness. com/review/allies/cleaver/us/tmcsb2c3.htm.

Reynolds, Clark G. *Famous American Admirals.* Annapolis, MD: Naval Institute Press, 2002.

Reynolds, Clark G., *The Fast Carriers: The Forging of an Air Navy.* Annapolis, MD: Naval Institute Press, 1968.

Rottman, Gordon, *Saipan & Tinian 1944: Piercing the Japanese Empire.* Botley, Oxford: Osprey Publishing, 2004.

Rottman, Gordon L., *World War 2 Pacific Island Guide: A Geo-Military Study.* Westport, CT: Greenwood Press, 2002.

St. John, Philip A., *USS Essex CV/CVA/CVS-9.* Paducah, KY: Turner Publishing Company, 1999.

Scarborough, Capt. William E., USN (Ret.), *The Neutrality Patrol: To Keep Us Out of World War II,* Naval Historical Center, United States Navy.

Sears, David, *Pacific Air: How Fearless Flyboys, Peerless Aircraft, and Fast Flattops Conquered the Skys in the War with Japan.* Cambridge, NA: First Da Capo Press, 2011.

Second Action Report: Stalemate II: Southern Philippines,

September 9–10, 1944, Commanding Officer USS Essex, October 1, 1944, WWII Archives Foundation, Incorporated.

Shaw, Henry I., Jr., Bernard C. Nalty and Edwin T. Turnbladh, *History of U.S. Marine Corps Operations in World War II, Volume III: Central Pacific Drive,* Historical Branch, G-3 Division, Headquarters, U.S. Marine Corps, 1966.

Shaw, Henry I., Jr., Bernard C. Nalty and Edwin T. Turnbladh, *Part IV Saipan: The Decisive Battle, Chapter 1, Background to Forager, Central Pacific Drive, History of U.S. Marine Corps Operations in World War II,* Historical Branch, G-3 Headquarters, U.S. Marine Corps.

Sherman, Captain Forest, *After Action Report Part 1,* davidmclellan0.tripod.com/id20.htm.

Sherman, Frederick Carl (1888–1957), The Pacific War Online Dictionary, pwencycl.kgbudge.com/S/h/Sherman_Frederick_C.htm.

Ship Information, Commander Naval Surface Group U.S. Pacific Fleet, public.navy.mil.

Sicard, Dictionary of American Naval Fighting Ships, Navy Department, Naval History & Heritage Command, Naval Historical Center.

Silverstone, Paul, *The Navy of World War II, 1922–1947.* New York: Routledge, 2007.

Simpson, Joanne Cavanaugh, "The Funny Little Fuze with Devastating Aim," *John Hopkins Magazine,* April 2000.

Sims, Edward H., *Greatest Fighter Missions of the Top Navy and Marine Aces of World War II.* New York: Ballantine Books, 1965.

Stubblebine, David, *John McCain,* World War II Database, ww2db.com/person_bio.php?person_id=511.

Sullivan, Jim, *F6F Hellcat in Action,* Carrollton, TX: Squadron/Signal Publications Inc., 1979.

Taylor, Theodore, *The Magnificent Mitscher.* Annapolis, MD: U.S. Naval Institute Press, 1954.

Third Action Report: Stalemate II: First Visayas, September 12–14, 1944, Commanding Officer USS Essex, October 1, 1944, WWII Archives Foundation, Incorporated.

Thomas, Evan, *Sea of Thunder: Four Commanders and the Last Great Naval Campaign 1941–1945.* New York: Simon & Schuster, 2006.

Thomason, Tommy H., *U.S. Navy Aircraft History, Waving Them Aboard—The LSO,* thanlont.blogspot.com/2012/11/waving-them-aboard-lso.html.

Tillman, Barrett, *Clash of the Carriers: The True Story of the Marianas Turkey Shoot of World War II.* New York: NAL Caliber, 2006.

Tillman, Barrett, "The Navy's Ace of Aces," *Centennial of Naval Aviation,* Vol. 3 (Fall 2011).

Tillman, Barrett, and Lawson, Robert L., *U.S. Navy Dive and Torpedo Bombers of World War II.* St. Paul, MN: MBI Publishing Company, 2001.

Tucker, Spencer C., *Leyte Gulf, Battle of (23–26 October 1944),* ABC-CLIO'S Encyclopedia of World War II: A Political, Social, and Military History, www.historyandtheheadlines.abc-clio.com.

Tuscaloosa, Dictionary of American Naval Fighting Ships (DANFS), Navy Department, Naval History & Heritage Command, Naval Historical Center.

U.S. Army Corps of Engineers, Southeast and Pacific IMA Region, Site Inspection Report, Naval Air Station Melbourne, Brevard County, Florida, FUDS Project No. I04FL038601, May 19, 2011.

"Valdemar Greene Lambert," *The Monterey Herald,* August 29, 2008, www.legacy.com/obituaries/monterey herald/obituary.aspx?

Vego, Milan N., *The Battle for Leyte, 1944: Allied and Japanese Plans, Preparations, and Execution.* Annapolis, MD: Naval Institute Press, 2006.

Vice Admiral (Retired) William V. "Bill" Davis, Jr., United State Navy Biography, U.S. Navy Website.

Wasp, Dictionary of American Naval Fighting Ships, Naval Historical Center, Department of the Navy.

Waters, Dictionary of American Naval Fighting Ships, Navy Department, Naval History & Heritage Command, Naval Historical Center

What Is an LSO? History, Carrier Landing Consultants, History, carrierlandingconsultants.com/lso.php.

Willis, David, "Boeing B-29 and B-50 Superfortress," *International Air Power Review,* Vol. 22 (2007): 136–169, Westport, CT: AIRtime Publishing.

Woodman, Richard, *Malta Convoys 1940–1943.* London: John Murray.

Woodward, Comer Vann, *The Battle of Leyte Gulf: The Incredible Story of World War II'S Largest Naval Battle.* New York: Skyhorse Publishing, 2007.

World War II Service and Diary of John R. McKnight-Ex Rd M 3c USN, www.wright.edu/~jack.mcknight/diary/diary/44–04.htm.

WWII Forums, Theaters of the Second World War, War in the Pacific, Naval Warfare in the Pacific, Carrier Aircraft Navigation: How Did They Do It?, www.ww2f.com/topic/21346-carrier-aircraft-navigation-how-did-they-do-it.

Zimmerman, Dwight Jon, *Operation Vengeance: The Mission to Kill Admiral Yamamoto,* Defense Media Network, May 8, 2013, www.defensemedianetwork.com/stories/operation-vengeance-the-mission-to-kill-admiral-yamamoto.

Index